UNDERSTANDING AND CONDUCTING RESEARCH

APPLICATIONS IN EDUCATION
AND THE BEHAVIORAL SCIENCES

UNDERSTANDING AND CONDUCTING RESEARCH

APPLICATIONS IN EDUCATION AND THE BEHAVIORAL SCIENCES

SECOND EDITION

Emanuel J. Mason

Professor of Educational and Counseling Psychology
University of Kentucky
Lexington, Kentucky

William J. Bramble

South East Regional Resource Center
Juneau, Alaska

McGRAW-HILL BOOK COMPANY

New York   St. Louis   San Francisco   Auckland   Bogotá   Caracas
Colorado Springs   Hamburg   Lisbon   London   Madrid   Mexico   Milan
Montreal   New Delhi   Oklahoma City   Panama   Paris   San Juan
São Paulo   Singapore   Sydney   Tokyo   Toronto

This book was set in Times Roman by the College Composition Unit
in cooperation with General Graphic Services, Inc.
The editors were Philip A. Butcher, Judith R. Cornwell, and David Dunham;
the production supervisor was Denise L. Puryear.
The cover was designed by Rafael Hernandez.
The drawings were done by Fine Line Illustrations, Inc.
R. R. Donnelley & Sons Company was printer and binder.

UNDERSTANDING AND CONDUCTING RESEARCH
Applications in Education and the Behavioral Sciences

1 2 3 4 5 6 7 8 9 0 D O C D O C 8 9 4 3 2 1 0 9

ISBN   0-07-040703-7

Library of Congress Cataloging-in-Publication Data

Mason, Emanuel J.
   Understanding and conducting research: applications in
education and the behavioral sciences/Emanuel J. Mason
and William J. Bramble. — 2nd ed.
   p. cm.
   Includes bibliographies and index.
   ISBN 0-07-040703-7
   1. Psychology — Research. 2. Education — Research. 3. Social
sciences — Research. I. Bramble, William J. II. Title.
BF76.5.M37 1989
300'.72—dc19   88-38145

To Susan, Sara, Sandy, and
Ellen, Anne Marie, Shelley, Billy, and
Our Parents

CONTENTS

THE EXPECTATIONS OF SOCIETY
THE SCOPE OF THE RESEARCH ENTERPRISE
SPECULATIONS FOR THE FUTURE
CONCLUSION
SUMMARY
REFERENCES
SUPPLEMENTARY READINGS

PREFACE

This book is intended to introduce beginning graduate-level students to the spectrum of thinking on research in education, the behavioral sciences, and related fields. However, unlike many of the other books in the field, this is not a cookbook of research techniques. It is not our view that research is a set of principles, activities, or methods that can be applied mechanically to any problem or situation. Research is about finding, structuring, and understanding the complexities of knowledge. This knowledge may be used to build theory, to develop policy, to support decision making, or just to find out something. Too often students dwell on the accoutrements of the researcher, such as statistics, measurement, or computers, thus reducing research to an affectation that lacks the riches and excitement of the real thing. The commitment is to look like a researcher, rather than to find dependable knowledge. It is hoped that the presentation, the many examples, and the issues raised in this book will help the student to appreciate research as a knowledge-building process with purposes, contexts, values and perspectives, and very definite limitations.

As was the first edition, this text is written for two groups of students. The first group includes graduate students in education and the behavioral and social sciences who are planning to become teachers, psychologists, counselors, managers, administrators, nurses, and other kinds of practitioners. They will not be likely to contribute extensively to the research literature, but in order to maintain their currency in their careers, they will require a modest level of literacy about scientific research. The second group to whom this text is directed includes the students who are preparing for careers that will be more directly involved in doing research.

We approached our task realistically. We expect many of the students who read this book will not have had extensive backgrounds in statistics, mathematics, philosophy of science, or even the social sciences. Every effort was made to keep the level of discussion sophisticated while not assuming extensive technical background on the part of the student. For example, this text is not intended to be a textbook on data analysis suitable for a statistics course; but since statistics is used in much research, some attention has to be given to statistical analysis. The focus of the chapters on statistics is on the meaning of various statistical techniques as they are applied in research. We leave the chore of teaching how to derive and apply those techniques to courses in statistical analysis. We have found in our teaching that students benefit from a discussion of how statistics can be applied in research, regardless of whether or not they have taken courses in statistics. A similar approach was taken in other technical areas such as measurement and computer applications.

We feel that skill in research (reading about it as well as doing it) will only come with practice. For this reason, questions have been provided in the chapters. These questions can be answered by students individually, or they can be used as a basis for class or group discussions. Where appropriate, answers (or suggested answers) have been provided in Appendix C. Students should also get in the habit of critically reading the research literature in their fields as they go through the book.

Much of the material included in the first edition has been changed, not because of dramatic upheavals in the research field, however, but because of the subtle changes since 1978, comments we received from colleagues in formal and informal reviews, and considerable feedback from students. A number of relatively new research strategies have been mentioned, such as exploratory data analysis, meta-analysis, and new ways to use computer technology in research. Chapters have been restructured, and the order of presentation has been changed. The orientation of the experimental design chapters (Chapters 4 and 5) more clearly emphasizes design principles rather than the strengths and weaknesses of preexisting designs. A new chapter (Chapter 11) discusses putting together all the various parts, the thinking, the tools, and the procedures, to create a research study. In addition, there has been a general updating of references, discussion, and illustrative material.

The book is divided into three parts. Part One establishes the foundation for the material covered in the book. To use a rather worn metaphor, Part One sets the stage for the rest of the book. How the researcher reasons, thinks, perceives, and knows are discussed. Further, the scientific method and examples of descriptive, experimental, historical, and evaluation research are presented. Part Two introduces the tools of the researcher. First the vocabulary of the researcher is explained, and there is a short discussion on the use of the library. Then there are chapters on experimental and quasi-experimental design, statistical analysis, measurement, observation, scaling, and computer applications. Chapters in Part Three are designed to help the student understand how the techniques discussed in Part Two are used to produce, recognize, evaluate, and write about research. In addition, such topics as research funding, ethics, and the social context of research are covered in the final chapters.

As with any book, a number of people besides the authors have made contributions and should be recognized for them. In the case of the present text, a complete list would be too extensive. However, certain contributions cannot be overlooked. We are particularly in the debt of the many students in EDP 656, Introduction to Research Methods in Education, who over the years have told us how this text should be written. We hope we learned those lessons well. We also wish to express our appreciation to some of our colleagues for their reviews of parts of the manuscript as it was being prepared, most notably, Phil Berger, James R. Barclay, and Tim Smith, were supportive in their willingness to discuss with us our ideas. Chia Hsin Lin helped by suggesting many of the recent illustrative examples from the literature. We wish to express our appreciation to our families, and to all the others whose patience and support helped make the completion of the final manuscript possible.

Emanuel J. Mason

William J. Bramble

UNDERSTANDING AND CONDUCTING RESEARCH

APPLICATIONS IN EDUCATION AND THE BEHAVIORAL SCIENCES

PART ONE

THE FIELD
OF RESEARCH:
AN OVERVIEW

Part I, consisting of two chapters, provides an introduction to the diversity and flavor of the spectrum of research in education and the behavioral sciences. Chapter 1 presents an introduction to such fundamental concepts as the relationship between philosophy and science, causation, basic versus applied research, and the kinds of reasoning used by researchers. In Chapter 2, the scientific method is portrayed as a way of thinking about and systematically investigating a problem area. Chapter 2 also provides specific illustrations of how the scientific method is applied by presenting examples from the literature. These two chapters provide a background for topics that come later.

CHAPTER 1

SCIENCE AND RESEARCH

Research is concerned with finding answers. Some forms of research are commonplace in everyday life. For example, a commuter wonders, "What is the quickest way to get to work?" Elsewhere a chef is asking, "How much salt should go into the soup?" At an elementary school, a teacher planning daily routines inquires, "When is the best time of day to recess the class?" and in a laboratory, a physicist wants to know, "What is the maximum velocity of an object in space?" Each of these people is asking questions of varying degrees of complexity and general importance and, by asking the questions, suggesting that answers can be found. *Research* may be defined simply as "the search for answers to questions." Thus if the commuter, the chef, the teacher, and the physicist search for the answers to their questions, they will each be doing research. Their research may be carefully and systematically done, or it may be haphazard. Perhaps the commuter and chef, preferring the trial-and-error approach, will not follow a carefully prescribed program to find solutions, but the physicist will probably organize the investigation carefully. In this text, we will emphasize the kind of systematic organized search for knowledge used in scientific investigations in education and the behavioral sciences rather than the more haphazard approaches many of us use for everyday problems.

Research activities can be viewed from three perspectives. For example, a pharmacologist might do some research on the side effects of a certain medication. A person who does not have an extensive background in biology or medicine reads about the finding in the newspaper and feels that the work is interesting but does not affect him or her personally very much. That person's physician, however, alters the prescriptions he issues as a result of the report.

The physician in this case plays the role of *consumer*. The person reading the newspaper is more of a *spectator,* while the pharmacologist is a *participant* in the research activity.

Understanding the principles and techniques of research can be useful to spectators and consumers as well as to participants in the research process. In education and the behavioral sciences, three categories of involvement in research also exist. Specifically in education, on the front line so to speak, consumers of research are the guidance counselors, teachers, school psychologists, and social workers, who offer direct services as part of the school program. The spectators, often with more than a passing interest, may be parents, taxpayers, and politicians. Participant researchers attempt to provide answers to the questions raised about education and schools.

THE CHARACTERISTICS OF SCIENCE AND RESEARCH

To most people, the word *science* brings visions of test tubes, microscopes, complicated laboratory equipment, and expressionless white-coated people turning dials, peering into glass tubing, and briskly jotting notes on clipboards. There is an air of mystery surrounding the whole scene. Another mistake that people make is to give the status of science to the tools that scientists use. For example, behavioral scientists commonly use tests, computers, and statistics as tools in their work. These tools assist in the scientist's work. Few people would confuse sawing wood with the highly skilled craft of furniture making. Similarly, definitions of *science* that focus on what some scientists do or the instruments they use are lacking in utility.

Probably the most parsimonious definition of *science* is that it is "the systematic development and organization of a body of knowledge." The material is organized to provide structure by which phenomena can be explained. By *phenomena,* we mean facts or events that can be observed. Thus Sir Isaac Newton, well known for his seventeenth-century work concerning the physics of moving objects, based his explanation of gravity upon observations he and others made about falling objects. Newton was able to integrate these observations into a universal explanation in the form of a mathematical relationship that indicated that the force of gravitation between two masses equaled the product of the masses multiplied by a constant and divided by the squared distance between the masses.* The use of a simple mathematical relationship to explain a phenomenon occurring naturally is a good example of the content of the physical sciences. The behavioral and social sciences have not yet been able to develop explanatory relationships that are quite so elegant in their simplicity.

It would be natural to ask at this point "Why have science? What is its purpose?" The answer to such a question is not a simple one. There are at

---

* Andrade, E. N. da C. (1958). *Sir Isaac Newton.* Garden City, NY: Doubleday (Anchor Books).

least two purposes, depending upon one's audience. The lay person usually looks toward science to improve the quality of life. According to this view, science holds the key to elimination of disease, the solution of social and economic problems, and the improvement of life generally. Many scientists, however, do not share this view. They think that improvement of life may be a useful by-product of science, but it cannot be the main purpose. Rather, the purpose of science, according to this position, is the formation of general explanatory principles explaining the relationships among phenomena that occur naturally. These principles can then be utilized to predict future events. Underlying this position is the proposition that knowledge is important in itself and that the significance of a piece of information is not tied to its applicability to the problems of everyday life. Another way of stating this aim would be to say that the purpose of science is to develop *theory,* which can be defined as "a set of formulations designed to explain and predict phenomena." We will have more to say about theories later.

One might ask, "Where does research fit into science?" To answer this question, we must go back to the definition of *research* given earlier, "the search for answers to questions." We could say that research is the process that scientists use to find the knowledge they need to formulate and evaluate theories. But that would be true for only some research. Other research does not have a scientific purpose at all. Consider, for example, research to determine the effectiveness of an advertising campaign for a certain brand of toothpaste. The researcher might look at the sales record of the product and also survey the attitudes of a sample of consumers to determine whether the advertising was effective. But he or she is probably not interested in developing generalizable knowledge, knowledge that can be used to formulate a theory of advertising to explain consumer reaction to a product. More likely, the researcher's sole interest is in being able to recommend to company executives the continuation or discontinuation of the advertising campaign.

Clearly, then, it is possible for a particular research investigation to be designed for reasons other than to support the aims of science. To clarify further what we mean by the term *research* in this text, we will restrict our interest to research that is scientific. However in this context, *scientific* does not necessarily mean "science." Rather, it refers to a manner of doing research known as the *scientific method.* We will go into the scientific method in some detail in Chapter 2. For the present, we will simply state that the scientific method provides for *systematic* investigation of a question or problem. The scientific method is extremely versatile. It has been adopted for use in virtually all kinds of research. Indeed, historians, physicists, and psychologists all use basically the same steps in conducting their investigations, although the specific techniques they use to observe, gather, and interpret data may be very different.

We have stated that we will emphasize scientific research in this book. Research that is not systematic would be haphazard. Occasionally a scientific discovery is precipitated by a serendipitous finding. Pasteur's chance finding of a vaccine for cholera in chickens is often cited as such a discovery.* Before this kind of discovery can be treated as scientific knowledge, however, it must be subjected to verification through systematic and thorough research.

SOURCES OF KNOWLEDGE

Researchers use a number of different sources of information. For example, people have long obtained knowledge from *individuals in positions of authority*. History is replete with examples of monarchs and clerics who have dictated truth, as they have interpreted it, to the masses. This kind of source is still used. A certain college of education, for example, has completely individualized and modularized its degree programs because its dean told the faculty that this was the best way to train an educator. The difficulty with using an authority as a source is that if the authority's knowledge is faulty, the information will be inadequate. For example, the dean we just mentioned may very well be correct in saying that individualized teacher education is the most effective method of training teachers. But without a comprehensive theory of teacher education, or at least a systematic body of knowledge regarding the process of teacher training, the dean's position must be regarded as nothing more than speculation. The reason that he can influence a whole college of education faculty to respond to his speculation is that he is in a position of authority. If he were not dean but, rather, a junior assistant professor or graduate student, his supposition very probably would have little effect on the rest of the college.

Tradition is another source of knowledge. Many of the things we think we know have come from tradition. For example, in the United States, children begin formal education at about the age of 6. When this practice is questioned, the response is usually that 6 has always been regarded as the best age to begin formal education. When traditions are valid, they are dependable sources of knowledge. However, traditions based upon false beliefs will result in faulty knowledge.

When we have legal problems, we seek the services of a lawyer. If we are sick, we consult a physician. When a child is not learning to read as well as his or her classmates, we call a reading specialist. These are examples of the use of *expert opinion,* another source of knowledge. Too often, expert opinion is taken without question as fact. We have all heard the admonition to seek opinions of at least two different physicians before agreeing to undergo surgery. This is not to say that the opinion of one expert is worth more than the opinion of another. To be sure, much of what experts offer really should be called sophisticated guessing based on a feeling for the subject rather than direct knowledge. However, there often can be more than one view of things, and researchers should be particularly aware of this point.

---

* De Kruif, Paul (1940). *Microbe hunters.* New York: Pocket Books, 1940.

Personal experience from observation is another source of knowledge quite familiar to most of us. For researchers, however, personal experience can be misleading. For example, there may be a tendency to omit evidence that does not support, and to find evidence that agrees with, prior beliefs. This is the well-known problem of achieving objectivity when using human judges. Anyone who has ever asked a new mother gazing at her hours-old firstborn whether she thought the child was attractive knows how a person's involvement and beliefs can influence perceptions. Another problem with personal experience is the subjective quality of the perception and interpretation of the experience.

Often people gain knowledge by resorting to reason. Sometimes the reasoning is from general observations to specific cases. This kind of reasoning is called *deduction*. For example, a student about to leave for class might notice that the day has become very dark, the wind is blowing, and there is a heavy dampness to the air. In general, when such conditions appeared on other days, a rainstorm followed. Thus the student reasons from general observations that it would be wise to wear a raincoat. On the other hand, reasoning can be *inductive,* or from the specific to the general. A teacher might reason that all classes enjoy hearing passages from "The Wizard of Oz" read at the end of the day because one of his previous classes enjoyed this experience. We will have more to say about reasoning later in this chapter.

When discussing how people know, it is difficult to avoid mentioning *common sense.* Everyone uses common sense, yet it is difficult to define. The major problem with common sense is that it is not a systematic method of gaining knowledge. Because of this lack of a systematic basis, common sense is not an acceptable way of gaining scientific knowledge.

The final source of knowledge to be discussed we shall call *documentation.* This source consists of the knowledge that society keeps stored in various forms. For example, we might obtain statistics concerning the average number of years of public education of male adults in the United States by referring to the data collected in the last census. Another kind of documentation can be obtained from records of legislation, court decisions, and written laws. Thus a student of the history of school finance would probably explore laws and court decisions. Records maintained by government offices and other agencies may also be used for documentation. When considering documents as sources of knowledge, the way the document or its content becomes available must be considered. For example, if we wish to investigate the rise in the proportion of black students at various colleges in the past 20 years, we could review the enrollment records of the past 20 years at the institutions of concern. This would be using *primary documentation.* But what if the information at one institution had been lost in a fire 2 years ago? We might ask people who filed the information to tell what they remember about the data that were lost. Such information is *secondary documentation,* and it is of course not always as dependable as primary sources. In this text, we will also consider the direct observation that occurs in laboratories and other experimental settings as a form of documentation.

THE RELATIONSHIP BETWEEN PHILOSOPHY AND SCIENCE

The ordinary person often thinks of philosophy and science as almost completely divorced from one another. Philosophy is thought to be primarily concerned with ideas and values, whereas science deals with "what is known." Yet they are not really quite that separate; they actually complement and support one another to a great degree. Specifically, both are concerned with the development, organization, and application of knowledge. Scientists tend to seek knowledge by observing phenomena under controlled conditions; philosophers tend to be concerned with the meaning, value, and impact of that knowledge. One of the arguments that has raged among nuclear physicists, for example, has little to do with the science of the atom. Rather, the debate concerns whether or not physicists have a moral responsibility not to investigate phenomena that could lead to discovery of knowledge that might be used in ways that are destructive. An example of such a discovery, of course, is the harnessing of nuclear energy to produce extraordinarily powerful bombs, each capable of destroying a whole city.

Many scientists believe that their role is to search for knowledge that would increase our understanding of the world about us. The knowledge itself is neither good nor bad. It is what people do with the knowledge that may be good or harmful. According to this view, the question of the value of knowledge is not one for the scientist but rather one for the philosopher. In this respect, philosophy might be considered the conscience of science. But it has another role as well, a role that is important if the goals of science are to be realized. Philosophy helps to organize the perspectives, activities, and findings of the scientific world. The branch of philosophy concerned with the values and structure of science is often called the *philosophy of science.*

A major problem of philosophers of science concerns the nature of knowing. The psychologist Joseph Royce (1974) argues that society has developed three different approaches to knowing. The first, the *metaphorical,* may be the oldest form of knowledge. It involves knowledge based upon intuitive or symbolic thought. An example of this might be the knowledge that a particular landscape is beautiful or a certain phrase profound. It represents evaluation against some internal standard. A second kind of knowing, the *rational,* is also an internal source of knowledge, but it is based more on the principles of logic. A rationalist, for example, would reason that since there is a preponderance of school failure among lower-socioeconomic-class children and since those children usually have diet deficiencies, providing a balanced meal each day should improve school performance. Of course, a good rationalist would realize that this is supposition rather than truth. Finally, knowledge can also be investigated *empirically;* that is, by observing objectively. The traffic engineer who determines whether the highway needs widening by counting the number of cars traveling it during a peak period is taking an empirical approach. Of course we must assume that our perceptions are correct, but they may not be. For example, the student with the slow watch who is always late to class never really knows the time, although he gathers empirical data by looking at his watch regularly.

Using Royce's conceptualization of the three methods of knowing, which approach to knowledge do you suppose is best for education and other behavioral applications? Is the most dependable knowledge what we think we know (metaphorical), or what we have reasoned that we know (rational), or what we have observed (empirical)? The answer, of course, is that we need all three to explore fully the complex relationships that characterize any human endeavor. For example, a narrowly empirical approach to how a student learns mathematical concepts would probably result in little more than a collection of observations of children doing mathematical tasks. A metaphorical thinker might conceptualize and symbolize the observations, suggesting further empirical work by classifying, ordering, and interpreting the data. A rationalist, using logic, might suggest relationships that would not otherwise be realized. Good research thus requires all three approaches.

The method the scientist uses in approaching knowledge will be reflected in the research findings. We should not expect the purely empirical researcher to be well prepared to discuss ethics, values, or even the implications of his or her work. For this reason, the pure empiricist may not be as valuable to society and the profession as is the scientist with a broader view of knowledge. This could also be said of the purely metaphoric or the purely rational researcher. Unfortunately, there seems to be a tendency among researchers in the various disciplines to downgrade approaches to knowledge other than their own.

WAYS OF REASONING

Reasoning, or the rational approach, is fundamental to the research process. Therefore, it will serve our purposes here to spend some time on the ways to reason. *Deductive thinking* was originally devised by the Greek philosopher Aristotle and his followers. It is the form of reasoning in which one goes from general knowledge to specific knowledge. For example, consider the following argument:

> All books have pages.
> This is a book.
> Therefore, this book has pages.

This form of discourse is called a *syllogism*. It contains a major premise (all books have pages), a minor premise (this is a book), and a conclusion (therefore, this book has pages). This argument is valid because the major and minor premises are both true and show a logical relationship to the conclusion. Notice that using the device of the syllogism, we have attributed a characteristic of all books to a specific one. To say it another way, we have *deduced* that this book has pages because all books have pages.

In the valid deduction in Figure 1-1, the major premise is the most encompassing. The minor premise is contained in it. This book is contained in "all books have pages," and therefore, this book has pages.

Now compare this with the next argument.

All books are printed in French.
What you are reading is a book.
Therefore, what you are reading is printed in French.

Notice that the first premise is false, and the argument is not correct. Figure 1-2 shows the case where the book you are reading is not printed in French. Of course, you could find a large number of books printed in French, and if they were the only books you ever saw, you might not question the logic of the discourse. But once you know of a book printed in a language other than French, you immediately see the fallacy in the argument. Thus, one of the limitations of deductive reasoning is that it depends upon the adequacy of the major premise. If the major premise is faulty, the deduction based upon it will lack validity.

Does this mean that we cannot reason accurately when we have partial or inadequate information about the general case? Not at all, for that is precisely the purpose of the method of *induction,* whereby the characteristics of the particular are attributed to the general. Induction depends upon observation. For example, if we wanted to know whether boys learn tumbling exercises faster than girls, we could take a sample of boys and girls, teach the group tumbling, note the speed of acquisition of skill for boys and girls, and attribute what happened in our sample to boys and girls in general. Certainly there are problems

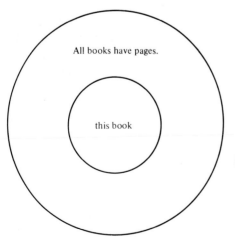

All books have pages.

this book

FIGURE 1-1
Diagram of an argument in which the minor premise is contained in the major premise.

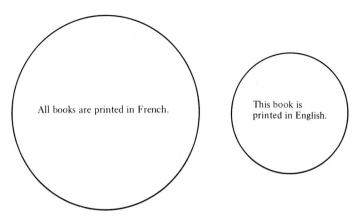

FIGURE 1-2
Diagram of an argument in which the minor premise is not contained in
the major premise.

with this method. Our sample of boys and girls might have been unusual and
not representative of boys and girls in general. There are other problems as
well. Should we assume that we mean all tumbling exercises, for example? Obviously, there are some limitations and problems associated with inductive
reasoning. Both induction and deduction are used by behavioral scientists and
educational researchers to organize facts, describe results, posit new relationships, and suggest new research.

THE CONCEPT OF CAUSATION

When we say that the objective of science is to discover information and organize it into principles explaining the relationships among naturally occurring
phenomena, we are not necessarily referring to discovering cause-and-effect
relationships. The concept of causality is not as simple as one might expect.
For example, if we strike a match, it may light. If it does, we may assume that
it is because of the striking. However, there are probably processes affected
by the striking of the match, such as heat generated by rubbing the match
against the rough surface and the position of the tip of the match during the
strike, that facilitate the ignition of the chemicals on the match tip. Yet it is
convenient to say that the lighting of the match was caused by the striking.
Furthermore, we notice that the striking does not always result in the match
being lit. Therefore, when we speak of striking as the cause of the match being
lit, what we really mean is that *on the basis of our observations,* striking the
match will *probably* result in the match becoming lit. We realize that we are
not directly observing all the processes involved and can only come to conclusions based upon what we see. Furthermore, the statement is made using

probability because we do not observe the identical effect each time the match is struck. That is, sometimes the match lights, but other times it does not.

John Stuart Mill was a philosopher of science who proposed canons that attempted to identify cause-and-effect relationships. The canons (Mill, 1916) were five methods of demonstrating causation. For example, the first canon, the *method of agreement,* suggests that if the same outcome occurred in two or more instances under investigation and each instance had only one common factor, then that factor was the cause (or the effect) of the phenomenon. This is similar to saying that if all people who attend a concert have admission tickets, then the ticket was the cause (or the effect) of attending the concert. This is obviously not true. Someone who had a ticket but who did not wish to hear the program might very likely not attend. Furthermore, people sitting in the audience did not get their tickets by attending the concert. Therefore, having a ticket is neither a cause nor an effect of attending the concert.

Mill's second canon, known as the *method of difference,* is sort of a corollary of the first. Mill suggested that if the phenomenon under investigation occurs in one instance but not another, and both instances have identical characteristics with one exception, that exception is the cause, or effect, or a part of the cause of the phenomenon. The method of difference suffers from much the same kind of deficiency as the method of agreement. For example, let's say that we are interested in knowing what causes one person to become an English teacher and someone else to become an accountant. We find a pair of identical twins. One is an accountant; the other is an English teacher. These twins are virtually identical in every way that we can imagine. They dress alike, eat similar foods, live together in the same house, and so on. We find, however, that the English teacher is right-handed; the accountant, left-handed. The method of difference would lead us to conclude that handedness is a cause (or part of a cause) or an effect of being an English teacher and an accountant. The difficulties in reasoning this way are obvious. First, despite our exhaustive study of the twins' traits, it is very likely that we did not include all the necessary characteristics. But, more important, we can surely find left-handed English teachers and right-handed accountants. Furthermore, the specific causes of something like vocational choice are so complex and interwoven as to make any attempt to search for them all an exhausting and futile exercise. Mill's other canons, the *joint method of agreement and disagreement,* the *method of residue,* and the *method of concomitant variation,* suffer from some of the same kinds of problems. The canons, however, were an important step in the development of the philosophy of science, for they served to crystallize thinking about the nature of causation.

A more contemporary view of the nature of causality was given by another well-known philosopher of science and physics, Rudolf Carnap (1966). Carnap argued that single factors do not cause specific events; rather, processes are caused by processes. To illustrate this point, let us return to the situation mentioned earlier where everyone at the concert had a ticket. The process of obtaining the ticket, with its own multiplicity of causes (wanting to hear the concert, having enough money to pay the price of admission, length of wait in line at the box office, etc.), would be said to have caused the process of attending the concert, which also can be attributed to other processes (having time to go, having transportation, not having a conflicting commitment, etc.).

Notice that the concept of causation is further complicated by the multiplicity of causes which may act to produce a single effect alone and in combination. In the behavioral sciences and education, most of the phenomena studied are so complex that the search for simple causes is not very useful. Consider the example of the high relationship between score on a reading test and score on an IQ test. Does one's IQ result in a certain level of reading performance? Does one's level of reading skill tend to produce a particular IQ score? Is there an external process—let's call it motivation to read well—that is related to both IQ and reading and that causes the apparent high relationship between IQ and reading? There is yet another possibility. Perhaps IQ and reading skill each have a multitude of common processes causing both of them. For example, some of these processes might be verbal ability, background experience, the quality of previous teaching, peer values, and parental educational level. These possibilities are depicted in Figure 1-3. There are others, of course. Notice that causal relationships are depicted by arrows that point from the proposed cause to the effect.

FIGURE 1-3
Some possible cause-and-effect relationships between IQ score and reading.

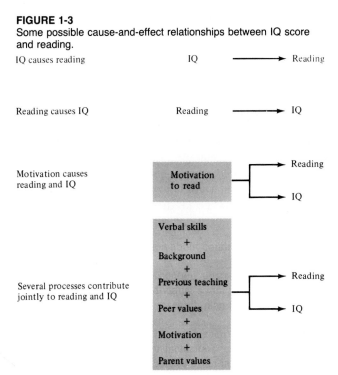

Despite the difficulties associated with interpretation of the concept of cause, it is still useful to the scientific researcher. (See Cook and Campbell, 1979, pp. 30–33, for an excellent summary of the meaning of *cause* in scientific research.) For example, causal relationships, such as the relationship between turning a key and starting an automobile or pressing a switch and hearing a radio, help one to know something about how to live in and, to some degree, control one's environment. Further, these causal assertions are testable as to their correctness in the scientific sense even when little is known about all the smaller processes involved (e.g., the mechanics of the car or the electronics of the radio). Because causal relationships are based on numerous complex and interrelated processes, they are probabilistic at best. Thus if the battery in the car is dead, or a terminal connection has worked loose, turning the ignition key may not start the car. Further, multiple causes, sequenced effects, or a combination of these might be causal to a given effect. In addition, causal relationships may be easier to research in highly controlled laboratory settings than in more natural field settings. Yet much research in education and the behavioral sciences must be conducted in settings that are more like the field than the laboratory.

Generally, it can be said that causes will precede effects. However, in some relationships the cause and the effect may be interchangeable. For instance, a psychologist might correctly suggest that an infant with a calm disposition will cause a more relaxed relationship between the parents than will an infant who is more irritable. On the other hand, the lack of stress between the parents might be the cause of the child's calm disposition.

Part of the scientist's concern about cause has to do with manipulation to create effects. For example, in research on school discipline, it has been found that when a child sees a model (e.g., a teacher, a classmate, a character in a film, etc.) performing in a certain manner, that child is more likely to show that behavior (Charles, 1985). Therefore, implicit in the research on modeling behavior for school discipline has been the idea that discipline could be controlled through effective manipulation of the models presented to a child in the classroom.

When scientists speak of "causation," they are often referring to a kind of prediction. That something can be predicted does not mean that it is necessarily caused by the information that led to the prediction. For example, if we predict that State University will win its next basketball game, the prediction may be meaningful to some degree. That is, it may be meaningful in terms of the ardor of the student making the prediction, the past record of the team, or the quality of the players. However, none of these will *cause* State University to win. Predictions can be considered to reflect cause only when *all* the relevant information is considered. Of course, we can never know *all* the relevant information, so our predictions are consequently presumptive. Hence the disillusionment in science with the concept of *cause*. Scientists do use the word "cause" from time to time, but do not be misled into thinking that they mean "cause" in the absolute sense.

CLASSIFICATION OF THE SCIENCES

If you were to construct a classification system for the divisions of science, would you say that there are a few broad divisions, such as the physical sciences, the biological sciences, and the behavioral and social sciences? Perhaps you might choose to classify further into physics, chemistry, astronomy, biology, psychology, education, sociology, economics, etc., partly because university faculties are usually organized that way. Exactly how sciences should be classified is a difficult question. However, Jean Piaget, well known for his work in the development of thinking and reasoning processes in young children, noted that the organization of university faculties is not standard among countries, and so any attempt to use such a system leads to difficulty (Piaget, 1974). Furthermore, even within countries, there are differences in the organization of the academic departments among universities. For this reason, Piaget suggested putting all disciplines involved with the study of human activities under the heading of "human sciences."

Piaget offered a system for further classifying the human sciences into four groups. The first group, the *nomothetic sciences,* includes those disciplines that involve the identification of relationships that are fairly constant and can be expressed in terms of quantitative functions or logical structures. Piaget would place much of the research activities of psychologists, sociologists, and economists into the nomothetic category. The nomothetic sciences are distinguished by the use of quantitative relationships, the tendency to use experimental research methods, focus of interest upon a few variables at a time, and concern for the development of principles using an empirical basis.

The *historical sciences,* the second classification, take the perspective of events across time. They may be concerned with the sequence of events leading up to the founding of a charitable institution or the impact of some great personality upon society. Piaget notes that although the historical scientist, unlike the nomothetic scientist, may be interested in quantitative data and underlying principles, the fundamental purpose of the historical scientist is to *reconstitute* reality rather than to break it down into distinct relationships. Thus the historian is rarely concerned with only one facet of an event; interest is focused on a variety of antecedent conditions. For example, historical study of the involvement of the United States in World War II would go beyond the single event of the Japanese attack on Pearl Harbor to include public opinion in the United States at the time; attitudes towards the war in Europe; the economic and political situation in the world; the level of technology available for communication, logistics, and waging battle; the personalities of world leaders; and so on.

The third major division of the human sciences, according to Piaget, is the *legal sciences.* This category of science concerns the duties and obligations of members of society which, in the form of laws, remain valid even when they are violated. For example, in our society it is considered a violation of law to steal from another person. Even though there are instances of robbery taking place, the validity of the law is not questioned. Compare this with the kind of "law" nomothetic science develops, which is usually expressed in the form of a theory that is tested empirically and, when contradicted by evidence, is considered invalid. The fourth division of the human sciences, according to Piaget—the *philosophical sciences*—is most difficult to characterize because of its diversity of scope and interest. The philosophical sciences are concerned with the critical evaluation of acquired knowledge in terms of human values and convictions.

So far we have seen that the sciences can be classified along the traditional divisions of university departments or faculties or by using the four-category system suggested by Piaget. There are other approaches as well. However, any system of classification will have difficulty dealing with specific research activities and types of investigations. Researchers must choose the techniques or strategies most appropriate to the knowledge they seek. They should not feel particularly wedded to a classification or category if it inhibits their effectiveness in searching for answers to research questions.

RELATIONSHIPS AMONG THE SCIENCES

All sciences have in common a singular purpose, to increase knowledge and organize what is known to facilitate understanding of phenomena as they occur naturally. All sciences are related also by their use of the systematic approach known as *the scientific method* to develop this knowledge. Another common ground is the use of the techniques of deductive and inductive reasoning. But although the various sciences use the same methods and have similar purposes and modes of reasoning, they differ in many ways. For example, the techniques researchers use vary considerably across disciplines. Surely the methods of testing a compound in qualitative chemistry would not be suitable for testing a child in the classroom. Furthermore, some sciences are much older than others. In the natural sciences of chemistry and physics, important breakthroughs were being recorded centuries before the first scientific exploration in psychology and education.

Another difference between the various fields of sciences involves their origins. Generally, human research activities begin with some form of curiosity about phenomena that probably reflect the status and quality of life at the time. For example, early people were very interested in maintaining their food supplies. This prompted questions about natural phenomena that affected crops and herds, such as weather, climate, and soil conditions. When humans began to find that by cooperating among themselves more could be accomplished, curiosity about phenomena that were needed for a functioning society began to emerge. People became curious about economics, law, and government. In this way, the differing needs of people and the developing of society led to curiosity concerning specific questions. The curiosity generally reflected a need for better understanding. Historically, the behavioral sciences had to wait for human curiosity to mature to the point where it could be directed toward the less obvious and, at the time, somewhat less pressing concerns of education and the behavioral sciences. This can readily be seen in the history of educational research. When society was less complex and technological than it presently is, there were many philosophies of education, but there was little interest or effort in developing methods to improve education because a person could live a relatively useful life even if he or she could not read or write well. A complex industrialized society, however, has greater need for educated individuals to operate its machines and institutions and to be citizens and leaders. Under this kind of pressure, society became curious about why certain children did not learn to read, write, or perform addition as well as other children, and a science emerged to promote better understanding of the educational processes.

Thus behavioral sciences differ from the physical and natural sciences not only in terms of the time when they emerged, but also in terms of the kinds of questions that brought them into being. Moreover, these newer sciences may be much more complex than the earlier ones. The ordinary person usually ranks physics and chemistry as among the most complex of human understandings. Yet when the newer sciences of human behavior and education further mature as sciences, they may very well be regarded as the most demanding. The sophistication that the natural and physical sciences have been able to attain may be due to the simplicity rather than the complexity of the phenomena they study. Of course, all this is conjecture now, but the degree to which human thinking had to mature before developing the capability to investigate social, behavioral, and educational phenomena scientifically certainly suggests that these sciences are concerned with abstract and complex phenomena.

The various sciences can be further distinguished on the basis of the kinds of phenomena they investigate. The natural sciences deal with objects and phenomena that occur in nature. Herbert A. Simon (1969) has contrasted these sciences with what he calls ''artificial'' sciences, which concern the nonnatural world created by humankind. For example, the laws of gravity and inertia exist regardless of which political party is in power or what the native language of the country may be. However, the concerns of the ''nonnatural'' sciences are very much subject to such influences. An illustration is provided by Barclay and Wu (1980), who reported that concepts such as *introversion* and *extroversion* clearly do not mean the same things in the United States and the Republic of China. Specifically, their research suggested that some behavior which would be considered extroverted in Taiwan classrooms would be looked upon as rather introverted in schools in the United States.

This concept of the artificial is useful in discussing another point of separation between natural and behavioral sciences. Simon uses the term *interface* to refer to the problem more clearly. Specifically, all complex systems, either man-made or natural, function according to the demands of an ''inner'' and an ''outer'' environment. The interface occurs between the inner and outer environments and represents the area of focus of the artificial sciences. For example, as we watch a child sitting in school during a mathematics lesson, there is a certain inner environment to which the child responds. It includes the complete physiology, anatomy, and biochemistry of sitting in school and learning. On the other hand, there is an outer reality which influences the child's behavior. It includes the teacher, materials in the room, the hiss of the radiator, the other children, and everything else in the external environment. Between the inner and outer environment the behavioral scientist will "create" areas of study which are "artificial," such as motivation, intelligence, and learning, to explain what goes on between the inner and outer environment and to predict future behavior of the child. This concept of the artificial provides an approach to the scientific study of complex systems, such as human behavior, without having to deal with the complexities of the inner and outer environments.

We will discuss one last way in which the behavioral sciences and education differ from the natural sciences. It has to do with instrumentation. The natural sciences use relatively precise measurement devices and instrumentation to record and observe. For example, such devices as the spectrograph, the high-powered telescope, the electron microscope, quartz clocks, and the micrometer have greatly aided natural scientists in their work. By comparison, the instrumentation of the behavioral sciences and education is primitive. To estimate intelligence or achievement, we compare people to one another and assume that differences between people reflect similar differences on the trait being measured. Another approach to measurement is to try to identify all the aspects of a particular trait. Then, by randomly selecting items for a test of the trait, it is hoped that the trait is being adequately measured. Tests of human functioning in psychology and education often do not give consistent results and occasionally do not measure what they were intended to measure very adequately because the interface between the inner and outer environment has proved difficult to specify.

BASIC VERSUS APPLIED RESEARCH

The terms *basic research* and *applied research* are widely used. However, their exact meaning is obscured by the many perspectives that can be taken in approaching research. Part of the difficulty has to do with stereotypes some people have of the two kinds of research. To many people, basic research is clean, complex, and respectable, but not useful. On the other hand, applied research connotes a real-world setting and is thus perceived as being difficult to control, inaccurate, useful, but not respectable. Unfortunately, these stereotypes do little to clarify basic and applied research. A more accurate way of determining whether a research study is basic or applied is to examine not the setting but the purpose of the investigation. The major purpose of basic research is to develop a base of knowledge upon which theory can be built. The major purpose of applied research is to answer practical and useful questions about policies, programs, projects, procedures, or organizations.

This distinction between basic and applied research is not always useful, however, when looking at a particular piece of research. For example, consider an architect who conducts an investigation into the ways that people form working relationships in an office environment for the purpose of designing a new building that will house the company headquarters. The architect's only interest in doing this research is to develop knowledge specific to a situation. A theory of employee interaction in the work place is clearly not the purpose of the research. Yet another researcher, interested in developing such a theory, might use the results of this study as if it were basic research.

Another way to look at the differences between basic and applied research is to consider the various roles played by those who do the research. The basic researcher studies phenomena in controlled settings for the purpose of trying to understand the relationships involved and to be able, ultimately, to make general statements about these relationships that can form the basis for a theory. Such a person usually works at a research institute or university. The applied scientist tries to test the findings of the basic researcher in applied settings. The applied researcher may also be employed by a university or research institute or may be found in private industry or working for a government agency. In the field of education, such a person might be employed by a curriculum publishing company, a state department of education, or a college of education at a university. Applied researchers are also found in settings in which the application or practitioner role is primary. This is where the teachers, clinical psychologists, school psychologists, social workers, physicians, civil engineers, managers, advertising specialists, and so on are found. Many of these people receive training in doing research, and they use this knowledge for two purposes: (1) to help practitioners understand, evaluate, and use the research produced by basic and applied researchers in their own fields; and (2) to develop a systematic way of addressing the practical problems and questions that arise as they practice their professions. For example, a teacher who notices that a segment of the class is not adequately motivated in science might look at the research literature on teaching science and then systematically try some of the findings suggested by the research.

The relative importance of basic and applied research has been argued. Some say that fields like education are so complex that there is no possibility of developing a theory. The only valuable knowledge research could generate in this kind of setting is in answer to applied questions. Others argue that without theory-oriented basic research, knowledge in the field will have no order or structure and will always have a random hit-or-miss quality.

In an effort to explain further the role of basic research, it might be useful to consider in greater detail some of its characteristics. The purpose of basic research is to advance understanding. This is done by exploring phenomena in very controlled, often artificial circumstances. As a body of knowledge develops, the findings are organized and integrated into theoretical propositions explaining the phenomena in question. Skinner's early laboratory work with learning in pigeons is an example of how basic research can lead to useful applications. Skinner found that the behavior of pigeons could be molded or shaped by reinforcing successive movements that were parts of the total movement (Hilgard and Bower, 1981). Thus, a pigeon could be made to turn in clockwise circles by reinforcing it each time it turned to the right. This notion of shaping learned behavior has been applied with considerable success to programmed educational materials for children and adults. The structure that basic research findings provide should be useful in developing further basic knowledge and also in forming predictions that may be applied in practical settings. However, all this systematic research takes time and money. Many of the problems in education and psychology require decisions now and cannot be delayed until such time as theories become available. Since applied research offers methods for finding solutions to current problems, it is important to contemporary society.

Some of the recent foci of applied educational research have been grading practices, collective bargaining for school personnel, curriculum content, instructional procedures, educational technology, and assessment of achievement. These topics have been investigated with an applied approach because the questions raised in these areas generally have limited or no body of knowledge or theory we can draw upon directly to aid in decision making. On the other hand, the basic research approach to problems such as how learning occurs, the nature of the social climate in a classroom, and the stages of cognitive development in the preschool child seems to be needed for theory development.

In short, a balanced research establishment that includes both basic and applied activities seems most desirable. Graduate training institutions play an important role in guaranteeing this balance by providing training in both kinds of research. Furthermore, federal and private funding sources also play an important role. When funding agencies overemphasize applied research, the basic science interests fade among the professional research community. Unfortunately, there is a tendency for this to occur since the aims of applied research are more readily understood by politicians, government bureaucrats, and the general public. It should be emphasized, however, that distinctions between basic and applied research are often difficult to make. For example, a research project might have been conducted in answer to specific applied questions about the best way to teach spelling. Yet because of the design and conceptualization of the study, its results may have some basic research qualities and be useful in theory formation. In the final analysis, the distinction between basic and applied research often depends more on the intentions and perspectives of the researcher or person reviewing the research than on the methodology used or the setting in which the work was done.

THE INFLUENCE OF THE RESEARCHER

One aspect of research often ignored in textbooks is the researcher. Because research in the behavioral sciences and education is a social process involving interactions among people, the researcher may inadvertently become a part of the research investigation. The researcher can affect the results of the investigation in at least four ways: (1) the selection of a topic, (2) the design of the experiment, (3) the interaction between the researcher and the experimental conditions, and (4) interpretation of the results.

To illustrate the effect of topic selection, let us look at some research reported by Pascarella, Smart, Ethington, and Nettles (1987) concerning the effects of academic and social experiences on the self-concept of black and white men and women. Using a complex statistical procedure, the researchers studied the self-concepts of adults nine years after they had last attended college in terms of their precollege self-concepts, academic and social experiences in college, certain characteristics of the colleges they attended, their early occupational status, and their educational attainments. To be sure, a college education and life's experiences can affect many different aspects of a person. Therefore, in order to do this particular study, Parscarella et al. had to have some interest in self-concept. Furthermore, while the researchers included a number of facets, not all possible variables were studied. For example, the effects of IQ, birth order, or previous success in athletics were not included. Certainly one could name many phenomena that might contribute to the self-concept of college graduates. Of course, the study would have become too large and expensive if a great many different kinds of information had been included. Therefore, the researcher in some sense influences the findings by choosing the topics to be studied.

The researcher can also influence the findings through the design of the experiment. This happens when the researcher chooses the measurement or assessment, data-collection, and data-analysis strategies. We will deal with these topics in depth later in this book. Here, an example will illustrate this aspect of the influence of the researcher upon the findings. Suppose that a researcher were interested in ascertaining the relationship between a male student's athletic ability and his academic performance. If the researcher chose to do his study at a school in which the athletic program was secondary to academic considerations, the findings might be very different than if the study were run in a school that put a premium on athletics. Furthermore, if the researcher were interested in quality of academic performance, the grade-point average might not be the best criterion. Also, the time it takes for the student to run the mile may not be an accurate reflection of general athletic ability. Clearly, in designing an investigation, the researcher makes certain decisions that affect the outcome.

Researchers may be conscious of these problems, but there are experimenter effects that may not be consciously noticed. These have been discussed at length in *Artifact in Behavioral Research,* edited by Rosenthal and Rosnow (1969). Such effects manifest themselves in two ways. First, the experimenter may inadvertently not report events objectively as they happen. Rosenthal (1969) pointed out, for example, that when experimenters make inadvertent computational errors, they usually make them in favor of their expectation of the outcome of the research. The second source of researcher bias in experiments emerges from the interaction of the experimenter and the subject. Rosenthal termed this the *experimenter-bias effect* (EBE). The EBE may be characterized as a self-fulfilling prophecy effect. That is, what the experimenter expects the outcome of his research to be influences the nature of the results. Rosenthal, in reviewing research pertaining to EBE in a variety of settings, even reported experimenter-bias effects in studies with animals and very small aquatic worms, called *planaria*.

A less subtle problem than experimenter bias comes into play when the researcher's own values and needs affect the design, analysis, and interpretation of research. The importance of objectivity in every part of the research process cannot be overemphasized. The purpose of doing research, whether applied or basic, is to find true and dependable information that was not evident before the research was done. However, occasionally researchers or their colleagues may, for various reasons (a need to support a position involving a personal investment, political or financial commitment, the pursuit of fame, or even laziness) forget their objectivity and the purpose of doing the research. Biasing influences may be introduced into the design of the research or, at the extreme, data may be invented.

For example, the sales department of XYZ, Inc., decides to come up with research to show the superiority of one of their new products, a hand cleaner, over that of their competitors. However, they know that their product is really no different from those already on the market. They decide to have a sample of the company's employees try the new item and a similar product of the competition at their place of work. To ensure that the employees will respond in the desired manner, the labels are left on the products. Since no employee wants to jeopardize his or her position in the company, they all report that they prefer XYZ's version. The sales department then reports that 100 percent of the users in their study preferred the XYZ product over that of the competition. The problem with this fictitious study may be obvious, but such difficulties might be concealed in a real setting. Researchers can bias their results by not reporting data that conflict with their views, by selecting samples that can be expected to respond in a certain way, or even by fabricating data. These practices are, of course, misleading, and they undermine the purpose of research. They are also unethical by most accepted standards (e.g., Principle la of the Ethical Principles of Psychologists of the American Psychological Association, reprinted in the *American Psychologist*, 1981, Vol. 38, pp. 633–638). Readers are cautioned to be aware of the occasional occurrences of these improper practices.

Even when a study is done carefully to avoid the introduction of bias or inaccuracies, the researcher can unduly influence interpretation of the research results. Specifically, when one feels that something should have occurred and it did not, there is a strong temptation to say that it did. For example, a graduate student reported to his research supervisor that their experiment was "mildly successful." When the supervisor asked for an explanation, the student reported that the results were in the expected direction to support the theory they were trying to test, but the data were "inconclusive."

The supervisor would have been misled into thinking the data were supporting the theory if the additional explanation had not been requested. On the other hand, the student did not realize the inconsistency in what he had reported. Either the experiment was successful, or it was not. Inconclusive data suggest no conclusion.

Another manifestation of researcher effects in interpretation is ''going beyond the data.'' For example, a researcher who is interested in linguistic competence might design a study to test how much time it takes for subjects to name an object in a picture. On finding that there is a relationship between a subject's response time and the amount of ambiguity in the picture, the researcher might erroneously report that the level of a person's linguistic performance is a function of the abstractness of the material discussed. This would be too general a statement to make on the basis of the study done. Thus researchers must be careful to stay within the boundaries of the data obtained and the study performed when interpreting the results of a study.

In conclusion, there are many ways that a researcher can inadvertently or deliberately influence the findings of a research investigation. Although the research on experimenter effects is not complete, researchers should be aware of the problem. It is generally possible to avoid unintentional biasing of experimental results by using data collectors who do not know the purpose of the study. Furthermore, the effects of the way the researcher conceptualizes the problem and designs the research can be minimized by providing a clear and objective description of the subjects, materials, and procedures. However, the reader should bear in mind that the particular way in which a researcher conceptualized a study is probably not the only way it could have been done. In addition, honest interest in obtaining the truth on the part of the researcher is essential if the study is to be objective and valid. Further, care should be taken to emphasize objectivity when research data is interpreted.

SUMMARY

In this chapter, we have presented a broad overview of science and research. Science has been defined as the systematic organization of knowledge. Science has two purposes, the improvement of the quality of life and the development of explanatory relationships, called *theories*. Research is simply the search for knowledge. Research activities may be undertaken in support of the aims of science, or they may be designed to discover knowledge to aid in answering specific questions or in decision making. Scientific research is systematic and follows the steps of the scientific method.

Researchers obtain knowledge from a variety of sources, among them individuals in a position of authority, tradition, expert opinion, personal experience, reason, common sense, and documentation. For the scientific researcher, personal observation and documentation serve as typical sources of information. However, care must be taken to ensure the accuracy of the information.

Philosophy and science are complementary. Philosophy serves to organize and provide structure for scientific activity and to study the impact and value of scientific knowledge. Three kinds of knowing, metaphorical, rational and empirical, are important in scientific research. Metaphorical knowledge refers to intuitive or symbolic thought. Rational knowledge involves reasoning according to the principles of logic. Empirical knowledge involves knowing based upon objective observation.

Reasoning is a fundamental process performed by researchers. *Deductive* reasoning involves going from general knowledge to the specific case. For example, if we know that all dogs are animals, then we can look at any specific dog and identify it as an animal. *Inductive* reasoning involves going from the specific to the general. It is a useful approach when knowledge about the general case is weak or incomplete. This kind of reasoning is extensively used in research in the behavioral sciences and education. Typically, some question is asked regarding the general characteristics of a group. A small representative sample of the group is chosen for study, and characteristics of this small group are attributed to the larger group. Whether reasoning deductively or inductively, the researcher should be aware that faulty premises will lead to faulty conclusions.

Discovery of cause-and-effect relationships is not a primary concern of science. This is because cause-and-effect relationships are difficult to find. Mill's canons, which suggested procedures for isolating cause-and-effect relationships, are considered outmoded by modern philosophers of science. However, the concept of *cause* has some useful qualities in research. Implicit in cause is the connotation that the environment can be manipulated to produce effects. Further, cause-and-effect relationships can assist in formulating predictions that may be tested.

There are several ways of classifying the sciences into separate disciplines. One method parallels the divisions of university faculties but is not satisfactory because of the great diversity of organization across universities and in different countries. Piaget (1974) suggested division into the *nomothetic, historical, legal,* and *philosophical* sciences.

All sciences have in common the scientific method of research and the goal of theory development. They all have further common ground in their use of deductive and inductive reasoning. However, the various sciences differ in a number of ways as well. First, they vary in techniques of data collection, measurement, and interpretation. Furthermore, certain sciences are older than others. Human interest and understanding had to mature to a point in history when certain questions could be asked, and their answers could be appreciated. Thus questions concerning food and shelter were primary in early civilizations. As society developed, questions about economics, law, and philosophy began to emerge from more complex lifestyles. Eventually, questions concerning human behavior, development, learning, and education began to increase in importance with the increasing needs for an educated populace created by a highly complex technological society. Another distinction between the various disciplines of science has been suggested by Simon (1969), who focused upon the nature of what is studied. Specifically, Simon identifies as *natural sciences* those disciplines concerned with objects and phenomena that occur in nature. He contrasts those sciences with what he calls *sciences of the artificial,* which concern the nonnatural world created by humankind and society. A final distinction between the sciences concerns measurement. That is, some sciences measure phenomena directly, others in varying degrees of indirectness. For example, in physics, measurements may be made very accurately in units such as grams, foot-pounds, and amperes. However, psychology and education must measure characteristics indirectly by comparing the performances of individuals and assuming that performance reflects traits.

Basic research is concerned with searching for knowledge that is fundamental and generalizable. It is typically the kind of research that can contribute to theory formation. *Applied* research is more concerned with knowledge that has immediate applications and would be useful in formulation of decisions and policies. It may be difficult to classify a given study as *basic* or *applied* without knowing the purpose of the research. Even when the purpose of the research is clear, a study intended to be applied might contribute findings useful to the theory of a basic researcher. On the other hand, a study done as basic research might have direct implication for use in an applied setting.

The researcher is an important part of any research and deserves consideration as such. The researcher can influence the results of investigations by (1) selection of the topic, (2) design of the experiment, (3) interaction between the researcher and experimental conditions, and (4) interpretation of the data. Researchers are typically aware of the effects of the first two problems but often not the third or fourth. Specifically, researchers can influence the results of investigations by having expectations for certain outcomes that cause those outcomes to be observed and by inadvertently making biased interpretations of observations. The values and personal needs of the researcher can have profound effects on the research. Objectivity and an honest interest in finding the truth are essential for valid research.

PROBLEMS FOR THOUGHT AND DISCUSSION

1 Are the following deductive arguments correct? Why?
  a All cows are animals
    This is a cow
    Therefore, this is an animal.
  b All students with high grades study diligently
    This is a student with high grades
    Therefore, this student studies diligently.
  c All students who complete these assignments are compulsive
    This student has not completed this assignment
    Therefore, this student is not compulsive.
2 Are the following inductive arguments correct? Why?
  a This is a cow

Cows are usually animals
I am reasonably certain that this is an animal.

b This is a student who studies diligently
Students who have high grades tend to study more diligently
He probably has high grades.

c Students who complete their assignments tend to be more compulsive than those who do not
This student completed his assignment
He is probably more compulsive than other students.

3 What kind of problems could be most usefully considered inductively? What kind of problems should be considered using deductive methods? Which kind of argument is more powerful?

4 Identify the kind of reasoning the researcher is doing in each of the sentences below in italics.

The researcher reads several reports of studies that suggest that the behavior of problem children can be controlled in the psychological clinic by using behavior-modification techniques. *He reasons that it is the behavior modification and not the setting which controls the child's behavior.* Following this idea, *he reasons that behavior modification can be used similarly with problem children in the classroom.* He decides to set up an experiment to test this. Four problem children in a third-grade classroom are selected as subjects in the study. The researcher decides to control their behavior by providing tokens for good behavior. The child can trade the tokens in at the end of the day for a small toy or candy. He finds that the maladaptive behavior of the children in the study is reduced 60 percent. He reasons that, *based upon his observations, behavior modification is useful in classrooms for children with behavior problems.* However, realizing some of the shortcomings of his work, the researcher makes some recommendations. For example, since he did not include all grade levels in his research and since children are noticeably different in other grade levels, *he reasons that the experiment should be repeated with older and younger children before the findings are generalized to those groups.*

5 For each of the following studies, indicate whether, in your opinion, the research described is basic or applied. Give reasons for your choice.

a In a classic study of group dynamics, three leadership styles (democratic, authoritarian, and laissez-faire) were used with groups of students in the classroom. It was noted that the three styles corresponded to differential levels of aggression of the group members (Lewin, Lippitt, & White, 1939).

b As part of a larger project designed to bring secondary educational programs to rural Alaskan communities, the effectiveness of computer-based instruction was compared to other media in classrooms across the state. It was found that computerized instruction was more effective (Mason & Bramble, 1982).

c A sample of Mexican-American and Anglo-American children was tested with the Peabody Picture Vocabulary Test. A small number of items on the test was found to be easier for one group or the other. However, results suggested that the overall score on the test was not unfavorably biased toward either group (Argulewicz & Abel, 1984).

6 Describe how the researcher can deliberately or inadvertently affect each of the following stages in the development of a study.

a selection of a topic

b selection of research sample or subjects
c selection of observation or measurement procedures
d design of procedures for doing the study
e collection of the data
f analysis of the data
g interpretation of the results

REFERENCES

Argulewicz, E. N., & Abel, R. R. (1984). Internal evidence of bias in the PPVT-R for Anglo-American and Mexican-American children. *Journal of School Psychology, 22,* 299–303.

Barclay, J. R., & Wu, W. T. (1980). Classroom climates in Taiwanese and American elementary schools: A cross-cultural study. *Contemporary Educational Psychology, 5,* 65–72.

Carnap, R. (1966). *An introduction to the philosophy of science.* New York: Basic Books.

Charles, C. M. (1985). *Building classroom discipline* (2nd ed.). New York: Longmans.

Cook, T. D., & Campbell, D. T. (1979). *Quasi-experimentation: Design and analysis for field settings.* Chicago: Rand McNally.

Hilgard, E. R., & Bower, G. H. (1981). *Theories of learning* (5th ed.). Englewood Cliffs, NJ: Prentice-Hall.

Lewin, K., Lippitt, R., & White, R. (1939). Patterns of aggressive behavior in experimentally created "social climates." *Journal of Social Psychology, 10,* 271–299.

Mason, E. J., & Bramble, W. J. (1982). A computerized solution to delivery of education in Alaska. *AEDS Monitor, 21*(3), 33–36.

Mill, J. S. (1916). *A system of logic* (8th ed.). London: Longmans.

Pascarella, E. T., Smart, J. C., & Nettles, M. T. (1987). The influence of college on self concept: A consideration of race and gender differences. *American Educational Research Journal, 24,* 49–77.

Piaget, J. (1974). *The place of the sciences of man in the system of sciences.* New York: Harper Torchbooks.

Rosenthal, R. (1969). Interpersonal expectations: Effect of the experimenter's hypothesis. In R. Rosenthal & R. Rosnow (Eds.), *Artifact in behavioral research.* New York: Academic.

Royce, J. R. (1974). Cognition and knowledge: Psychological epistemology. In E. C. Carterette & M. P. Friedman (Eds.), *Handbook of perception,* Vol. 1. New York: Academic, 149–176.

Simon, H. A. (1969). *The sciences of the artificial.* Cambridge, MA: M.I.T.

SUPPLEMENTARY READINGS

Anderson, R. C. (1984). Some reflections on the acquisition of knowledge. *Educational Researcher, 13* (9), 5–10.

Broudy, H. S., Ennis, R. H., & Krimerman, L. I. (Eds.) (1973). *Philosophy of educational research.* New York: Wiley.

De Kruif, P. (1940). *Microbe hunters.* New York: Pocket Books.

Kuhn, T. S. (1970). *The structure of scientific revolutions* (2nd ed.). University of Chicago Press.

McCain, G., & Segal, E. M. (1977). *The game of science* (3rd ed.). Monterey, CA: Brooks/Cole.

Monte, C. F. (1975). *Psychology's scientific endeavor*. New York: Praeger.

Phillips, B. N. (1987). On science, mirrors, lamps, and professional practice. *Professional School Psychology, 2,* 221–229.

Popkowitz, T. S. (1984). *Paradigm and ideology in educational research: The social functions of the intellectual*. New York: Falmer Press.

Rosenthal, R., & Rosnow, R. (Eds.), (1969). *Artifact in behavioral research*. New York: Academic.

Rudner, R. S. (1966). *Philosophy of social science*. Englewood Cliffs, NJ: Prentice-Hall.

Russell, B. (1917). *Logic and mysticism*. London: G. Allen.

Turner, M. B. (1967). *Philosophy and the science of behavior*. New York: Appleton-Century-Crofts.

CHAPTER 2

MODES OF RESEARCH AND THE SCIENTIFIC METHOD

In the last chapter, we reviewed the goals of science. We found the fundamental aim of science to be the development of explanatory conceptualizations, called *theories*. Furthermore, we noted that not all research has in common with science this goal of theory development. For example, applied or decision-oriented research does not have the development of theory as its objective. However, this kind of research may still be scientific in that the methods of science are used to explore the phenomena systematically.

Let us consider an example of scientific research that does not seek to further the aims of science. It is done only to find specific knowledge for decision making. One morning, a college student who liked to fix automobiles decided to take the family car to school. However, when he turned the key in the ignition, the car did not start. The student reasoned that the problem could be in the electrical system; otherwise, he would have heard the motor turning over when he tried to start the automobile. He guessed, first, that the problem had to do with poor battery connections or a dead battery. However, after checking the output of the battery and the cables connected to it, he decided that the problem was not there. He next suspected that the wire connections to the electric starter motor might be the source of the problem. Perhaps they had worked loose or become wet in the heavy rain of the night before. Finding that this was not the case, he checked the fuses, suspecting that one of them had blown. He did find a blackened fuse in the fuse holder, and when it was replaced, the car started immediately. On the way to school, the student reasoned that fuses blow out when electrical circuits become overloaded. Since faulty electrical connections or wires can often cause this to happen, he decided to check the electrical circuitry for possible defects after he returned from classes.

Notice that the student proceeded *systematically* to solve the problem of getting the car started. We commonly use this kind of approach in solving the problems that we meet daily. Some other aspects of this approach, besides its systematic nature, bear mentioning. Specifically, the student focused on one aspect of the problem at a time. Considerations that did not bear directly on the problem were treated as extraneous and ignored. Thus while the fuel system, the transmission, the valves in the engine, and so on, may be important in the operation of a motor vehicle, they were not considered at all in getting the car to start in this case. In a sense, the student *controlled* these considerations in his investigations by determining that they were extraneous to the particular problems he faced. Because controlling extraneous influences is an important aspect of scientific research, the methodology for control will be dealt with in detail in later chapters.

Another aspect of the student's investigations in getting his car started is that he (1) proposed a solution, (2) investigated it by observation, and then (3) rejected or accepted his proposed solution based on observations. He followed this procedure with each solution he proposed until he found one that was supported by his observations. Notice that the student sought to integrate what he learned about the blown fuse into his general knowledge of electrical problems.

These aspects of scientific research—systematic investigation, control of extraneous considerations, selection of solutions based upon observations, and interpretation of findings—can be found in disciplined inquiry of all kinds. Historians, physicists, educational researchers, and engineers all use the same kind of approach to finding solutions. Of course, the kind of proposed solution, the type of observations made, the techniques of observation, and the interpretations vary greatly among the different fields of study. However, all scientific research has in common the scientific method of finding solutions.

THE SCIENTIFIC METHOD

The scientific method is usually described in five steps. However, some identify only three or four steps, while others say there are six or seven steps (see, for example, True, 1983; Jones, 1973). The number of steps is not important. What is important is the process that the researcher follows (a hypothetico-deductive paradigm). The scientific method should not be regarded as a series of steps but, rather, as a set of overlapping and interdependent procedures for systematically studying phenomena and revealing knowledge. In other words, it is a way of thinking when doing research. In fact, the philosopher John Dewey referred to the scientific method as a "habit of mind" (Dewey, 1910). The steps of the scientific method described here need not be followed in order, although researchers usually write up their reports as if they were. They do this more to meet the conventions of research writing established over the years and to show that each of the steps was attended to in their research than to show that they began with the first step of the process. To illustrate the steps in the scientific method of research, we will refer to the previous example of the student whose car would not start.

Step 1 The first step in the scientific method is usually characterized as the sensing or realizing that some problem exists through familiarity with a topic. For example, something might happen that cannot be easily explained, or the way to accomplish some goal may not be evident. The realization that the car did not start even though it had worked previously served to establish the existence of the problem for the student.

Step 2 The problem is clarified; that is, the nature, scope, and specifics of the problem are identified. In our example, the student recognized the problem to be, simply, "How do I get the car started?" The problem is a question that determines, to a large extent, the direction the investigation will take. For example, had the student recognized his problem as "How will I get to school today?" or "Whom shall I ask to fix the car?" his subsequent behavior would have been very different.

Step 3 The third step is devising the plan for the research. To do this, a statement describing a possible solution to the problem is made, and procedures are identified to test the plausibility of this tentative solution. Going back to our example, the student first thought that the problem might be with the battery, and so he developed a strategy to test that possibility. Finding that solution to be implausible or unsupported by his observations, he reasoned that the problem might be due to damp terminals on the starter motor, and he proceeded to test this. He continued to make plausible guesses about the cause of his inability to get the car started until he found one that was supported by what he saw in his investigations. Each guess he made led to a *strategy,* a plan for investigating the plausibility of the solution.

Step 4 This step is decision making. Based upon the data collected in the previous step, the researcher evaluates the adequacy of the proposed solution. If the data support the solution, it is accepted as reasonable. The student in our example rejected the reasonableness of two possible solutions before he found one that was adequately supported by his observations.

Step 5 The final step involves interpretation and generalization of the findings into the larger body of knowledge about the phenomenon. This might involve consideration of previous knowledge in terms of the new knowledge or further experimentation. Both consideration of what is already known and further experimentation in light of the new knowledge might be appropriate. We saw this in our example when the student replaced the worn-out fuse. In a sense, he was investigating whether or not the car would start with a new fuse in place of the old one. Furthermore, as he was driving to school, the student considered his knowledge about the fuse in his car in terms of what he knew about blown fuses in general and, therefore, determined to search for a short circuit.

Many different kinds of studies are typically conducted in education and the behavioral and social sciences. We will find the scientific method implicit in much of this research. In this chapter, four broad categories are described: (1) historical research, (2) descriptive research, (3) experimental and quasi-experimental research, and (4) policy research and evaluation.

These categories of research are not as precise or as mutually exclusive as one might suspect on first glance. We have tried to provide definitions and examples of the various categories below; however, different people might put the same research in different categories. For this reason, the important points to gain from the descriptions of the different kinds of research are (1) the pervasiveness of the scientific method and (2) the variety of approaches taken to research in education.

HISTORICAL RESEARCH

Historical research is a specialty in itself. Considerable training and skill are required to perform this kind of research effectively. For this reason, we are not able to cover it extensively in the present text. However, a brief discussion and an illustrative example is presented in order to permit comparison of it with other research approaches common in education and related fields. Historical research is often grouped together with legal research. This is done for a couple of reasons. First, to gain a complete understanding of one, the other will probably have to be considered. For example, to understand why there is a shortage of mathematics teachers during a particular period, it might be necessary to look at the state statutes that existed at a previous time regarding the provision of funds to help college students study mathematics education. Further, laws often originate as the codification of past practices or out of a need arising from events that may be studied historically. A second reason for grouping legal with historical research is that some of the methods for doing research in history and law may be similar.

However, the attitudes, goals, and perspectives of researchers in history and law are necessarily different. While the historian seeks to document and verify what really happened in the past, a legal researcher may be more concerned with establishing past events in the context of some legal precedent or law. In the present discussion, we will concentrate on historical research. Students interested in legal research may pursue this topic elsewhere.

The purpose of historical research has changed considerably since the ancient Greeks conducted historical studies to discover and describe past events. In the present century, historical research has acquired a more sophisticated purpose: interpretation of the present. Thus historical research can provide a perspective for understanding the customs, traditions, and facts of the present by studying the events of earlier times. Furthermore, characteristics of present society may be traced to earlier practices and influences. In addition, research into the past can often be useful in formulating predictions for the future.

In the recent past, historical research in education was not popular. Part of the reason for this may be that good historical research is not easy; it tends to be slow, painstaking, and exacting when compared to some other kinds of research. Perhaps the commitment to methodical scholarly activity is so great that few researchers in our fast-moving, technology-oriented society are able to find the time or the patience to immerse themselves in problems requiring historical study. This is unfortunate because there are certainly lessons to be learned from the past.

To clarify the discussion of historical research, we shall consider a paper on the history of Canadian public education presented by F. Henry Johnson (1969) during the centenary year of Canada's independence. Johnson studied a variety of information relating to the beginnings of public education in Canada. By studying various sources (books about the period, letters written by educators of the time, old records maintained by school boards, and articles and books written by scholars of the educational system), Johnson was able to suggest that the early Canadian schools were relatively progressive for their time. Johnson found, for example, that in the 1860s, Canadian teachers were concerned about placing too much pressure on students to memorize material. In addition, teachers were encouraged to use "positive" means to control or manage their classes. For example, the Ontario schools experimented with giving merit cards that could be traded in for prize books for appropriate performance and behavior. These practices predated the beginning of the scientific study of the psychology of learning by about 10 years and Skinner's earliest work by more than half a century. Furthermore, Hewett (1964) is credited with applying what is essentially the merit-card approach in what he called the "engineered classroom" about a century later. All this does not suggest that Canadian schools of the 1860s were superior to today's schools. On the contrary, there were relatively few schools, teachers were poorly trained, and materials available for use in the classrooms were inadequate. Furthermore, class size tended to be very large; in some cases, as many as 150 pupils were taught by a single teacher. Finally, Johnson found that there was a respect for the importance of education in molding society and an emphasis on compulsory schooling at the time of Canada's confederation.

In addition to institutions such as schools, historical perspective can be applied to curricula, organizations, individuals, laws, scientific discoveries, innovative practices, and a variety of other topics. The steps of the scientific method can be detected in historical investigations, but the nature of the data requires some techniques peculiar to historical research. Initially, the problem is formulated. It might concern a need for more suitable interpretation of past events in relation to the conditions of the present, or it might result from gaps in knowledge about the past. An important consideration in formulating the problem is the availability of the necessary data. Of course, the researcher may not be aware of what data are available until after he or she has done some research.

In the second stage, historical data, or source materials, are collected. The researcher obtains source materials in a variety of ways. The library, of course, is a very important resource. In addition, court records, old newspapers, museum collections, government reports, personal letters, government statistical files, eyewitness accounts, and anything else the researcher can find to shed light on the problem will be surveyed.

After the information is collected, it is subjected to careful scrutiny. This constitutes the third stage of historical research, the stage in which the *authenticity* and *accuracy* of the material is determined. Establishing authenticity of historical material is called *external criticism*. In doing this, the researcher investigates the genuineness of the material. For example, if, in the course of studying the emergence of the position of county superintendent of schools, a historian locates a 75-year-old letter from the dean of the teacher training school of the state university to the governor about the importance of qualified administrators at the county level, he must establish the authenticity of the letter. To do this, he might have the paper and ink analyzed to ensure that they conform to materials in use three-quarters of a century earlier. He might also compare the dean's signature on the letter to his signature on other documents. Furthermore, the writing style would be carefully reviewed to ensure that it is representative of the language of the time the letter was allegedly written. The historian must be sure that the conclusions he reaches are based upon genuine data. Once the authenticity of the information is established, *internal criticism* is performed to determine the meaning and trustworthiness of the message in the document. Suppose, for example, that the historian had two authentic letters instead of one. One was from the dean as described above, and the second was from a banker to his Aunt Martha who lived in a neighboring state. One suspects that the opinions expressed in the letter from the dean should be given more weight in determining what happened. However, this might not be true if the banker were also an elected member of the state assembly.

An element of criticism with regard to the accuracy of historical data is the relationship of the source of the message to the past events under study. For example, one might not be as inclined to believe a newspaper's or encyclopedia's account of an event as one would to believe congruent descriptions of several witnesses. Furthermore, descriptions of objects given by others usually do not convey as much information as does studying the objects directly. Thus sources of historical information have been classified into two groups, primary and secondary. *Primary* sources are those closest to the subject under study, such as eyewitness accounts and actual objects. *Secondary* sources are accounts offered by those who did not actually see the object or event but obtained information and provided descriptions of what they learned. Typical secondary sources are newspapers, encyclopedias, and magazine articles. In a court of law, a distinction is made between direct and hearsay evidence. Direct evidence is similar to primary source information, whereas hearsay evidence is analogous to secondary source data. Direct evidence is considered more important in court proceedings than hearsay. Historical researchers usually try to maximize the amount of information that they get from primary sources. For this reason, in tracing the early development of education in Canada, Johnson used several annual reports to the Department of Education as sources rather than trying to locate the same material summarized in history books.

In the fourth stage of historical research, the data that have been accumulated and evaluated are further analyzed. Knowledge gleaned in this stage is integrated and synthesized into explanations. Connections between facts are reasoned, and causes and relationships are inferred. For example, in reviewing the various approaches to the study of human behavior prevalent in the early part of the twentieth century, Snelbecker (1985) was able to conclude that as a result of structuralism, functionalism, behaviorism, Gestalt psychology, and the psychoanalytic movement, the field of psychology became more experimental and objective.

In the fifth step of the historical research process, the data and interpretations of previous steps are integrated to form a more general concept. For example, Snelbecker's findings on the origins of objectivity and experimental approaches in psychology might be generalized to other behavioral sciences, such as education. Of course, such generalizations cannot be fully accepted unsupported. Thus the generalizations in the fifth step of the historical process will usually result in reformulation of the problems and hypotheses suggesting directions for further exploration.

Historical research is unique among the various types of research in that the sources of data being studied are usually not available for the researcher's direct scrutiny. The researcher bears a special burden of impartial interpretation. Furthermore, the researcher must be sure that he understands the perspective of the sources of information. For example, one would expect a police officer's perspective of a riot to be different from that of one of the rioters. Furthermore, if the historical researcher were a police officer or a rioter, he might not be completely objective in ascertaining the necessary facts.

DESCRIPTIVE RESEARCH

We will use the term "descriptive research" to represent a broad range of activities that have in common the purpose of describing situations or phenomena. These descriptions may be necessary for decision making or to support broader research objectives. For example, if a school board wants to plan adequately for implementing a new and effective science program, its members must know how many children will be in each of the grade levels to use the program for the next few years. They also need to know the number of teachers who are not familiar with the new program. Research activities designed to meet these needs can facilitate decisions about the number of books and science kits to be bought and the number of teachers to attend a workshop on use of the program materials.

Descriptive research is also conducted to advance the broader aims of science. In this context, it is usually performed to develop knowledge on which the problems and explanations of subsequent research will be based. For example, a researcher may be interested in the effects of culture on reading achievement. But first he must describe what he means by "culture." He begins by studying two cultures to find the ways in which they are similar and different. He discovers that one culture has a diet consisting largely of vegetables, a written language based on phonic symbols, and a polytheistic religion. The other culture has more meat and fish in its diet, its written language is pictorial, and its religion is based upon sun worship. Our researcher may now know enough about the two cultures to begin to develop problems for research on reading and culture. (However, he still must explain what "reading" means.) The census studies performed every decade by the United States government provide descriptive data that commonly clarify problems for researchers. For example, the finding that a type of occupation contains a disproportionate representation of a particular ethnic group might suggest research problems to an industrial psychologist.

In the present discussion, we divide descriptive research into two broad categories representing quantitative and qualitative approaches. *Quantitative descriptive research* uses measurement and statistical principles and models familiar to many natural and physical scientists. In other words, quantitative research involves quantification of the phenomena under study. In contrast, *qualitative research* deals with the observations, impressions, and interpretations of researchers and is, therefore, more difficult to define succinctly. "It is at best an umbrella term covering an array of interpretive techniques which seek to describe, decode, translate and otherwise come to terms with the meaning...of certain more or less naturally occurring phenomena...." (Van Maanen, 1983, p. 9). Of the types of studies included in this chapter, case and field studies and perhaps action research might be classified as *qualitative* relatively more often, while ex post facto research, correlational research, developmental research, and survey research might be more often classified as *quantitative*. Archival research might be either kind. However, one would have to look carefully at a given study to determine whether it was quantitative or qualitative and would probably find that most research had elements of both.

Each approach has a long tradition in scholarly research. The quantitative tradition emerges from the positivist view that order exists among elements and phenomena in the world regardless of whether humans are conscious of the order. The job of the researcher is to expose that order. On the other hand, the qualitative researcher believes knowledge is constructed symbolically, based on conventions widely held within the community. Thus the qualitative approach is said to stem from the conventionalist view (Hatch, 1985).

Considerable debate has raged over which tradition is more appropriate for the study of education, psychology, and related areas. This debate has, on occasion, been referred to as "the quantoids versus the smooshes" (Hatch, 1985). In the past, quantitative research was held in higher esteem by most social and behavioral scientists and educational researchers. There was a tendency to associate quantitative methods with the "hard" or "real" sciences and qualitative methods with humanism, soft thinking, and shoddy research. Of course, neither stereotype was justified. More recently, it has been argued that models of research that fit the agricultural and physical sciences (e.g., where one can empirically determine the number of cabbages a field produces or how fast an object is moving over a distance) are often not well-suited to the kinds of questions one addresses in the social and behavioral sciences and in education (see, for example, Broudy, 1983; Eisner, 1984; Shulman, 1981). Our position in the present text is that there must be a place in the study of human behavior for a variety of methodologies and approaches and for consideration of the contexts in which observations were made. In the presentation of descriptive approaches that follows, various kinds of studies are identified. The reader should be aware that these classifications may be difficult to apply in a strict way to any single study because it is likely that a given study includes elements of several classifications. The purpose of describing phenomena or events and the systematic approach represented by the scientific method are common threads that run through these studies.

Action Research

Research designed to uncover effective ways of dealing with problems in the real world can be referred to as *action research*. This kind of research is not confined to a particular methodology or paradigm. The example we present here is a study of the effectiveness of training teenage parents to care for their infants (Field, 1981). The study is based on statistical and other evidence that infants of teenage mothers seem to be exposed to more risks than are other infants. The mothers and children were recruited for participation in the study while the children were still in the neonate period. Mothers were trained at home or in an infant nursery. A control group received no training. The mothers trained at home were visited at 2-week intervals over a 12-month period. Those trained in the nursery setting attended 3 days per week for 6 months, were paid minimum wage, and assisted as staff in the center. Results of the study suggested that the children of both groups of trained mothers benefited more in terms of their health and cognitive measures than did the control children. Generally greater benefits were realized by children of the mothers trained in the nursery than were realized by children of the mothers trained at home.

Field's study illustrates several points about action research. First, the results of such research have direct application to real-world problems. Second, elements of both quantitative and qualitative approaches can be found in such studies. For example, quantitative measures of weight, height, and cognitive skills were obtained in this study. However, primarily from personal impressions and observations and without the benefit of systematic quantitative data, the researcher was able to say that the mothers in the nursery center showed some unexpected vocational aspirations to become nurses. Third, treatments and methods that are investigated are flexible and might change during the study in response to the results as they are obtained. Thus, action research is more systematic and empirical than some other approaches to innovation and change, but it does not lead to carefully controlled scientific experiments that are generalizable to a wide variety of situations and settings.

Ex Post Facto Research

Very often, research is conducted on effects that have taken place in the past. This kind of research is usually called *ex post facto* since it is "after the fact." Because such investigations are sometimes conducted to search for causes of things that have already happened by comparing previously established conditions, this kind of research is also often referred to as *causal comparative*. An example should help to clarify what is meant by ex post facto research.

Backman (1972) studied patterns of mental abilities in four ethnic groups. She further broke down the ethnic groups into upper-middle and lower-middle socioeconomic status (SES) and males and females and looked at six different kinds of mental abilities in a sample of 2925 twelfth-grade students who had taken part in Project TALENT in 1960. Backman reported that black subjects tended to have lower average scores than the other groups and that Asian subjects tended to have the highest average scores. Furthermore, Backman reported that differences in mental ability between SES groups were not impressive enough to interpret. However, sex of the student was found to be closely related to pattern of mental abilities.

A careful review of the Backman study illustrates several important points about ex post facto research. First of all, the researcher had no control over the data that she studied. That is, subjects could not be assigned to a particular ethnic group, sex, or socioeconomic level by the experimenter. Since the investigator could not control these variables, she could not be sure about their effects. This is true of ex post facto research in general. To understand this point better, consider the finding that males and females had different mental abilities. Would it be acceptable to say that being a male or female had certain effects upon mental abilities from these results? Or would it be more correct to say only that there was a relationship between sex of the student and pattern of mental ability? Clearly it would be better simply to recognize the association than to attribute effects. One cannot tell whether the biological effects of being a male or female or the many experiences and characteristics that go with being male or female in our society caused the differences. Notice that this study is primarily descriptive. That is, based upon results of the study, the researcher attempted to describe the mental abilities of high school students.

The ex post facto study is particularly useful when the variables being investigated cannot be controlled by the experimenter. Another context in which the ex post facto study is useful is when the investigator could control what is being investigated but to do so would be irresponsible or unethical. For example, there has been concern that artificial food colorings may cause hyperactivity and learning problems in young children. An experiment could be designed to test this in which some children are given heavy doses of food coloring, others are not, and then, after a period of time, the behavior and performance of the two groups are compared. Of course, such research could be dangerous to the children involved and is therefore inhumane and unethical. An investigator could use the ex post facto approach to study the diets of children who demonstrate known behavioral and learning problems and to compare their diets with those of children who do not have such problems. The degree to which greater problems are consistently found among children who have large amounts of artificial food coloring in their diets would suggest conclusions about the relationship between food coloring and learning and behavior problems.

The major weakness of the ex post facto approach is that characteristics researched outside the laboratory are very complex. In Backman's study, for example, it cannot be said that there is a simple effect that can be traced to ethnic group membership. Specifically, being Asian does not imply being exposed to a single set of cultural influences. One can be Asian and be Chinese, Japanese, Korean, Vietnamese, Malaysian, etc. Moreover, third- or fourth-generation Asian-Americans are probably more like other groups of Americans than like first-generation Asian-Americans, and it is probably easier to maintain Old World customs and traditions in ethnic neighborhoods in large cities than in rural areas. So, although it may be interesting to note differences among the ethnic groups in patterns of mental abilities, it is difficult to tell what these differences really mean. Since fewer Asians are usually found in rural areas than in urban areas of the United States, perhaps Backman's study of ethnic groups was really comparing rural to urban students.

Another problem, somewhat related, concerns appropriate sampling of subjects. Since the researcher must confine the investigation to the available data, generalizing to the whole population might be difficult. Again, let's look at the Backman study for an illustration. Twelfth-grade students who participated in the Project TALENT study in 1960 were tested, and Backman reported on one phase of the results. If the study were done today, would the same results be found? Backman's most important finding related to differences between males and females. Certainly, society has changed since 1960 regarding attitudes towards sex roles. But have these changes affected patterns of mental ability? Clearly this cannot be answered by the 1960 Project TALENT data.

Notice that ex post facto research is useful because it allows for investigation of problems that would not otherwise be suitable for study. However, there are difficulties in using this approach to find definite answers. It is likely that the primary value of the method is in raising specific questions about general problems that can then be explored more systematically using other methods.

Case and Field Studies

Case and field studies are very similar. Usually, case studies involve in-depth consideration of one person, group, project, institution, agency, or other entity. They are basically intensive investigations of the factors that contributed to characteristics of the case. In a sense, the physician who investigates the condition of a patient is performing a case study. The same can be said for the work of the psychologist, social worker, marriage counselor, efficiency expert, and school administrator when they study a specific person, group, institution, or school.

Field studies are similar to case studies except for the point of view of the researcher. Specifically, researchers who conduct case studies tend to be practitioners who are interested in understanding a condition so that it can be treated or altered in some way. In addition, many case studies are conducted to foster understanding of how current conditions or characteristics developed for practical reasons (e.g., to provide better public services or a more effective economic basis for those services or to make a medical diagnosis). On the other hand, those who conduct field studies tend to be more interested in fostering general understanding of the phenomena involved and may have little interest in changing the situation. For example, sociologists who study social trends in a society might approach the society as if it were a case. That is, they would use methodology similar to the practitioner's approach in performing a case study. Similarly, anthropologists interested in studying the origin of moral concepts in a culture will also approach the culture, whether it is an ancient city-state, a tropical island society, or a large multiethnic urban high school as if it were a case.

The case-study approach to research in the behavioral sciences is well established. Increased emphasis on it has been advocated to handle the particularly complex problems of education by Lutz and Ramsey (1974), who suggested that some of the information required of educational researchers may not be available using any other method. For example, the qualitative aspects of how teachers interact with parents, students, and administrators in a school district during a time of community crisis would be best assessed by a participant observer who is trained to be objective and impartial in recording and describing the nature of social climate and interaction. Warren's (1967) anthropological study of education in a German village and Grant's (1979) study of the Soviet educational system are examples. These two studies are different in interesting ways. While Warren focused on a single circumscribed setting within a country, Grant's work was designed to capture the nature of a whole nation's educational system. Both tell about school experiences, but they tell their stories differently.

A Case Study in Reading Acquisition

As an example of a case study, we will look at a study of six preschool children ranging in age from 2 years, 9 months to 4 years, 10 months who learned to read without instruction. The research, really an integration of six case studies, was done to determine whether there was a pattern of learning to read without instruction that all the children followed. In this study, reported by Anbar (1986), parents had to verify that their children were able to read and had not received systematic reading instruction in the past. The children also were required to read 24 words (arranged in short sentences) with no more than three errors in order to be included in the study.

In an attempt to discover the processes by which these children had learned to read, Anbar interviewed the parents intensively on two occasions. The first interview was open-ended and less structured than the second. The two interviews were designed to explore specific relevant information and, at the same time, to allow each pair of parents an opportunity to provide insight about any unique or unusual conditions that existed in a particular situation. In addition, each child was administered an intelligence test and a test of picture recognition (the Peabody Picture Vocabulary Test). After the parental interviews and assessments of cognitive and reading status were completed, the data were compiled and analyzed in the form of a case study for each child. The case studies were then summarized in tabular form. From these tables, the researcher was able to identify seven stages followed by the children in the process of learning to read. The process began with the children becoming engaged in activities that increased their awareness of books and print. This was typically followed by learning letters and increasing sight vocabulary. Following this, the children went on to learn sounds for the letters and then to make words by putting together letter blocks, plastic letters, and other similar toys. After some practice in making words and reading from familiar books, the children began to try to sound out unfamiliar words. Reading for enjoyment did not seem to occur before the age of 4 in any of the children. Further, although the parents had reported that their children had not had systematic reading instruction in the past, Anbar was able to determine that the parents had all engaged in a considerable amount of activity with the children that was related to reading (e.g., playing letter games, coaching children in vocabulary development, teaching letter sounds, etc.). Anbar concluded that the role of the parents was essential to the children's early reading acquisition.

A Field Study: Communication in the Classroom on an Indian Reservation

Our example of a field study is an investigation by Philips (1983) of how language usage by Indians living on a reservation in central Oregon is culturally unique. This research was facilitated by the fact that most residents of the reservation spoke English as their first language. Supporting the study was evidence that children on the reservation performed much worse than did other students in academic achievement testing and scored lowest of all in language areas. The researcher gathered her data primarily through observation. That is, she sat with, observed, and followed the children in and outside of the classroom. She interviewed and observed many members of the community, visited homes, and lived in the community, all the while taking notes and tape-recording. This kind of study, long done by anthropologists, is called *ethnographic research.*

In order to determine the effects of culture on language, Philips observed four classrooms (two first- and two sixth-grade classes) in depth. Two of the classrooms were on the reservation and consisted of 95 percent Indian students; for comparison purposes, the other two classrooms were in the nearby town and consisted of 95 percent Anglo students. Philips found that like other youngsters, Indian children learn socially acceptable communication patterns at home and in their communities from adults with whom they interact and whom they observe. Thus, by the time they arrive at school at the age of 6, they have adapted to the Indian cultural patterns of communication. Yet school is oriented toward Anglo patterns of communication. For example, Philips reported major differences between the two cultures in the degree of emphasis on verbal communication skills for younger members of the community. In the Indian culture, words were used by young people primarily to transmit information. While older members of the community participated relatively more in verbal interaction in large group activities (by running council meetings, making speeches, discussing politics, etc.), verbal communication among young people tended to be limited and efficient. Younger members of the community were more involved in activities using visual communication (athletics, rodeo competitions, ritual dancing, etc.). Young people in both cultures were physically active, but Indian children were given less incentive than were Anglo children to participate verbally in the adult culture. Other differences involved the use of phrases, attention behavior, ways of designating speaker change in conversations, and other aspects of verbal socialization.

Using the participant observer technique enabled Philips to record considerable data that would otherwise have been missed. For example, she was able to observe whether eye contact was maintained in certain kinds of communication or whether the muscles around the eyes were tightened to communicate attention to a speaker. Further, she was able to show how teachers from outside the Indian culture, who did not understand the subtleties of communication within the culture, had difficulty communicating with children in the classroom.

The Significance of Case and Field Studies   The case- and field study approach contrasts sharply with other research strategies in the behavioral sciences in several ways. In the case study, an attempt is made to study a multitude of factors by limiting the number of cases observed. In most other kinds of behavioral research, a few factors are studied in a large sample of cases. For example, in the Backman (1972) study that we discussed earlier, only SES, ethnic group, sex, and mental abilities were studied in a sample of 2925 subjects. On the other hand, the preschool reading study we just reviewed had only six subjects, whose background, behavior, and social environment had been intensely studied.

Another distinguishing feature of case and field research when compared to other kinds of research is that the factors under study are usually not oversimplified. That is, they tend to be studies of phenomena as they exist in the natural setting. To illustrate what we mean here, we will contrast the Philips study with the Backman research mentioned earlier. In the Backman work ethnic-group membership was considered de facto to mean cultural-group membership. No further definition of *cultural group* was given. However, in the Philips study, the meaning of culture was carefully detailed to include language, socialization, family relations, child rearing, geographic environment, economics, food preferences, and community roles, among other concerns.

The case- and field-study approach is generally useful in bringing to light relationships that can be further studied in other ways. In order to ask research questions, one must know that a problem area exists. Very often, suggestions for more tightly controlled research are garnered from intensive case studies. Moreover, this process can also work the opposite way. That is, research conducted in more tightly controlled artificial circumstances can produce findings that would then be subjected to carefully designed case and field studies. Indeed, the Philips work we just reviewed may be traced to earlier basic research in linguistics. Regarding the Anbar preschool reading study, one might raise the question of how children who show early reading skill relate to their peers in school settings when they reach first grade. Such a question might be approached with an ethnographic participant-observer model of the kind Philips used in her study of Indian classrooms. The ethnographic technique is difficult to do well because the researcher must be both an objective observer while, at the same time, participating fully in the setting. Considerable training is required to master this technique.

The case-study approach has certain obvious limitations. Because such a small sample is involved, generalization of findings to other cases is hazardous. Another very important problem concerns bias. A case study can be seriously biased in two ways. First, in selecting a case to study, the researcher might bias outcomes by using a case in which the findings can be fairly dependably predicted. Second, bias can be introduced when the researcher begins to collect and interpret observations. It is the open-ended nature of the case study that causes this particular problem.

Correlational Research

Would it not be useful to be able to know whether variations in one trait or characteristic correspond with variations in another? For example, if we knew what a person's score was on a test of mathematical concepts, it would be nice to know whether that corresponds in a systematic way to his ability to use mathematical skills on the job as an accountant. This is the kind of problem addressed in correlational studies. Here we will discuss correlational methods only briefly. However, the topic will be considered in greater detail in Chapter 6. Table 2-1 depicts three of the different possibilities for the relationship between score on a mathematics test and performance on the job as rated by a supervisor on a scale of 1 to 5, with 1 meaning very incompetent and 5 meaning very competent. In each case, a person's score on one measure is paired with his score on the other. For instance in the first example, the first person scored 10 in math and 5 in performance, the second scored 9 in math and 4 in performance, and so on. We can plot each pair of scores as a single point on a graph (see Figure 2-1). Notice that the point represented by each pair of scores is found by drawing a line through the mathematics axis perpendicular to it at each mathematics score. At each corresponding performance score, another line is drawn perpendicular to the performance axis. Where the two perpendicular lines cross locates the point for that pair of scores. This has been done on the graph for example 1 with two points. Drawing points in this manner results in a kind of graph called a *scattergram* or *scatter diagram*. Real-life data rarely exhibit the straight-line relationships that we see in Figure 2-1.

TABLE 2-1
THREE EXAMPLES OF MATHEMATICS TEST SCORES AND
SUPERVISOR'S PERFORMANCE RATINGS

Mathematics	Performance Rating
Example 1	
10	5
9	4
8	3
7	2
6	1
Example 2	
10	5
9	2
8	5
7	2
6	5
Example 3	
10	1
9	2
8	3
7	4
6	5

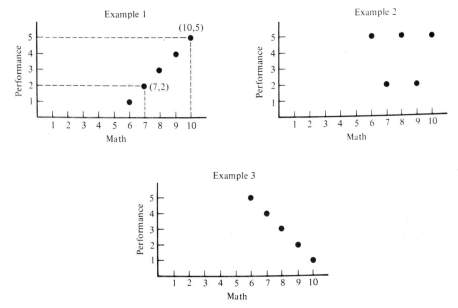

FIGURE 2-1
Pairs of scores plotted as points from three examples in Table 2-1.

More often, data collected in actual situations will look more like the examples shown in Figure 2-2.

We use an index called the *Pearson product-moment correlation coefficient* to summarize the relationship that exists between two variables. The symbol for this is r_{xy} and it is read "the correlation of X and Y." When variables X and Y are perfectly related, as in example 1 in Table 2-1, then $r_{xy} = +1.00$. This value is the maximum positive value of a correlation coefficient. The plus indicates that higher scores on one variable are paired with higher scores on the other. Of course, lower scores also correspond on both variables. Example 3 shows a correlation of -1.00. Can you tell why? The answer, of course, is that the points are arranged along a straight line and that is the reason for the 1.00, and the negative sign in front of the 1.00 reflects the fact that higher scores on one variable correspond to lower scores on the other. Example 3 represents the maximum negative value of the correlation coefficient. Thus r_{xy} can be any value between $+1.00$ and -1.00. Now what about example 2 in Table 2-1? Since there is no real relationship between the two variables, $r_{xy} = 0.00$. An r_{xy} of 0.00 means that there is no relationship.

Now let us turn to the scattergrams in Figure 2-2. Notice that in example 1 $r_{xy} = .92$. This means that there is a high degree of relationship between the two variables. Since the sign of the correlation is positive, higher scores on one variable tend to be paired with higher scores on the other. Example 2 in

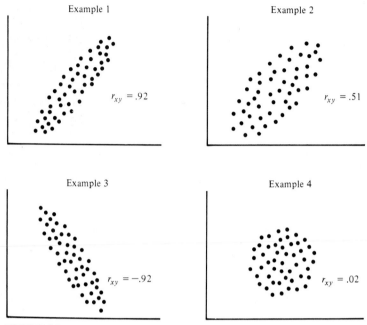

FIGURE 2-2
Scatter diagrams from four sets of realistic data.

Figure 2-2 shows an even wider scatter of the points. Therefore, less relationship is indicated than in example 1. In example 3, we see a strong negative relationship. The −.92 means that higher scores on one variable correspond to the lower scores on the other. Data in example 4 demonstrate almost no relationship. This is reflected in the scattergram and the correlation coefficient.

We will have more to say about correlation in later chapters, but for the present this discussion should have provided enough background for an understanding of correlational studies. These studies seek to discover how variations in scores on one factor correspond to scores on other factors. This purpose is readily apparent in research reported by Hoge and McKay (1986). The research concerns the relationship between scores on the Child Behavior Checklist-Teacher's Report Form developed by Edelbrock and Achenbach (1982) and teachers' and parents' assessments of overall school adjustment in four areas (work, behavior, learning, and happiness). The study was based on a sample of 172 boys in the first through the sixth grade drawn from 12 classrooms. From among 96 volunteers, 22 parents were selected to be interviewed for the study. In general, the researchers found moderate correlations between the parents' ratings of adjustment and their children's total scores on the Child Behavior Checklist-Teacher's Report Form. Similar results for teachers' ratings were obtained. Correlations of the parents' checklist total scores with ratings of the four adjustment areas ranged from −.34 to −.64; for teachers, the correlations ranged from −.55 to −.66. The negative correlations suggested that the more behavior problems attributed to a child, the lower his adjustment rating.

Would Hoge and McKay have been correct to conclude that a boy's adjustment ratings were a result of his behavior in class? Or could the reverse be the case? This is an important point about correlational studies. They do not reflect cause-and-effect relationships; only direction and degree of association can be shown in such studies. From the Hoge and McKay study, we know the size and the direction of the relationships between the adjustment and behavior variables, but we do not know that one caused or even preceded the other.

Correlational studies do not always use the product-moment correlation coefficient. There are many other ways to show association. We will not list them in this chapter, nor could they all be included in the present text because the number of methods of showing association is very great.* Any study may be classified as *correlational* if it attempts to describe relationships between variables but not to show that variations in one cause variations in another. For this reason, studies which attempt to predict one kind of score from another when the two scores are correlated are also considered correlational studies. Thus if we know that the correlation of a certain IQ test and a particular achievement test is .95, then we can estimate a student's IQ from his achievement score by finding the IQ usually obtained by students who score similarly in achievement.

Developmental Research

Research that focuses on changes that can be observed over time is usually referred to as *developmental research*. This kind of study can focus on products, people, institutions, or organizations. Developmental studies may be designed for various purposes. For example, one purpose of developmental study is to seek origins of behavior; another is to seek interrelationships among factors affecting growth. In addition, sequences and patterns of influences upon growth may be studied. Further, developmental studies may be conducted to establish the nature of trends in the past and to use these trends to make predictions about the future. Developmental studies contribute to decisions made about automobile insurance rates, enrollments at the state university 15 years into the future, and estimates of food requirements for the population.

The most common application of the developmental approach to research in education and the behavioral sciences occurs in the area of human development. Obviously educators must know something about human growth and development if they are to be successful. Developmental studies of human

---

*Readers interested in knowing more about these methods are referred to the Freeman (1965), the Glass and Hopkins (1984), and the Pedhazur (1982) references listed in the Supplementary Readings section at the end of this chapter.

growth have focused on the growth of reasoning, intelligence, emotions, interpersonal relationships, comprehension, physical characteristics, social needs, and many other facets that would be of interest to those who work with children and adults.

Developmental research conducted by Kifer (1975) centered upon the relationship between school achievement and personality characteristics. Kifer proposed that a student's emotional development depends to a large degree upon his past patterns of academic achievement. That is, a student's cumulative background of success and failure over a period of time contributes to the formation of personality characteristics. To test this proposition, the investigator collected data from a sample of students in the second, fourth, sixth, and eighth grades who were in the top 20 percent or the bottom 20 percent of their classes, based upon grades in academic courses. The students in the second-grade sample were chosen solely on the basis of their second-grade records. Students on all other levels were chosen if they were in the top 20 percent or the bottom 20 percent every year that they attended school. Subjects were administered three tests designed to assess self-concept, self-esteem, and something called Intellectual Achievement Responsibility. The analysis of the data led Kifer to conclude that success in school coincides with positive personality characteristics, whereas consistent failure is associated with poor regard for one's own self and abilities. Also related to this was the pattern of support and encouragement the child received at home. That is, personality traits and achievement were better for students from homes that provided more support and encouragement.

An important feature of the Kifer study was the role that age and grade level played in the results. This is a typical focus of developmental studies. Usually these studies take time into consideration by using a cross-sectional or a longitudinal approach. The *longitudinal approach* involves studying the same group of subjects over a period of time. *Cross-sectional studies,* on the other hand, involve looking at phenomena in different groups of subjects who are at different ages or stages of development. For example, we might look at the reasoning ability of children from 4 to 8 years old longitudinally or cross-sectionally. If we were to seek a longitudinal perspective, we would plan our investigation so that we would study the same group of children over the 5-year period from age 4 to 8. However, if we were to take a cross-sectional approach, we could collect all our data at one time, using separate samples of 4-, 5-, 6-, 7-, and 8-year-olds. The two approaches to developmental research are illustrated in Figure 2-3, where different reasoning abilities are indicated by lowercase letters that represent scores on a reasoning test. If we were to perform a cross-sectional study, we would collect data all at once on the five different age groups. This would be similar to describing how 4-year-olds perform, then 5-year-olds, then 6-, 7-, and 8-year-olds. It would be as if we ran five separate studies at the same time. On the other hand, if we approached the problem longitudinally, we would find a group of 4-year-olds, administer our reasoning test to them, locate the same group one year later and test them

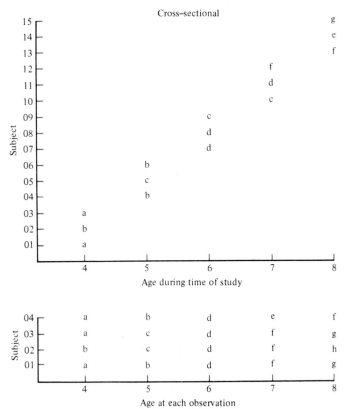

FIGURE 2-3
Cross-sectional and longitudinal plans for research.

again, and repeat this when the subjects reached 6, 7, and 8 years of age. Which approach did Kifer use in his study of personality and patterns of achievement?

There are advantages and disadvantages to both kinds of developmental research. There are obvious benefits in being able to trace later developments from earlier characteristics in a single group of subjects using the longitudinal method. However, in longitudinal research, it is often difficult to follow all subjects over a period of years. Subjects may move from the area, lose interest in participating, become ill, or even die; and the researcher has no control over how loss of subjects will influence results. Another problem the longitudinal researcher faces concerns the control of factors which over time can influence his sample. For example, a group of students participating in a longitudinal study attends a school whose principal thinks that the arts and humanities should be emphasized rather than the sciences. The students in this school who are participants in the longitudinal study might reflect the interest of the principal rather than growth influences which occur naturally. Furthermore, with repeated administrations of the same tests, subjects tend to learn about the test, and it is difficult to establish whether familiarity with the test or natural growth processes are precipitating observed changes over time. Finally, the researcher must have the time and resources available to perform longitudinal research.

Cross-sectional studies are, of course, easier to conduct and control than are longitudinal studies. Generally they can be performed with less effort and expense. By definition, they require less time than do longitudinal studies. However, the subjects sampled at the different grades, ages, or stages may not be comparable. Thus the differences might be due to group membership rather than maturation. For example, if we surveyed attitudes towards careers in an inner-city high school, we might find differences between the ninth, tenth, eleventh, and twelfth grades. Could we conclude that these differences were due to maturation if we were aware that the four groups of students were different in fundamental ways, such as ethnic makeup, IQ scores, past achievement, or interest in academics? Of course, we could not say conclusively what caused differences in attitudes between the groups of students. Thus, while the growth of characteristics over time is of primary concern in developmental studies, this aspect can generally be evaluated speculatively at best in cross-sectional studies.

Archival Research

Records of past occurrences exist that can be used to study relationships scientifically. For example, a school psychologist who systematically reviews the cumulative record folders of a group of academically talented students who did poorly in mathematics in high school and a similar group who did well in mathematics to seek a possible explanation for the difference in performance is doing archival research. The sociologist who systematically examines the published literature, tax records, municipal departmental reports, and proceedings of the city council to study the effects of economic stress on the social structure of a small town is also doing archival research. Archival research may be the best or the only way to answer many types of research questions.

One of the distinguishing characteristics of many archival studies is that their data were often collected for purposes other than the research. In contrasting this kind of research to ex post facto research, for example, the TALENT data were collected for research purposes, although Backman's (1972) study might not have been specifically on the minds of the designers of the project. Another feature of archival research that should be stressed, although it may at first seem obvious, is that the researcher must be familiar with the data sources in order to know that the necessary information exists to address the question.

A variety of sources may be used in conducting archival studies. Statistical information collected by government agencies such as the Census Bureau or the U.S. Office of Education might be used. In addition, records of a university on the annual characteristics of faculty and students and statistical data banks maintained by state departments of education are also potential sources of archival research. Other potential sources include the communications media (e.g., newspapers, magazines, professional journals, videotaped news reports, etc.), personal files and records of key people involved in the matter under study, and other written or recorded materials.

Using a combination of sources, Pion and Lipsey (1984) studied changes in the psychology profession from the late 1960s through the 1980s. The purpose of the study was to investigate the effects of changes in society on the profession of psychology and the specialties within the profession. Among their sources were statistical data from the U.S. Bureau of Labor Statistics, the National Science Foundation, the National Research Council, and the American Psychological Association. They also reviewed a variety of written reports from sources such as the National Academy of Sciences, the National Center for Educational Statistics, and the U.S. Office of Management and Budget. In addition, articles from professional journals such as the *American Psychologist* and *Public Opinion Quarterly* were used. From their research and analysis, Pion and Lipsey were able to relate changes within the profession of psychology to social and economic trends. For example, since the end of World War II there has been an enormous increase in the number of people employed in service-related industries in the United States; by 1979, this segment had come to represent about 70 percent of the labor force. At the same time, there have been increases in both government employment and in dependence on specialized technical and scientific knowledge throughout society. The number of people obtaining graduate education increased during this period as well, and the major source of employment for these individuals is no longer the academic world but business and government. These movements within society resulted in a growth in the practitioner specialties within psychology (clinical, counseling, and school psychology). The more research-oriented members of the profession (e.g., experimental, developmental, and cognitive psychologists) were less inclined to take advantage of the new opportunities in industry and government. This resulted in a growth in the proportion of psychologists providing clinical services and a decrease in the proportion of psychologists primarily engaged in research and teaching in the academic environment.

Archival researchers must often deal with the problem of plausible rival explanations for their conclusions because they have no control over the settings in which their data developed. For example, Pion and Lipsey emphasize the increase in the size of the service sector of the economy as a factor in the move in psychology toward increased emphasis on professional services. However, one might argue that other influences were at work. The period during which psychology was increasing in the service sector was also the period of Lyndon Johnson's "great society." It was a time of increased funding for graduate education in the social sciences and education and for programs for the educationally and otherwise handicapped. One might argue, therefore, that it was this increased funding for training and services that was the catalyst for the changes the profession of psychology was experiencing, not the increasingly service-related orientation of the country's economy.

Generalizing findings to other groups and settings is another difficulty in archival research. First, since the data may be gleaned from diverse sources, the conditions under which various segments of the data were developed may differ. When all these diverse elements are pieced together, it can be difficult to describe who the data represent. For example, part of the Pion and Lipsey data included information on doctorates in psychology. Since most doctoral programs in psychology tend to be given in the colleges of arts and sciences on most university campuses, studies may overlook the fact that many doctoral programs in psychology (especially in such areas as educational, school, counseling, industrial, medical, and rehabilitation psychology) may be offered elsewhere within an institution of higher education. This may result in underestimating the representation of certain fields in the total population studied. When data from several sources are used, some that include all psychology programs regardless of location on campus may be combined with others that only consider those with arts and sciences affiliation, and the combined data set would therefore not be representative of any population. Thus the researcher must be careful about combining archival sources. Despite these problems, archival research, when suitable sources of information exist, is an important way to study certain problems for which other techniques may not be available.

Survey Research

Survey research is used to study the distribution of characteristics in a population. Questionnaires and interviews are usually used to collect information in survey research. Surveys may be administered via face-to-face interviews with respondents, by mail, or by telephone.

Questions in a survey may be open-ended or they may be highly structured in the way they permit respondents to answer. For example, an open-ended survey question dealing with how parents supervise their children's homework activities might be worded as follows:

How much supervision do you provide when your child does homework?

The same question could be structured as follows:

Circle the statement below that best describes the amount of supervision you provide your child when he or she does homework.

a I sit with him (or her) until the assignment is finished.
b I sit with him (or her) for a while to make sure it's done.
c I occasionally sit with him (or her) if I am asked to do so.
d I check it after it's finished.

e I ask about homework assignments, but I do not interfere.

f I do not supervise because I believe homework is the child's responsibility.

While the first way of asking the question permits a more complete response and more individual expression, it can be difficult to summarize the wide range of possible answers. The second format has the advantage of permitting easy tabulation, but it may not provide the respondent with a completely satisfactory choice.

Survey research is common in sociological and political-attitude research. Survey research in education may be done to determine views or attitudes for the purpose of planning or decision making. Phi Delta Kappa (PDK), a society of professional educators, often does surveys to study attitudes or perceptions of some aspect of education (e.g., Gallup, 1984, 1985). In 1987, PDK sponsored a survey to determine public attitudes towards some of the educational policies of the Reagan administration (Gallup & Clark, 1987). A sample of 1571 adults from across the country was selected to be interviewed in April 1987. The sample was carefully selected to be representative of the entire population of Americans over the age of 18. The survey questionnaire included a number of structured questions about attitudes towards and perceptions of schools and education. Among the findings of the survey was that the great majority of the adults responding felt that schools should raise their standards for academic achievement. Further, a similar percentage seemed to feel that increasing the competition among schools and states by revealing test scores would be an effective method of improving schools. The survey results suggested a preference for local over federal control of schools. A majority of the respondents indicated they were more satisfied with their local schools than they were with schools across the nation in general. In addition, although teachers generally received high grades from the respondents, those with children in school rated teachers more favorably than did those without children in school. Yet 72 percent favored establishing higher standards and requirements for entry into the teaching profession. Seventy-six percent favored including sex education in the curriculum. Another interesting finding was that although the public was faced with forming opinions about many of these issues, few of the respondents had heard or read about them.

A study like the Phi Delta Kappa survey is only useful if the sample of respondents is representative of the population as a whole. In the case of the PDK survey, representativeness was assured by using a random-selection procedure for choosing respondents. Specifically, various categories of respondents were identified based on the most recent census. Then people were chosen randomly from those categories. For example, if it were determined from the census that a certain percentage of the population was from the middle west and had completed four years of college, then the sample would include that same percentage of randomly selected midwestern college graduates. Because they carefully designed the sample to be representative, the PDK survey researchers were justified in attributing the findings from the sample to the population as a whole. For example, if it were found that 76 percent of the respondents felt sex education should be part of the school curriculum, it could be assumed that a corresponding percentage (within some range, perhaps 71 to 81 percent) of the population of adults in the United States felt the same way. We have more to say about the important issue of sampling in Chapter 4.

EXPERIMENTAL AND QUASI-EXPERIMENTAL RESEARCH

Only a brief introduction will be given here to familiarize the student with this experimental and quasi-experimental research. More complete treatment is reserved for Chapters 4 and 5. Experimental research is the most tightly controlled of the various kinds of research we have discussed so far. It involves systematic manipulation of experimental conditions in which extraneous influences are controlled or eliminated. Experimental is different from descriptive research in terms of purpose and perspective as well. That is, in experimental research, the position is taken that the effects of one variable upon another can be investigated by isolation and study of those variables. Usually these effects are not stated in definite cause-and-effect terms because, as we said in Chapter 1, whether causes can ever be identified is problematic.

A study by Rosenthal and Fode (1963) will serve to illustrate these points. In this study, the experimenter's influence on the outcome of an experiment was investigated, using a group of psychology students as experimenters in a study of maze learning with laboratory rats as subjects. Half the experimenters were told that their rats were bred to be "maze-bright," and the remaining experimenters were told that their rats were bred from a "maze-dull" strain. According to Rosenthal and Fode, animals believed to be brighter by the student-experimenters performed better from the first day of the study. In addition, at the end of the experimental period, student-experimenters who were told that they had brighter rats tended to describe their rats in more favorable terms. Rosenthal and Fode concluded that the beliefs of the student-experimenters were associated with the performance of the rats. They were *not* saying that the experimenters' beliefs directly caused the rats' behavior; a number of intermediate events could have occurred to cause the allegedly "maze-bright" rats to perform better.

The experimental study is designed to minimize alternative explanations for the obtained results. That is, if we do an experiment in which we compare two teaching methods, unless all factors which might contribute to a difference between the two methods are controlled, the experiment is not very useful. Look at the investigation illustrated in Table 2-2. Notice that the average scores of the two groups are different. Could one conclude from these results that method A was better? Probably not! Disregarding the small size of the samples, the difference in performance between the two classrooms may have been due to a difference in teachers, students, or various other factors.

TABLE 2-2
TEST SCORES AFTER TWO TEACHING METHODS
IN TWO MATCHED CLASSROOMS

	Classroom 1 Method A	Classroom 2 Method B
	6	1
	8	3
	7	5
	9	4
	10	2
Average Score	8	3

Experimental studies involve comparing conditions under various stages of the treatment. In a simple experiment, a collection of subjects might be divided into two groups, one to undergo a treatment condition, the other to receive a neutral treatment (or *control*). The two groups are compared after the treatment is applied using a criterion measure. If there is a difference in the measure between the groups, it may be attributed to treatment effects only if the two groups were similar on the measure before the treatment conditions were applied.

To illustrate some of these points, we will consider a study by Clements and Gullo (1984). In this study, 18 first-grade children were randomly divided into two groups of 9 students each. The children in each group were then given a series of tests to determine their pretreatment level of performance in vocabulary and cognitive style (reflectivity and divergent thinking). Then the children worked on the computer for 80 minutes per week (two sessions, each 40 minutes) over a 12-week period. Children in the experimental group were taught to program the computer using the Logo language (a programming language designed to permit children to control and learn about the computer and programming). At the same time, the control group was exposed to computer-assisted instruction (CAI) using a variety of commercial program packages. At the end of the 12-week period, all the children were administered a variety of posttreatment tests. Results suggested that the Logo group improved on some of the cognitive style measures while the CAI group did not. Further, the Logo group performed better in a number of measures than the CAI group.

Clements and Gullo attributed the differences in performance between the two groups to the differential effects of the experimental and control conditions. They felt justified in doing this because the subjects were randomly assigned to the two groups and so the only systematic difference between the groups should have been the treatment conditions. Although other issues can be raised about maintaining group equivalence over the duration of the study, we save discussion of these issues for later in the book. The important point here is how randomized assignment was used to control unwanted influences in the experiment.

Unfortunately, because of the nature of the real-life situations in which behavioral scientists and educational researchers collect their data, many studies have to be conducted under less than controlled conditions. Researchers often find that they cannot select their subjects or assign treatments as they would like and may therefore design what they call *quasi-experimental studies,* which are similar to experimental studies but are used when complete experimental control is not a realistic possibility or would be too costly. A quasi-experimental study must be designed so that all outside influences are controlled. It is the responsibility of the experimenter to design the study to fit the situation in which the research is being done. We will have more to say about this kind of research in Chapters 4 and 5.

POLICY RESEARCH AND EVALUATION

Policy research can be defined as "the development of a foundation of information to be used as a basis for making plans and decisions that will impact policy." For example, if a school board wishes to establish a policy concerning contracting with local universities for an annual program of in-service teacher education, it would want some research done to describe the kinds of in-service training that local teachers might require each year. Among the studies the district might conduct are a survey of teachers, principals, and parents; a cost analysis comparing the proposed contract method to other approaches; and a study to see what other districts do for annual staff training.

A simple but reasonably encompassing definition of evaluation might be as follows: *Evaluation* is "the process of determining the value or worth of something." Evaluation studies of government-funded community projects, school curricula, school administrators, students, university counseling centers, nutritional programs, advertising campaigns, television programs, the federal Social Security system, and insurance-company actuarial procedures are done routinely. Evaluation studies themselves may sometimes be evaluated. An evaluation of an evaluation is called a *meta-evaluation* (Worthen & Sanders, 1987).

There is no single policy study or evaluation design or research method; rather, evaluators and policy researchers commonly use an array of methods, some of which we have mentioned in this chapter (e.g., archival research, case and field studies, experimental research, etc.). Both types of researchers are primarily interested in finding the necessary information and will gather that information in any way they can. The primary distinction between evaluation and policy study is in the orientation of the researcher. That is, while the purpose of one study is to evaluate, the purpose of the other is to support planning and decision making in forming policy within the context of the political, social, and economic realities of the time and setting (Yudof, 1984). For this reason, policy research is more integrated with economic and political issues and social needs than is evaluation.

Policy research and evaluation have many similarities and often share the same data and methodology. However, policy studies are usually done in governmental, political, or managerial settings, while evaluation is more commonly found "on the front line," in settings such as schools, universities, and mental health and health facilities. We will focus more on evaluation when we return to these issues in Chapter 11.

Evaluation and policy research occupy a peculiar position among research activities. Many researchers do not feel that they should be classified as *scientific inquiry*. On the other hand, many evaluators are not aware that there is a difference between scientific research, policy study, and evaluation. Figure 2-4 shows this often misunderstood relationship. Notice the overlap. Some evaluation and policy-study activities meet all the standards of systematic and rigorous scientific research; others do not. Moreover, some scientific research can be seen to be very much like evaluation or policy study when carefully scrutinized.

The misunderstanding probably arises because policy research and evaluation tend to use many of the same methods as other kinds of research. As can be seen in Figure 2-4, evaluators and other researchers use the historical, descriptive, and experimental methodologies we have been discussing in this chapter. How then can they be differentiated? The difference between them is one of purpose. That is, based on our definitions of *research* and *evaluation*

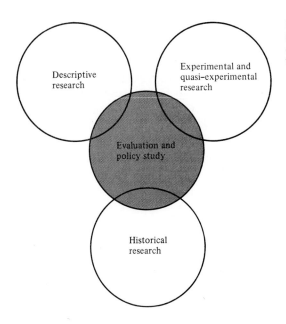

FIGURE 2-4
Overlapping relationship between evaluation and policy study and other forms of research.

given earlier, we can say that research is performed either to accumulate facts or to increase knowledge and understanding. On the other hand, evaluations are done to see whether or not programs are working or products or objectives are adequate, and policy studies are done to support planning and decision making.

We will finish this brief discussion of evaluation with a well-known example that has raised considerable controversy: the evaluation of the preschool program Head Start created by the Westinghouse Learning Corporation and Ohio University (1969). This evaluation has had important implications for federal policy regarding compensatory education programs. The question asked in this evaluation was whether Head Start programs had an impact on the emotional and intellectual development of participating children. The evaluation therefore did not consider other important questions concerning the effectiveness of Head Start, such as the influence of the program on nutrition, health, or families of the children. To investigate the effects of Head Start on the emotional and intellectual development of the children, a sample of first, second, and third graders who had attended preschool Head Start programs for educationally disadvantaged children in 104 centers across the United States was matched with a similar sample of disadvantaged children who had not participated in Head Start. A battery of paper-and-pencil tests designed to assess emotional, cognitive, and intellectual status was administered to the children. It was found that children who attended Head Start were still considerably below national standards in testing. However, when compared to similarly disadvantaged children, there were slight differences in favor of the Head Start children who had attended full-year programs but not for those who had attended summer programs only. On the basis of the evaluation, policy decisions were made. It was recommended that full-year Head Start programs be continued but that summer programs be eliminated. In addition, it was recommended that certain improvements be made in the full-year programs.

This evaluation study was paid for by the federal government. Currently, most federally funded programs, projects, and institutions have some provision for evaluation built into their structures. In addition, administrators and management-level executives are beginning to require evaluation in their organizations and institutions in private industry. Schools have been using evaluation studies for some time. Furthermore, curriculum and educational product development projects almost always contain an evaluation component. Thus, whether evaluation and policy study qualify as research or something separate is really not as important an issue as the need for a general understanding of the complexity, diversity, and demands of these kinds of studies.

WHICH TYPE OF STUDY IS BEST

The question of which type of study is best is not a simple one; to answer it, we must look at the questions being asked, the resources available, and the nature of the previous work in the field. Moreover, one of these considerations may be more important in some situations than others.

When a problem concerns the origin of present structures in society, the best method of investigation would probably be the historical study. To do a descriptive survey of attitudes or a case study of a politician's rise to office probably would not satisfactorily address the problem. Furthermore, even though the experimental study is probably the most appealing of the methodologies from a rigorous scientific point of view, it clearly would not be appropriate in this case.

The most appropriate method of addressing the problem suggests the best type of research to use in a situation. Thus the kind of research to be done must be capable of responding to the questions being raised. To be sure, if a particular research strategy requires funds, resources, or technical skills that are not available to the researcher, a compromise must be made. In such cases, the research methodology used may be less than desirable, but if the problem is an important one, at least something can be done. This type of compromise is often made in research situations. For example, if a sociologist is interested in knowing how the attitudes of high school students have changed over the past 25 years, he would of course like to have access to *complete* information on the attitudes of *all* high school students in the past 25 years. Not only is that information unavailable, but the amount that is presently available on attitudes of 25 years ago is based upon survey or attitude instruments of the time. They might not be completely useful for the sociologist's purpose. Also, they might not be easily interpretable in today's culture. The sociologist would have to compromise further on the sample that is studied. Since complete data on the population may not be available 25 years later, only data that can be found can be used in the study. Furthermore, the sociologist probably has not the time, funds, or resources to get attitude responses from the present population of high school students. Some plan for sampling a representative group is needed. Thus, the answer to the question of which type of study should be done depends upon the problem being investigated, the resources available, and what is already known about the phenomenon to be investigated.

SUMMARY

Most scientific investigations in education and the behavioral sciences fall into one of four categories. That is, research may be historical, descriptive, experimental, policy-oriented, or evaluative. Each of these different types of research has in common with the others an adherence to the steps of the scientific method.

1 Identification of a problem area
2 Clarification and definition of the problem

3 Proposal of a plausible solution and observation according to an approach designed to test the solution

4 Decisions on the adequacy of the proposed solution based upon the data gathered and observations made

5 Comparison of the proposed solution with previous findings and other observations to determine how the solution may be integrated with what is already known (needs for additional research might become apparent)

The steps of the scientific method may not always be followed in sequence. However, scientists usually describe their research by discussing the events that occurred at each stage. The reader is reminded that not all types of research are included in this chapter. There are other research strategies that may be of particular use in specific situations. Also classifiable as research are the traditional scholarly activities of philosophical analysis and integrative literature review, for example. The particular type of research to be conducted depends upon the nature of the research problem. The researcher also takes into consideration the resources and what is known about the field in designing a research study.

PROBLEMS FOR THOUGHT AND DISCUSSION

1 Identify the steps of the scientific method represented in the examples of descriptive research that were given.

2 You are a researcher interested in studying the relationship between educational level of attainment of an adult and annual income. Identify some of the descriptive research approaches you might take. Briefly describe some studies you might conduct to investigate the relationship.

3 The findings in a descriptive research study can be influenced by the type of study that is made. Can you think of a hypothetical example?

4 Find an article in a professional journal that reports on a research study. Usually, research articles are written in a format that reflects the scientific method. The first section usually describes the background and purpose. This is usually followed by a summary of the subjects, the materials used, and the procedures followed. Then the results are presented. Finally, the conclusions are given. See whether your article follows this format, and then match the parts of the article to the scientific method.

5 A researcher was interested in studying the development of laws pertaining to schools in his state since the Civil War. He proceeded by developing a 30-item questionnaire. Each item contained a statement of a social issue relating to the schools. For example, the first item was "Industry requires an educated public from which to hire a capable working force." A random sample of people whose names appeared on the voting registers across the state were asked to rate the significance of each of the items in terms of contribution to the present structure of school law. Ratings were made on a 5-point scale from *very important* to *very unimportant*. When the data were all collected, the investigator concluded that certain items were more important than others in forming the present state laws pertaining to public education.

   a What kind of study did the researcher conduct? Was it appropriate to the problem?

   b Were the researcher's conclusions correct? Why?

c How could this problem have been studied?

d What did the researcher's data really mean?

6 A company that publishes educational curriculum materials is interested in assessing the effectiveness of a textbook.

a What kind of research is involved?

b What specific knowledge is sought in such an investigation?

c Describe the steps one might go through in setting up and doing such a study.

d Does this kind of study regularly contribute to the goals of science?

7 Obtain a copy of an issue of a journal that publishes research reports from your field. For each research report in the issue, see whether you can

a identify the type of study that was done.

b recognize the steps of the scientific method.

c evaluate the adequacy of the method in answering the questions towards which the research was directed.

8 Scan several issues of a research journal from your own field of interest. Is there a particular type of research study that predominates? Can you think of some reasons why that is so?

REFERENCES

Anbar, A. (1986). Reading acquisition of preschool children without systematic instruction. *Early Childhood Research Quarterly, 1* (1), 83–87.

Backman, M. E. (1972). Patterns of mental abilities: Ethnic, socioeconomic, and sex. *American Educational Research Journal, 9,* 1–12.

Broudy, H. (1983). Predicaments, problems, puzzles, and paradoxes. *Educational Theory, 33* (1), 33–39.

Clements, D. H., & Gullo, D. F. (1984). Effects of computer programming on young children's cognition. *Journal of Educational Psychology, 76,* 1051–1058.

Dewey, J. (1910). Science as subject-matter and a method. *Science, 31,* 121–127.

Edelbrock, C. S., & Achenbach, T. M. (1982). *Scoring format for the Child Behavior Checklist-Teacher's Report Form: Boys aged 6–11.* Burlington: University of Vermont, Department of Psychiatry.

Eisner, E. (1984). Can educational research inform educational practice? *Phi Delta Kappan, 65,* 447–452.

Field, T. (1981). Intervention for high risk infants and their parents. *Educational Evaluation and Policy Analysis, 3,* 69–78.

Gallup, A. (1984). The Gallup poll of teachers' attitudes toward the public schools. *Phi Delta Kappan, 66,* 97–107.

Gallup, A. (1985). The Gallup poll of teachers' attitudes toward the public schools—Pt. 2. *Phi Delta Kappan, 66,* 323–330.

Gallup, A. M., & Clark, D. L. (1987). The 19th annual Gallup poll of the public's attitudes toward the public schools. *Phi Delta Kappan, 69,* 17–30.

Grant, N. (1979). *Soviet education (4th ed.).* New York: Penguin.

Hatch, J. A. (1985). The quantoids versus the smooshes: Struggling with methodological rapprochement. *Issues in Education, 3,* 158–167.

Hewett, F. A. (1964). A hierarchy of educational tasks for children with learning disorders. *Exceptional Children, 31,* 207–214.

Hoge, R. D., & McKay, V. (1986). Criterion-related validity data for the Child Behavior Checklist-Teacher's Report Form. *Journal of School Psychology, 24,* 387–393.

Johnson, F. H. (1969). Canadian public education at the time of the confederation. In M. Gillet (Ed.), *Readings in the history of education*. New York: McGraw-Hill, 265–273.

Jones, R. (1973). The nature of research. In R. H. Jones (Ed.), *Methods and techniques of educational research*. Danville, IL: Interstate.

Kifer, E. (1975). Relationships between academic achievement and personality characteristics: A quasi-longitudinal study. *American Educational Research Journal, 12,* 191–210.

Lutz, F. W., & Ramsey, M. A. (1974). The use of anthropological field methods in education. *Educational Researcher, 3* (10), 5–8.

Philips, S. U. (1983). *The invisible culture*. New York: Longmans.

Pion, G. M., & Lipsey, M. W. (1984). Psychology and society: The challenge of change. *American Psychologist, 39,* 739–754.

Shulman, L. (1981). Disciplines of inquiry in education: An overview. *Educational Researcher, 10* (5), 5–12, 23.

Snelbecker, G. E. (1985). *Learning theory, instructional theory, and psychoeducational design*. New York: University Press.

True, J. A. (1983). *Finding out: Conducting and evaluating social research*. Belmont, CA: Wadsworth.

Van Maanen, J. (1983). Reclaiming qualitative methods. In J. Van Maanen (Ed.), *Qualitative methodology*. Beverly Hills, CA: Sage.

Warren, R. L. (1967). *Education in Rebhausen, a German village*. New York: Holt.

Westinghouse Learning Corporation & Ohio University. (1969). *An evaluation of Head Start on children's cognitive and affective development (executive summary)*. Springfield, VA: Clearinghouse for Federal Scientific and Technical Information (ERIC Document Reproduction Service No. ED 03632).

Worthen, B. R., & Sanders, J. R. (1987). *Educational evaluation: Alternative approaches and practical guidelines*. New York: Longmans.

Yudof, M. G. (1984). Educational policy research and the new consensus of the 1980s. *Phi Delta Kappan, 65,* 456–459.

SUPPLEMENTARY READINGS

Baker, R. L., & Schutz, R. E. (1972). *Instructional product research*. New York: American Book.

Campbell, D. T., & Stanley, J. C. (1968). Experimental and quasi-experimental designs for research on teaching. In N. L. Gage (Ed.), *Handbook of research on teaching*. Chicago: Rand McNally.

Cohen, M. L. (1971). *Legal research in a nutshell*. St. Paul, MN: West.

Cook, D. R., & La Fleur, N. K. (1975). *A guide to educational research* (2nd ed.). Boston: Allyn and Bacon.

Freeman, L. C. (1965). *Elementary and applied statistics: For students in behavioral science*. New York: Wiley.

Glass, G. V., & Hopkins, K. D. (1984). *Statistical methods in education and psychology (2nd ed.)*. Englewood Cliffs, NJ: Prentice-Hall.

Hughs, H. S. (1964). *History as art and as science: Twin vista on the past*. New York: Harper & Row.

Husen, T. (1984). *Educational research & policy: How do they relate?* Oxford, England: Pergamon.

Pedhazur, E. J. (1982). *Multiple regression in behavioral research (2nd ed.).* New York: Holt.

Popkowitz, T. S., & Tabachnick, B. R. (Eds.) (1981). *The study of schooling: Field based methodologies in educational research and evaluation.* New York: Praeger.

Start, K. B. (1975). Reality for the researcher. *Educational Researcher, 12,* 323–336.

Travers, R. M. W. (1983). *How research has changed American schools: A history from 1840 to the present.* Kalamazoo, MI: Mythos.

Van Maanen, J., & Dabbs, R. R. (Eds.) (1982). *Varieties of qualitative research.* Beverly Hills, CA: Sage.

Warren, R. C. (1973). *Context and isolation: The teaching experience in an elementary school* (technical report No. 35, Stanford Center for Research and Development in Teaching). Stanford, CA: ERIC Document Reproduction Service No. ED 080 512.

PART TWO

THE TOOLS OF THE RESEARCHER

The correct tools are essential in any craft. Just as the carpenter could not put a fine finish on a piece of furniture with an axe and a mechanic could not determine tire pressure with a measuring cup, a journeyman researcher cannot do the job without the right tools. This does not necessarily eliminate the creative use of old tools for new purposes, but whatever the tools, they must be the appropriate ones for the task at hand. In Part II, we look at the researcher's tools. They include a specialized vocabulary, a research library (Chapter 3), experimental design and research validity (Chapters 4 and 5), statistical techniques (Chapters 6 and 7), measurement and observation (Chapters 8 and 9), and computers (Chapter 10). The reader is encouraged to think about how the various tools have different purposes and can be used with different kinds of questions, perspectives, and requirements for information. For example, the experimental study will produce somewhat different information than will the in-depth interview, data might undergo subtle changes as it is prepared for computerized analysis, or a measurement technique may be reliable and valid for some applications and not for others. We will see that research design is concerned with selecting the best combination of tools to do the job in a given situation.

CHAPTER 3

MAKING PROBLEMS
RESEARCHABLE

The language of the researcher is specialized; like all technical languages, it involves the use of certain words in the ordinary vocabulary in markedly specific ways, and it includes words created to meet specialized needs. Although it is impossible to cover the entire lexicon of the social and behavioral sciences here, we will give it attention in terms of planning, conducting, and reporting on research studies. The relationship between this specialized vocabulary and the structure of research will be discussed. In addition, we will consider the purpose, construction, and documentation of research problem statements. In doing so, we will briefly consider use of the library and other sources for documentation of a problem. Finally, hypothesis statements will be viewed in terms of their relationship to problem statements, their construction, and their use in research investigations. Throughout the chapter, it will be evident that researchers are constantly reducing complex issues and problems to simpler ones. This process of reduction facilitates investigation and explanation in science and research.

LANGUAGE AND THE STRUCTURE OF RESEARCH

Language provides a structure for research. That is, stages in the research process and its results are given certain descriptive labels. For example, a psychologist looking for a *theory* of attitude formation develops a *construct* called credibility, then states a *hypothesis:* "As the social status of the person making a statement increases, the credibility of what is said increases." "Theory," "construct," and "hypothesis" are words used to label and organize the work of the researcher. We will look at such words and their specialized meanings in the following sections.

Variables and Constructs

Since many of the terms that we will be defining involve variables and constructs, it is a good idea at this point to specify what we mean by these terms. *Variables* are characteristics of persons, things, groups, programs, etc., which can take on values. These values can be categorical, such as eye color or racial group, or they can be quantitative, such as height, IQ, or batting average. Depending upon the hypotheses being tested, the researcher may assign a variable, as with method of instruction, or a preexisting variable may be identified using some kind of measurement such as height or intelligence.

In stating problems and hypotheses, researchers recognize three different kinds of variables. The first kind, *independent variables,* are manipulated by the researcher or are seen as contributing to the observed effects. For example, if we want to compare the effects of taking aspirin for a headache to taking another pill, the type of medication taken is the independent variable. *Dependent variables* are those variables upon which the measurements of effects are made. Thus, the dependent variable in the headache study might be the degree to which research subjects reported that their headaches subsided. *Intervening variables,* sometimes called *nuisance variables* or *extraneous variables,* are those that contaminate or obscure the results of an experiment. Some intervening variables in the aspirin study might be the subjects' willingness to cooperate, the accuracy of the subjects' reports of their symptoms, and the time of day that the subjects were interviewed. Researchers try to *control* intervening variables so that their effects on the results of an experiment will be minimized.

Variables are more specific than *constructs.* A construct is a concept or idea that has been devised for a specific scientific purpose. For example, the word "intelligence" is a construct that can be defined as "the ability to adapt to the environment." Notice that although the construct is devised for scientific purposes, there is an uncomfortable vagueness to it. We can see this in our definition of *intelligence.* What do the words "ability" and "adapt" mean exactly? This definition is not very useful to a researcher because it is not *operational.* Intelligence could be made more operational by defining it as a score on an IQ test. Such a definition may make intelligence a useful research variable, but it changes the meaning of intelligence considerably. Researchers try to avoid using definitions of variables that are so vague as to be meaningless or so specific as to be trivial. Therefore, the definition of constructs and variables is a major concern for researchers.

Variables may be operationally defined in two ways. The first, already mentioned, is to describe the variable in observational terms. Thus, the variable "mechanical aptitude" becomes defined by the score on a mechanical aptitude test. It is easy to see how the nature of the test can influence the character of a variable defined in this way. For example, some mechanical aptitude tests emphasize knowledge and experience with mechanical concepts; others emphasize spatial reasoning or comprehension of the principles of mechanics (Anastasi, 1982). Operational definitions could also be based on behavior. For example, mechanical aptitude could be assessed by timing performance in putting a series of simple puzzles together. As with definitions based on specific tests, the meaning of the operationalized variables would depend on the behavioral criteria established. A second way to define a variable operationally is to manipulate conditions to create it. For example, if the variable to be defined operationally is training effectiveness, subjects who underwent a prescribed training procedure can be compared with a group of subjects who were not so trained.

From the discussion so far, it should be clear that operational definitions are necessarily incomplete representations of constructs. Just as no single intelligence test score could represent all aspects of the construct of intelligence and no one experimental manipulation (e.g., receiving a medication versus not receiving one) could represent the richness of conditions involved in administering medication, an operational variable cannot represent all that is in a construct. One of the reasons why research investigations are often found to have been repeated frequently in the literature is because of the need to study a construct with different perspectives resulting from various operationalizations of the variables. There is more discussion of this issue in the chapters on experimental design and measurement.

Laws

A *law* in science is a statement about the relationship between two or more variables when that relationship is so constant as to constitute a dependable statement of the relationship. Laws must not be in conflict with observations, and they must be free of inconsistencies. They should be stated in the simplest possible terms and be abstract and general enough to apply in a wide variety of situations. In addition to providing explanations, laws should be useful in predicting outcomes.

An important aspect of laws is that they can be changed or refined when conflicting facts and information are found. For example, recent work in physics relating to Einstein's general theory of relativity may indicate a need for refinement of Newton's statement of the law of gravity, which refers to how objects tend to fall toward the center of the earth. True scientific laws are difficult to find in the behavioral sciences and education.

Theory

A *theory* is "a set of formulations designed to explain and predict facts and events which can be observed." The formulations might include empirical facts, definitions, or propositions related in some meaningful way to facilitate explanation and prediction of phenomena that are observed. Thus theories are statements that may not have the elegance or simplicity of laws. Nor do they have the same degree of certainty. Yet they must be verified by substantial observation. Furthermore, laws may provide the basis for explanation and structure within theories.

Theories can serve to give structure and direction to research by pointing to constructs and variables relevant to study. For example, a theory of successful attainment in the educational system might emphasize background, attitudes, peer relationships, values, quality of schooling, and educational opportunity. Variables such as average rainfall in the region where the student lives and altitude of his or her house above sea level would be ignored. Theories also serve to clarify and give structure to concepts and facts by expressing relationships. This suggests another use of theory, the summarizing of what is known about a phenomenon. For example, using theory, we do not have to make long-drawn-out statements like "In 1932, 16 children who spoke French fluently were not given an opportunity to speak the language for two years, and they lost their fluency. This was also found with another sample in 1946," and so on repeating the process for every kind of human skill and knowledge. Rather, on the basis of what is known, we could simply develop a theory of forgetting, which says that knowledge that is not used will eventually be forgotten.

Models

"Model" is a word often used in ways similar to "theory" and "law." To most people, the word "model" means something smaller than the real thing, such as a model train or a model car, or an exemplar, as when a person is referred to as a "model" father or a "model" teacher. To the scientist, however, the word has a slightly different connotation. It means the representation of the abstract ideas of a theory in real terms. As such, models are less general and succinct than are theories and laws.

Models take different shapes and forms for different types of scientists. For an engineer, a model might be a small-scale prototype of an airplane in a wind tunnel; for a physicist, it might be a model of the structure of the atom. High school science teachers are familiar with models of the solar system that permit demonstration of the movements of the planets and the arrangement of the sun, moon, and earth during eclipses. Psychologists commonly use computer models to test problem-solving methods because the processes that occur in the human brain cannot be easily observed. University admissions officers use statistical models to predict success in college studies based on such criteria as high school grades, standardized test scores, and rank in class.

Scientists and researchers find models useful for reducing reality to a manageable scale. Often models are used to guide research. For example, suppose a psychologist is asked to design a model for learning to operate a computer-aided manufacturing system in a light-bulb factory. The model is based on previous research in human learning in which the rate of acquisition of a cognitive skill is dependent on commitment to learn the skill and prior knowledge and skill in related areas. Due to the nature of the skill to be learned, the psychologist initially decides to include three constructs in the model: reading ability, mathematics knowledge, and motivation. She proposes a model which can be expressed in the two ways illustrated in Figure 3-1. First, the relationship between the three contributors to rate of acquisition is shown in the form of a flowchart. Although this representation is easy to read and understand, it has a certain amount of vagueness. For example, it is not clear whether each of the arrows represents the same amount of contribution. Further, the constructs in the model are not operational in the present form. The relationship is also shown as a mathematical statement in Figure 3.1. The relationship shown as a mathematical function has some of the same gaps in clarity as the flowchart. With current information, the researcher does not know how to set up an equation (e.g., should the terms all be added, weighted in some way, or multiplied by a constant?).

The <u>models</u> in Figure 3.1, with all their faults, <u>accomplish two things</u> for the psychologist. <u>First, they help to organize her ideas</u> (e.g., the variables that are dependent are shown as dependent and those that are independent in the relationship are shown that way). <u>Second, they help the psychologist clarify what is not known.</u> This helps her design the research. For example, one study might involve archival research of the records of employees who have been trained to operate the system. One would need measures of reading ability (e.g., highest educational level attained), mathematics knowledge (e.g., preemployment screening test), and motivation to learn the task (e.g., volunteered versus assigned) as well as some estimate of rate of acquisition (e.g., weeks to complete training). Other research might involve comparative studies based on manipulation of the independent variables. As the psychologist learns more about the model through analysis of various descriptive and ex-

A.

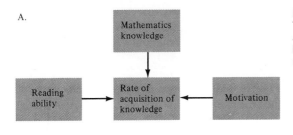

FIGURE 3-1
Two ways of expressing a model about the relationship of prior knowledge, reading ability, and motivation to rate of acquisition.

B.

$$Y = f(RA, MK, MO)$$

Where:　Y = rate of acquisition skill
RA = reading ability measure
MK = measure of prior knowledge in mathematics
MO = measure of motivation

perimental studies, changes that would clarify or improve the specificity of the model may be suggested. However, model building is rarely a smooth process, and there will probably be many false starts, cul-de-sacs, puzzles, and predicaments along the way.

Hypothesis Statements

A *hypothesis* is a tentative declarative statement about the relationship between two or more variables. In other words, it is an educated guess. Hypotheses are usually based on a theory or model, but it is not uncommon to see hypotheses that are based simply on the existence of a question that needs to be answered. This is particularly true in evaluation research. For example, a hospital administrator may run an experiment to determine whether carpet is better than floor tiles. The hypothesis for the study could be that carpeted floors are cheaper to maintain than tiled floors. There is no underlying theory or model involved, and the experiment is designed strictly to evaluate the relative advantages of carpeted floors. An important characteristic of hypotheses is that they must be *testable*. How this is done will be discussed in a later section of the chapter.

Relationships among the Terms

Figure 3-2 illustrates the relationships among laws, theories, models, and hypotheses. The higher levels of the figure represent progressively more abstract and more generalizable statements. Thus the greater the generalizability of the statement, the less useful it is in everyday terms. Furthermore, statements near the bottom are more tentative than those closer to the top.

FIGURE 3-2
Relationships among laws, theories, models, and hypotheses.

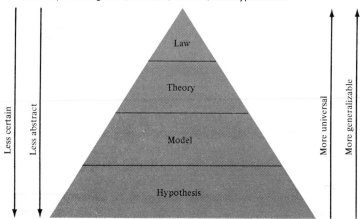

Many behavioral scientists and educational researchers would argue that the triangle depicted in Figure 3-2 should be flat on top rather than pointed. That is, when looking at the behavioral and social sciences as well as education, examples of good laws are hard to find or do not now exist, nor are there many valid theories either. Most current theoretical formulations in the behavioral sciences and education are really more similar to models than to laws as natural scientists understand them.

From Model to Hypothesis: An Illustration

In order to illustrate the relationships among the terms we have been discussing, we will turn to a theoretical approach that has widely influenced much of the thinking in education and the behavioral sciences, the social cognitive theory of Albert Bandura (Bandura & Walters, 1963; Bandura, 1977, 1986). We can use this approach to illustrate much of what has been said about theories, models, and hypotheses. However, a brief review of Bandura's position is necessary before we can do this.

According to Bandura, learning comes from observation. It occurs in two distinct stages: acquisition and performance. For example, a child watches the teacher demonstrate how to plant seeds in a flowerpot. This is the acquisition phase. Then, in the performance phase, the child goes back to his desk and plants seeds in a flowerpot he is given. The teacher serves as a model for the child. According to Bandura, modeling leads to vicarious learning through observation and imitation of the experiences of others in the following four stages:

1 *Attentional processes* focus on what is perceived and explored from the array of events in the environment that have the potential for being modeled.

2 *Retentional processes* involve placing experiences in memory. Memories serve as the basis for producing responses and for internally correcting responses when they are given.

3 *Production processes* concern making connections between the representative symbol of an act or event in memory with physical response mechanisms.

4 *Motivational processes* determine whether the behavior will be performed. A person will be more likely to perform the behavior if he or she is motivated to do so. Motivation might be based on a pleasurable expectation, anticipated reward, or perhaps avoidance of punishment or discomfort.

Figure 3-3 shows Bandura's four stages in the context of a student learning to multiply numbers in arithmetic class.

According to Bandura, environment plays a critical role in learning. However, as can be seen from an analysis of the four steps listed above, the person (or *self*) and the nature of the behavior involved play equally essential roles in the process of learning. Bandura proposes an ongoing interrelationship between these three components. In other words, each component is continually

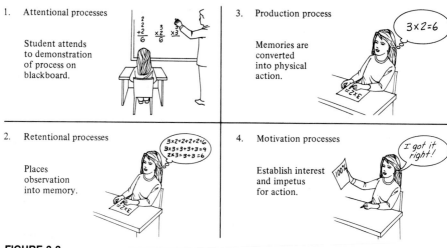

FIGURE 3-3
Bandura's four stages of learning.

influencing the other. A pictorial model of this interdependency is shown in Figure 3-4. The model can be activated in a variety of ways. For example, an event in the environment might trigger the behavior. On the other hand, the person, in response to something previously learned, might initiate the behavior. At any rate, the self component is capable of analyzing and judging the efficacy of the response in view of environmental conditions, which, in turn, shape the behavior.

Bandura's theory has wide applicability. For example, it can be used to explain how people develop their social skills, language, patterns of interpersonal behavior, cultural traditions, values, and the personality and skills to perform academically (Bandura, 1986; Zimmerman, 1985). The theory has been widely used as a basis for interventions, treatment programs, and research in psychology and education.

The Bandura position is typical of the kind of theory found in the social sciences. While it has some of the properties of theories in the natural and physical sciences, such as generalizability to a wide range of phenomena and utility in providing explanatory relationships, it is relatively vague when compared to

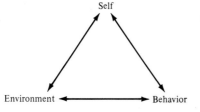

FIGURE 3-4
Bandura's three-component model.

theories found in physics or chemistry. Although the stages of learning and the three components displayed in Figures 3-3 and 3-4 are elegant in their relative simplicity and broad generalizability, *self, environment,* and *behavior* are not as clearly defined as are the components of Einstein's model (energy, mass, and the speed of light). Thus this kind of theory is a sort of "middle theory" when compared with some other scientific theories. Yet "middle theory" is about the most structured kind of theory found in psychology and the social sciences.

Bandura's three-component model, shown in Figure 3-4, can be used to generate testable hypotheses about how specific kinds of learning occur. To illustrate this, we turn to research by Zimmerman and Kinsler (1979), who investigated whether a videotape of a child being punished for playing with toys could influence the behavior of a child who viewed the tape and then was placed in a similar setting. (There were other aspects to the study, but, for our purposes, focusing on this portion is sufficient.) In this research, a group of 108 children in kindergarten and first grade were randomly assigned to treatment conditions. The children's behavior was observed for 15 minutes after they had viewed the tape and again one week later. Figure 3-5 shows how the variables in the study were related to the constructs of Bandura's three-component model (*environment* includes the videotaped model; *behavior* refers to playing with a specific set of toys).

Although Zimmerman and Kinsler did not say so precisely, a major hypothesis of their study might be stated as follows:

> Children who view a videotape that shows a child being punished for playing with toys will, when placed in a similar situation, play with the toys less than will children who have not seen the videotape.

The data were found to support the above hypothesis. The relationship between this hypothesis and the three-component model can be seen in Figure 3-5. Also noteworthy is the inferred role of the self component. Zimmerman and Kinsler refer to what goes on in this component as "The children's degree of internalization of the standard of conduct..." (p. 390). In other words, the

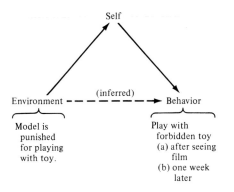

FIGURE 3-5
The three-component model in the Zimmerman and Kinsler study.

children stored the behavior of the model and the consequent punishment in their memories. The memory then served as a standard for behavior. This standard was used in their judgment of their own behavior. Since memories and other internal psychological processes cannot be observed directly, they must be inferred. In this case, the inference is based on the consistency in performance immediately after viewing the videotape and one week later.

From the Bandura theory and the three-component model, Zimmerman and Kinsler were able to derive a meaningful hypothesis and test it. The theory gives a context and structure to the findings. Variables are not drawn randomly from a satchel. They are operationalizations of constructs that fit together to form explanations. Other researchers who look at the findings can place the results in this context and carry the research further. Without structure, progress in research is difficult. There are other theories and models that could be mentioned. However, the emphasis here is not on any theory or explanation but, rather, on using structures like theory and models to guide one's research. We now turn to one of the most difficult aspects of doing research, finding a problem and stating testable hypotheses that address that problem.

STATEMENT OF THE PROBLEM AND HYPOTHESIS

We now turn our attention towards the statement of research problems and hypotheses. We noted earlier that a *hypothesis* is "a tentative declarative statement about the relationship between two or more variables." It is stated to suggest a solution to a problem. Thus there must be a problem before a hypothesis can be formulated. The problem may originate from a conceptual framework, such as a theory or model. When this is the case, the purpose of the research is usually to improve our power to explain or predict scientifically. For example, the theory of transfer of training suggests that material similar to that which has been previously learned will be easier to learn than material not related to what is already known. From it, a problem might be suggested and hypotheses formulated regarding the relevance of this theory for the development of educational materials. Problems can also originate from a need for information. A school administrator who is asked to select textbooks is faced with the problem of finding the most effective texts.

Developing an adequate statement of the problem is one of the most important and difficult tasks in research. It begins with an interest in an area about which knowledge is not complete. It is not uncommon for a researcher to spend years studying an area before feeling ready to state a problem. A problem may derive from a theory or model, a state of affairs, or systematic observations and research. For example, in the case of the Zimmerman and Kinsler study cited above, the problem was based on Bandura's model and might be stated as follows: "Would behavior presented on a television screen be enough to influence behavior?" Problems are generally stated as questions concerning the nature of the relationship between two or more variables. Sample problems are given below.

1 What are the components of leadership among school principals? (Pitner & Hocevar, 1987)

2 How does racial bias influence the decisions of jurors? (Klein & Creech, 1982)

3 Are the differences in mathematics performance between male and female high school students due to differences in the pattern of experience with quantitative course work? (Pallas & Alexander, 1983)

4 Does information about research on changing test responses affect students' attitudes, reasons for changing answers, and test performance? (McMorris, DeMers, & Schwartz, 1987)

But research problems are not merely questions. Thus "Is service in the military character-building?" and "Do parental attitudes foster creativity in students?" may be discussed by philosophers and popular writers and may be important issues, but they are far too vague to be suitable as research problems.

Problem statements should be evaluated on the basis of three characteristics. First, a problem should raise a question about a relationship between variables. Second, the relationship between the variables should be stated clearly and concisely. Finally, the problem statement should suggest a method of researching the question. For example, the four problem statements given above each imply that an empirical study could be designed to test the question. (See if you can visualize a study suggested by each problem statement.) The requirement that a way to test the problem should be suggested in the problem statement is generally the most difficult to satisfy. It is the one that determines the suitability of the problem for research. Since the nature of a research project is implicit in the way the problem is stated, such statements are crucially important.

FORMULATING PROBLEMS AND DOCUMENTATION

Problems are special kinds of questions that arise in areas in which knowledge is needed. They may ask questions of practical concern, or they may refer to the development or refinement of basic theory. Whatever the origins of a problem, they must be documented.

Have you ever tried to ask a question about something for no reason? To do so would be similar to stating a problem without documentation. Something must be known about the problem for it to have meaning. This is the purpose of documentation, to couch the problem in a context that provides purpose to the question. Literature reviews, reports of scientific research, writings on theoretical and philosophical issues, and various other sources of information are useful in developing a problem statement. In this section, we will look briefly at documentation of problems, using the library and other sources of information.

Using the Library

There are a number of centralized sources of information available in a good reference library with which the researcher must be familiar. Among these, the

Educational Resources Information Center (ERIC) and *Psychological Abstracts* *(PA)* are perhaps the most important for educational and behavioral science researchers.

 ERIC   ERIC began as a project of the U.S. Office of Education (USOE) in 1964 to collect, store, and make available information about education and research relating to education. It was operated at first as a division of the National Institute of Education (NIE), and then put under the Office of Educational Research and Improvement (OERI) within the U.S. Department of Education. ERIC supports a number of clearinghouses across the United States (usually between 15 and 20, depending on funding availability and changing priorities). These clearinghouses collect, abstract, and index information concerning education. This information may be drawn from journals, conference proceedings, government reports, unpublished manuscripts, or elsewhere. Materials collected in the clearinghouses are forwarded to central offices in the Washington, D.C., area, where the full texts are stored on microfilm and indexes are created for retrieving the information.

ERIC publishes two different indexes. The *Current Index to Journals in Education (CIJE)* is compiled monthly from materials found in published journals relevant to the field of education. *Research in Education (RIE)* is the second ERIC index. It contains abstracts of research from sources other than journals. Many libraries have the complete up-to-date files of *RIE* available on microfiche or hard copy. If your library does not have *RIE* on file, documents may be ordered from ERIC, using procedures described in *RIE*.

The *ERIC Thesaurus* contains descriptors of keywords that can be utilized to assist in locating information. Documents are assigned keywords when they are abstracted and placed in the index. These keywords can then be used to locate the documents. Keywords and information about them may be found in the *Thesaurus* organized under subject areas. For example, under the descriptor "Competency Based Education," one might find various kinds of information, such as the number of items to which this descriptor refers in the ERIC collection and a definition of the scope of the descriptor. Terms that could be used to tailor a search might also be included. Thus, under "Competency Based Education," terms such as "Individualized Instruction," "Performance Criteria," "Testing," etc. might be used to narrow the field of a search. The *ERIC Thesaurus* is published in volumes that are updated annually.

The researcher can go directly from the *Thesaurus* to the volumes of *CIJE* and *RIE* on the shelf to find information. While a search can be done by hand, most modern research libraries are able to provide a computerized search of the ERIC system as a service. Due to the ever-increasing size and complexity of the ERIC database, comprehensive computer searches require that the user have some sophistication about ERIC. For this reason, most libraries offering computerized search services will provide a specialist to help a researcher design a literature search. When this kind of specialized consultation is available, the researcher should take advantage of it. Entries in *CIJE* are found in three separate sections: the subject index, the author index, and the main-entry section. An article may be found by locating its number in either the subject or author index and then looking up the complete listing in the main-entry section. Documents listed in *RIE* are indexed according to author, institution, and subject. Many libraries at larger universities now have computer-search capabilities for the *CIJE* and *RIE* files.

Psychological Abstracts (PA) *Psychological Abstracts* is similar to ERIC in terms of the services it provides and its organization; however, the information it contains is somewhat different. *PA* is published monthly by the American Psychological Association. Each issue contains an index and literally thousands of abstracts or citations from the world's literature in psychology. *Psychological Abstracts* contains an English language abstract for each article cited, even when foreign journals have not provided one. Abstracts are generally included for research articles; but books, lengthy reports, monographs, dissertations, and other works may only be cited with a full bibliographic reference.

The coverage of the psychological literature is very broad in *Psychological Abstracts*. For example, under "Marriage & Family" in the Social Psychology section, it would not be surprising to find items about topics such as employment trends among women, patterns of adoption of black children in the United States, approaches to financing early childhood education in England, and a description of relationships between French mothers and infants during play. To further illustrate the breadth of coverage in this resource, one might find, under Educational Psychology, entries or problems of foreign children in German special education classes, the reading skill of gifted children, students' opinions of math lecturers in Papua, New Guinea, memory devices for learning nonsense words, evaluation of a music education program, and the relationship between the teacher's personality and a student's performance in class.

There are 16 major categories of entries in *Psychological Abstracts,* and literally hundreds of subcategories. Because of its breadth in defining the area of literature relating to psychology, *PA* is an extremely useful resource for most educational and behavioral science researchers. Even researchers in other fields such as medicine, dentistry, law, social work, physiology, and certain areas of engineering find *PA* to be a useful resource.

Like ERIC, *PA* can be searched by hand or by computer. Also like ERIC, *PA* publishes a thesaurus of keywords and descriptors called *The Thesaurus of Psychological Index Terms*. Many research libraries can access the *PA* databank, called PsychINFO. In addition, searches can be requested from PASAR (PA Search and Retrieval), a service of *Psychological Abstracts*. A computer search requires careful selection of the appropriate keywords. Many research libraries can provide assistance with designing and conducting a computerized search of *PA*.

Performing a Computerized Search Computerization of library resources is becoming a necessity. Consider for a moment the number of individual items indexed by a major data base such as ERIC or *Psychological Abstracts*. The

Current Index to Journals in Education (*CIJE*) reviews about 780 of the world's journals in education to index about 1500 articles per month. Another 33,000 or so entries per year are included in *PA*. A researcher simply could not sift through all that material in a reasonable amount of time. Further, with the informational data base increasing in size daily, the need for computerization is obvious.

The computerization of literature searches can be a mixed blessing. While computerization saves a considerable amount of time, it does rely on a machine and the design of the program to find what is needed. If a search is not designed properly, the most appropriate literature may be missed. A graduate student who worked with one of the present authors found that when she searched the literature for her dissertation research, the computer did not locate any of the literature she knew existed on the topic but, instead, came up with a number of irrelevant citations. For example, since her topic was the development of reasoning in children and its relationship to educational performance, she began her search with the keyword "education," used the subcategory "development," and, under this, listed "reasoning." What she obtained from the system surprised her. It gave her numerous citations dealing with planning and designing fund-raising projects in education! What she did not know was that many educators use the word "development" to describe fund-raising activities. With the help of a librarian familiar with the system and the field of education, the student was able to rearrange her keywords to obtain a search of more appropriate literature. Thus the way the search is designed is critical, and sometimes the help of a knowledgeable librarian may also be critical to the design of a useful computerized literature search. Figure 3-6 lists a possible sequence of steps to follow when making a computerized search of the literature.

Other Research Indexes, Bibliographies, and Other Sources   Although ERIC and *PA* will cover most of the literature of interest to educational and behavioral science researchers, other bibliographic sources might be consulted for additional information. For example, the *Exceptional Child Education Resources* (*ECER*), published by the Council for Exceptional Children, indexes journals relating to topics in special education. *Dissertation Abstracts International,* published by University Microfilms, contains abstracts of doctoral dissertations from most of the major institutions in the United States and Canada. Copies of the dissertations listed may be obtained on microfilm or in photocopy form.

Education Index is another useful source of published information about education. It indexes articles and books about education that have appeared in periodicals. *Education Index* is published monthly.

Many other sources contain abstracts of a variety of publications useful for the educational researcher. Most of these sources index their entries by subject and author and contain short abstracts describing the publication. Sources of abstracts useful to educational and behavioral science researchers are, *So-*

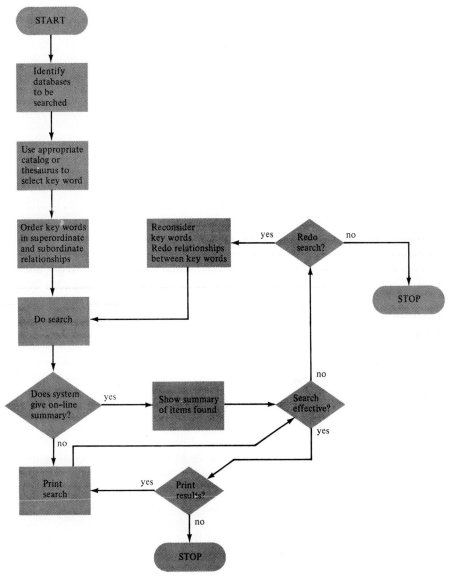

FIGURE 3-6
A plan for a computerized literature search.

ciological Abstracts, Mental Retardation Abstracts, Educational Administration Abstracts, and *Child Development Abstracts.*

Several publications specialize in reporting reviews of the literature available on a topic. Perhaps the most important to educational researchers is the *Review of Educational Research (RER).* Between 1931 and 1969, this periodical published reviews on specific topics in education chosen by the editorial board. However, since 1970, it has been publishing unsolicited reviews of educational topics. *Review of Research in Education (RRE)*, and the *Encyclopedia of Educational Research* contain reviews of topics in educational research. These sources can provide an overview of a topic that will summarize the literature in an area rather thoroughly. Similar reviews can be found in the *NSSE Yearbook,* published annually on a particular topic in education by the National Society for the Study of Education. Two sources in psychology that publish comprehensive reviews of specific topics are *Psychological Bulletin* and the *Annual Review of Psychology.*

The *Science Citation Index (SCI)* (for literature in the fields of science, medicine, agriculture, technology, and the behavioral sciences) and the *Social Science Citation Index (SSCI)* (for literature in the fields of the social, behavioral, and related sciences, often including education) take a rather different approach to literature searching than do most of the sources cited thus far. Specifically, they allow one to find the articles that have cited a particular reference. A researcher who uses *SCI* or *SSCI* would first identify a reference that is the key to progress in a particular area. The whole index can then be searched for other works that cite that reference.

Other centralized reference sources are the *Handbooks of Research on Teaching* (1st ed., Gage, N. L., ed., Chicago: Rand McNally, 1965; 2nd ed., Travers, R. M. W., ed., Chicago: Rand McNally, 1973; and 3rd ed., Wittrock, M. C., ed., New York: Macmillan, 1986) which summarize research in various fields of education. The *Mental Measurements Yearbook* contains reviews of various psychological and educational tests and discusses research concerning those tests. Many other yearbooks and handbooks of this type are published.

These reference sources, along with the tests, periodicals, government reports, and other holdings make the library a particularly important resource to consider when formulating and documenting research problems. Libraries are organized to permit access to the material they contain. Sometimes computers are used to find information; other times, the indexes and files of the library must be used. Librarians can be very helpful to researchers seeking literature. Researchers must know how to use a library facility and be familiar with the many services that it offers.

Outlines and Notes

Good note-taking skills are important if one is to make maximum use of the information gleaned from the various resources in the library. Just as important as note-taking skills, however, is the organization of the effort and material. To facilitate organization, a preliminary outline is developed. Most outlines are organized using Roman numbers to identify major topics. Capital letters are used to identify subtopics to be discussed under each main topic. Further identification of subareas to be included utilizes Arabic numbers and lowercase letters. An example of the typical outline structure is shown in Figure 3-7 for the beginning of a paper on the relationship between education and home environment. The author will write the paper using the outline as a guide. It will ensure that all the identified material is covered in a meaningful sequence.

The outline should be formulated before the library work is completed because it will serve as a useful guide, ensuring that information needed about each topic will be considered. Information must be recorded at the time and in the way it is found to ensure accuracy. One of the most popular methods of recording information is to use an index-card file. This method requires two different sets of cards, one for bibliographic data and the other for recording

FIGURE 3-7
The beginning of a sample outline showing organizational structure.

```
            Education and the Home Environment
                         Outline
    I. Introduction
        a. Background
            1. Social factors
            2. Economic factors
            3. Educational factors
                a. Resources
                b. Personnel
            4. Philosophical influences

        B. Present Context
            1. Social factors
            2. Economic factors
            3. Educational factors
            4. Contemporary trends in philosophy

    II. Review of Research Literature
        a. Research on social factors
            1. Research in social factors
                a. The family stu...
```

the information available in the article. Figure 3-8 shows an example of reference cards using this system.

The bibliographic index should contain reference information in the form to be used for typing the references. For example, in Figure 3-8, the bibliographic card is written in the style recommended for reference citations by the journals published by the American Psychological Association. On the back of the card, additional data about the reference may be recorded as necessary, such as the library call number, the pages reviewed, or the section of the library in which the reference was found in case it is needed later. Bibliographic cards should be filed in alphabetical order so that they may be consulted quickly. The information index-card entries are filed according to the outline developed for the topic. These cards contain the name of the author and the data of the reference followed by the relevant information. There can be several cards for

FIGURE 3-8
Examples of a bibliographic entry and an information-card entry.

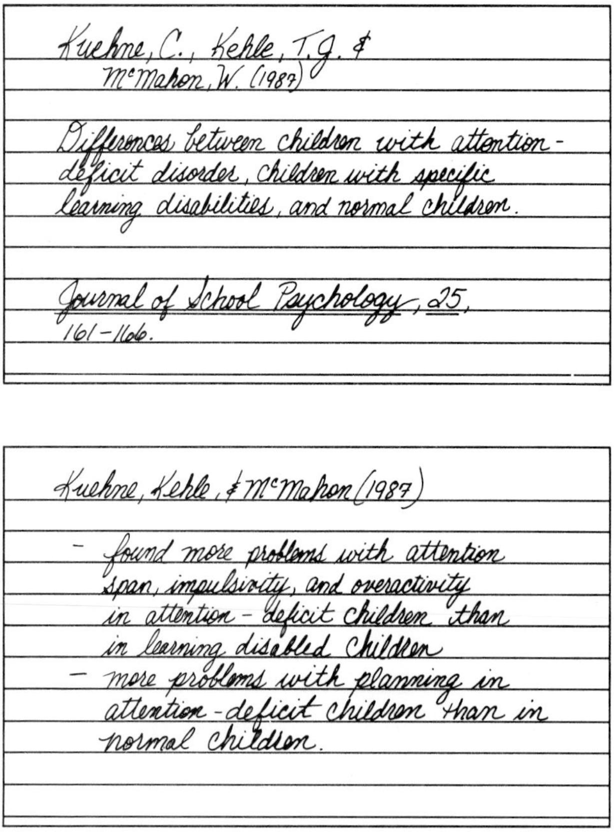

Kuehne, C., Kehle, T.J. & McMahon, W. (1987)

Differences between children with attention-deficit disorder, children with specific learning disabilities, and normal children.

Journal of School Psychology, 25, 161–166.

Kuehne, Kehle, & McMahon (1987)

- found more problems with attention span, impulsivity, and overactivity in attention-deficit children than in learning disabled children
- more problems with planning in attention-deficit children than in normal children.

a single reference when several pieces of information are derived from the same source.

Documentation by Research

We have discussed documentation of a problem when useful information is available in a library; but what can we do when we are interested in a problem that has not been previously researched very extensively? Must we find a new problem to investigate? Not if the problem is worthwhile. Since information about the problem is not available from published sources, the researcher must develop the documentation that is needed to state and delineate the problem. This can be done using research techniques such as the pilot study.

The *pilot study* is a small-scale version of the proposed study, with a restricted sample of subjects. Often a student beginning work on a dissertation finds that there is little information available to answer specific questions about the design of the research or a suitable measurement instrument. A pilot study might be run to find answers to questions such as, "Are the measurements sensitive enough?" and "Are the treatments valid?"

Interviews, surveys, and expert opinion are other sources of documentation of problem statements. Some problems require obtaining information directly from people who are familiar with the topic. For example, in one research project related to improvement of health care for hypertensive patients, area residents were surveyed regarding their preferences for method of delivery of services. Local physicians, nurses, and pharmacists were interviewed to determine needs. Finally, public health and medical administration experts were consulted. As a result of this documentation, the problem was stated with considerable precision even though the library did not contain very much information on the problem.

Putting It All Together in a Problem Statement

The sequence of events in developing a research problem is as follows:

   1 Become interested in a topic.
   2 Investigate the topic. Find out as much of what is known about it as possible. This might involve working in the library or collecting data in the field.
   3 On the basis of the previous step, specify an operational problem statement.
   4 Integrate what is known to support the problem as it has been stated. This might require going back to the library or doing more field research.

Many research reports begin with a section that contains the problem statement and the documentation that leads up to and supports the problem. Where appropriate, this documentation may be referred to as "review of the literature."

THE HYPOTHESIS STATEMENT

In previous sections of this chapter, we looked at hypotheses from the perspective of variables, constructs, models, theories, and laws. In this section, we will relate the hypothesis to the statement of the problem and then discuss stating and testing hypotheses.

Relationship between a Hypothesis and a Problem

A hypothesis statement is derived directly from the statement of the problem. The *hypothesis* is actually a guess at a solution to the problem. Since it is a solution, it is stated in declarative form. Furthermore, since it is a proposed solution, it should be testable or verifiable. Moreover, if the guess is to be an intelligent one, it ought to be based upon what is known about the topic of the problem. The review of the literature, past research, and personal experience contribute to this knowledge.

The hypothesis is more operational than the problem statement. We discussed the meaning of the word "operational" earlier in this chapter in reference to variables and constructs. Consider the following problem statement, suggested by Hendel (1985):

> Does a structured undergraduate curriculum lead to better academic performance and program satisfaction than an unstructured curriculum does?

If this problem were operational, we would not have questions about the meaning of terms like "structured" and "unstructured" curriculum, "academic performance," and "program satisfaction." Hendel defined a *structured program* as one for which the institution has specific requirements, and an *unstructured program* as one that permits students to design their own course of study. Academic performance and satisfaction were defined by a systematic procedure of transcript review and a questionnaire administered to the students. Hendel did not state a specific hypothesis in his journal article, but, had he done so, it would probably have been something like the following:

> Students who complete unstructured (individually designed) courses of study in their undergraduate programs will demonstrate greater program satisfaction and better academic performance than will students who complete structured (established institutional curricula) programs.

It should be obvious that the hypothesis suggests an answer to the problem. Further, since the terms "program satisfaction" and "academic performance" are operationalized with specific instrumentation in the study (by a questionnaire and transcript analysis procedure), the statement is more operational than is the problem. Finally, the hypothesis suggests comparing two groups as a way of testing it. Because of these features, the hypothesis serves to structure the research investigation.

Stating the Hypothesis

Stating the hypothesis can be rather easy once the problem is known. In fact, a good statement of the problem usually suggests rather directly the nature of the hypothesis statement. We have already discussed five characteristics of good hypothesis statements.

1 Hypotheses should be stated in declarative form.
2 Hypotheses should describe a relationship between two or more variables.
3 Hypotheses should be testable.
4 Hypotheses should be operational in that there should be no ambiguity in the variables or the relationships proposed.
5 Hypotheses should reflect a guess at a solution or outcome to a problem based upon some knowledge, previous research, or identified needs.

Using these five characteristics as a guide, let us take a look at two actual research problems and corresponding hypotheses. Petroski, Craighead, and Horan (1983) researched the following problem:

Can the grooming behavior of mentally retarded women be improved through training?

In the Petroski et al. research, one of the hypotheses could have been stated as follows:

Mentally retarded women who are shown sequential photographs of *themselves* performing grooming behaviors will not engage in more *grooming behavior* than will mentally retarded *women shown pictures of other women* performing the behaviors or a *control group* of mentally retarded women given verbal grooming instruction.

The italicized pharases identify the independent and dependent variables. Have all five criteria of hypothesis statements been met? Clearly the hypothesis has been stated in a declarative sentence as a relationship between two or more variables. Furthermore, the way it is written suggests that it is testable by setting up groups of subjects who will be shown photographed sequences of a woman (either themselves or another person) performing grooming tasks (combing her hair, washing her face, etc.) or will be assigned to a control group that receives verbal instruction on grooming. However, it does not yet seem that the variables are sufficiently operational. For example, the exact nature of the grooming tasks, the number of photos in a sequence, and the specifics of the verbal instruction for the control group is not clear. Further, the criteria for mental retardation in the study were not specified in the hypothesis. Much of this information can be found in the article. In order to avoid unnecessarily long hypothesis statements, it is not uncommon for researchers to further operationalize the variables under study in the section of the research proposal or report where the methods for conducting the study are described. The fifth criterion, that the hypothesis reflect a solution or outcome to a problem based upon previous knowledge or research, is satisfied. Not only is the relationship of the hypothesis to the problem obvious, but Petroski et al. reviewed social learning theory (including the theoretical position of Bandura cited earlier) and related research with retarded and normal subjects.

Very often, a researcher will not report both the research problem and hypothesis in a published research article because of space and style limitations imposed by the publications. Consider the example of the study reported by Hollon and Gemmill (1976, p. 82) regarding a comparison of the roles of male and female community-college professors. The authors, after a review of the literature, say that the purpose of the study was to explore how female and male professors differ in the amount that they "perceived participation in decision making, job related tension, job involvement, and overall job satisfaction." That statement implied the following problem:

Do male professors differ from female professors in their perceived participation in decision making, job-related tension, job involvement, and overall job satisfaction?

The authors follow this implied problem with four specific hypotheses. It was hypothesized that

"Female teaching professionals in academe will, in comparison to their male counterparts, experience: (1) less perceived participation in decision making in the immediate work environment; (2) greater job related tension; (3) less job involvement; and (4) less overall job satisfaction" (p. 82).

Hollon and Gemmill followed the statement of the hypotheses with explicit descriptions of the measuring instruments to be used in the study. Review the five criteria of good hypothesis statements listed earlier and determine for yourself the adequacy of the four hypotheses of Hollon and Gemmill. You can see that the hypotheses are stated in declarative form and express relationships among variables. Furthermore, the hypotheses do seem to follow from the problem. The criteria of testability can be met by comparing male to female professors in terms of the dependent variables. However, the hypotheses in their present state may not be as operational as they should be. For example, operational definitions for terms like "job involvement" and "job-related tension" should be included in the article.

Kinds of Hypotheses

The hypothesis statements we have been discussing to this point have been of the kind generally referred to as *substantive or research* hypotheses. If one conducts qualitative or historical research, a substantive hypothesis statement may be all that is needed. However, if a problem is to be investigated empirically, another kind of hypothesis must be stated in terms of the quantities to be investigated. For example, we might hypothesize that children in a class taught by teaching method A will perform differently on a test than will children taught by method B. Here we are stating a hypothesis about average performance in the two groups. That is, we are saying that the average test score of those taught by method A is going to be different from that of those taught by method B, and thus an empirical hypothesis is suggested. An *empirical hypothesis* is simply a translation of a substantive hypothesis from words into a statistically meaningful relationship.

In statistical testing, a particular kind of hypothesis, called the *null hypothesis,* is tested. It is called *null* because it usually reflects the "no-difference" or "no-effect" situation. A simple example of a null hypothesis is as follows:

$$H_o : \mu_A = \mu_B$$

where H_o = null hypothesis

μ_A = the average score of group A (μ is the lowercase Greek letter mu)

μ_B = the average score of group B.

This hypothesis is read as follows: "The population mean of group A is no different from the population mean of group B." Using various statistical techniques discussed in later chapters, we can test this hypothesis. We will have more to say about statistical hypotheses and how to test them in Chapter 7.

SUMMARY

A very general but highly predictive statement about a relationship among variables is called a *law*. *Theories* are less elegant, less simple, and less certain statements than laws. *Models* are less parsimonious and general than theories. *Hypotheses* are declarative statements about a specific relationship among certain *variables* under precisely defined conditions. *Problem statements* must be made before clear statements of hypotheses can be developed.

Figure 3-9 presents the ideal situation in the formulation of research investigations. Notice that two different starting points are included for simplicity. In actual research situations, the process may begin at any stage and recycling may be called for (e.g., the results of the hypothesis test may call for a new statement of the problem or, alternatively, for a reconceptualization of the theory). More will be said about this later. For the moment, however, we are considering the ideal version of the research process beginning at one of the two indicated starting points in Figure 3-9. Depending upon the purpose, research

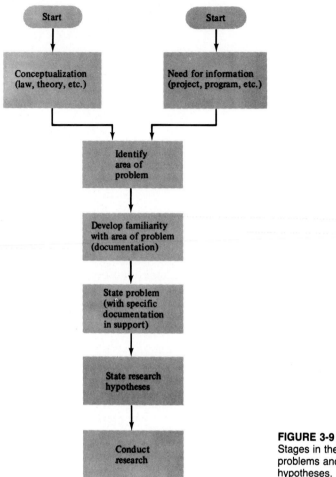

FIGURE 3-9
Stages in the formulation of
problems and the testing of
hypotheses.

may originate in abstract conceptualizations such as laws, theories, or models. Research might also emerge from a need for information in an applied setting, which could then result in conceptualizations such as models and theories, although this may not be necessary with all types of research.

A good library can be an essential tool for documentation of a research problem. Several services and indexes of bibliographic material exist to help the researcher locate pertinent material. These resources can be accessed by using computerized techniques or through more traditional library catalogs. Among the major index and abstract services for researchers in education are the ERIC indexes (*RIE* and *CIJE*) and *Psychological Abstracts* (*PA*).

After the problem area is identified and documented, the problem can be stated as a question. The hypothesis is stated as a solution to that question and suggests the manner in which it will be tested. Finally, a research investigation is designed and conducted to test the hypothesis. The diagram in Figure 3-9 represents the ideal situation because science and research often do not proceed in so orderly a fashion. For example, a researcher may be investigating one problem when another emerges from the data, or, once into a test of the hypothesis, the researcher may realize an important variable was not considered in the review of the literature. However, the thorough researcher tries to follow the steps identified in Figure 3-9 as closely as possible and to proceed in an orderly manner in investigations.

PROBLEMS FOR THOUGHT AND DISCUSSION

1 C. Northcote Parkinson (1957) stated the following as a scientific law: "Work expands so as to fill the time available for its completion" (p. 2).
   a Does this statement possess the characteristics of a law?
   b Would you classify it as a theory, model, hypothesis, or none of these? Why?
   c Suggest some variables which might be used to formulate testable hypotheses about Parkinson's law.
2 From your area of interest, select a field of research.
   a Identify any relevant laws, theories, principles, models, or paradigms.
   b Trace the development of hypotheses for specific research studies which you know about to the theories, models, paradigms, or other higher-order generalizations from which they originate.
3 For each of the following problems, develop at least one hypothesis statement:
   a Is there a relationship between a physical education student's ability to jump vertically and the ability to run a mile?
   b Do people with college degrees make better salespeople?
   c Do schools in countries with democratic forms of government produce students who are more creative?
   d Does an iron-deficient diet influence children's ability to perform on problem-solving tasks?
4 Select a published research article of interest to you. Trace the steps outlined in Figure 3-9 in the development of the study. Can the sequence be followed in the article?
5 What are the criteria for a good problem statement?
6 Locate the *PA* volume for a recent year. Look up the entries listed under "teacher personality" in the subject index. Note the titles and the journals of the entries. Compare with listings under "teacher personality" for the same year in *Education Index* and *CIJE*.
7 Discuss the resources available at your reference library with the librarian. Include periodicals that are available, the organization and location of materials, the actual card or computerized catalog, computerized searching, and any special resources or services provided.
8 Develop an index-card file on a topic that interests you by reviewing library sources. Be sure to keep the bibliographical entries and the information entries separate.
9 A teacher states to a psychologist that based on his observations, students today are better able to solve problems creatively than were students 10 or 15 years ago. The psychologist wishes to do some research to determine whether this statement is jus-

tified. How should she proceed? What kinds of difficulties might she encounter in forming researchable problem and hypotheses statements?

10 Find several hypothesis statements in the literature, and evaluate them according to the five criteria of good hypotheses listed in this chapter.

11 It has been suggested by some researchers that stating a problem or hypothesis before seeing the data is not a good idea because the researcher will not know what statements the data will support. Discuss this position in view of the considerations presented in Chapter 3.

12 Identify the deficiencies of the following hypotheses, and offer some suggestions for improving them:

a Girls are no brighter than boys.

b Do Graduate Record Examination scores increase after students have attended one year of graduate school?

c Japanese children are better mathematics students.

d Impulsive people do not read as well as do reflective people.

REFERENCES

Anastasi, A. (1982). *Psychological testing (5th ed.).* New York: Macmillan.

Bandura, A. (1977). *Social learning theory.* Englewood Cliffs, NJ: Prentice-Hall.

Bandura, A. (1986). *Social foundations of thought and action.* Englewood Cliffs, NJ: Prentice-Hall.

Bandura, A., & Walters, R. H. (1963). *Social learning and personality development.* New York: Holt.

Hendel, D. D. (1985). Effects of individualized and structured college curricula on students' performance and satisfaction. *American Educational Research Journal, 22,* 117–122.

Hollon, C. J., & Gemmill, G. R. (1976). A comparison of male and female professors in decision making, job related tension, job involvement, and job satisfaction. *Educational Administration Quarterly, 12,* 80–93.

Klein, K., & Creech, B. (1982). Race, rape, and bias: Distortion of prior odds and meaning changes. *Basic and Applied Social Psychology, 3,* 21–33.

McMorris, R. F., DeMers, L. P., & Schwartz, S. P. (1987). Attitudes, behaviors, and reasons for changing responses following answer-changing instruction. *Journal of Educational Measurement, 24,* 131–143.

Pallas, A. M., & Alexander, K. L. (1983). Sex differences in quantitative SAT performance: New evidence on the differential coursework hypothesis. *American Educational Research Journal, 20,* 165–182.

Parkinson, C. N. (1957). *Parkinson's law and other studies in administration.* Boston: Houghton Mifflin.

Petroski, R. A., Craighead, L. W., & Horan, J. J. (1983). Separate and combined effects of behavior rehearsal and self–other modeling variations on the grooming skill acquisition of mentally retarded women. *Journal of Counseling Psychology, 30,* 279–282.

Pitner, N. J., & Hocevar, D. (1987). An empirical investigation of two factor versus multifactor theories of principal leadership: Implications for the evaluation of school principals. *Journal of Personnel Evaluation in Education, 1,* 93–109.

Zimmerman, B. J. (1985). Theoretical foundations of school psychology: Past and present. In J. R. Bergan (Ed.), *School psychology in contemporary society: An introduction.* Columbus, OH: Merrill.

Zimmerman, B. J., & Kinsler, K. (1979). Effects of exposure to a punished model and verbal prohibitions on children's toy play. *Journal of Educational Psychology, 71,* 388–395.

SUPPLEMENTARY READINGS

Dillon, J. T. (1984). The classification of research questions. *Review of Educational Research, 54,* 327–361.

Gage, N. L. (1985). *Hard gains in the soft sciences.* Bloomington, IN: Phi Delta Kappa.

Greenwood, L. (1985). *Literature searching in education: A primer for beginning scholars.* Lexington, KY: Willowood Press.

Harris, R. J. (1976). The uncertain connection between verbal theories and research hypotheses in social psychology. *Journal of Experimental Social Psychology, 12,* 210–219.

McCain, G., & Segal, E. M. (1977). *The game of science* (3rd ed.). Monterey, CA: Brooks/Cole.

Phillips, D. C. (1987). *Philosophy, science, and social inquiry.* New York: Pergamon.

Snelbecker, G. E. (1985). *Learning theory, instructional theory and psychoeducational design.* Lanham, MD: University Press of America, chap. 1, "Psychology and Education: Problems of Application; chap. 2, "An Introduction to Theory and Theory Construction."

Snow, R. E. (1973). Theory construction for research on teaching. In R. M. W. Travers (Ed.), *Second handbook of research on teaching.* Chicago: Rand McNally, 77–112.

Turner, M. B. (1965). *Philosophy and the science of behavior.* New York: Appleton-Century-Crofts.

4

UNDERSTANDING AND DESIGNING EXPERIMENTAL STUDIES

In this chapter, we will focus our attention on the kind of study in which the researcher is interested in learning about the effects of certain conditions (*independent variables*) on other conditions (*dependent variables*) in controlled settings. Such studies are called *experiments*. Let us begin this discussion with an example.

Suppose we wish to assess the effectiveness of a television commercial for a certain brand of shaving cream. First, we ask a sample of people to take a test of their knowledge about the product. Then, we expose them to the advertisement. Finally, we readminister the test to the same sample of subjects. We find that on the second testing, after they have heard the commercial, the subjects seem to know more about the product. At first glance, the conclusion that the commercial effectively increased their knowledge about the product may seem justified. However, after thinking a bit more, we may begin to wonder about such things as whether two exposures to the same questions caused the higher scores on the second administration. We might also question the nature of the sample used in the study. For example, does the sample include a disproportionate number of young children or women who do not use shaving cream, would be unlikely to know much about it initially, and would probably not purchase the product in any case? Such considerations might lead us to question the meaning and value of the research. If our shaving-cream study had been well-designed, we could not as easily have raised those questions about the effects of testing or the nature of the sample.

The purpose of this chapter is first, to show you what to look for in determining the worth of research designs you read about, and second, to help you select designs for your own research efforts. We will consider the ways that variables are controlled in experiments. In addition, we will look at the differences between experimental and nonexperimental designs.

Experimentation in the social and behavioral sciences is a relatively recent development. Danziger (1985) discusses the historical evolution of the psychological experiment from the late nineteenth century. In early experiments in such fields as psychology and hypnosis, the researchers themselves served as subjects. In later studies in these fields, less participatory roles for the experimenter were considered appropriate.

Experimental research can yield convincing information if it is well designed. If it is poorly designed, no matter how good the execution, the resulting information will be of questionable or no value. In designing experiments, attention must be paid to the setting, purpose, procedures, and conclusions of the intended experiment. Poor design can lead to a problem all too common in educational and social science research—that the conclusions expressed are not possible from the study that was done. *Experimental validity* is the term used to refer to the degree to which an experiment answers the questions asked or, to put it another way, the degree to which the conclusions follow logically from the study.

JUDGING THE VALIDITY OF RESEARCH DESIGNS

In judging the worth of a research design, validity must be our primary consideration. There are at least four aspects of validity of an experiment, and each aspect must be evaluated to determine the worth of the design. The first aspect is the internal logic of the experiment; this is called *internal validity*. The second aspect is *external validity,* the degree to which the results can be generalized beyond the confines of the specific study. The third and fourth aspects are the data analysis and interpretation and the operationalization of constructs (Cook & Campbell, 1979). Internal and external validity are addressed in the present chapter; the other forms of validity are covered in later chapter on statistics and measurement.

Campbell and Stanley (1963) noted that internal validity is the basic requirement without which an experiment cannot be interpreted. It answers the question: "Did in fact the experimental treatments make a difference in this specific experimental instance?" (p. 175). In a study of a new programmed text for mathematics instruction, the question of internal validity would be: "Do the students in the study really know more about mathematics because of the programmed text?" In a study of a new program to reduce the high school dropout rate in a school district, the question of internal validity would be: "Is there a reduction in the dropout rate because of the new program?"

To be at all useful, a study must have internal validity. However, internal validity is no guarantee that external validity will be present. The questions of external validity are: "Can the results of the experiment be generalized to other samples at other times and settings from the population being studied?"

and "Do the results generalize to other populations at other times and different settings?" Thus, in the study of the programmed mathematics text referred to earlier, we might ask the question, "Would the improvement in performance in mathematics attributed to the text be true for other groups of students in other schools?" In the study of the program to reduce the number of high school dropouts, we might ask, "Would this program be as effective in other school districts as it was in the one studied?"

A study that tests a hypothesis and has internal validity is called a *true experiment*. A study that has no internal validity is called *preexperimental* and is not very useful. A third kind of experimental study, the quasi-experiment, is used when a true experimental design is not possible. The quasi-experiment is covered in more detail in the next chapter. In designing any experiment, the researchers must be aware of the factors that threaten its validity.

THREATS TO INTERNAL VALIDITY

Campbell and Stanley (1963) identified eight different types of influences that can threaten the internal validity of a research design. These influences, if not properly controlled, can become *confounded with* (i.e., entangled with and not separable from) the effects of the treatment variable or variables. When these influences are not controlled, it is impossible to determine whether the treatment variable has produced the particular effect observed or whether that effect is due to something else. The eight threats to internal validity are

History. This involves the influence of events that may occur in the time span between measurements. Generally, the longer this time span, the greater the probability that something can happen in the subjects' environment to affect the results.

Maturation. During an experiment, the subjects themselves can change. They may grow tired, hungry, bored, or, in the case of a longer experiment, older.

Testing. Taking a test beforehand can cause a person to have a higher score the second time because of familiarity with the test. Thus, in a pretest-posttest situation, the practice provided by the pretest can result in a higher score on the posttest.

Instrumentation. When changes in the measurement or observation occur during the experiment, they can influence the experimental results. Such changes can occur when observers or scorers change or become tired or bored or when different scoring criteria are used because subjects are older.

Statistical Regression. There is a tendency for groups chosen on the basis of extreme scores to score closer to the average subsequently. For example, a group composed of subjects who scored extremely high on a test will probably average a lower score on a second administration of the test regardless of the treatment.

Selection. When groups are to be compared to determine the effects of different treatments, but the groups are systematically different from the start, selection can become a problem.

Experimental Mortality. Experimental mortality can be a problem when subjects withdraw from the comparison groups at differential rates. That is, groups that were comparable at the start may not be similar by the end of the experiment because of differential withdrawal of subjects from the treatment groups rather than as a result of treatment effects.

Interactions among Factors. Factors can operate together to influence experimental results. That is, threats to internal validity such as instrumentation, selection, and experimental mortality could operate in combination to affect the results of a study.

The threats to internal validity can be illustrated by using a study in which racial prejudice is the dependent variable. A measure of prejudice is administered to a random sample of white adults immediately before and one year after the implementation of a court-ordered busing program designed to achieve greater racial balance in a large metropolitan area. The major finding of the study is that there is a significant decline, pretest to posttest, in the average prejudice scores. Now for the question of internal validity: "Is the observed decline in racial prejudice due to the busing project?" We answer the question by looking at the threats to internal validity and asking whether each type could account for the decline in prejudice scores rather than exposure to the experimental variable (the busing program).

History

First, we look at historical events. Could certain events other than the experimental ones occurring between the first and second administrations of the prejudice test account for the experimental findings? The answer here is that historical events can offer competing explanations for the decline in prejudice. Thus history is a threat to the internal validity of the research findings. For example, suppose that in the interim between the first and second observations of the sample, a particularly successful housing integration program was implemented and an integrated professional sports team from the city won a league championship. These factors could have contributed to the decline in scores on the test, and the researcher would have no way of determining the actual cause of the change in scores.

Maturation

Maturation could also offer an alternative explanation of the results. Perhaps the trend in the prejudice scores of urban whites has shown a continuous decline over the last 10 years as the population has gained in education and sophistication. Thus, taking two measurements of prejudice separated by a period of 1 year any time during this 10-year period would very likely reveal a significant drop in scores no matter what intervening variables were present.

Testing

A third alternative explanation for the experimental finding, and hence a third threat to the internal validity of the study, is testing. Suppose that some of the subjects of the experiment realized after they completed the pretest that it measured their racial prejudice. Since it is not socially desirable to appear prejudiced, the second time they took the test they made a conscious effort to answer the items in such a way as to seem less prejudiced. Hence the decline of scores on the second test may be the result of testing.

Instrumentation

A fourth threat to the internal validity of this experiment is instrumentation. Let us suppose that the test of prejudice had to be individually administered to each participant by someone trained to do it and that a certain degree of interpretation was called for in the process of translating statements the participant made into a score on the test. When it was time for the second measurement of prejudice, it was difficult to obtain the services of the same person who administered the pretest. Even if the same person was available, it may have been difficult to administer the test exactly the way it was administered the first time. Any change in scores on the second administration may thus be entirely due to instrumentation.

Statistical Regression

To adequately illustrate the fifth threat to experimental validity, statistical regression, we need to change the study of prejudice somewhat. Suppose the researcher took particular care to select only very prejudiced individuals in the sample to be studied. The rationale may have been that if the attitudes of this group of individuals changed after the busing program, then the attitudes of the rest of the population of the area would certainly also change. The individuals were selected in the following way. The prejudice test was administered to a very large sample of individuals before the busing program, and those who scored in the top 10 percent of the sample were selected for the study. This group is referred to as an *extreme group* because only persons with extreme scores on the test were included. (Note that an extreme group could also be a group with low scores.) The threat of statistical regression occurs wherever an extreme group is selected for study. The effect of statistical regression is that the scores of an extreme group will move (or regress) toward the average score of the whole group on a second testing. Thus the decline in the average score, or *mean,* on the posttest for the highly prejudiced group is expected because of statistical regression regardless of treatment effects.

Since this concept may be rather difficult to grasp, we will develop it here in more detail. The basic rationale is as follows. The measurement of prejudice by the test chosen in the study is not perfect. The score for each person probably varies from day to day depending on extraneous variables such as the person's mood, the events of that particular day, the level of care in answering items, etc. All these things serve to introduce a certain amount of "error" into the person's score. This is typical of the measuring instruments used in educational and behavioral science research, all of which contain varying amounts of error. The errors, when averaged across all individuals in the population, tend to cancel each other out and thus may be handled by statistical methods such as those described in Chapters 6 and 7. However, when an extreme group is used, these errors tend to be more often in the direction of the extremity than in the direction of the mean. To say this another way, the scores of the high extreme group on the prejudice test are more often too high rather than too low because of the measurement errors. Thus, on the second administration of the same test, not so many of the errors are likely to be as large and the scores will tend not to be as extreme. The average of the extreme group will fall closer to the average for everybody than did the pretest mean of the extreme group.

Regression toward the mean can also raise the average score. For example, a group of second-grade students who read extremely poorly may have been selected for a special program to improve their reading skills. Regardless of the effectiveness of the program, the mean score of these students on a standardized reading test administered the following year will tend to be closer to the overall group mean due to statistical regression. Thus their performance will appear to improve on the second test. Figure 4-1 illustrates regression to the mean for these two cases.

Selection

Selection is a threat to internal validity when differences exist between comparison groups before the treatments are applied. To illustrate selection, we return to the study of the change in prejudice scores resulting from court-ordered busing, but we must first make a slight alteration in the study to demonstrate selection effects more clearly. Suppose we chose another city, city B, that was very similar to the city in which the busing occurred (city A). We would need to show that no change in prejudice occurred in city B over the same period of time in order to be able to conclude that changes observed in city A were due to busing. However, we could never be sure that the differences observed were not due to internal differences between city A and city B that had nothing to do with busing. It would even be possible to select the two cities to produce certain results. For example, the two cities selected might be similar in size and economic character, but one might be a multiethnic city on

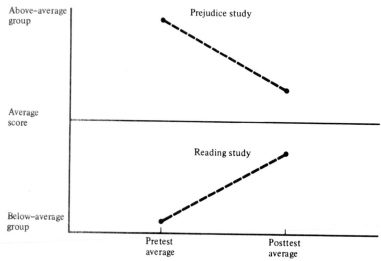

FIGURE 4-1
Illustrations of statistical regression towards the mean.

the West coast while the other is located in the middle West or South and relatively homogenous ethnically. Further, at the same time the busing issue was in the forefront in city A, city B was experiencing labor disputes and major problems in its public housing programs. It would be difficult in such a situation to determine whether differences in prejudice scores between the two cities were due to busing or to numerous other factors.

Experimental Mortality

Suppose that only half of the pretested subjects in the busing study were willing to take the posttest. We would have no way of knowing whether the posttested group was systematically different from the group who began the study. Thus because of the subjects who dropped out of the study (the *mortality rate*), there would be no way to be certain that the decline in prejudice scores was an effect of the busing. The remaining posttested respondents could have been the least prejudiced in the sample from the beginning.

In studies that involve comparing two or more groups, differential mortality can be a major threat. Even when groups are initially equivalent, the composition of the groups may change to the point where they are not comparable by the end of the study. For example, in the study of prejudice in the two cities mentioned above, if the population of one city were in a period of rapid change—with middle-class residents moving to distant suburbs and being replaced by poor members of ethnic minorities—and similar movements were not occurring in the other city, mortality might provide as plausible a rival explanation for the observed attitude changes as busing. Researchers should be aware of the potential for differential mortality among treatment groups, particularly in experiments that occur over a period of time, and should recognize when attrition affects the character of a sample.

Interactions among Factors

An interaction occurs when two or more influences function in combination to result in an effect upon the dependent variable that is mistakenly taken as the effect of the treatment variable. Thus, in the prejudice experiment, the presence of different types of individuals in the two cities might have had a special effect on the prejudice variable because of the differing rates of maturity in the different types of individuals. Perhaps there was a gradual lessening of prejudice in the adult white populations of both cities (a maturational process) but the change was greater among middle socioeconomic-status (SES) than among lower SES whites (selection). Thus, if a greater proportion of middle-class whites is found in city A, the maturational change in prejudice scores during a year's time should be greater in that city. This threat to internal validity represents a whole class of possible interactions in which combination effects of any of the first seven factors may occur. In actual practice, however, the only interaction threatening internal validity that occurs with any regularity is that between selection and maturation.

Other Threats to Internal Validity

The threats to internal validity discussed thus far have been the ones emphasized by Campbell and Stanley (1963). However, more recent analyses have recognized additional sources of invalidity that may be internal to an experiment. In general, these threats deal with diminishment of the distinction between the treatment conditions. The factors discussed by Cook and Campbell (1979) are diffusion or imitation of treatments, compensatory equalization of treatments, compensatory rivalry by respondents receiving less desirable treatments, and resentful demoralizing of subjects in less desirable treatment groups.

Diffusion or Imitation of Treatments   When the members of the treatment groups can communicate with each other during the course of the experiment, they may exchange information that could unintentionally make the treatments very similar. This is particularly true when different information is given to each treatment group to establish the conditions of the treatment. For example, consider a study of the effects of different approaches to counseling persons with marital problems. If the clients in the experimental groups communicate between sessions, they may discuss their problems, their therapists, and their experiences in treatment. This could have the effect of inadvertently reducing the uniqueness of what each client is gaining from the experimental treatments.

Compensatory Equalization of Treatments When one treatment condition seems more desirable to those who are responsible for administering the experiment (or to the school, institution, or other setting in which the experiment occurs), there may be a tendency to compensate in the other treatment conditions. For example, two similar schools are chosen to participate in an experiment designed to determine the effects of a federal program providing free lunch to children from poor families. The effects of the program will be determined by observing the general health level of the children and their behavior in class, particularly during the afternoon hours. The federal support program is implemented in one school and not in the other. However, the school district administration, realizing that the poor children in the community will not get a balanced lunch if they are not in the school receiving federal support, establishes a fund to ensure that each child in the comparison school will eat a proper meal during the lunch period. Since it is likely that a child's health and behavior are more dependent on the quality of the nutrition received than on the source of funds for the lunch, it will be impossible to tell whether the federal lunch program has any effect.

Compensatory Rivalry by Respondents Receiving Less Desirable Treatments When it is common knowledge among the subjects of an experiment that one of the treatment groups is expected to perform better than the other, a competitive environment may result in which the underdog group tries not to be beaten.

For example, in one experiment, computers were used to provide drill to special education students, and the teachers were told that if the computers proved effective, they would be used for other instructional tasks while the computers provided all the drill. The teachers, viewing the computers as a threat to their livelihoods, worked extraordinarily diligently to beat the computer during the experiment. In a competitive environment like this, rivalry can be more influential in producing the results than is the treatment, and the internal validity of the experiment must therefore be suspect.

Resentful Demoralizing of Subjects in Less Desirable Treatment Groups When subjects in one treatment group feel that they are clearly receiving less benefit than are those in another treatment group, it may lead to demoralization and resentment that can influence the outcome of the experiment. To illustrate, suppose that a research project was designed to investigate the effects of different dieting programs on weight loss. In one treatment condition, subjects were given measured portions of food free for each meal on a daily basis. To stay on the diet, all they had to do was prepare and serve the measured portions and refrain from snacking between meals. In the comparison condition, subjects had to purchase, prepare, and serve the meals described in a guidebook. If the subjects in the two treatment groups were able to communicate easily, it would not be surprising if the group that was not receiving the free meals became resentful. This might affect the way in which they followed the diet, with obvious consequences for the internal validity of the comparison.

Coping with Threats to Internal Validity

The basis for measuring internal validity is the degree to which treatment groups are equivalent in every respect except the treatment. Several approaches for insuring the internal validity of experiments have been advocated. Among the most prevalent of these approaches are random assignment of subjects to treatment groups, use of control groups, and statistical covariance (Cook & Campbell, 1979; Elashoff, 1969). The control and randomization approaches will be discussed here. More will be said about covariance in Chapter 7.

   Random Assignment   Consider a class of students who will participate in an experiment with two treatment conditions. We could divide the group so that all the males were in the experimental treatment group and all the females were in the other. However, that would not be satisfactory because we could not be certain whether the results were due to the effects of the experimental treatment or the gender of the subjects. If we instead assigned one-half of the males and one-half of the females to each group, the groups might still differ in characteristics such as learning ability, health, ethnic background, or parents' educational level. Even if we were able to equate the groups on all these variables, we might still be worried about equivalence on any number of other variables. The list of ways in which people can differ is literally endless.

It is a deceptively difficult problem to establish and maintain the equivalence of groups of people used as subjects in experiments. Randomly assigning individual subjects to treatment conditions is one way to attempt to equalize treatment groups.

In order to assign subjects randomly, we must first identify a pool of people from which to sample. They can be students in a class, a sample chosen to represent a population of seventh graders, volunteers solicited through a newspaper advertisement, or some other group. Each individual is then selected to be in one of the treatment groups by a random procedure (e.g., flipping a coin, throwing dice, having a computer make the random assignments, etc.). The criterion that must be satisfied in such a procedure is that each subject must begin with an equal probability of being assigned to each group. Thus, if there are two experimental groups, each subject should be just as likely to wind up assigned to one group as to the other.

Random assignment tends to create equivalent groups for the following reason. When you consider all the individuals to be assigned to two or more groups, there will be many ways in which the individuals in the sample can vary. For example, some individuals will have high numerical aptitude, some moderate, and some low. Some individuals will be high on verbal fluency, some moderate, and some low, and so forth for many, many traits that may have some bearing on the final performance of individuals on the dependent variable. In the process of assigning randomly, each individual with a particular pattern of aptitudes, interests, etc. has an equal chance of being assigned to each of the groups in the experiment. Hence, as we construct each group, individuals in a group who possess a great deal of a certain kind of aptitude, interest, etc. tend to be counterbalanced by individuals low on the same trait. The cumulative effect of this process is that the groups tend to be equivalent. Then if we observe differences between groups after the administration of the experimental treatment conditions, we may infer that the differences are due to the treatment conditions.

We are not *guaranteed* that groups will be made equivalent through randomization. Some samples will turn out by *chance* to be quite unusual. However, extremely deviant groups obtained through randomization should be rare. If we insist that the results of an experiment be replicated with regularity over successive repetitions of the same experiment, we will, in a sense, protect ourselves against unusual samples that can occur through randomization in a single experiment. In addition, there are times when randomization is impossible. This is common in field experiments when the researcher does not have control over the setting in which the research is conducted. When studies are done in schools, hospitals, prisons, and other settings, random assignment is often not possible because of requirements for providing service or maintaining organization. In these situations, true experimentation cannot take place because equivalence of the treatment groups cannot be assured through random assignment. However, by careful analysis, the researcher may be able to recognize many of the threats to internal validity and design them out of the study. Such a study is called a *quasi-experiment.* We cover the design of quasi-experiments in Chapter 5.

Control Groups The purpose of a control group is to establish a standard against which an experimental treatment can be compared. A control group must be treated in exactly the same way as the experimental group except for the specific factor in the treatment condition that is being tested. For example, a researcher is interested in the effects of teaching mathematics with pictures and diagrams rather than the more traditional methods using equations and prose for explanations. He sets up an experiment in which the experimental group is taught by his novel approach while a control group is taught with a traditional method that is similar to the experimental method in all ways except the specific instructional program. Thus the two groups would be about the same size, would study mathematics at the same time of day, would get similar amounts and kinds of homework, etc. The only difference between the two groups would be the pictorial content as opposed to the more traditional explanations relying on equations and prose.

Some threats to internal validity are not susceptible to elimination by random assignment of subjects. Generally, experiments requiring a lengthy period of time have the greatest number of threats to validity that cannot be reduced through random assignment. For example, the problems of compensatory equalization of treatments, experimental mortality, and diffusion or imitation of treatment can become more pronounced when an experiment must be conducted over a long period of time (as in a test of curriculum materials during an academic year). Borg (1984) suggested that this type of problem be addressed by using control groups that meet certain criteria. Briefly, the control-group conditions should have the following characteristics:

1 They should be as desirable to the subjects as are the treatment-group conditions.

2 They should be similar in duration and procedure to the experimental-treatment conditions.

3 The control conditions should be concerned with variables unrelated to the treatment effects under study.

Control conditions should be designed keeping the hypothesis to be tested in mind. It may be necessary to have two or more controls when the treatment is complex. To illustrate, suppose a researcher wished to compare the effects of counseling families with a handicapped child. In such families, it is not uncommon for the other children to feel ignored or unappreciated. The researcher is interested in comparing the effectiveness of individual counseling with each member of the family to counseling in which the whole family is seen as a group by the therapist. Since counseling is a complex process involving many personal and interpersonal factors, the researcher decides that a control group is necessary to compare the progress of families receiving the two kinds of therapy with families receiving no therapy. However, the kind of conditions to build into the control group is a problem. The researcher reasons that both therapy approaches are providing attention as well as therapy to the clients. Therefore, a good control condition might be one in which the clients are given attention by a nonprofessional on a weekly basis for about the same amount of time as the experimental groups are receiving. The researcher further reasons that a second control group should get no attention at all from an outsider in order to determine how no intervention compares to the attention of a nonprofessional. Of course, there are ethical as well as research concerns to be considered in such a decision to withhold treatment. Ethical issues are addressed in Chapter 10.

INTERNAL VALIDITY AND THE DESIGN OF EXPERIMENTS

Internal validity is an extremely important aspect of an experiment. If a study does not have some degree of internal validity, the value of the results will be questionable at best. Therefore, before we go on to consider external validity and the generalizability of research, we will pause to look at how the concerns raised about internal validity apply to specific research studies. In order to simplify the discussion, a method of symbolically representing the design of an experiment will be presented.

Symbolic Representation of Research Designs

A symbolic system for representing experimental designs is useful for diagramming experimental designs. The diagrams can then serve as an aid for analyzing designs and identifying their strengths and weaknesses. The symbols we will use are standard in the field of experimental design (Campbell & Stanley, 1963). These symbols are easy to understand. The symbol X is used to represent the administration of the experimental variable (*treatment*), and the symbol O is used to represent observation of the subjects on the outcome measure. When we say *observation* here, we are referring to any of a range of scores such as attitude, achievement, and aptitude scores as well as observational ratings. In designs where the subjects are observed on several occasions, these separate observations may be indicated by subscripts. Thus, if there are two observations, they are indicated by O_1 and O_2; three observations are indicated by O_1, O_2, and O_3, etc. The temporal sequence of the various events that take place for an experimental group is represented from left to right. Thus, if the design includes a single group observed before and after the administration of a treatment, we write

$$O \ X \ O$$

If the single group is observed only once (after the treatment), we write

$$X \ O$$

Where there are two or more groups, we distinguish between groups that are nonequivalent (e.g., two different classrooms of students) and equivalent (where subjects have been randomly assigned to groups). To illustrate, consider an example of a design involving two groups and a posttest only. The case of nonequivalent groups is represented using a broken line as follows:

$$\frac{X \ O}{O}$$

In this design, the first group receives the experimental treatment and is observed after the treatment. The nonequivalent second group does not receive the treatment but is observed at the same time as the first group. In this case, the first group is the experimental group, and the second group is the control group. A design in which random assignment to groups is used in an effort to equate the groups is represented as follows:

$$R \ X \ O$$
$$R \ \ \ \ O$$

The symbol R represents the process of randomly assigning subjects to the two groups. There is no broken line separating the two groups because the groups should be equivalent as a result of the randomization. The first group, the experimental group, receives the experimental treatment and is observed after the treatment. The second group, the control group, does not get the experimental treatment but may perform some appropriate innocuous task. The control group is then observed at the same time as the experimental group.

Occasionally, it is useful to make a distinction between different kinds of control conditions or various treatments in a design. We will use two kinds of symbols for control groups. The first, no symbol or a blank, is used to indicate a control in which no conditions are established by the experimenter. The second, (X), is used to indicate a control in which almost all of the experimental setting is matched in the control group except for the specific treatment. Further, different treatment conditions are represented by subscripted Xs. To illustrate use of these symbols, we will consider a study of the treatment of job-related stress in office workers. In this study, two treatment conditions are compared with two control conditions. The first treatment condition involves training subjects to do deep breathing and other relaxation exercises when they feel stressed at work. The second treatment condition involves similar training; however, it is done after work and is intended to help the worker relax at home. The dependent variables in this study include a variety of stress-related measures (i.e., blood pressure, heart rate, the frequency of psychosomatic complaints experienced in the past year, and a general anxiety). The two control conditions are a no-treatment condition (nothing is done with this group) and a lecture condition. The lecture group meets as frequently as the training groups and is lectured on the menaces of stress in one's life. A sample of workers is identified and, after a pretest, randomly assigned to a control group or an experimental group. This design could be summarized with the following diagram:

$$R \; O \; X_1 \; O$$
$$R \; O \; X_2 \; O$$
$$R \; O \; (X) \; O$$
$$R \; O \qquad O$$

where O = the dependent observations

R = randomly assigned subjects

X_1 and X_2 = the treatments

(X) = the lecture control

the blank = the no treatment control

The diagram can be viewed as a blueprint of the study. We now turn to some common preexperimental and experimental designs.

PREEXPERIMENTAL DESIGNS

The preexperimental designs we will discuss are designs in which a single experimental group or nonequivalent experimental groups are used. These designs have been seen frequently in educational research. However, they are extremely weak in the necessary quality of internal validity and therefore are not generally recommended.

The One-Shot Case Study

In this design, a single group is studied subsequent to some treatment or agent assumed to cause change. The design is represented as follows:

$$X \; O$$

As Campbell and Stanley (1963) correctly point out, this design is essentially worthless. Comparisons are possible only insofar as the researcher's experience allows knowledge of what the observed scores would have been without exposure to the treatment. This type of comparison is of dubious value, however.

Here is an example of such a study. Suppose that a one-week workshop is offered for guidance counselors just prior to the beginning of the school year in a large school district. The workshop focuses on the development of group-counseling skills. At the conclusion of the workshop, the participants are asked to fill out a questionnaire which measures, among other things, their attitude towards group-counseling techniques. The average scores are judged to be high, and the workshop is therefore considered a success.

Is such a study internally valid? Certainly not. Since the participants have the option of choosing whether or not to come to the workshop, they are likely to be a select group, probably with some particular interest in the group-counseling approach. Their favorable responses on the questionnaire may reflect, to some extent, their positive attitude towards the technique prior to the workshop and may not be a result of the workshop. Thus a threat to the internal validity of the design is selection. Likewise, mortality poses a threat to the internal validity of the design. This occurs because the questionnaire is administered only to those who complete the workshop. The lack of responses from those who dropped out of the program or refused to fill out the questionnaires may have biased the results.

History and maturation also are threats to the internal validity of this design. History, for example, could pose a threat in the following way. Suppose, during the workshop, a favorable newspaper story on the success of group-counseling techniques in a neighboring school district came to the attention of most of the participants. It would be impossible to determine whether the positive attitude of participants was due to the treatment or to the unique intrasession history. Maturation might threaten the internal validity of the design in the following way. The positive scores of the participants are judged to be high based on the researcher's experience. That is, the comparison is based upon the perceived typical score of guidance counselors he or she has known who were not workshop attendees. It may be that the population of guidance counselors is gradually becoming more enthusiastic about group-counseling approaches. This could occur because the technique is advocated by prominent individuals and presented in the press in a favorable light, because favorable research findings have been published, etc. The increasing enthusiasm and high scores of the workshop participants may thus reflect the maturation of professionals in the field towards the group approach rather than the effect of the workshop itself.

The remaining factors that threaten the internal validity of designs do not threaten the internal validity of the one-shot case study. Testing and instrumentation are not threats because there is no pretest used in the design. Statistical regression is not a threat. The interaction of selection and maturation is not a threat to internal validity. The reason for this is complicated but stems from the fact that neither difference scores nor group comparisons are used in determining the results of the study.

One-Group Pretest-Posttest Design

The second preexperimental design to be presented is the one-group pretest-posttest design. The symbolic representation of this design is as follows:

$$O \; X \; O$$

In a study employing this design, a single group of subjects is observed, the treatment is administered, and the group is observed again after treatment. The effect of the treatment is judged by the change in observed scores between the pretest and the posttest.

An example of this design is found in a study of the effects of high school consolidation conducted by Rivers (1973). The subjects were from the graduating class of a newly formed consolidated high school in south central Appalachia. They were asked before and after attending the consolidated high school whether they intended to attend college or a postsecondary vocational school. The factors that threaten the internal validity of this design include history, maturation, testing, instrumentation, and the interaction of selection and maturation. Regression would be a threat if the single group being studied were an extreme group. Since the group was actually the entire population of public high school students in the area, regression does not appear to pose a threat in this instance. History and maturation are dangers for essentially the same reasons that they threaten the internal validity of the one-shot case-study design. Selection itself is not a factor threatening internal validity. Although the group may have an extreme pretest or posttest mean due to the effects of selection, the pretest-to-posttest gain is not affected by selection alone. However, selection can interact with other factors such as maturation to produce unique pretest-to-posttest differences, and thus the interaction of selection and maturation becomes a threat to the internal validity of this design. Experimental mortality, the production of pretest-to-posttest differences among groups due to differential dropout rates of individuals from groups, is not a factor threatening validity because there is but a single group used in the design. In summary, however, this design is so lacking in internal validity that it is also lacking in external validity. The discussion of factors affecting external validity is therefore not included here.

Static-Group Comparison

The static-group comparison is a design in which two nonequivalent groups of individuals are studied on a posttest-only basis. One of the groups in such a design has been exposed to the experimental variable, and the other has not. The static-group comparison study can be represented as follows:

$$\frac{X\ O}{O}$$

The design represents an improvement of sorts over the two earlier designs in that a reference point is provided by the control group for determining the effect of X on the performance of the experimental group. However, this design is still classified as preexperimental because there is no real way of knowing whether the two groups are equivalent initially. Of course, the static-group comparison design may involve more than two groups. For example, there may be two different treatment groups and a control group, and so forth. There also may be several experimental groups but no real control group. In this case, the purpose might be to compare several competing treatment methods rather than to compare one experimental group to a control group.

A study reported by Schwartz and Oseroff (1975) serves to illustrate the static-group comparison. The experimental treatment in their study was the Florida State University Clinical Teacher Model, an alternative noncategorical teacher preparation program in special education. Classes of children taught by teachers who had completed a master's program under the Clinical Teacher Model formed the experimental group. A nonequivalent control group was formed using classes of children of teachers from nearby schools who were certified to teach mildly handicapped children. The children in the study were classified as mildly handicapped (educable mentally retarded, learning disabled, emotionally disturbed). Student performance was measured with the Metropolitan Achievement Test (MAT) reading and arithmetic subtests. The students of the Clinical Teachers were found to score higher on the reading and arithmetic tests, and this was attributed to the program under which their teachers were trained.

The design used in this study does deal with several threats to internal validity. By virtue of the fact that a comparison group is included, history, testing, and instrumentation may have been controlled. Since extreme groups were not selected, statistical regression is controlled. Maturation may be a problem in a design such as this. In this instance, we do not expect it to be because the groups are measured once and are of about the same age. Selection, however, is a problem because the two groups of teachers and students are not equated through randomization. Likewise, there may have been a selection-maturation interaction if the students of the Clinical Teachers were, as a group, less handicapped and matured faster during the experiment. On the external validity side, selection and the experimental treatment could also combine in this study to produce an interactive threat. However, with this design, as with designs 1 and 2, external validity is a moot point because of the lack of internal validity of the study. Thus, though the results of the study may accurately reflect reality, there is no way of being sure that they actually do. The findings of the study, despite the amount of work involved, must be regarded as largely unsubstantiated.

TRUE EXPERIMENTAL DESIGNS

The three true experimental designs presented here are regarded as superior to the preexperimental designs for two reasons. First, they each involve at least one comparison group in addition to the experimental group. Second, random assignment of subjects to groups is used in an effort to establish the initial equivalence of the groups. The internal validity of these three designs tends to be high. The eight factors subject to random assignment jeopardizing internal validity are usually controlled in all of these designs.

Pretest-Posttest Control-Group Design

This design is represented as follows:

$$R \ O \ X \ O$$
$$R \ O \quad \ O$$

As with the static-group comparison design, the pretest-posttest control-group design may include more than two groups. The basic design, however, involves two groups formed through random assignment. Both groups are observed at some initial point (pretest) and then again after the treatment is administered to the experimental group (posttest).

We will illustrate the pretest-posttest control-group design with a study of the effectiveness of training in the management of anxiety and stress (Daley, Bloom, Deffenbacher, & Stewart, 1983). The subjects were undergraduate psychology students identified by their anxiety-test scores who had volunteered to participate. The students were randomly assigned to one of three groups: (1) a large group (27 members), (2) small groups (10 or 11 members), and (3) a control group (people waiting to be given the training). All three groups were pretested with a number of instruments. Then a structured training program covering topics such as relaxation with deep breathing, relaxation focusing on muscles, and so on was given over a seven-week period to both treatment groups. Posttesting was done one week after treatment and in a seven-week follow-up. The small groups showed somewhat better performance (lower general-anxiety scores) on the posttest and the seven-week follow-up than did the other groups. Large-group subjects and controls scored similarly. The researchers concluded that small-group training was more effective than was large-group training or no training.

This study provides considerably more control of the threats to internal validity than do the preexperimental designs. For example, history and maturation should not present problems because their influence should be equal in treatment and control groups. Selection should have been controlled internally by assigning the subjects randomly. Mortality was also probably controlled by randomization because the researchers reported only a small number of subjects who did not complete the study. Since extreme groups were not used in the study, regression was not a problem. Both groups were pretested, so testing should not raise concerns. In addition, since selection was controlled, interaction of factors does not appear to present any further threats. Thus randomization accounted for much of the potential for invalidity of this experiment. However, the threats that are not affected by randomization must be looked at separately. They deal primarily with the potential decay of the differences between the treatment and control conditions over time. Since the subjects were taking the same psychology course on a university campus, it is not unlikely that they had opportunity to discuss the training they were (or were not) receiving. This could have reduced the effectiveness of the large-group condition through resentful demoralizing of the less desirable treatment groups, or it could have enhanced the control condition by compensatory rivalry. Further, if any of the control (waiting-list) subjects became severely anxious or came under considerable stress during the seven-week period of the study, they might have informally sought help from their peers in the treatment groups, thus raising the threat of diffusion or imitation of treatments.

Posttest-Only Control-Group Design

This design is, without a doubt, the most desirable and most widely used of the true experimental designs. The design is represented as follows:

$$R \ X \ O$$
$$R \quad \ O$$

Again, the design may include more than two groups and is presented here in its simplest form. The current research literature abounds in examples of this design. The threats to internal validity are controlled to the same extent as the pretest-posttest control-group design. Our example of the posttest-only control-group design is a study by Benware and Deci (1984) designed to compare the effects of different learner expectations on motivation, attitudes, and amount learned. In this study, 43 students in an introductory psychology course were randomly assigned to two groups. Both groups were given an article on brain functioning to take home and study. Each subject was treated individually rather than as part of a group. The control group was told that they would be tested on the material, while the experimental group was told that they would be asked to teach the contents of the article to another student. Two weeks later, both groups completed a questionnaire assessing motivation and attitudes towards the article and the experiment. They also took a 24-item test of what they had learned from the article. As a result of the data obtained, the experimenters concluded that subjects who study in order to teach are more interested in the material, enjoy the experience more, and are more willing to return for the experiment. Further, concept learning is greater for experimental subjects, but rote learning is similar for the two groups.

An analysis of the threats to internal validity in this study suggests a rather tight design. History, maturation, and selection are all controlled by random assignment. Randomization also probably led to control of mortality (three subjects dropped out of the experiment—two in the experimental group and one in the control group). Since there was no pretest, testing could not have been a problem. Similarly, regression could not have threatened internal validity because extreme groups of subjects were not used. Instrumentation was controlled because (1) the observational instruments were objective (rating scales, true/false, multiple choice, etc.), (2) experimenter interaction with the subjects was minimal, and (3) the treatment was established by a standard set of written instructions. Further, using the criteria suggested by Borg (1984) discussed earlier, it would seem that much of the threat to internal validity that might be due to the decay of the difference between the control and experimental conditions were countered by the design of the control group. However, the design would have been even stronger against threats of this kind if questions had been added to the instrumentation to help the experimenter determine whether the control and experimental subjects communicated across treatment groups during the two weeks between the application of the treatment and the posttest. On the whole, this design presents some fairly convincing evidence that students who expect to teach something learn with a more positive attitude than do students who expect only to be tested on it. This convincing evidence was obtained without investing time and resources on a pretest.

A further word about this design is needed here. When the design is not used in favor of the pretest-posttest control-group design or the Solomon four-group design that we are soon to discuss, the reason is usually the reluctance of the experimenter to give up the notion that a pretest is needed to do a study. This reasoning is largely outmoded because group comparisons are usually the primary interest rather than the particular amount of gain in each group, a quality usually measured with a "rubber yardstick" anyway in educational re-search (see Chapter 8 for a discussion of the problems encountered using gain scores). Thus the posttest-only design, with its economy and efficiency, is usu-ally the best choice in situations calling for an experimental design.

Other Experimental Designs: Variations on a Theme

Many variations on the two true experimental designs just discussed are pos-sible, providing opportunities for the specific kinds of group contrasting needed in some situations. For example, in some research on counseling psy-chology, there may be ethical concerns about denying treatment to a control group that could benefit from counseling. In some of these situations, a delayed-treatment control-group design may be used. Such an approach was taken in the Daley, Bloom, Deffenbacher, and Stewart (1983) study cited ear-lier as an example of the pretest-posttest control-group design. Actually, the control group got treatment on a delayed basis after the experimental data were collected from the treatment groups. The design of the study was as fol-lows:

$$R \ O \ X_1 \ O$$
$$R \ O \ X_2 \ O$$
$$R \ O \quad \ O \ X_1 \ O$$

This delayed-treatment design has certain advantages over a pretest-posttest control-group design. First, it allows the researcher to use a control group that will not be deprived of a treatment that may help them. Second, it provides a test of change in the control group under the treatment condition. One would expect the control group to respond as did the treatment 1 group. Of course, other variations of a delayed-treatment design are possible. For ex-ample, a second control group could have received treatment 2 on a delayed basis.

Another variation of the experimental designs, the Solomon four-group de-sign, is actually a combination of the pretest-posttest control group and the posttest-only control group designs. Two experimental and two control groups are used. Pretests are administered to two groups and not administered to the other two. The design is represented symbolically as follows:

$$R \ O \ X \ O$$
$$R \ O \quad O$$
$$R \quad X \ O$$
$$R \quad \quad O$$

This design is rarely used in educational and psychological research but offers more information than does any other design discussed in this chapter. Com-parisons between the experimental groups (1 and 3) and the control groups (2 and 4) allow for the determination of the effect of the treatment variable. Gain scores for the experimental treatment can be evaluated with groups 1 and 2. The effect of testing alone can be determined by comparing the scores of groups 2 and 4. The interaction of testing and the treatment variable can be determined by comparing the difference in posttest scores between the pretested groups (1 and 2) with the difference in posttest scores between the unpretested groups (3 and 4). Thus the design is very attractive in terms of the information it provides. However, this additional information is expensive because two additional groups must be included in the design. In addition, the design is difficult to analyze, and the specialized information is largely unnecessary if the posttest-only control-group design is used, since there is no pretest.

The application of the Solomon four-group design is illustrated with a study of the effects of videotaped microteaching on the self-concepts of social studies teachers (Randall, 1972). The study involved a large number of student teachers randomly assigned to four groups. Two groups participated in a televised microteaching experience and completed a posttest in self-concept, but only one of these two groups completed the pretest prior to the microteaching experience. There were two control groups. Both completed the posttest, but only one completed the pretest. The results of the study were that no significant differences in self-concept were found among the groups. No evidence was found of a testing effect or a testing by treatment interaction.

EXTERNAL VALIDITY

The degree to which the results of an experiment may be extended to other samples from the same population and to other populations is known as *external validity*. The method used to select a sample and the design of a study can have a major impact on the external validity of the study. Thus we must learn something about how samples are chosen and the design threats to external validity.

Choosing a Representative Sample from a Population

Sampling is the act of drawing a sample from a population. Usually the sample is considerably smaller than the population, though in the case of a relatively small population, the sample may be nearly the same size. An adequate sample must be large enough to provide fairly accurate estimates of the parameters of interest. It should also be representative of the population being studied and not of some atypical, or biased, part of it. A biased sample will lead to inappropriate conclusions about the population. It is surprisingly easy to find such samples. One of the best known examples occurred in 1948 when Harry S. Truman was elected president. His opponent, Thomas E. Dewey, had been predicted to win on the basis of a large poll of voters conducted prior to the election. Explanations for this erroneous prediction vary.* In addition to a late shift to Truman among undecided voters, better educated persons were overrepresented in the samples. Seemingly small sources of bias such as this may produce entirely unrepresentative results.

At this point, we should make a distinction between randomly assigning subjects to experimental groups (discussed in regard to internal validity) and selecting a sample from a population for study. Random sampling involves selecting a group of subjects to be randomly assigned to treatment groups. In other words, we are referring to two different processes. Ideally, first we select them, then we assign them (see Figure 4-2). We say *ideally* because random selection is so expensive and time-consuming that convenience samples are frequently used in educational, behavioral, and social science research. It is more difficult to generalize to other samples and populations from convenience samples. However, the internal validity of an experiment will not be affected by use of a convenience sample so long as the treatment groups are assigned to be equivalent. A number of techniques have been developed for choosing representative samples, among them simple random sampling, stratified random sampling, and cluster sampling.

Simple Random Sampling

Simple random sampling is a way of selecting subjects in which every element (or person) in the population has an equal opportunity to be chosen. For example, in a study of graduates from a single year in a college of engineering, a sample of 75 out of 150 was chosen. Such a sample could have been chosen in a number of ways, such as assigning each person in the population a number and then choosing numbers to include in the sample from a table of random numbers (see Table B-1 in Appendix B) or random digits generated by a computer. Any random procedure is acceptable, even choosing cards from a shuffled deck in which each card contains the name of one person in the population. The major concern in determining the randomness of a sample is that every subject in the population have an equal opportunity of being selected.

Stratified Random Sampling

Simple random sampling, though useful in many instances, is not appropriate for all research problems. A given population may often be more usefully studied by considering its parts rather than the population as a whole. In studying the graduates of the college of engineering, it may be more useful to study various types of engineering graduates (e.g., chemical engineers, mechanical engineers, civil engineers) separately. The types of engineers constitute *strata* of the population of engineers. A stratum is analogous to a subset. Thus, if the

---

* Mosteller, F. (1949). *The pre-election polls of 1948: Report to the committee on analysis of pre-election polls and forecasts.* New York: Social Science Research Council Bulletin 60.

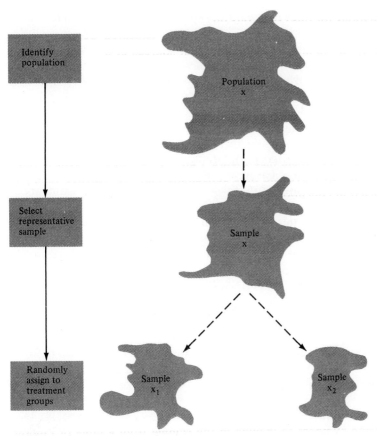

FIGURE 4-2
Ideally, samples will be representative of the population.

engineering graduates are represented as set G and the strata of the population are represented by the subsets C (chemical engineers), M (mechanical engineers), and R (civil engineers), the following diagram describes the population of engineering graduates and its strata:

When the research problem involves gathering information for each of the strata in a population, a sample of sufficient size must be obtained from each stratum. This is called *stratified sampling*. If the random sampling approach is used, the procedure is called *stratified random sampling*. In this procedure, separate random samples are drawn from each of the strata. The sizes of the samples drawn from each stratum depend upon the number of individuals in the stratum and the precision with which the parameters are to be estimated. The larger the sample size, the more precise estimates tend to be.

Cluster Sampling

Another procedure commonly used is grouping individuals in a population into clusters or aggregates (usually based on physical proximity) rather than into strata (based on common class). In a school district, for example, students in a single grade are often grouped into classrooms. Classrooms can be thought of as clusters of students and not strata unless the students are assigned to classrooms based on characteristics such as previous achievement level or scores on an IQ test. Often it is easier to do a study or experiment using children from only some of the classrooms (clusters) in a district (containing the population of students). For example, there may be 50 classrooms in a district, and a researcher may only be able to get useful information from 15 of these. When the procedures for simple random sampling are applied to clusters, a random cluster sample is obtained, which is a random sample of classrooms. Each classroom has the same chance of being selected. However, if the number of students per classroom varies, cluster samples do *not* provide random samples of students. For this reason, cluster sampling sometimes produces greater error in estimation of parameters than does simple random sampling. There are ways of achieving precise estimate with the cluster technique. This and other topics in sampling, because of the degree of complexity involved, will be left to textbooks on sampling such as Kish (1965), listed in the supplementary readings at the end of this chapter.

Validity of a Sample

An additional point should be made about sampling. When a sample is obtained, it is possible, to some degree, to determine whether results from that sample are likely to be valid indicators of the population parameters. This is done by comparing the characteristics of the sample with those of the population, using characteristics other than those actually being investigated in the study. For example, a sample of schoolchildren is selected from children in a particular school district in order to determine the level of reading achievement in the district. Obviously, valid information about reading achievement of the population is not already available as a check on our results, but demographic information and other test results may be available for the entire population of schoolchildren. Using these other data, it would be possible to see whether the students in the sample are typical of those in the entire population and then infer whether the results on reading achievement are likely to be valid.

Using sample data to generalize to a different population brings with it a new set of concerns. For example, if a representative sample of third graders were taken in a large midwestern city in 1987, the population to which the sample data is suitable for generalization is this population of third graders. Technically, these data could not even be considered generalizable to third graders in the same city in 1985, 1988, or any other year except 1987. However, the difficulty in generalizing to other groups is relative. Clearly, one would be in a better position to extend results from the 1987 midwestern sample of third graders in that same city in 1989 than to third graders in Zurich or Hong Kong in 1900.

Generalization of findings to particular subgroups within the population is also difficult. Consider the problem of generalizing from a representative sample of the adult population of the United States to adult American Indians living in the southwestern part of the country. The population for which the sample is representative is not the population of Indians, even though Indians are contained in the population of the United States and, as such, were represented in the sample.

Finally, as stated earlier, most research in education and the behavioral sciences is done with convenience samples. This is because obtaining a random sample can be difficult and costly. In some cases, it may even be impossible to locate a random sample because of the lack of clear limits to the population (e.g., the population of kindergarten students in New York City includes all students who ever have or ever will attend kindergarten in that city). Researchers use convenience samples with greatly differing characteristics over many studies. In some instances, generalization of research findings to diverse groups can be enhanced by replicating studies many times, using diverse convenience samples.

Threats to External Validity within the Design of the Experiment

In addition to the effects of sampling on the generalization of results, the nature of the experimental conditions might influence generalizability. Factors which Campbell and Stanley (1963) cite as threats to the external validity or generalizability of a study are the following:

Reactive or Interaction Effect of Testing. Treatment effects may not be generalizable when there is a pretest that sensitizes the subjects to the treatment. That is, the findings regarding the treatment may only be generalized to those situations in which the pretest is administered.

Interaction of Selection and the Experimental Variable. When subjects are selected who might be unusually susceptible to the effects of the experimental variable, the results would not be generalizable to the larger group.

Reactive Effects of Experimental Arrangements. This threat to external validity concerns the setting of the study. Findings observable in the laboratory may not be directly applicable to real-life settings.

Multiple-Treatment Interference. When multiple treatments are applied sequentially, subjects are likely to experience cumulative effects. That is, it would be difficult to separate the effects of subsequent treatments from those of prior ones.

To discuss the factors that jeopardize the external validity of an experiment, we return to the random sample of adults who were administered a test of racial prejudice before and after the implementation of court-ordered school busing in their city. To illustrate the points we wish to make about external validity more clearly, we will assume that we randomly divide our sample into two groups: one receives human-relations training designed to reduce prejudice, the other gets no training between the pre- and posttests. The experiment was designed to see if the human-relations training could reduce prejudice. We will now consider the threats to external validity of this hypothetical study.

Reactive or Interaction Effect of Testing   First, consider the interaction of testing and the experimental treatment. This is another interaction effect, but, in this case, the interaction is the special effect of taking a pretest upon the treatment variable. The treatment variable is the human-relations training program. If a pretest of racial prejudice were included in the experiment, it could sensitize the respondents in some way to the human-relations training so that they would benefit from it in a way they might not have if they had not been pretested. If this were to occur, the results obtained would be specific to pretested populations and would not generalize to unpretested populations. In an experimental design in which there is no pretest, external validity of the experiment would not be jeopardized by the interaction of testing and the experimental treatment.

Interaction of Selection and the Experimental Variable   Another factor that may jeopardize the external validity of an experiment is the interaction of selection and the experimental variable. This occurs when the individuals who constitute the experimental group are special in some way; that is, not entirely representative of the larger population being considered. It may be that their special nature makes them more susceptible or better able to take advantage of the experimental treatment. In the racial-prejudice and human-relations-training experiment, you may feel that since the subjects were randomly selected from white adults living in the city and since there was random assignment to treatment groups, there is no possibility of an interaction between selection and the treatment variable except by an accidental quirk of the random assignment producing nonequivalent groups. This is not the case, however, if the subjects in the experiment are assumed to represent all residents in similar cities or even the same city over a period of several years. The subjects in the study may be unique and somehow specially able to take advantage of the experimental treatment. Thus the possibility of an interaction of selection and the experimental variable exists as a threat to the external validity of this experiment.

Reactive Effects of Experimental Arrangements   A third potential threat to the external validity of a study is the reactive effects of experimental arrangements. This threat concerns all the ways that the settings of research investigations are different from real-life settings. For this reason, reactive effects are sometimes referred to as *threats to ecological validity*. One example of this kind of threat is the well-known *Hawthorne effect.* This effect, named because it was first reported at the Hawthorne Works of the Western Electric Company in the 1920s (Madge, 1962; Parsons, 1974), is produced by subjects' knowledge that they are being treated in a special way as part of an experiment. The effect is not produced by the experimental variable per se but, rather, by the very fact that the subjects know they are participating in an experiment. This effect is especially noticeable in laboratory experiments, where subjects are in a totally unfamiliar environment and where the experimental setting and tasks are highly artificial. However, the effect is also noticed in experimentation conducted in natural settings unless the subjects and the experimental observers are unaware that an experiment is being conducted. In either case where reactive effects of experimental arrangements exist, findings are not generalizable to nonexperimental settings.

Another concern within reactive effects might be due to subjects' perceptions of how they should behave in an experiment. Rather than perform as they would naturally, subjects in an experiment can pick up cues about what the experimenter wants to know or how they are expected to perform and behave accordingly. This happens because subjects want to be considered "good" subjects by the experimenter. When subjects are behaving in this way, it is said that they are responding to the *demand characteristics* of the experiment.

In the experimental study of racial prejudice and human relations, would reactive effects of the experiment constitute a possible threat to the external validity of the experiment? The answer is, possibly. If the subjects are aware that they are participating in an experiment to determine the effects of human-relations training on prejudice, reactive effects may occur, and group differences may be attributable to these effects rather than to the experimental treatment of human-relations training.

Multiple-Treatment Interference   The final threat to external validity is called *multiple-treatment interference*. This threat arises whenever several treatments are sequentially applied to the subjects and where prior treatments interact with subsequent ones. This threat is most severe in experiments involving the sequential application of several treatments to the same subjects (see, for example, some of the quasi-experimental designs discussed in Chapter 5). However, even in a study like the one focusing on human-relations training and racial prejudice, multiple-treatment interference can be a problem if other studies have been or are being conducted with the same group simultaneously. Thus the researcher should always be alert to this final threat to external validity.

EXTERNAL VALIDITY AND DESCRIPTIVE DESIGNS

Much of what we have covered in regard to external validity of experimental studies applies also to descriptive research. In fact, when determining the usefulness of a study, external validity may be a more serious concern for some types of descriptive studies than it is for experimental studies because the usefulness of the latter is more dependent upon internal validity. For example, consider survey research to determine attitudes towards providing sex education in public high schools. One way to do such research might be to gain the cooperation of a group of religious institutions across the country that will make it possible to do the survey in Sunday schools, thus greatly facilitating the collection of data. The plan might be to mail survey forms to randomly selected member churches for administration on a particular Sunday in all classes for adults and students of high school age.

Analyzing such a sex education survey in terms of population and threats to external validity would reveal many threats. First, the target population to whom the results would be generalizable is not clear. Generalization to all high school students and adults across the country could not be made because many people do not attend church or Sunday school at all and those who do may not belong to a church that is a member of the group that participated in the survey. Even generalization to the population of people whose churches participated could not be made because not even all of these church members attend Sunday school. Further, since the surveys would be administered in Sunday school, the answers might differ from the answers given by the same people if the survey were administered elsewhere, thus suggesting the potential for reactive arrangements. In short, there are enough threats to external validity in this survey to make the results of limited use at best.

SUMMARY

The focus of this chapter has been on the design and validity of experimental research studies. Two types of validity were distinguished: internal and external. The question answered by consideration of internal validity is "Did the experimental treatment really have an effect?" A design must have internal validity. Without it, the results cannot be interpreted and there can be no external validity. External validity is assessed by answering the question "Can the results of this study be generalized to other samples from the population being studied?" Or, stretching it further, "Can the results of the study be generalized to similar populations?" Generalization to other groups is never fully justified, but the degree to which it may be possible to generalize is related to the type of research design employed.

Preexperimental and true experimental designs were discussed in this chapter in terms of the degree to which they control for threats to internal and external validity. Factors that can jeopardize internal validity and external validity were considered. The preexperimental designs were found to be so weak in internal validity that they are virtually worthless for research. The experimental designs were found to be strong in internal validity, although some problems in external validity are possible. The experimental designs were typified by the use of comparison groups to which subjects were randomly assigned. The most highly recommended of these designs is the posttest-only control-group design, a design that has become common in current research literature.

PROBLEMS FOR THOUGHT AND DISCUSSION

1 In research studies A and B described below,
  a Diagram the research design, using the symbols provided in this chapter.
  b Analyze the threats to internal validity.
  c Discuss the external validity and generalizability of the results.
  d Suggest ways to improve the study.

Research Example A

Delclos, V. R., Burns, M. S., & Kulewicz, S. J. (1987). Effects of dynamic assessment on teachers' expectations of handicapped children. *American Educational Research Journal, 24,* 325–336.

Sixty subjects (20 teachers and 40 teacher trainees) who were taking courses at a university in the southeastern part of the United States were randomly assigned to one of two treatment groups in a study designed to investigate the effects of dynamic assessment on teachers' expectations for student performance. *Dynamic assessment* is a method of studying students' learning potential by observing them in a learning situation. Both groups of subjects were shown a child in a videotape being administered a traditional assessment (i.e., tests). Then, the treatment group was shown the same child in a dynamic-assessment setting while the control group saw the same child in another traditional testing session. Each subject then completed a questionnaire designed to reveal expectations for the academic performance of the child in the videotape. It was concluded that expectations for the child's performance were higher after viewing the dynamic assessment.

Research Example B

Hegarty, W. H. (1975). Changes in students' attitudes as a result of participating in a simulated game. *Journal of Educational Psychology, 67,* 136–140.

Four sections consisting of 109 students in a course in business policy were divided into two groups randomly. Two sections were assigned to participate in a noncomputerized simulation game that represents a completely open society. The remaining two sections comprised the control group. The experimental group participated in the simulation game during a five-week period during regular class meetings, while the control group attended more traditional class sessions during the same time period. All four sections were pretested using measures of community integration and civic responsibility. Using the excuse that the data had been lost, subjects were readministered the same items at the end of the study. While the control group did not show any change in the dependent variables, the students who participated in the simulation game showed an increase in the community integration score. It was concluded that participation in the simulation game tends to lead toward greater commitment towards community integration.

2 A school principal is interested in knowing whether a modern mathematics curriculum is more effective with high-ability or low-ability students. He selects the students scoring in the top 20 percent and the bottom 20 percent on the last group achievement test in mathematics and provides them with a one-semester curriculum in modern mathematics. He then has both groups tested with the same achievement test. On the basis of the average number of items correct shown below, he concludes that bright students gain less in a modern mathematics program than do students with lower ability.

	Pretest	Posttest
High ability	75	80
Low ability	32	51

   a Discuss the threats to internal and external validity in this experiment.
   b Discuss the influence of regression effects upon the principal's conclusions.
3 Design an experimental study to test the hypothesis that voters who meet a candidate who is running for office (in person) are more likely to vote for that candidate than are voters who only see the candidate on television.
4 Find a report of experimental research in a professional journal. Diagram the study, using the procedures described in this chapter; then, analyze the study for internal and external validity.

REFERENCES

Benware, C. A., & Deci, E. L. (1984). Quality of learning with an active versus passive motivational set. *American Educational Research Journal, 21,* 755–765.

Borg, W. (1984). Dealing with threats to internal validity that randomization does not rule out. *Educational Researcher, 13* (10), 11–14.

Campbell, D. T., & Stanley, J. C. (1963). Experimental and quasi-experimental designs for research. In Gage, N. L., (Ed.). *Handbook of research on teaching.* Chicago: Rand McNally.

Cook, T. D., & Campbell, D. T. (1979). *Quasi-experimentation: Design and analysis issues for field settings.* Chicago: Rand McNally.

Daley, P. C., Bloom, L. J., Deffenbacher, J. L., & Stewart, R. (1983). Treatment effectiveness of anxiety management training in small and large groups. *Journal of Counseling Psychology, 30,* 104–107.

Danziger, K. (1985). The origins of the psychological experiment as a social institution. *American Psychologist, 40,* 133–140.

Madge, J. (1962). *The origins of sociology.* New York: Free Press.

Parsons, H. M. (1974). What happened at Hawthorne? *Science, 183,* 922–932.

Randall, R. W. (1972). The effects of videotaped microteaching on the self-concepts of social studies teachers. Unpublished doctoral dissertation. Lexington: University of Kentucky.

Rivers, J. E. (1973). The effects of high school consolidation on lower class students' achievement and aspirations: An Appalachian case study. Unpublished master's thesis. Lexington: University of Kentucky.

Schwartz, L., & Oseroff, A. (1975). *The clinical teacher for special education: Final report* (Vol. 2). Tallahassee: Florida State University.

SUPPLEMENTARY READINGS

Cronbach, L. J. (1982). *Designing evaluations of educational social programs.* San Francisco: Jossey-Bass.

Kish, L. (1965). *Survey sampling.* New York: Wiley.

Michael, M., Boyce, W. T., & Wilcox, A. J. (1984). *Biomedical bestiary: An epidemiologic guide to flaws and fallacies in the medical literature.* Boston: Little, Brown.

Rosenthal, R., & Rosnow, R. L. (1969). *Artifact in behavioral research.* New York: Academic.

CHAPTER 5

QUASI-EXPERIMENTATION— WHEN THERE CAN BE NO RANDOM ASSIGNMENT

In Chapter 4, we discussed preexperimental and experimental designs for research. Following Campbell and Stanley (1963), we considered the various factors that can endanger the internal or external validity of studies using these designs. The preexperimental designs were found so lacking in internal validity that they should not be used in educational and behavioral research. Experimental designs, particularly the posttest-only control-group design, were found to have much to recommend them. In fact, these designs are quite commonly used in educational and behavioral research. However, to use them, the experimenters must have absolute control over the measurements and exposures to experimental treatments. In particular, they must be able to assign individuals randomly to the treatment and control groups they plan to include in the design. This degree of control is not always possible.

For example, a researcher may know that a collective bargaining agreement will be implemented in school district A and wish to determine the effect of this arrangement on teacher morale. A sample of teachers from the district is thus selected and morale measured before and after the implementation of the agreement. A sample of teachers from a comparable district (district B) is selected simultaneously with the selection of the first sample and teacher morale is measured at the same points as for school district A. Such a study is similar to the pretest-posttest control-group design but does not involve random assignment of subjects to groups. Thus the groups may not be equivalent, and the results from the study more open to question than they would be if the pretest-posttest control-group design had been used. However, as we shall see in this chapter, a design such as this can furnish useful information if viewed in the proper light.

A second example of a design that does not coincide with one of those already discussed, i.e., a design that is neither a preexperimental or true experimental design, is the time-series study. In this type of study, a sample of individuals is observed repeatedly on a number of occasions. Prior to the introduction of the experimental variable, a base line of response is established. At a particular point, the experimental treatment is applied and the researcher continues taking measurements on a number of subsequent occasions in an effort to see what effect the treatment has had. Elaborations of this design are possible when two or more samples of individuals are included in the experiment. Designs such as these are common in clinical situations, in which individuals are treated in particular ways over extended periods of time and a series of observations is made.

Quasi-experimental designs provide an alternative to experimental designs in that they can often be carried out in field settings and do not require that the experimenter have the ability to equalize groups by random assignment of subjects. Since they can be used in field settings, they avoid some of the pitfalls that can result from the artificiality of the laboratory. On the other hand, since they do not have the same degree of control as experimental designs, the information that these designs yield must often be regarded as imperfect.

Much research in education and the social and behavioral sciences is done using complex treatments (e.g., curriculum innovations, different counseling approaches, training programs, etc.) in real-life settings rather than in highly controlled laboratory situations. Therefore, quasi-experimentation represents a major portion of the research effort in these fields. In this chapter, several of the more common quasi-experimental designs are reviewed. In addition to using groups of subjects, we will consider experimental research with one subject. Although some established quasi-experimental designs are presented, the reader is cautioned about using these designs in cookbook fashion. As we shall see, quasi-experimental situations require analysis of the validity threats discussed in Chapter 4 and design of an experimental process appropriate to the objectives of the research and the characteristics of the setting and sample. A more thorough treatment of design of quasi-experiments can be found in Cook and Campbell (1979).

THE NEED FOR ALTERNATIVES TO EXPERIMENTAL DESIGN

If a fairly definitive experiment can be performed using an experimental design why, you might ask, would a researcher want to use a quasi-experimental design? The answer to this question is partially that the researcher may prefer to carry out a study in the natural setting or else may be forced, due to the nature of the experimental variable, to conduct the experiment in the setting where the experimental event actually occurs. For example, a researcher may know that a certain computer-assisted instruction (CAI) works in the laboratory after having done several experiments using it in that setting. However, the researcher may wish to determine if certain effects of the CAI can be observed in actual school settings. To pose another example, a researcher may be interested in determining the effects of a program in special education that is to be implemented in 20 percent of the schools in the state during the next school year. Even without any control over which students, classrooms, or schools participate in the program, the researcher wishes to carry out a meaningful study. In these instances, quasi-experimental designs can be useful.

In considering the worth of quasi-experimental designs, we must go back to the purposes of research identified in Chapter 1. We indicated at that time that systematic research has two basic objectives: (1) to increase knowledge or answer questions and (2) to advance the development of theory. When we find answers to questions that are raised in a highly controlled laboratory setting, the resultant knowledge may not be as useful as we wish because phenomena tend to occur differently in natural settings. It is the burden of the behavioral, social, and educational sciences that their theories and important questions must deal almost exclusively with complex natural phenomena. Of course, some knowledge is better than none regarding these phenomena in natural settings. Since the researcher does not have total control in these settings, quasi-experimental techniques developed to deal systematically with the threats to internal and external validity are useful.

How do we find dependable information when we must use quasi-experimental techniques? Part of the answer has already been given. That is, we design our quasi-experiments recognizing the threats to internal and external validity. The rest of the answer, also applicable to true experiments, is replication. As we shall see in Chapter 7, when statistical hypotheses are tested, the results are regarded in terms of accepting or rejecting null hypotheses. Results of single experiments never "prove" or "disprove" null hypotheses. This means that experimental results must be consistently replicated before they can be considered dependable. Thus, by requiring quasi-experimental results to be replicated in other settings, we are not making any greater demands than are made of findings in experimental studies. A carefully designed quasi-experiment is certainly worth doing if the null hypothesis is sufficiently tested by the design. As Campbell and Stanley (1963, p. 205) have noted, quasi-experimental studies are "well worth employing where *more efficient probes are unavailable.*"

QUASI-EXPERIMENTAL DESIGNS

We now turn to four of the quasi-experimental designs discussed by Campbell and Stanley: the nonequivalent-control-group design, the counterbalanced design, the equivalent-time-samples design, and the time-series design. Careful attention must be paid to the threats to the internal and external validity in quasi-experimental designs because the factors that threaten the validity of these designs depend somewhat on the particular research application.

Nonequivalent-Control-Group Design

The nonequivalent-control-group design is similar to the static-group comparison, with the difference that in this design, both groups take a pretest as well as a posttest. The nonequivalent-control-group design is represented as follows:

$$\frac{O \; X \; O}{O \qquad O}$$

In this design, a group exposed to the experimental variable (X), is compared to a similar group not exposed to X. The differences between O_1 and O_2 in the two groups are compared to determine whether X had an effect on the performance of the experimental group.

We look at two examples of the nonequivalent-control-group design. The first example is a study reported by Nelson, Lowe, and Dalrymple (1975). Their study focused on new home economics curricula for disadvantaged students. In particular, the study focused on the development of a new curriculum design to prepare participants for dual roles as homemakers and wage earners. The literature in the area suggested that vocational home economics programs have traditionally been found in rural schools and their effectiveness for disadvantaged students in urban areas was not known.

Though the study was, in fact, more comprehensive, we can concentrate on two basic groups and a single dependent variable. A special course was constructed that focused on the dual roles of homemaker and wage earner. This constituted the treatment (X). Disadvantaged urban students in schools in several Eastern and Midwestern states took this course. Most subjects were 15 to 17-year-old girls who met the criteria specified in the study for disadvantaged status. The control groups took a home economics course that focused on clothing and did not include the content of the experimental course. One of the outcome measures was a scale devised to assess attitude towards work. There was a more positive pretest-to-posttest change in attitude in the experimental than in the control students. The researchers concluded that the course had a favorable impact on students' attitude towards work.

In the Nelson et al. study just described, a threat to internal validity from the selection by maturation interaction arises from the possibility that the subjects chosen would have developed a more positive attitude toward work without any treatment. Though it seems unlikely, it is possible that students interested enough in the home economics course to sign up for it may have matured more rapidly in the area measured by the dependent variable. In this way, the possibility of a selection by maturation interaction threatens the internal validity of the study.

There could be a regression threat to this design. The extreme nature of the groups—both are disadvantaged and may tend to have extreme scores on the pretest measuring attitudes toward work—could have led to a regression effect that might be mistaken for the effect of X. Though this is possible, the groups were not selected for their extreme scores on the attitude test in this study. Further, the two groups of subjects were selected initially because they were quite similar in background. Our guess here is that if there were a regression effect, it would occur equally in the two groups and would therefore not constitute a severe threat to the internal validity of the study. We note here also that the design controls for history, maturation, testing, instrumentation, selection, and mortality at least partly by concentrating on the amount of change in each group rather than the absolute differences between the groups on the posttest. However, the problem of diffusion or imitation of treatments was not handled by the design. There is no evidence to show that the students or the teachers did not communicate with each other about the experiment. Nor is there evidence that teachers and students did not do something in addition to the experimental procedures in class that would reduce the distinction between the experimental and control conditions over the course of the experiment. Overall, this design, although weaker in internal validity than its experimental counterpart (the pretest-posttest control-group design), can provide useful data about whether the treatment variable had an effect in the study.

The external validity of the design is somewhat more questionable. As in any of the designs where a pretest is included, the possible interaction between testing and the experimental variable is not controlled. It is always possible that the effect of the special home economics course would only be observed on a pretested population of students and does not generalize to one that is not pretested. Likewise, there exists the possibility of an interaction between selection and X (the experimental group subjects may be especially susceptible to the treatment variable), and reactive effects (the more positive attitudes towards work on the part of the students in the experimental course may result from the knowledge of both teachers and students that the course was somehow special).

Our second illustration of the nonequivalent-control-group design is provided by Sassenrath, Croce, and Penaloza (1984) in their longitudinal study of differences in achievement between students in public and private schools. In this study—part of a larger study to validate a multicultural testing procedure—a very large number of students was tested initially in 1972. About a decade later, during a retesting of the same students, it was noted that 49 of the original group had switched from public to private schools. The range of time spent in private school settings by these students was from 2 to 10 years, with an average of 5.5 years. Sassenrath et al. located 49 students from the large sample who had spent all their time in public schools and could be matched with the 49 that had had private school experience. The matching was based on gender, socioeconomic status, ethnicity, age, and IQ score. The group that had remained in public schools was considered the control group, while those who had spent time in private schools were considered the experimental group. The researchers found that the two groups showed nearly identical performance on math and reading achievement tests shortly before graduation from high school. On the basis of this finding, the researchers posited no advantage from attending private school.

Since this study found no difference between the groups, any threats to internal validity that exist might have served to mask real differences that would have been revealed if the threats were not present. Analysis of the internal validity of the Sassenrath et al. study suggests a considerable amount of control. History would probably not present problems because both groups would have been exposed to similar events over the 10-year period. Maturation was probably controlled by matching the subjects or age. Testing probably was not a problem because of the long time span between the pretesting and the posttesting and because the testing was probably inobtrusive in that it was perceived as part of the total academic program. However, selection and regression could have been responsible for the finding of no difference between public and private schools. For an explanation, consider a scenario in which students who were sent to private schools were doing poorly in their studies at the public schools. In a sense, they formed a low-scoring extreme in achievement. Despite financial hardships, their parents sent them to private school until their grades improved. In this case, the performance of the private school group could have reflected regression towards the mean. Further, the performance of the private school attendees could conceivably have resulted from a better experience than these same low-scoring students would have had had they remained in the public schools. In other words, if the regression explanation is correct, the private school experiences really were not advantageous. On the other hand, if selection provides the explanation for the results, then the private schools did, indeed, contribute to better achievement. Although this explanation based on selection and regression may, in fact, be incorrect, we have no way of knowing from the information given. As this study illustrates, matching subjects to gain equivalence of comparison groups rarely achieves that equivalence.

Other threats to internal validity in the Sassenrath et al. study might result from selection interacting with other factors, such as maturation, history, and instrumentation (e.g., public schools may give more practice in standardized testing of the type used as a dependent variable). The study did control for the threats of compensatory rivalry, imitation and diffusion of treatments, compensatory equalization, and resentful demoralizing because the subjects did not know they were being compared on the basis of school and probably did not interact with each other because of the size of the original sample and the small likelihood that they knew one another.

Reviewing our two examples of the nonequivalent-control-group design provides us with an important lesson about quasi-experimental research. That is, despite the similarity in the design of the Nelson et al. and Sassenrath et al. studies the general similarity of threats to their validity (e.g., selection, possibly regression, etc.), each one had unique characteristics and posed potential pitfalls that the other did not. For example, regression was a more definite concern in the Sassenrath et al. study than in the Nelson et al. study. For this reason, internal and external validity should be considered on a study-by-study basis. It cannot be assumed that studies using similar designs will handle all threats to validity with the same effectiveness. With this caveat in mind, the nonequivalent-control-group design can be fairly high in internal validity relative to other quasi-experimental designs. This design and the preexperimental static-group comparison (see Chapter 4) are tempting designs for researchers engaged in field-based research because there are many naturally occurring situations in which the effects of interesting treatment variables can be studied by comparing existing groups exposed to varying treatments or situations. In such cases, one naturally occurring group is used as a treatment group and a comparable group of individuals serves as a control. Studies involving both of these designs appear frequently in the research literature. Considering the threats to internal and external validity, the preferred choice between the two designs is the quasi-experimental design involving both a pretest and a posttest.

Counterbalanced Design

A *counterbalanced design* is one in which there are several treatments and several respondents and each respondent is presented with each treatment condition in random order. This design can be symbolized as follows:

Group or Subject	Time or setting			
	1	2	3	4
A	$X_1 O$	$X_4 O$	$X_3 O$	$X_2 O$
B	$X_2 O$	$X_3 O$	$X_4 O$	$X_1 O$
C	$X_3 O$	$X_1 O$	$X_2 O$	$X_4 O$
D	$X_4 O$	$X_2 O$	$X_1 O$	$X_3 O$

We will use a research study by Robertson, De Reus, and Drabman (1976) as an example of the counterbalanced design. In this study, 16 children from a class for low-achieving and disruptive second-grade children served as subjects. Four types of tutoring were administered in random order to four groups of four subjects each in a 4 × 4 counterbalanced design after base-line and feedback periods were concluded. The four tutoring conditions were as follows:

1 Noncontingent peer tutoring—children were tutored by a fifth grader.

2 Contingent peer tutoring—children were tutored by a fifth grader only when they had earned a ticket for their behavior earlier in the day.

3 Noncontingent college tutoring—children were tutored by college students.

4 Contingent college tutoring—children received tutoring from college students only when they had earned a ticket earlier in the day for their behavior.

Thus the design for the Robertson, et al. study may be diagrammed as follows:

Group	Tutoring phases			
	1	2	3	4
1	X_1O	X_2O	X_3O	X_4O
2	X_2O	X_3O	X_4O	X_1O
3	X_4O	X_1O	X_2O	X_3O
4	X_3O	X_4O	X_1O	X_2O

where X_1 = noncontingent peer tutoring

$\quad X_2$ = contingent peer tutoring

$\quad X_3$ = noncontingent college tutoring

$\quad X_4$ = contingent college tutoring

The investigators reported that there were no significant group effects or significant effects across tutoring methods. Further, fifth graders and college students were equally effective as tutors. However, contingent tutoring was more effective than noncontingent tutoring in reducing disruptive behavior. There were no noteworthy effects of the treatment combinations of type of tutor (college versus peer) and contingent versus noncontingent tutoring.

Internal validity is reasonably high with this design, with the possible exception of the selection and maturation interaction. History, maturation, testing, instrumentation, and most of the other threats to internal validity should be adequately controlled by the random assignment to treatments. However, interaction of selection and maturation could present problems for internal validity. This would be most likely to occur when the groups are not equivalent prior to the experimental procedures and might cause differential effects across treatments that were not due to the treatments themselves. For example, assume for the moment that group 1 in the experiment just discussed was composed of retarded second graders and that the students in the other groups were normal. Those in group 1 could be expected to mature during the course of the study at a slower rate than the rest of the students. This, of course, could have an effect on the results that is quite unrelated to the treatment effects. Another source of invalidity could arise from the possibility of the subjects (or the tutors) across treatments communicating about the study.

External validity can be well controlled in a counterbalanced study, but special care must be taken to accomplish this. Because of the diversity of treatment situations to which each subject is exposed and the diversity of situations in which each treatment is applied, it is likely that a true treatment effect will be exposed in a counterbalanced design. This is particularly true in larger counterbalanced designs, when a large diversity of subject groups is represented. Can you see how this would enhance generalizability?

Equivalent-Time-Samples Design

The *equivalent-time-samples design* is a quasi-experimental design in which each subject serves repeatedly under the experimental and control conditions of an experiment. The design can involve the alternation of experimental and control conditions shown below.

$$X_1O \ X_0O \ X_1O \ X_0O, \ etc.$$

Here, X_1 represents the application of the experimental variable and X_0 represents the control condition or some alternate condition. The pattern of X_0 and X_1 applications may be randomized rather than alternated for what would perhaps be a more effective version of the design.

An example of an equivalent-time-samples design was reported by Carnine (1976). The study is entitled "Effects of Two Teacher Presentation Rates on Off-Task Behavior, Answering Correctly, and Participation." The subjects were low-achieving first-grade children during beginning reading instruction. The alternative treatments were X_1, a fast rate of presentation by the teacher during instruction, and X_0, a slow rate of presentation by the teacher. In the slow rate of presentation, there was a delay between the children's response on a given task and the introduction of the next task; in the fast rate of presentation, there was no delay. The entire design used in this study is given below.

$$X_1O \ X_0O \ X_1O \ X_0O \ X_1O \ X_0O$$

Three pairs of fast and slow presentations were given. One of the findings of the study was that fast-rate presentation was accompanied by less off-task behavior. The results clearly show that the percentage of off-task behavior was greater under the slow presentation than under the fast.

Let us turn now to the question of internal and external validity for this design. Does the fast rate of presentation have the effect of producing less off-task behavior (greater attentiveness), and can this effect be generalized to other samples from the same population? This design is generally very high in internal validity. Careful inspection of the design reveals that though many of these factors could threaten the design if it were

$$X_1O \quad or \quad X_0O$$

the repeated introduction of the treatment variable alternated with the control condition makes variables such as history, maturation, etc., unlikely rival explanations for the results obtained. Since there is only one group of subjects, threats to internal validity due to such influences as diffusion or imitation of treatments or compensatory equalization of treatments do not exist in this design so long as the experimenter maintains the integrity of the treatment conditions each time they are applied.

The generalization of the effects of X to other samples from the same population or to other populations is risky, however. Generalization is obviously possible only to frequently tested populations. The threat to external validity posed by the testing by X interaction is clear. With such frequent testing and changing of experimental conditions, the teacher and students in such a study are bound to have a feeling of being treated specially; and thus the threat of reactive effects exists. However, this problem might be reduced in studies such as the one Carnine reported if the observation could be made unobtrusively; that is, without being obvious to the teachers and students. With the constant alternation or random application of experimental treatments, multiple-treatment interference is possible. Finally, there is the threat to external validity presented by possible interaction of selection and treatment. If the subjects are special in some way (i.e., not representative of the population studied), they may be especially susceptible to the treatment. The subjects in the reading study were selected because they were representative of the group of slow readers. However, they may have represented this group in some special way, and the results of the experiment may not generalize to all slow readers. In the Carnine quasi-experimental study, evidence is presented to support the hypothesis that a fast rate of presentation produces less off-task behavior. The hypothesis has stood up to the probe presented by the study. Additional probing is needed to ensure the plausibility of the hypothesis.

Time-Series Design

Time-series designs involve periodic measurement of subjects or groups. The experimental treatment is introduced among the observations, and any subsequent change in the pattern of scores is attributed to the treatment. Thus the time-series design may be symbolized as

$$O_1 \ O_2 \ O_3 \ O_4 \ X \ O_5 \ O_6 \ O_7 \ O_8$$

Figure 5-1 shows some of the possible outcomes of this design. Notice that more is required than a simple increase in score between the measurements taken just prior to and right after the application of the treatment. For example, the impact of the treatment may be inferred in A and B of Figure 5-1. However, this is not the case in C and D.

The major threat to internal validity for the time-series design is history. This is because there is no way to tell whether changes noted after the treatment is applied may be due to some factor that was present at the same time the treatment was administered. External validity is less secure, however. The design does not control for the interaction of testing and treatment. Depending upon how the sample subjects were selected, there may be an interaction of the characteristics of the subjects and the treatment. Furthermore, with all of the observations being made, it may be difficult to avoid a reactive-

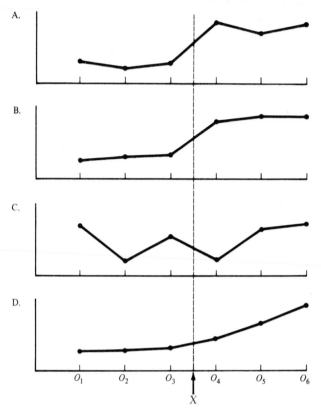

FIGURE 5-1
Some possible patterns of results in a time-series experiment.

effects problem in which the subjects' natural response to the treatments is altered. If the measures are made unobtrusively and the subject is not aware of
them, this problem may be avoided.

For an example of a time-series experiment, we turn to a study reported by
Bornstein and Quevillon (1976) on the effects of a self-instructional package on
the on-task behavior of three overactive preschool boys. Each boy was observed during the first eight days of the study. Then the first child was given
the training program, which lasted about two hours, and his behavior was observed on subsequent days. The second boy received the training after 16
days. The third boy underwent the training period after 24 days. Observed on-
task behavior for the three boys averaged between 10 percent and 14.6 percent
before the treatments. After the treatments, the change was dramatic. The average on-task behavior was between 70.8 and 82.3 percent. These percentages
continued through the fortieth day. Furthermore, subsequent observations at
60 and 90 days suggested the behavior was being maintained. However, what
is important to note from this study is the remarkable improvement in on-task

behavior after administration of the treatments, suggesting that the treatment was effective.

SINGLE-SUBJECT INVESTIGATIONS

Practitioners (special educators, clinical or school psychologists, guidance counselors, speech therapists, rehabilitation counselors, and psychiatrists) who design therapeutic interventions for individual children or clients often find the group approach to research insufficient for the questions they must address. Their concern is not how the average person in a group will perform after undergoing treatment and control conditions but, rather, how the treatment will affect an individual. Therefore, such practitioners often prefer to do their research using a single subject in both the treatment and control conditions. Single-subject research designs are related to the time series designs we covered earlier in this chapter.

Psychology and education have rich traditions in single-subject research. In fact, much of the earliest research in scientific psychology, the research of Wundt, Ebbinghaus, and Pavlov, took a single-subject approach. Researchers interested in reinforcement and behavior have developed single-subject designs extensively (Herson & Barlow, 1976; Kratochwill, 1978). Although many specific designs have been developed, only two single-subject designs will be described here; the reversal design and the multiple-base-line design. The concerns about the validity of experimental and quasi-experimental designs mentioned earlier also apply to single-subject designs.

Reversal Designs

Consider the psychologist who is called to a classroom to help Tom, a withdrawn child, become more socially confident with his peers. The psychologist decides that a good measure of social confidence is the number of interactions the child initiates with peers during the day. She has the teacher keep track of these interactions for one full week (five school days). This establishes a base line of the behavior and serves as a control. This is condition A. The next week, the psychologist establishes the experimental condition (condition B). Each of the other children in the class and the teacher are told to smile whenever Tom initiates a social contact either by saying something or by some action (smiling, participating in games, etc.). Tom's rate of social-contact initiation goes up considerably during the experimental period (see Figure 5-2). However, history and maturation may provide explanations for the change. The treatment effects would be more plausible if the social-initiation behavior became less frequent when the treatment was removed (i.e., when the teacher and classmates stopped smiling in response to social initiatives). This is where the term *reversal* originates. Figure 5-3 shows the decline in desirable behavior when a third week without the treatment condition was included in the design.

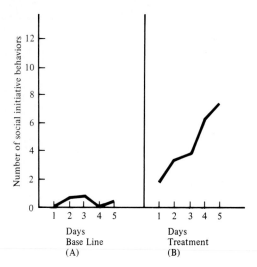

FIGURE 5.2
Number of social initiatives during
baseline and treatment conditions.

FIGURE 5.3
Number of social initiatives during baseline, treatment, and reversal.

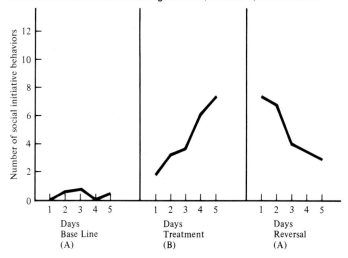

If the behavior increased when the treatment returned, the design would be
even more convincing. Thus, a reversal design is sometimes identified as an
ABA or ABAB design.

Multiple-Base-line Designs

When two or more behaviors are to be trained as part of a larger treatment, a
multiple-base-line design might be used. For example, suppose that an over-

active child is being trained to be more productive during school sessions. The psychologist working with the child identifies three behaviors that would lead to increased productivity: (1) not calling out answers in class unless requested to respond by the teacher, (2) not hitting or pushing other students, and (3) spending more time on learning tasks in class. Each of these behaviors is treated at different points during the course of the experiment. Thus the calling-out behavior might be treated after a base-line period of five days. After five days of this treatment, the treatment switches focus to aggressive behavior towards other children. Base-line levels of aggressive behavior would be determined during the control and experimental periods of the calling-out behavior. Further, the time spent on classwork would be monitored for base-line levels while the other treatments and controls are taking place, with the final treatment being applied to this behavior. Figure 5-4 shows the pattern of behavioral change for this multiple-base-line experiment. Thus the treatment

FIGURE 5.4
Multiple-base-line, single-subject study.

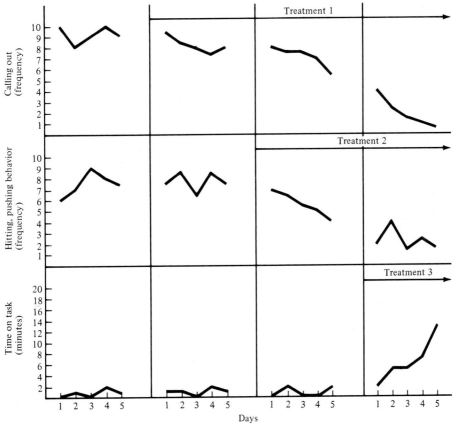

of each behavior is essentially an AB design. The multiple base line provides evidence that the treatment is affecting behavior. A multiple-base-line design is usually preferred to reversal design when there are ethical questions about whether to remove a treatment from a subject when the treatment seems to be working effectively.

Research with single subjects has a place in educational and behavioral science research. The methods used in this kind of research are becoming more sophisticated. A number of good references on the topic are provided at the end of this chapter.

OTHER QUASI-EXPERIMENTAL DESIGNS

Quasi-experiments are designed when true experiments cannot be conducted because the researcher does not have the opportunity to equalize the treatments and control groups by random assignment of subjects at the start of the study. Not all of the quasi-experimental designs that are possible have been discussed in this chapter. Campbell and Stanley (1963) and Cook and Campbell (1979) list several more, and still others exist.

One might think, from the discussion in this chapter so far, that there are a few research designs (e.g., the pretest-posttest control-group design, the time series design, etc.) that are used whenever an experimental study is done. Thus, to find a proper design for a given situation, a researcher need only look up a list of designs in a source like Campbell and Stanley and select one. The threats to internal and external validity would be automatically controlled by the design. Unfortunately, it is not that easy. The threats to internal and external validity are difficult to eliminate and must be analyzed in the context of each new setting and hypothesis.

The reader should take careful note that one *designs an experiment* rather than selects a design. This is because each quasi-experiment must be designed to uniquely fit the conditions of the situation in which it will be used. The purpose of the design process is to minimize the threats to internal and external validity. It is perfectly permissible for the researcher to be creative in designing a quasi-experiment in order to fit an existing setting so long as the design can be shown to have validity. With this in mind, we now turn to the process of designing experiments. Our approach will be to analyze threats to validity systematically in order to build the design that will produce results that are as unambiguous as possible.

DESIGNING EXPERIMENTAL RESEARCH

Designing experimental research can be thought of as a process similar to designing a bridge or building. Invalidity will make the structure fail. Each attempt to counter a threat to the internal or external validity of an experiment can be thought of as a reinforcement of the structure. A designer of research will follow a pattern of thinking about and analyzing the threats in order to create a solid, dependable structure. However, the process of building a design is not entirely mechanical. Building a research design requires a sensitivity towards the experimental environment. For example, the researcher should sense how various threats like selection or mortality might affect the results and what might be done in designing the study to avoid the problems. This requires that the researcher be familiar with the field in which the research is being done.

Figure 5-5 shows an analysis sheet for developing an experimental design. It lists the various threats to internal validity and gives the researcher an opportunity to consider each one. Completion of the design-analysis sheet requires consideration of the way in which a threat will affect the study and what might be done to avoid the problem. The design-analysis sheet can be used to critique an existing study as well as to develop a design for a new one. The design-analysis sheet should be considered as part of the overall process of developing and doing a research investigation. This process is discussed more fully in Chapter 10.

We will briefly discuss the use of the design-analysis sheet in the context of developing a study to test the hypothesis that college students who are trained to provide tutoring to their peers have better interpersonal and teaching skills than do those who are not trained to be tutors. Brandwein and DiVittis (1985) reported on a similar study done at the Baruch College in New York City.

The researcher began by identifying the treatments, measures, and comparisons needed to test the hypothesis that training makes a college student a more effective tutor. This is shown at the top of the design-analysis sheet in Figure 5-6. To determine the effects of the training, subjects were presented paragraphs that described tutoring situations. Subjects were then asked to select a statement that most closely reflected their probable action should they find themselves in similar situations. Thus the dependent variable was not actual tutoring performance but a paper-and-pencil measure of response choice. The initial plan was to compare a treatment group that had received training with a no-training control group. The comparison is shown in the space titled ''Proposed Design'' at the top of the design sheet in Figure 5-6. Initially, the design appears to be the preexperimental static-group comparison identified in Chapter 4.

After diagramming the design, the researcher asked ''If I did the study with this design, what would be the sources of invalidity of the results?'' Then threats to internal and external validity can be considered one at a time by going through the list on the design sheet. From notes made in Figure 5-6, it can be seen that the original static-group design was very weak. After analysis of all the potential threats to the validity of the design, changes were developed to eliminate as many threats to experimental validity as possible, given the situation in which the research would be conducted. As a result, a new design, shown at the bottom of the design-analysis sheet, was proposed. Instead of calling for a comparison of a trained group with a group who volunteered for training but did not receive it, the new study calls for dividing the volunteers randomly into two groups. One group would be trained as tutors; the other

Design Analysis Sheet for Research Designs

Hypothesis: _____

_____

Type of sample and population: _____

Is random assignment to treatment groups possible?   Yes   No

Proposed design:

Internal validity	How it operates in this case	Effective counter to avoid problem
1. History		
2. Maturation		
3. Testing		
4. Instrumentation		
5. Statistical regression		
6. Selection		
7. Experimental mortality		
8. Interactions among factors		
9. Diffusion or imitation of treatments		
10. Compensatory equalization of treatments		
11. Compensatory rivalry		
12. Resentful demoralizing		
External validity		
13. Random sample of population		
14. Reactive or interaction effect of testing		
15. Interaction of selection and the experimental variable		
16. Reactive effects of experimental arrangments		
17. Multiple treatment interference		

Revised design:

FIGURE 5.5
Design analysis sheet.

Design Analysis Sheet for Research Designs

Hypothesis: *College students who are trained as tutors will be more effective in tutoring peers than untrained college students.*

Type of sample and population: *Undergraduate volunteers*

Is random assignment to treatments groups possible? (Yes)   No

Proposed design: X _ _ _ O
　　　　　　　　　　　　　O

Internal validity	How it operates in this case	Effective counter to avoid problem
1. History	Exper. & control groups treated differently.	(1) Random assignment (2) Run exper. & control at same time
2. Maturation	different groups – effect unknown	(1) Random assign (2) Run exper. & control at same time
3. Testing	OK – no pretest	———
4. Instrumentation	Subjects choosing behaviors objective scoring – ok	———
5. Statistical regression	OK – no extreme groups	———
6. Selection	Both groups volunteers undergrad – problem caused by major?	Randomly assign subjects
7. Experimental mortality	possible over the course of the semester	(1) Monitor both groups for mortality (2) Random assign ss
8. Interactions among factors	Selection mortality? Selection maturation?	Random assignment
9. Diffusion or imitation of treatments	Students can compare notes and help each other	(1) Make control "treatment" condition comparable. (2) Encourage subjects not to share materials and information. (3) Name courses differently.
10. Compensatory equalization of treatments	no treatment control	Make control condition equivalent task.
11. Compensatory rivalry	//	//
12. Resentful demoralizing	//	//
External validity		
13. Random sample of population	No. Subjects must be volunteers	No. Therefore generalization to other samples is risky (also to other populations).
14. Reactive or interaction effect of testing	OK – no pretest	———
15. Interaction of selection and the experimental variable	Volunteers may make better tutors	replicate with nonvolunteers in another study
16. Reactive effects of experimental arrangements	Subjects know they are in a research study	(1) Make treatment and control conditions as unobtrusive and normal as possible. (2) Set up treatments as courses given for credit.
17. Multiple treatment interference	OK – no multiple treatments	Ethical problems of no treatment taken care of by reversal with no observations.
Revised design:	R X O (x) R (X) O X	

FIGURE 5.6
Design analysis sheet completed for tutoring study.

143

would get training in small-group decision making. The two courses would be offered for credit. Further, the courses would have different titles, and subjects in the experimental and control conditions would have no way of recognizing that they were participating in the same study, thus avoiding threats due to diffusion or rivalry. Both groups would receive both kinds of training over two semesters, but the research would be based only on data collected in the first semester.

The new design, shown at the bottom of Figure 5-6, is improved by random assignment to groups and a control training group that does not receive any training in tutoring but does receive training in something (in this case, group decision making). While the control group does not receive the same training, it is equivalent enough to differ only in the content of the training. These two alterations in the design converted a weak study into a rather strong one. The reader should carefully review the discussion of the threats to internal and external validity in Figure 5-6 to see how the study was improved with the changed design.

The design-analysis sheet can also be used to critique existing research. In addition to identifying strengths and weaknesses, it can help find ways in which an experimental study could be improved. (Try to use the design sheet to come up with an effective quasi-experimental design for the tutoring study when random assignment of subjects to treatments is not possible.)

SUMMARY

Quasi-experimental designs are used when the researcher does not have complete control over the experimental variables or when subjects will not be assigned to treatments randomly. These designs provide methods for investigating hypotheses with fairly valid results even when complete control is not possible. When a researcher must use a quasi-experimental design, the one selected should minimize the alternative explanations of the results by maximizing internal validity. Although external validity considerations are secondary, they are important for generalization of findings.

In this chapter, selected quasi-experimental designs have been presented, including the nonequivalent-control-groups design, counterbalanced design, equivalent-time-samples design, and time series designs. In addition, single-subject investigations were described. Building a design to counter threats to invalidity, rather than selecting designs in cookbook fashion, was emphasized. A design-analysis sheet that can help the researcher design experimental studies was presented.

PROBLEMS FOR THOUGHT AND DISCUSSION

1 A researcher was asked to design a study that would permit comparison of the reading programs in two different elementary schools. In one school, the reading program was based on the children's interests. Teachers assigned materials and individualized

reading experiences based on what the children said they would like to read. The other school had a more traditional reading program, based on a textbook series and reading materials designed for use with whole classes. The researcher was not able to assign students randomly to schools and classes but was able to effect an exchange of materials between the schools during the year as part of the procedures of the study.

a Develop a design that would allow for a comparison of the schools with some degree of internal validity.

b Analyze the internal and external validity of the design, using the design-analysis sheet.

2 A classic study by Morphett and Washburne (1931) is generally credited with providing a basis for a widespread belief that children should not begin first grade until they are 6 years old (Downing, 1973). To summarize the study, all 141 first-grade students in Winnetka, Illinois, were given intelligence and reading tests early in the school year. Mental age was then correlated to reading progress and sight-word scores. It was found that children with mental ages between 6 and 6½ years made the most satisfactory progress. Although this study is correlational rather than experimental or quasi-experimental, threats to external validity still apply to the conclusions.

a Evaluate the generalization of the findings to all children starting school.

b Using the design-analysis sheet, design a study to test the hypothesis that 6 is a better age to begin first grade than is 5 or 7.

3 Locate a quasi-experimental study reported in a professional journal in your own area of interest. Evaluate the study in terms of its internal and external validity, using the design-analysis sheet.

REFERENCES

Bornstein, P. H., & Quevillon, R. P. (1976). The effects of a self-instructional package on overactive preschool boys. *Journal of Applied Behavioral Analysis, 9,* 179–188.

Brandwein, A. C., & DiVittis, A. (1985). The evaluation of a peer tutoring program: A quantitative approach. *Educational and Psychological Measurement, 45,* 15–27.

Campbell, D. T., & Stanley, J. C. (1963). Experimental and quasi-experimental designs for research. In Gage, N. L. (Ed.). *Handbook of research on teaching.* Chicago: Rand McNally.

Carnine, D. W. (1976). Effects of two teacher-presentation rates on off-task behavior, answering correctly, and participation. *Journal of Applied Behavior Analysis, 9,* 199–206.

Cook, T. D., & Campbell, D. T. (1979). *Quasi-experimentation: Design and analysis in field settings.* Chicago: Rand McNally.

Downing, J. (1973). Cultural expectations. In Downing, J. (Ed.). *Comparative reading: Cross-national studies of behavior and processes in reading and writing.* New York: Macmillan.

Herson, M., & Barlow, D. H. (1976). *Single case experimental designs: Strategies for studying behavior change.* New York: Pergamon.

Kratochwill, T. R. (Ed.) (1978). *Single subject research: Strategies for evaluating change.* New York: Academic.

Morphett, M. V., & Washburne, C. (1931). When should children begin to read? *Elementary School Journal, 31,* 496–503.

Nelson, H. Y., Lowe, P.K., & Dalrymple, J. I. (1975). Preparing disadvantaged pupils for homemaker and wage-earner roles. *Home Economics Research Journal, 4,* 102–114.

Robertson, S. J., De Reus, D. M., & Drabman, R. S. (1976). Peer and college-student tutoring as reinforcement in a token-economy. *Journal of Applied Behavior Analysis, 9,* 169–177.

Sassenrath, J., Croce, M., & Penaloza, M. (1984). Private and public school students: Longitudinal achievement differences? *American Educational Research Journal, 21,* 557–563.

SUPPLEMENTARY READINGS

Cronbach, L. J. (1982). *Designing evaluations of educational programs.* San Francisco: Jossey-Bass.

Shumway, R. H. (1988). *Applied time series analysis.* Englewood Cliffs, NJ: Prentice-Hall.

Trochim, W. M. K. (Ed.) (1986). *Advances in quasi-experimental design and analysis.* San Francisco: Jossey-Bass.

CHAPTER 6

SOME FUNDAMENTAL QUANTITATIVE TOOLS

It is difficult to describe research in education and the behavioral and social sciences without mentioning statistics. Although many people do not recognize statistics as a familiar part of their everyday lives, we do encounter statistics frequently. We often hear reference to a batter's *average* or the *average* number of points per game in basketball. Students talk about grade-point *averages*. Government bureaus furnish daily reports about things such as employment *rates* and *median* income. Guidance counselors refer to test-score *norms* and *rank* in class when discussing a student's academic potential. These are all common examples of *statistics* that are widely used in our society. Statisticians, however, are often seen as people who play with numbers in order to be able to lie to or mislead the public. This unfortunate view reflects a lack of understanding of the aims and methods of statistics. Statisticians and researchers use numbers to make informative, concise statements about quantitative data. Computing batting averages, median income, and a student's rank in class are but three examples of what statisticians do with data.

There are two major branches in the field of statistics. *Descriptive statistics* is concerned with the organization, display, and interpretation of data. Census Bureau reports that summarize its studies of the population of the United States are examples of the descriptive use of statistics. Specifically, statisticians working with census data are able to *describe* the characteristics of the population in terms of measures such as the average number of children in a family or the average educational level of males above the age of 21. *Inferential statistics,* the other branch of statistics, enters our lives in a less obvious but still important way. Here, the emphasis is on using data from a sample of individuals to infer one or more properties of the whole population. For example, most television commercials are screened for effectiveness by the advertising agencies producing them. This is done by having a fairly small group of persons view the commercial and make comments. The agency can then draw inferences regarding the probable effectiveness of the advertisement for the population of potential viewers. Another example of the use of inferential statistics is provided by the automotive industry. It would be far too expensive to survey every person who might buy a car in order to design comfortable seating accommodations. Therefore, samples of consumers are studied, and the characteristics found in the samples are inferred to be those of the entire consumer population.

Notice that in both examples, the reasoning goes from the specific to the general. This type of reasoning was identified in Chapter 1 as *inductive*. Its results do not lead to certainty, but if the sample is chosen carefully, the inference about the general case will probably be accurate enough to make sound decisions. Since the application of inferential statistics involves making inferences about the general case (the population) from a specific case (the sample), inductive reasoning characterizes inferential statistics. Let us say that the zoo in which an elephant named Azuri lives wants to know if he is tall by elephant standards. A statistician, commissioned to find the answer, goes into the jungle, locates 12 elephants, and measures their height. Eleven of the elephants in the sample are taller than Azuri, so the statistician infers that Azuri is short compared to the elephant population. This pattern of making inferences from a sample to a population is fundamental in inferential statistics.

Descriptive and inferential statistics have significant effects on our daily lives. For example, to a large extent, they determine our insurance costs; the availability of certain consumer products; radio and television programming; and the character of schools, government, and politics. In addition, statistical techniques are essential to quantitative research in the behavioral and social sciences. Researchers use descriptive or inferential statistics extensively. For example, if a school board asked an educational researcher to report on the performance of students on an achievement test administered in the district, the researcher would probably develop the report with descriptive statistics. If a political scientist was commissioned by a political party in a large state to assess the general attitude towards its candidates in an upcoming election, he or she would probably try to locate a representative sample of the population upon which to base inferences.

Consumers of research, as well as researchers, need some familiarity with statistics. For example, the student of the psychology of learning needs to know what the results of a psychologist's learning experiment indicate, the teacher needs to choose the best mathematics textbook for the class based on research evidence, and social planners need to make intelligent use of sociological research. It is impossible for us all to be expert at everything, but because statistics are so important in our everyday and professional lives, it is in our best interest to develop some appreciation and understanding of the field.

With this thought in mind, we provide an overview of statistics relating quantitative techniques to research methodology in this and the next chapter.

Since research depends heavily on observation and measurement, we begin the chapter with a general overview of the types of observational and measurement scales researchers use. As we shall see, the type of scale has implications for the statistical analysis that can be done. (Chapters 8 and 9 deal more specifically with the details of measurement and observation.) The focus of the present chapter is on the use of statistical techniques to describe data. We cover topics such as central tendency, dispersion, describing relationships, and exploration of data. Students are encouraged to practice with the examples in the chapter. However, it should be recognized that this and the next chapter are meant only to introduce the student to ways that researchers use statistics as a tool. This and the next chapter should not be considered an adequate substitute for formal preparation in statistics.

BASIC CONCEPTS IN MEASUREMENT

Measurement facilitates the use of statistical methods and the choice of an appropriate statistical method. *Measurement* is the process of assigning numbers to objects according to a set of rules. Measurements are made to codify information about characteristics or traits that objects or individuals possess. For example, we might classify individuals according to political-party affiliation and assign the number 1 to Democrats, 2 to Republicans, 3 to those who belong to some other political party, and 4 to independents. Another example of measurement would result if we assigned to each student in a chemistry class a score based upon the number of items answered correctly on a final examination. These examples are only two of many measurements that educators and social and behavioral scientists make. Measurement procedures allow us to quantify information about individuals and provide the basic data for statistical analyses.

There are basically four types of measurements, called *measurement scales*. They are as follows:

1 *Nominal scales* name objects, using numerals to identify them.

2 *Ordinal scales* provide information about the relative amount of some trait possessed by objects, in addition to naming them.

3 *Interval scales* have the properties of nominal and ordinal scales, and the intervals between consecutive points on the scale are equal.

4 *Ratio scales* incorporate the properties of nominal, ordinal, and interval scales and also include an absolute zero point at which there is a total absence of the trait being measured.

Nominal measurement is used to classify or name objects. The classification of individuals based on political-party affiliation is an example. Though this type of measurement may seem rather simple, many of the variables of greatest interest are nominal in nature. Among the more commonly studied scales are gender, religious preference, occupation, and geographic area of residence. Notice that when we assign numbers to categories on a nominal scale, they are nothing more than names. We cannot perform any arithmetic procedures upon those numbers. For example, if we assign the number 1 to pears and the number 2 to apples, it makes no sense to add, subtract, multiply, or divide these numbers. Therefore, when we have nominal data, we must be careful to use the numbers only as labels of categories and nothing else.

In ordinal measurement, numerals indicate the relative position of individuals within a group. Ordinal data are usually the result of ranking procedures. For example, five airline pilots may be ranked from highest to lowest based upon their proficiency. This results in a measurement scale that if accurate, indicates the relative degree of skill possessed by the pilots but does not provide information about the amount of difference between pilots at each rank. Thus the measurements do not indicate, for example, whether there is one outstanding and four rather mediocre pilots or four outstanding and one poor pilot. All that is conveyed is the relative positions of individuals with respect to skill. Again, although these measurements seem crude compared with others, ordinal measurements are frequently encountered in research in education and in the behavioral and social sciences. Remember, the numbers used in ordinal scales represent more than just labels. They also show order or rank. Thus 1 comes before 2, 2 before 3, and so on. Contrast this to the numerals from a nominal scale, which occur in no particular order. That is, on a nominal scale of types of fruit, peaches may be labeled 1 or 16 or 400. They will be peaches no matter what they are labeled. In ordinal scales, this is not the case. The numbers are ordered so as to designate relative positions within the group. With ordinal scales, however, we are still limited in the arithmetic procedures we are able to apply because we do not have a consistent amount of the trait between each rank score.

Interval measurement has the property of equal distances between consecutive points on the scale. Thus a final examination for a chemistry class might be used as an interval scale because between successive points on the scale is one item. That is, if each item is worth 1 point, the student who received a score of 28 had one more item correct than did the student who scored 27. And the student with 17 had one less correct item than did the student with a score of 18. Of course, we are being overly simplistic here. Items on the test may vary considerably in difficulty, and the difference between consecutive scores, while representing a single item, may not correspond to equal increments of actual chemistry achievement. As a general practice, however, this is ignored in education, and such measurements are considered to be interval. Note that a score of zero is possible on the chemistry examination, but this is not a true zero point. It does not necessarily correspond to absence of any achievement in chemistry. To satisfy yourself that this is true, imagine a test in chemistry so difficult that it takes an extremely good grasp of the subject matter to get even a single point.

Many measurement scales encountered in studies in education and the social and behavioral sciences are treated as interval. Most often, these measurements are scores derived by summing the correct responses to the items on a test. But these are not the only interval measurements. For example, the number of repetitions in a learning experiment, yearly income, number of books read in an academic subject area, and the time it takes to perform a task are all considered interval. Often, as with the chemistry test, scores are realized to be only approximately interval as far as the underlying trait is concerned but are used as if they were, in fact, interval. Interval scales are considered more sophisticated than nominal and ordinal scales because they have all the characteristics of nominal and ordinal scales and also have equal intervals between the points along the scale. This allows for arithmetic operations to be performed. For example, while we would never think of finding the average of nominal scores, we would not hesitate to find an average of chemistry test scores or an average number of errors for subjects in a learning experiment.

Ratio scales include the properties of the first three measurement scales as well as an absolute zero point. An absolute zero point indicates complete absence of the trait being measured. In a sense, the zero point is just before the point where the scale begins. Such scales are not uncommon in the physical sciences (length, height, mass, velocity). They rarely occur in the social or behavioral sciences because of the abstract nature of the constructs that are usually measured in these sciences. When they are encountered, they may be treated in the same way as interval data.

The characteristics of nominal, ordinal, or interval measurements help dictate the statistical techniques appropriate to the type of measurement represented in the data. Therefore, in discussing various statistical methods in research, we will emphasize the kind of measurement for which a technique is appropriate.

CENTRAL TENDENCY

Suppose we have given a test to a class of 30 students, and someone asks us how the class performed. What would be the best way to report performance? Although reading all 30 scores would indicate how each student had done, this would not convey much about the performance of the class as a group. We need a method of summarizing those test scores. One method might be to draw a graph. Figure 6-1 shows a graph of the test scores for the 30 students. Although graphing is an important method of reporting quantitative data, it will not be discussed extensively here. The reader should consult a basic text in statistics, such as those listed at the end of this chapter, for a thorough treatment. A second way would be to find one score that represents all the scores. Locating this kind of score is known as the *central tendency* approach. There are several different measures of central tendency, each with its own set of uses and characteristics. We will discuss three of the more popular ones in this section.

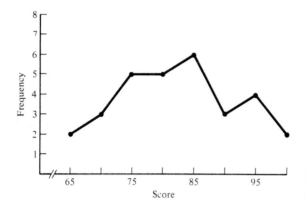

FIGURE 6-1
Test scores of 30 students in a class.

Mode

The choice of a measure of central tendency depends, to a large extent, upon the type of measurement scale used. If the data are nominal, the only available measure of central tendency is the mode. The *mode* is simply the most frequently occurring score. For example, a sample of 100 teachers who were asked whether or not they would be willing to join a teachers' union responded as follows:

Would join the union   73
Would not join the union   16
No opinion   11

Thus for this nominal scale, the *modal,* or most frequently observed, response from the sample was that they would join the union. If the numeral 1 had been assigned to "would join the union," 2 to "would not join the union," and 3 to "no opinion," the mode would have been 1; but this would not have changed the meaning of the mode.

Median

Because of the property of order present in ordinal scales, another measure of central tendency, called the *median,* is often used with ordinal data. The median is the score that occurs at the point on the scale below which 50 percent of the scores fall and above which the other 50 percent of the scores occur. For example, the following scores were obtained on a test of feelings of empathy in teachers:

   20, 19, 18, 15, 11, 4, 3, 3, 2

Note that when we arrange the scores by size, the middle score is 11. That is the score above and below which 50 percent of the scores occur (assuming, of course, that half the score of 11 goes with the upper group and half with the

TABLE 6-1
SCORES OF 10 STUDENTS ON A
MATHEMATICS TEST

Student	Score
1. Bill	15
2. James	12
3. Karen	12
4. Marianne	11
5. Helen	10
6. Louise	10
7. Logan	10
8. Donna	9
9. Joe	7
10. Edward	7

lower group). Thus 11 is the median. Since 3 is the most frequently occurring score, it is the mode. If one more teacher took the empathy test and got a score of 16, then the median would be someplace between the two middle scores, 11 and 15. The median would then be assigned the value of the midpoint between the two middle scores, or 13. The computation of the median becomes more complex when there are tied scores near the median in a list of data. However, we will leave discussion of that to texts designed primarily for courses in statistics.*

Mean

With interval data a third measure of central tendency, the arithmetic average, or the *mean,* may be used. The mean is computed by adding together all scores in a sample and dividing the total by the number of scores. The scores of 10 students on a mathematics test are presented in Table 6-1. These scores represent the number of correct answers on a 20-item test. Therefore, the scores will be considered interval in nature. The total of all 10 scores is 103. Since there are 10 scores in the sample, the sample mean is 103 ÷ 10, or 10.3. Since describing statistics like the sample mean verbally is cumbersome, statisticians represent the sample mean and the operations used to obtain it symbolically.

We can represent the variable of interest by the letter X. In the case of the data displayed in Table 6-1, X represents the score on the math test. A single score on that variable we will call X_i (read "X sub i"). The letter i is called a subscript and represents the position of a score in the list. Thus, for the data in Table 6-1, values of i range from 1 to 10 for the scores of the 10 students. This

---

* For example, the reader will find this material covered very well in Ferguson, G. A. (1981). *Statistical analysis in education and psychology.* New York: McGraw-Hill, or in Glass, G. V., & Hopkins, K. D. (1984). *Statistical method in education and psychology.* Englewood Cliffs, NJ: Prentice-Hall, pp. 32–33.

means that X_4 is the score of the fourth student, Marianne, and $X_4 = 11$. Donna's score, X_8, is 9. The symbol we will use for the mean is $\overline{X}$ (read "X bar"). Now, using these symbols, we can find the mean of the 10 scores as follows:

$$\overline{X} = \frac{X_1 + X_2 + X_3 + X_4 + X_5 + X_6 + X_7 + X_8 + X_9 + X_{10}}{10}$$

However, what would we do if we had a very long list of scores, say 500, and we wanted to find the mean? Obviously, it could become very tedious if we had to write $X_1 + X_2 + X_3 + \cdot \ \cdot \ \cdot + X_{499} + X_{500}$ to find the total of all 500 scores.

For that reason, the symbol Σ (uppercase Greek letter sigma) is used by statisticians to show summation of a list of scores. If we simply write

$$\sum_{i=1}^{10} X_i$$

it would be read as "the sum of scores on X for individuals 1 through 10." A symbol for the sum of that list of 500 scores just mentioned is simply

$$\sum_{i=1}^{500} X_i$$

Now, we are ready to develop a general formula for the mean that can be used for lists of scores of any length. We have already shown that

$$\overline{X} = \frac{X_1 + X_2 + X_3 + X_4 + X_5 + X_6 + X_7 + X_8 + X_9 + X_{10}}{10}$$

for 10 scores. Rewriting this, using the symbol for summation,

$$\overline{X} = \frac{\sum_{i=1}^{10} X_i}{10}$$

In general, where we have n subjects (whatever the number is) the formula for the mean is

$$\overline{X} = \frac{\sum_{i=1}^{n} X_i}{n}$$

Choosing a Measure of Central Tendency

With interval data, the mean, median, and mode can all be computed, although the most frequently used is the mean. Each conveys a different kind of information and should be used accordingly. For example, if an indication of the "most typical" score is required, all three might be useful. On the other hand, the mode is clearly the best choice to show the most frequently occurring score. Yet the mode may be an extreme score in the distribution and not really "central" in the usual sense of that word. This could happen if the modal response on an easy 10-item history quiz was 10, for example. In this case, more students would obtain a perfect score on the test than would obtain any other score. The median reflects the middle of a distribution of scores in the sense that half the scores fall above the median and half the scores fall below it. The mean represents the average score. Extreme scores can affect the mean but not other measures of central tendency. Consider, for example, the following two lists of scores:

	A	B
	1	1
	3	3
	3	3
	3	3
	5	15
Total	15	25

The mean, median, and mode of list A are all 3. For list B, however, the median and mode are still 3, but the increase of 10 in the last score resulted in the mean increasing to 5. Thus the mean is sensitive to extreme scores, and, for that reason, the median or mode is sometimes preferred to the mean.

MEASURES OF DISPERSION

Although a measure of central tendency provides us with useful information about a distribution, we need to know something about the "spread" of the scores in a distribution to be able to know how the scores vary around the measures of central tendency. Consider the following three lists of data, for example:

A	B	C
0	1	3
1	2	3
2	3	3
4	4	3
8	5	3
$\Sigma X_i = 15$	$\Sigma X_i = 15$	$\Sigma X_i = 15$
$\overline{X} = 3$	$\overline{X} = 3$	$\overline{X} = 3$

In each of the above lists, the mean is 3. Yet in list C, all the scores are 3, whereas in list A, none of the scores is 3; in fact, they vary from 0 to 8. In list B, the values of the scores are more homogenous than in A but less homogenous than in C. This is the kind of information we try to summarize with measures of dispersion.

No completely satisfactory measure of dispersion exists for variables measured on nominal scales. For these variables, often the best that can be done to describe dispersion is to construct a graph showing each category and its frequency.

When ordinal measurement is used, several measures of dispersion based on the idea of a *range* can be used. The simplest of these are the *inclusive* and *exclusive* range. The exclusive range is simply the highest score minus the lowest. Look at our lists A, B, and C. The exclusive range of scores in list A is 8 minus 0, or 8; in list B, it is 5 minus 1, or 4; in list C, it is 3 minus 3, or 0. Obviously, the lower the exclusive range, the less dispersion among the scores. The inclusive range is also very simple to compute. It is the lowest score subtracted from the highest score plus 1. This one unit is added so that all the values represented by the scores in the distribution (2.5 to 3.5 for the score of 3, for example) are included in the range; hence the name "inclusive." For list A, therefore, the inclusive range would be 9; for list B, it would be 5; and for list C, it would be 1. Again, the lower the inclusive range, the less dispersion in the scores. There are other range statistics, but we will leave a discussion of these to elementary statistics texts.

When a variable is measured with an interval scale, the mean may be the appropriate measure of central tendency. A way to show dispersion with this kind of data might be to show how far each score is from the mean. We can do this by subtracting the mean from each score. This is represented symbolically by

$$(X_i - \overline{X})$$

and we call this the *deviation from the mean*. We can find the size of this deviation for each score in a set of data. In Table 6-2, the scores from Table 6-1 are shown again. The mean for these scores is 10.3. The size of the deviation of each score from the mean is shown in the column labeled "Deviation." For example, Bill's score, X_1, is 4.7 greater than the mean ($15 - 10.3 = 4.7$), while Joe's score, X_9, is 3.3 less than the mean ($7 - 10.3 = -3.3$). On first glance, it would seem that the sum of these deviations would provide a good measure of dispersion. However, the sum of the deviations from the mean in a distribution is always zero. Thus

$$\sum_{i=1}^{n} (X_i - \overline{X}) = 0$$

This obviously will not reflect varying amounts of dispersion in different distributions. We can get out of this bind by squaring the deviations (which will eliminate the negative signs), and the total will then always be positive. The

TABLE 6-2
DEVIATIONS FROM THE MEAN ON THE MATHEMATICS TEST

Student	Score	Deviation	Squared deviation
1. Bill	15	4.7	22.09
2. James	12	1.7	2.89
3. Karen	12	1.7	2.89
4. Marianne	11	.7	.49
5. Helen	10	−.3	.09
6. Louise	10	−.3	.09
7. Logan	10	−.3	.09
8. Donna	9	−1.3	1.69
9. Joe	7	−3.3	10.89
10. Edward	7	− 3.3	10.89
Total	103	0	52.10
$\bar{X} = 10.3$			

squared deviations from the mean for the mathematics test scores are also shown in Table 6-2. For example, the squared deviation from the mean for Karen's score is $(X_3 - \bar{X})^2$ or $(12 - 10.3)^2 = 2.89$. The sum of squared deviations from the mean is

$$\sum_{i=1}^{n} (X_i - \bar{X})^2 = 52.10$$

This quantity reflects the amount of dispersion but is not itself an adequate measure of dispersion because the size of the quantity depends on the number of scores. To correct this, the sum of squared deviations from the mean can be divided by the number of scores to produce the variance, which we will represent as S_x^2. The variance is

$$S_x^2 = \frac{\sum_{i=1}^{n} (X_i - \bar{X})^2}{n}$$

The *variance* of a distribution is the average of the squared deviations from the mean of the distribution. Actually, if scores are only available for a portion (sample) of individuals from the population being studied, the correct formula for the variance is

$$S_x^2 = \frac{\sum_{i=1}^{n} (X_i - \bar{X})^2}{n-1}$$

The interpretation of variance computed by this formula is essentially the same as that for the earlier formula. The reason for using $n - 1$ in the denominator of the right-hand side of the equation is rather advanced for discussion at this point but is discussed in most elementary statistics books.

For the data in Table 6-2, the variance is

$$S_x^2 = \frac{\sum\limits_{i=1}^{n} (X_i - \overline{X})^2}{n - 1} = \frac{52.10}{9} = 5.79$$

A measure of dispersion for interval level variables that is closely related to the variance is the standard deviation. The *standard deviation*, S_x, is simply the positive square root of the variance:*

$$S_x = \sqrt{\frac{\sum\limits_{i=1}^{n} (X_i - \overline{X})^2}{n - 1}}$$

The standard deviation for the mathematics test is thus $\sqrt{5.79}$, or 2.41. As with the range as a measure of dispersion, the larger the variance or standard deviation, the more spread out the scores are. There is no one variance or standard deviation that is considered large, however. Interpretation of the size of the measure of dispersion is different for each set of data. Another point about the standard deviation is that it tends to be a number within the range of the set of scores, while the variance can be a very large number. This property of the standard deviation often renders it more satisfactory than the variance for interpretation of the dispersion in a list of scores.

PROBLEMS FOR THOUGHT AND DISCUSSION

1 Name the kinds of scales involved in each of the following:
  a Students lined up according to size, tallest in the rear, shortest up front
  b Colors of automobiles on the highway
  c Kinds of fruit for sale in a market
  d Height of a plant in centimeters
  e Height of a plant in inches
  f Scores on a spelling test in a third-grade class
  g Celsius thermometer readings
  h Infant mortality rates per year over a period of years

---

* For the sake of brevity, this formula is often written without subscripts. This has been done with the fifth problem for thought and discussion that follows.

i Years of teaching experience
j Classification of a country as having a high, moderate, or low literacy rate.
2 A foreman is asked to keep track of the number of units his crew worked on in a factory for 2 weeks and then report typical output. The foreman found the following output over 10 working days:

First week, units output		Second week, units output	
M	29	M	26
Tu	25	Tu	29
W	27	W	24
Th	29	Th	28
F	20	F	29

Would the foreman be better off reporting the mean, the median, or the modal output to his boss? Why? Which type of dispersion should be reported? Why?
3 A teacher has a class of 12 children which she wishes to divide into two reading groups based upon the following scores on a reading test:

Student	Reading score
1	10
2	10
3	3
4	8
5	9
6	3
7	10
8	10
9	1
10	5
11	10
12	5

Which of the three measures of central tendency provides the best rationale for splitting the group for reading instruction? Why?
4 What measures of central tendency and dispersion can be used with each of the following:
  a Scores on a spelling test
  b Ranks in a high school class
  c Racial backgrounds represented in a community
  d Annual income of wage earners in the United States
  e Stock market prices
5 Fifteen college students were asked to participate in a study designed to see how many trials were needed to learn a list containing 10 three-letter nonsense words in sequence. The number of trials for each of the students is listed below:

Student	Trials	Student	Trials
A	3	I	5
B	7	J	4
C	5	K	7
D	3	L	6
E	5	M	5
F	6	N	4
G	8	O	5
H	2		

a Find the mean, median, and modal number of trials
b Find the inclusive and exclusive range
c Find the value of the standard deviation using the formula:

$$S_x = \sqrt{\frac{\Sigma(X - \bar{X})^2}{n - 1}}$$

[Hint: Begin by calling the number of trials X, then make a column for $(X - \bar{X})$, and another for $(X - \bar{X})^2$. Sum the $(X - \bar{X})^2$ terms to obtain the value of $\Sigma(X - \bar{X})^2$.]

6 Complete the following table.

Nominal	Ordinal	Interval	Ratio
Definition			
Examples			
Measures of central tendency			
Measures of dispersion			

EXPLORATORY DATA ANALYSIS

Exploratory data analysis (EDA) is a relatively new approach to data analysis (Tukey, 1977). Used with more traditional analysis techniques, it can greatly expand the researcher's ability to understand and interpret data. The approach emphasizes visual display of data in different ways to highlight relationships and patterns existing within the data. In this way, a sensitive researcher can expose more and different information out of a set of data than would be possible using traditional methods alone. We will use one EDA technique, the stem-and-leaf, to illustrate the kind of approach EDA takes to investigating the meaning of data.

Assume a teacher gave an intelligence test to the class and the following list of scores was obtained:

115	118	129
120	123	121
116	121	117
121	116	109
132	118	114
101	112	130
111	140	

As it appears above, the list does not convey much information about the performance of the group. Rearrangement of the scores from lowest to highest will tell something about the range of scores in the sample. However, a sorted lists would not convey a sense of the shape of the distribution or the magnitude of differences between scores. Figure 6-2 shows the IQ scores in a stem-and-leaf display in which the first two digits (the "hundreds" and the "tens" columns) are listed to the left of the vertical line. To the right of the line are the

List	Ordered list	Stem–and–leaf
115	101	
120	109	
116	111	
121	112	10 | 1 9
132	114	
101	115	11 | 1 2 4 5 6 6 7 8 8
111	116	
118	116	12 | 0 1 1 1 3 9
123	117	
121	118	13 | 0 2
116	118	
118	120	14 | 0
112	121	
140	121	
129	121	
114	123	
121	129	
109	130	
117	132	
130	140	

FIGURE 6-2
List, ordered list, and stem-and-leaf display.

third digits in each score (representing the "ones" column). Notice how the data form a bar graph, or *histogram,* of scores, which immediately conveys, in a pictorial sense, the central range of scores and the extremes. This kind of information can help a researcher understand data more completely than can a mean or standard deviation alone.

Exploratory data analysis represents a new perspective when compared to more traditional ways of summarizing and studying data. As Hartwig and Dearing (1979, p. 13) insisted, "...exploratory data analysis is a state of mind...," in which numerical analysis (e.g., means, variances, correlations, etc.) is not the only way to analyze data. The stem-and-leaf display is only one of a number of richly revealing EDA techniques that can be applied to data along with traditional analysis procedures. A good overview of this topic is provided by Hartwig and Dearing (1979).

THE NORMAL CURVE AND STANDARD SCORES

Probably the most commonly encountered kind of data in educational and behavioral research is interval or nearly interval. For example, scores on achievement tests, IQ tests, and aptitude tests are usually considered to be interval. Distributions of a large number of these scores very often take on a bell shape. Such distributions are called *normal distributions.* A normal distribution of scores on an achievement test in spelling is pictured in Figure 6-3. Notice that scores near the center of the distribution occur rather frequently, while scores some distance from the center occur less often. Scores a great distance from the center occur only rarely.

Several aspects of the curve shown in Figure 6-3 deserve mention. First, a perfectly smooth symmetrical curve such as this does not ordinarily occur with real data, especially when a small number of cases are considered. However, don't let this convince you that the normal distribution is not useful. It may be an ideal that is never or rarely attained, but it offers an excellent perspective for viewing many distributions with large numbers of scores because often these large distributions tend to follow the shape of the normal distribution to a surprising degree. A second point is that this type of distribution is symmetric, and the mean, median, and mode all occur at the same point in the distri-

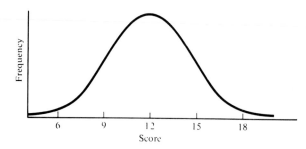

FIGURE 6-3
A normal distribution of scores on an achievement test in spelling.

bution. Third, the tails of the curve, though approaching the X axis for scores further from the mean in both directions, never quite touch the X axis.

Another property of the normal distribution is shown in Figure 6-4. From the graph it is clear that the mean of this distribution occurs at the score of 12. Furthermore, it happens that the standard deviation (square root of the variance) is 3. Knowing these two things, it is possible to discover some additional properties about the normal distribution. Again, referring to Figure 6-4, locate the point on the X axis that is 1 standard deviation above the mean (12 + 3 = 15) and the point 1 standard deviation below the mean (12 − 3 = 9). As indicated on the graph, about 68 percent of the scores in the distribution are within 1 standard deviation of the mean (between 9 and 15). Locate the points in the distribution which are 2 standard deviations below and above the mean. These points are at the scores 6 and 18, respectively. As indicated on the graph, approximately 95 percent of the scores in a normal distribution will be found within 2 standard deviations of the mean.

While the normal distribution is not obtained exactly in a sample, it is useful in thinking about the distribution of the entire population of scores. Earlier we referred to the mean and standard deviation as *statistics* when they were computed from samples of scores taken from the population. When we find values of the mean and standard deviation using the whole population of scores, we refer to them as *parameters*. Statisticians often distinguish statistics (computed on samples) from parameters (computed on populations) by using Roman letters for the statistics (e.g., $\bar{X}$, or S_x^2) and Greek letters for parameters (e.g., μ, or σ_x^2). Thus the formula for computing the population mean is

$$\mu = \frac{\sum_{i=1}^{N} X_i}{N}$$

where N = the   total   number   of   scores   in   the   population.

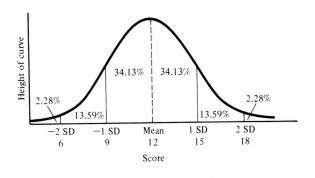

FIGURE 6-4
Normal distribution of scores on the spelling test.

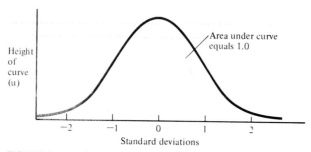

FIGURE 6-5
The unit normal distribution.

Similarly, the variance of the population is a parameter and is computed by

$$\sigma^2 = \frac{\displaystyle\sum_{i=1}^{N} (X_i - \mu)^2}{N}$$

When we know the values of μ and σ^2, and X is distributed normally, we can identify perfectly the normal distribution of scores.*

A special case of the normal distribution, shown in Figure 6-5, is the unit normal distribution. This is a normal distribution where the mean is zero and the standard deviation is one. Also, the total area under the curve in this distribution is equal to 1.00. Thus the area under the curve between -1.00 and $+1.00$ standard deviation units is approximately .68 and the area between -2.00 and $+2.00$ standard deviation units is approximately .95. Tables have been constructed to enable us to find the area under the normal curve to the left of any score in the unit normal distribution. Such a table is Table B.2 in Appendix B. In Table B.2 note that the area to the left of the score 0.00, which is at the mean, is .500. That means that half the distribution falls below 0.00, and that point of the distribution is equal to the median. The area to the left of the score -1.00 is .1587, and the area to the left of $+1.00$ is .8413. Thus the area between the scores of -1.00 and $+1.00$ is .8413 $-$ .1587, or .6826. This shows again that the percentage of the area under the curve that lies within 1

---

* The formula for the normal distribution developed by De Moivre is

$$u = \frac{1}{\sigma\sqrt{2\pi}} e^{-(X - \mu)^2/2\sigma^2}$$

The unfamiliar terms in this expression are u, the height of the curve above a particular score X; π, the constant 3.1416; and e, the base of the system of natural logarithms (a constant value of approximately 2.718). The mathematical manipulation of this formula is beyond the scope of this book, but the formula allows plotting a normal curve for any μ and σ^2 computed from a population of X that is normally distributed. With some rather advanced mathematical procedures the areas under the curve between any two scores can be determined using the formula.

standard deviation above and below the mean is approximately 68 percent. Areas to the left of all scores between -3.00 and $+3.00$ are included in Table B.2.

You might think that going to the trouble of constructing such a table for the case of $\mu = 0$ and $\sigma^2 = 1$ is a waste of time since for any real measure of achievement, attitude, and so forth, the chances of obtaining a population mean of exactly 0 and population variance of exactly 1 are extremely small. But it happens that for any normally distributed variable, the scores can be transformed so they have a mean of 0 and a variance of 1. Then areas under the curve to the left of various scores can be determined by using the adjusted scores and referring to the table of the unit normal distribution.

Converting a set of scores into a distribution that has a mean of 0 and a standard deviation of 1 is a simple process. Consider the following set of five scores as an example:

X

20
15
10
20
10

The mean is 15 and the standard deviation 5. Since 15 is the mean, we want it to be 0. Also, 20 is 1 standard deviation above the mean, and we want it to be $+1.0$, while 10 is 1 standard deviation below the mean, and therefore we want it to become -1.0. We can accomplish this adjustment using the following formula for the whole population:

$$z = \frac{X - \mu}{\sigma}$$

or, for a sample:

$$z = \frac{X - \overline{X}}{S_x}$$

Expressing each score as a value of z, the five scores with a mean of 15 and a standard deviation of 5 then become

X	$(X - \overline{X})/S_x$	z
20	$(20 - 15)/5$	1.0
15	$(15 - 15)/5$	0
10	$(10 - 15)/5$	-1.0
20	$(20 - 15)/5$	1.0
10	$(10 - 15)/5$	-1.0

If our sample of scores had come from a normally distributed population, we could use the values of the unit normal curve to estimate the proportion of scores which fall below a given score. For example, since 20 is 1 standard deviation above the mean, and about 84 percent of the scores fall below 1 standard deviation above the mean, 20 is better than 84 percent of the scores. Of course, we can only make this kind of interpretation when the population of scores is normally distributed. Another condition is that S_x and $\bar{X}$ are dependable *estimates* of σ_x and μ. When the sample size is large, this tends to be the case. However, when sample sizes are small, chance variation in the values of statistics can be large.

The z scores we have been discussing belong to a class of scores called *standard scores*. Standard scores are so named because of the fact that they are expressed in terms of the standard deviation. In z scores the standard deviation of the scores is used in the denominator of the equation

$$z = \frac{X - \bar{X}}{S_x}$$

Other standard scores are based upon z scores. For example, T scores, used in some achievement tests, may be formed from z scores using the equation

$$T = 10(z) + 50$$

This means that T scores have a mean of 50 and a standard deviation of 10. Can you see why? Another kind of standard score is used with the Wechsler Intelligence Scale for Children—Revised (WISC-R). In this kind of standard score, IQ is based on a normal distribution which has a mean of 100 and a standard deviation of 15. Therefore, WISC-R IQ scores are computed from z scores as follows:

$$WISC\text{-}R \ IQ = 15(z) + 100$$

A person who scored 1.2 standard deviations above the mean would have an IQ of 15(1.2) + 100, which equals 118. The various kinds of standard scores were designed to avoid dealing with the small numbers and decimal values that would be necessary in using z scores.

SUMMARIZING RELATIONSHIPS BETWEEN TWO VARIABLES

To this point, we have been discussing ways to summarize a single list of scores. However, it is not unusual in the social and behavioral sciences and education to consider more than one variable at the same time. In Chapter 2, for example, we reviewed a correlational study by Hoge and McKay in which the relationship of parents' ratings of educational adjustment and a child's school behavior was studied.

Let us begin our discussion of summarizing a relationship between two scores by looking at the scores of 10 students on a mathematics aptitude test

(X) and an achievement test in mathematics (Y). These scores are presented in Table 6-3. The aptitude test scores are arranged in order of size from smallest to largest. The scores on the achievement test tend to follow this ordering somewhat. Thus we can see in the scatter diagram in Figure 6-6 that low scores on the achievement test tend to be found in individuals who also have low aptitude scores, and high achievement scores appear for students with higher aptitude.

Now look at the number of errors made in maze tracing and the score on a map-reading test for 10 students. These scores are presented in Table 6-4 and graphed in Figure 6-7. Notice that the students who made more errors in maze tracing tended to get lower scores on the map-reading test. Also, students who made fewer errors tended to get higher scores in map reading. Now compare the relationship between the variables in Figure 6-6 with that between the variables in Figure 6-7. You can see that the direction of the relationship is different. Higher scores are paired with higher scores and lower with lower scores in Figure 6-6. But this is not the case in Figure 6-7, where those who made a higher number of errors tended to score lower in map reading. The relationship depicted in Figure 6-6 is said to be *positive* or *direct*, while the one in Figure 6-7 is called *negative* or *inverse*. We need a statistical method of summarizing this kind of relationship which will tell us two things. First, we want to know

TABLE 6-3
MATHEMATICS APTITUDE AND MATHEMATICS ACHIEVEMENT TEST SCORES FOR 10 STUDENTS

Student	Math aptitude (X)	Math achievement (Y)	$(X - \bar{X})$	$(Y - \bar{Y})$	$(X - \bar{X})(Y - \bar{Y})$
1. James	68	17	18	7	126
2. Cathy	62	12	12	2	24
3. Valerie	55	12	5	2	10
4. Chuck	52	14	2	4	8
5. Diane	51	8	1	− 2	− 2
6. Bob	49	9	− 1	− 1	1
7. Len	47	8	− 3	− 2	6
8. Judy	44	11	− 6	1	− 6
9. Amy	40	3	− 10	− 7	70
10. Ellery	32	6	− 18	− 4	72
Total	500	100	0	0	309

$$\bar{X} = 50 \qquad \bar{Y} = 10$$
$$S^2_x = 107.56 \qquad S^2_y = 16.44$$
$$S_x = 10.37 \qquad S_y = 4.05$$

$$S_{xy} = \frac{309}{9} = 34.33$$

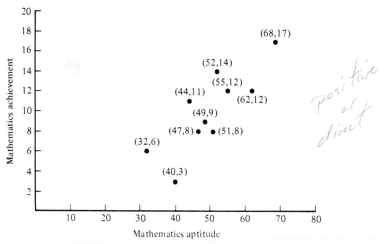

FIGURE 6-6
Scatter diagram for mathematics aptitude and mathematics achievement scores.

TABLE 6-4
MAP-READING TEST SCORES AND MAZE-TRACING ERRORS OF 10 STUDENTS

Student	(X) Maze-tracing errors	(Y) Map-reading score	$(X - \bar{X})$	$(Y - \bar{Y})$	$(X - \bar{X})(Y - \bar{Y})$
Jerry	10	75	− 6	8	− 48
Joe	11	77	− 5	10	− 50
Pete	14	71	− 2	4	− 8
Jane	14	70	− 2	3	− 6
Joyce	15	71	− 1	4	− 4
Arnold	18	69	2	2	4
Fred	18	65	2	− 2	− 4
Pat	19	62	3	− 5	− 15
Nate	20	60	4	− 7	− 28
Alice	21	50	5	− 17	− 85
Total	160	670	0	0	− 244
	$\bar{X} = 16$	$\bar{Y} = 67$			

whether the relationship is direct or inverse. Second, we must know how strong the relationship is. A strong relationship is one in which knowing something about one variable also conveys information about the other variable. For example, there is a strong relationship between the number of errors one makes on a test and the number of correct answers. If we know that someone made 10 errors on a 25-item test, then assuming all questions were answered, the score was 15. Conversely, a student who had 20 items correct made only 5

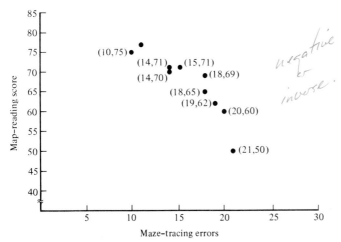

FIGURE 6-7
Scatter diagram for maze-tracing errors and map-reading scores.

errors. There is a less strong relationship between a person's height and weight. Specifically, if we know that a person is 5 feet 10 inches tall, we can guess that person's weight but would probably not be exactly right. If we guessed that the weight was between 135 and 190 pounds we probably would not be wrong, but if we tried to choose a specific number, we would probably make an error. Also, if we know a person is 240 pounds, we are pretty sure we are not dealing with a five-footer, but the exact height would be impossible to guess knowing only the weight.

First we will see how to determine whether a relationship is direct or inverse. To do this we look at each pair of X and Y scores in terms of the means of X and Y. The deviations of X and Y from the means of X and Y have been computed in Tables 6-3 and 6-4. Then the X and Y deviations in each pair are multiplied by each other. This has also been done in Tables 6-3 and 6-4. Notice that when the relationship is direct, the X's above $\overline{X}$ tend to be paired with the Y values above the mean of Y. Also, the X values below $\overline{X}$ and the Y scores below $\overline{Y}$ are paired. When the X and Y deviations are multiplied, the negative $(X - \overline{X})$'s are multiplied by the negative $(Y - \overline{Y})$'s, and the positive $(X - \overline{X})$'s are multiplied by positive $(Y - \overline{Y})$'s. This results in a positive total in the $(X - \overline{X})(Y - \overline{Y})$ column. Following the same reasoning you should see why the $(X - \overline{X})(Y - \overline{Y})$ total in Table 6-4 is negative, and why when that total is negative the relationship is inverse (negative).

Thus, the term which we shall call *sum of deviation cross-products,*

$$\Sigma(X - \overline{X})(Y - \overline{Y})$$

will tell us whether we have a direct or inverse relationship. Now, we need some way of summarizing the strength of the relationship. Obviously the sum of deviation cross-products will not do that since its size is dependent upon the number of scores. If we divide by the number of scores, we get a statistic called the *covariance*. However, when working with sample data, it is more correct to divide the sum of deviation cross-products by $n - 1$ for the same reasons we did earlier in computing the variance. Thus, the formula for covariance in a sample of scores, where S_{xy} stands for covariance, is

$$S_{xy} = \frac{\Sigma(X - \overline{X})(Y - \overline{Y})}{n - 1}$$

Unfortunately, covariance is not a good measure of the strength of a relationship either, because the larger the variance of X and Y, the larger the covariance will tend to be. We need an index that will be readily interpretable according to the same set of rules every time regardless of the variance of X and Y measurements. We get this standardization in a way that is familiar to us. Remember that dividing deviation scores like $(X - \overline{X})$ by the standard deviation created a distribution of scores where the mean was 0 and the standard deviation was 1.0 regardless of the range of scores in the data. We take this same approach to find an index of relationship. That is, we divide S_{xy}, the covariance of X and Y, by the product of the standard deviation of X and the standard deviation of Y to obtain the *Pearson product-moment correlation coefficient*. Using r_{xy} as the symbol for the correlation coefficient,*

$$r_{xy} = \frac{S_{xy}}{S_x S_y}$$

The correlation coefficient can be any value between $+1.00$ and -1.00. Though there are no strict rules for interpreting the size of correlation coefficients, correlations between .80 and 1.00 are considered high, while correlations between .30 and .60 are considered moderate.† Correlations which range between $+.30$ and $-.30$ are typically considered too low to be of importance. However, interpretations may vary in specific situations depending on sample size. A negative correlation indicates that a relationship is inverse. A relationship can be high and inverse, as in a correlation of $-.90$.

For the data in Table 6-3 the correlation coefficient is

---

* An easier and more widely used computational formula is

$$r_{xy} = \frac{\Sigma XY - (\Sigma X)(\Sigma Y)/n}{\sqrt{\left[\Sigma X^2 - \frac{(\Sigma X)^2}{n}\right]\left[\Sigma Y^2 - \frac{(\Sigma Y)^2}{n}\right]}}$$

†In interpreting the magnitude of correlations, the same conventions apply whether the correlation is inverse or direct.

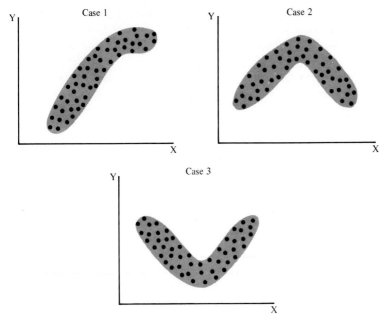

FIGURE 6-8
Curvilinear relationships between two interval-level variables.

$$r_{xy} = \frac{S_{xy}}{S_x S_y} = \frac{34.33}{(10.37)(4.05)} = .82$$

Since .82 is close to the maximum positive value r_{xy} can attain (1.00), it represents a high degree of positive relationship between the two variables.

The product-moment correlation coefficient is only appropriate when there is a *linear* relationship between two variables. What is meant by linear or straight-line relationship can be seen by referring to Figures 6-6 and 6-7. Contrast these to the curvilinear relationships shown in Figure 6-8. Perhaps you can see what happens to the covariance in these cases. Special statistical procedures are available which are sensitive to curvilinear relationships. In reading about or conducting research concerning the relationship between two interval-level variables, you should ask whether it is more likely that a linear or curvilinear relationship exists between the variables, or, better yet, plot the points on a scatter diagram. If the data are curvilinear, appropriate statistical techniques other than the Pearson product-moment correlation should be applied.*

---

* See Glass, G. V., & Hopkins, K.D. (1984). *Statistical methods in education and psychology* (2nd ed.). Englewood Cliffs, NJ: Prentice-Hall. This contains a good discussion of curvilinearity and its effect upon correlation coefficients on pp. 83–84, and a suggested measure of a curvilinear relationship on pp. 142–142.

Another caution in interpreting correlations concerns "artifact" correlations, which can occur because what appeared to be a single group was really two distinct groups. The data shown in Figure 6-9 illustrate this point. These data are scores on a verbal intelligence test (*X*) and an anxiety test (*Y*) for a sample of 100 boys and 100 girls in the fourth grade. This sample turns out in fact to be two samples since the boys tend to have both lower intelligence and lower anxiety scores than the girls. The effect of combining these two distributions is represented by the dotted line, and the resulting correlation coefficient would indicate the existence of a positive relationship. But if we had graphed boys' and girls' scores separately, we would have found no relationship between anxiety and intelligence.

REGRESSION TECHNIQUES

In education and behavioral research situations it is often useful to conduct *prediction* or *estimation* studies. In prediction, current characteristics are used to identify scores at a future time. Estimation involves identification of a present attribute from other traits or scores. For example, we would be predicting if we used Graduate Record Examination scores of college seniors to tell us what their grade-point averages would be at the end of graduate school. On the other hand, we would be estimating if we used the GRE scores of freshmen to identify their grade-point averages as freshmen. Although the concepts are different, the procedures used to predict and estimate are identical, and statisticians often use the two terms interchangeably.

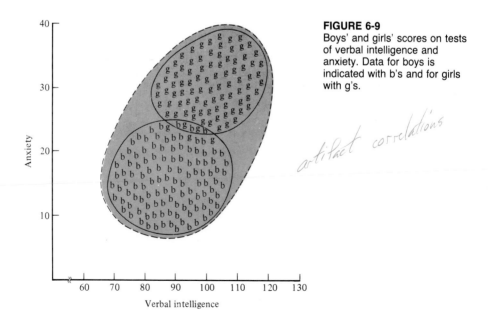

FIGURE 6-9
Boys' and girls' scores on tests of verbal intelligence and anxiety. Data for boys is indicated with b's and for girls with g's.

Earlier in this chapter, we looked at the Pearson product-moment correlation coefficient as a way of summarizing the degree of linear relationship between two variables. When two variables are correlated, one can be used to predict or estimate the other. This is called *simple* prediction. Furthermore, several variables can be used to predict a single variable by extending the notion of the correlation coefficient to situations involving more than two variables: this is termed *multiple* prediction.

Simple Prediction

Let us begin our discussion of prediction and estimation with two sets of X and Y data. One set has a correlation between X and Y of + 1.0, and r_{xy} for the other set is zero. These data are listed and graphed in Figure 6-10. The points in the perfectly correlated set of data form a straight line. We can move along the line, and at any point on the line construct two perpendicular lines—one to the X axis and the other to the Y axis. The value of Y at a certain value of X can be determined exactly. For example, where $X = 4$, $Y = 6$. This basically is how statisticians predict one value from another when there is a straight-line, or linear, relationship among the variables, a procedure known as *regression.*

FIGURE 6-10
Two sets of data and their scatter diagrams.

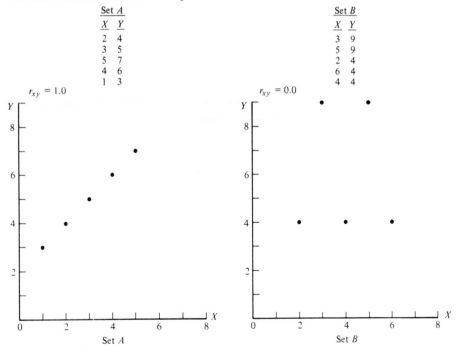

Set A

X	Y
2	4
3	5
5	7
4	6
1	3

Set B

X	Y
3	9
5	9
2	4
6	4
4	4

$r_{xy} = 1.0$

$r_{xy} = 0.0$

Now look at data set B in Figure 6-10, where $r_{xy} = 0.0$. There is no straight-line relationship among the pairs of X and Y scores. Figure 6-11 is a graph of nine paired mathematics (X) and science (Y) scores. Again, the prediction line has been drawn. We can use that line to predict science scores for other people who took the mathematics test only. For instance, let us say that there is a tenth student in the class who took the mathematics test and obtained a score of 40. We could estimate that student's science score by finding the point on the regression line corresponding to $X = 40$ and obtaining the value of Y at that point. Dotted perpendicular lines have been drawn from the point where $X = 40$ to the X and Y axes, and it can easily be seen that at that point $Y = 25$.

The problem with predicting this way is that accurate measurement on a graph is difficult. We can get more accurate estimations of predicted values of Y using the mathematical equation for a straight line. This equation can be written:

$$Y_i = \beta_0 + \beta_1 X_i$$

where Y_i is any value of Y and X_i is the corresponding value of X. The interpretations of β_0 and β_1 follow.

FIGURE 6-11
Scatter diagram of nine students' scores on a mathematics (X) and a science (Y) test.

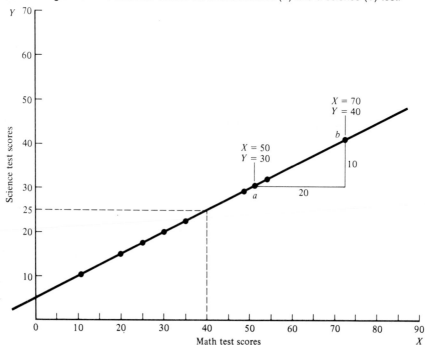

First let us consider β_1. It is the *slope* of the line and may be found using the formula

$$\beta_1 = \frac{Y_i - Y_j}{X_i - X_j}$$

where X_i and Y_i are values of X and Y for a point on the line, and X_j and Y_j are values of X and Y at another point on the line to the left of the first point. The slope is the difference between two points along the Y axis divided by the difference in X between the same two points. The slope tells us how much change in Y there is for each unit of change in X. Applying this to the line depicted in Figure 6-11, we find the slope by arbitrarily selecting two points a and b (in this case $X = 50$, $Y = 30$, and $X = 70$, $Y = 40$) and computing β_1 as follows:

$$\beta_1 = \frac{40 - 30}{70 - 50} = \frac{10}{20} = .5$$

The value of β_0 may be read directly off the graph in Figure 6-11. It is called the *Y intercept*, and is defined as the value of Y when $X = 0$. The value of β_0 at the point where $X = 0$ in our line is 5. Substituting these values of β_1 and β_0 in the formula for a straight line, we obtain

$$Y = 5 + .5X_i$$

Using this equation, we can estimate science test scores from mathematics test scores. For example, earlier in our discussion we estimated that a person who obtained a score of 40 on the mathematics test would score 25 in science from the line in Figure 6-11. Now we can estimate this using the formula

$$Y = 5 + .5(40) = 25$$

The problem with the method as described thus far is that most X and Y variables are not perfectly related. That is, variables are not typically correlated perfectly. Figure 6-12 shows a scattergram of two variables, achievement and aptitude, which are correlated about .82. When the data points do not conform to a straight line, it is more difficult to select a line to use for prediction purposes.

A line has been placed through the data points in Figure 6-12 that is supposed to represent the "best fitting" line for those points. This line was placed where it is for a special reason, to be described shortly. However, for the present, the reader may wish to question the line as not appearing to be the best fitting one for the points. Actually, there are an infinite number of lines which could have been selected. It should be apparent that our predictions will be less accurate for the data in Figure 6-12 than they were with perfectly correlated data. This introduces the concept of *error of estimate*. That is, we predict a value of Y from a value of X and it is different from the Y we had observed for that X. If we label predicted scores $\hat{Y}$, then $\hat{Y}$ may be lesser or

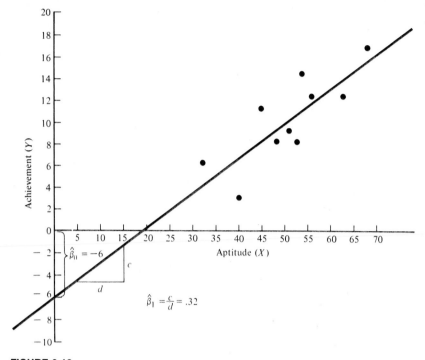

FIGURE 6-12
Mathematics aptitude and mathematics achievement scores, including the "best-fitting" regression line. ($\hat{\beta}_0$ and $\hat{\beta}_1$ are the least-squares estimates of the population values for β_0 and β_1.)

greater than Y, the corresponding observed score. The error of estimate is equal to the difference between Y and $\hat{Y}$, or

$$e = Y - \hat{Y}$$

To illustrate errors of estimate, let us say for the moment that the Y intercept and the slope for the line depicted in Figure 6-12 are -6 and .32, respectively. The equation for the regression line is

$$\hat{Y} = -6.0 + .32X$$

The achievement score of a student who scored 68 on the aptitude test can be computed using this equation. Thus,

$$\hat{Y}_1 = -6.0 + .32(68)$$
$$= +15.76$$

However, in Figure 6-13 it is seen that the student who scored 68 in aptitude actually scored 17.0 in achievement. Thus, the error of estimate is $17.0 - 15.76 = 1.24$.

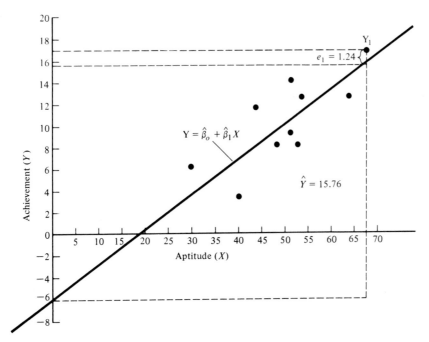

FIGURE 6-13
Graphic representation of the prediction of a student's scores on the mathematics achievement test from his score of 68 on the aptitude test.

With the understanding that each time we make a prediction there will be an error of estimate when the X and Y pair of scores do not fall exactly on the regression line, we are ready to proceed to explain why we chose the line we did for the data shown in Figure 6-12. Several possible criteria or rules exist for use in selecting a prediction line. We chose a line that would minimize the total squared errors of estimate. In other words, we predict a $\hat{Y}$ score for each obtained value of X. Then we get the errors of estimate, using

$$e = Y - \hat{Y}$$

and we square these. Finally we take the sum of the e^2. The prediction line that gives us the lowest possible value of Σe^2 is the one we choose. Using calculus we can find this line without having to try all possible lines, and it is called the *least-squares solution*. The formulas for the least-squares solution to β_1 and β_0 are as follows:*

---

* A preferable formula for calculating $\hat{\beta}_1$ is

$$\hat{\beta}_1 = \frac{\Sigma XY - \dfrac{(\Sigma X)(\Sigma X)}{n}}{\Sigma X^2 - \dfrac{(\Sigma X)^2}{n}}$$

$$\hat{\beta}_1 = r_{xy} \frac{S_y}{S_x}$$

$$\hat{\beta}_0 = \overline{Y} - \hat{\beta}_1 \overline{X}$$

where $\hat{\beta}_1$ = estimated slope of the least-squares regression line
r_{xy} = correlation between X and Y
S_y = standard deviation of Y
S_x = standard deviation of X
$\hat{\beta}_0$ = estimated Y intercept of the least-squares regression line
$\overline{Y}$ = mean of Y
$\overline{X}$ = mean of X

The data depicted in Figure 6-12 come from the correlation example given earlier in Table 6-3. Going back to that example, we find

$$S_x = 10.37$$
$$S_y = 4.05$$
$$r_{xy} = .82$$
$$\overline{X} = 50$$
$$\overline{Y} = 10$$

Applying these values to the formula for least-squares estimates of β_1 and β_0,

$$\beta_1 = .82 \frac{(4.05)}{(10.37)} = .32$$

$$\beta_0 = 10 - .32(50) = -6.0$$

Now you can see why we chose the line

$$\hat{Y} = -6.0 + .32X$$

for the data points depicted in Figure 6-12.

Determining the Usefulness of Predicting Y from X

If we were to predict values of a Y variable without knowing anything about X, our best estimate would be the mean of Y. Each time we estimated a Y score which is not exactly equal to $\overline{Y}$, there would be an error of estimate equal to

$$e = Y - \overline{Y}$$

The variance of the errors would therefore be

$$S_y^2 = \frac{\Sigma(Y - \overline{Y})^2}{n - 1}$$

which happens to be the variance of Y. In predicting Y from X we hope to reduce the size of this variance. We have already shown that the error of an estimate is

$$e = Y - \hat{Y}$$

Taking the variance of all these errors we get the variance error of estimate, which is

$$S_e^2 = \frac{\Sigma(Y - \hat{Y})^2}{n - 2}$$

The important question to ask when formulating a prediction equation is whether the equation does a better job of predicting than the mean of the criterion distribution. To test this, analysis of variance can be used. (See Chapter 7 for a discussion of this technique.) The approach is to test the null hypothesis that β_1 is equal to zero (from Chapter 3, presentation of hypotheses) or

$$H_0 : \beta_1 = 0$$

The reader can readily see why this is done by looking at the formula for the least-squares estimate of β_0. That is,

$$\hat{\beta}_0 = \overline{Y} - \hat{\beta}_1(\overline{X})$$

If $\beta_1 = 0$, then

$$\hat{\beta}_0 = \overline{Y}$$
$$\text{and } \hat{Y} = \overline{Y}$$

Also, an equation was given earlier in this discussion which shows the relationship of $\hat{\beta}_1$ to the correlation coefficient, r_{xy}. Specifically,

$$\hat{\beta}_1 = r_{xy}\left(\frac{S_y}{S_x}\right)$$

Therefore, if $r_{xy} = 0$, then $\hat{\beta}_1 = 0$. The higher the correlation between X and Y, the greater the value of $\hat{\beta}_1$. A description of the computational formula and procedures for testing the null hypothesis can be found elsewhere.† The reader

---

* See Edwards (1979), Chapter 2.
†Ibid.

should keep in mind that the value of $\hat{\beta}_1$ is computed from a sample, and is only an estimate of a parameter β_1. It is not the population value for $\hat{\beta}_1$.

Another important aspect of prediction concerns the amount of variance in the criterion variable which is accounted for by predicting Y from X. It can be shown that this proportion of variance is equal to the squared correlation of X and Y. Thus, if two variables correlate .90, 81 percent of the variance in Y is accounted for by predicting Y from X. This proportion reduces rapidly with lower correlation coefficients. Thus, when $r_{xy} = .60$, $r_{xy}^2 = .36$, and when $r_{xy} = .50$, $r_{xy}^2 = .25$.

When There Is More Than One Predictor Variable

Often in prediction problems the researcher wishes to predict the score on a dependent variable from a combination of several predictors rather than a single one. The intention is to improve on the simple linear-regression model by increasing the accuracy of the prediction through incorporating additional information from several independent variables. The simplest form of such prediction is the two-predictor case, in which the scores on two independent variables (X_1 and X_2) are used to predict the score on Y. The model for this is given as

$$Y = \beta_0 + \beta_1 X_1 + \beta_2 X_2 + e$$

where $\hat{\beta}_0$ = constant term or Y intercept
β_1 = weight for variable X_1 in the prediction equation
X_1 = score of an individual on the first predictor (independent) variable
β_2 = weight of the variable X_2 in the prediction equation
X_2 = score of the individual on the second predictor (independent) variable
Y = score of an individual on the criterion (dependent) variable
e = error of estimate

For example, a researcher might wish to predict the grade-point averages of mathematics graduate students from their scores on the quantitative and verbal portions of the Graduate Record Examination. A random sample of 30 graduate students in mathematics is selected. The scores of these students on the GRE quantitative (X_1) and GRE verbal (X_2) tests are obtained, as well as the students' current grade-point averages (Y). Through least-squares estimation procedures,* the estimates of β_1, β_2, and β_0 are found to be

$$\hat{\beta}_0 = 1.6$$
$$\hat{\beta}_1 = .0022$$
$$\hat{\beta}_2 = .0013$$

* The computational procedures required are beyond the scope of this text; see Edwards (1979), Chapter 4.

We can use the equation to predict the grade-point average of a student who scores 500 on the GRE verbal test (X_1) and 520 on the quantitative test (X_2). From the equation

$$\hat{Y} = \beta_0 + \beta_1 X_1 + \beta_2 X_2$$

we substitute our estimated values of β_1, β_2, and β_0 as follows:

$$\hat{Y} = 1.6 + .0022(500) + .0013(520)$$
$$= 3.376$$

Thus, we would expect a student with scores of 500 and 520 on the GRE to have a grade-point average of about 3.38.

For the two-predictor model an analysis of variance can also be performed to test whether each of the predictor variables is necessary in the model. However, a complication arises when using this model because X's are typically correlated with each other to some extent as well as with Y. Thus, if they share much variance with each other, they may to some extent each predict Y in the same way. That is, some of their common variance with Y may be shared between them. This is a problem because their common variance can be represented only once in the prediction model (not once for each predictor variable). Thus, when selecting the right set of variables to retain in the model through hypothesis testing, the order in which variables enter the model is important. This order must be made explicit in building the model and in the analysis of variance for testing the regression. A common procedure which takes into account the ordering of the prediction variables is summarized as follows. The model is evaluated by considering the first predictor of Y as the only one, then the second as a predictor of what remains of Y that is not predicted by the first. If there are more predictors, the third is tested as a predictor of what remains of Y which is not predicted by the first and second predictors. This procedure adds the best predictor into the model at each stage and continues until all the predictors in the multiple-prediction model are considered. Only those variables which account for a significant portion of the variance of Y are accepted for the final prediction model.

Multiple-prediction problems can become quite complex in that a number of predictors might be used to estimate a single criterion. The purpose of such studies is usually to enable the researcher to select a small number of variables, say 3 or 4, from a larger set, say 8 to 20, which predict the criterion adequately.*

---

* The reader interested in applying regression analysis for developing the "best" prediction model is referred to Draper and Smith (1981).

An Application of Multiple Regression

Welch, Anderson, and Harris (1982) used multiple-regression analysis to study the effects of schooling on mathematics achievement in a national random sample of 17-year-olds from the United States. In this study, eight background variables (such as percent of the community receiving assistance from welfare, percent of professionals living in the community, percent of racial minorities in the school, mean parental educational level of the school, etc.) and the number of semesters of mathematics completed by the students were used to predict scores on a mathematics achievement test. The researchers first used the background variables to predict the mathematics scores and found that about 24 percent of the variance in math test scores was explained by background. The addition of a single variable—the number of semesters in mathematics completed by the students—accounted for an additional 34 percent of the variance. The researchers checked these findings by replicating the results with two additional samples. From the study, they were able to conclude that while a student's background was important to mathematics achievement, the amount of mathematics the student actually studied was critical. On the basis of their analysis, the researchers suggested that the best way to increase mathematics performance was to study more math in school.

SUMMARY

Statistical procedures can be of great help to the researcher or to the consumer of research. Two basic kinds of statistics are *descriptive* statistics, involving the summarization of data, and *inferential* statistics, involving the inference of properties of a population from a sample of observations. Included in the discussion of descriptive statistics in this chapter were measures of central tendency and dispersion, the normal distribution, standard scores, simple graphing, and regression and correlation. These basic tools allow us to describe distributions of variables succinctly. Exploratory data analysis (EDA) takes a different perspective on data analysis than does traditional statistics. This method emphasizes visual display methods (such as the stem-and-leaf display) as a way of revealing information contained in a data set. In addition, regression procedures permit utilizing relationships that exist between variables to predict or estimate values of a variable from one or several others.

PROBLEMS FOR THOUGHT AND DISCUSSION

1 The following set of scores on a test of oral reading ability was obtained from a sample of 12 second graders. Determine the mean, median, and mode for the scores. What common information do these measures of central tendency convey? What different information do they convey?

Student	Score
1	36
2	31
3	30
4	28
5	30
6	29
7	27
8	26
9	22
10	18
11	9
12	6

2 Compute the appropriate measures of central tendency and dispersion in the following cases:

a Students in an urban high school are classified by race. The results are

Race	Numerical code	Frequency
White	1	30
Black	2	21
Oriental	3	7

b Several players on a professional football team are judged on the basis of skill. The results are

Player number	Relative skill
10	3
13	7
16	9
22	10
25	17
58	20
59	21
72	23
74	27

c The times in seconds required by a group of sixth graders to run the 40-yard dash are

Child	Time	Child	Time	Child	Time
Andy	10.0	Joel	13.1	Gary	10.6
Craig	9.3	Frank	10.8	Ronnie	9.9
Lowell	8.6	Howard	14.8	Alfred	8.9
Bob	9.9	Stewart	8.9		

3 The scores on a test of computational speed are normally distributed, with a mean of 76 and a standard deviation of 12.

a Compute a z score for the score of 70 on the test.

b What proportion of the scores in the distribution should fall below the score of 70? above the score of 70?

c Compute the z score for the score of 94 on the test.

d What proportion of the scores in the distribution should fall below the score of 94?

e What proportion of the scores in the distribution should fall between the scores of 70 and 94?

4 The following scores were obtained on a test of memory and on a verbal learning task. The verbal learning scores were the number of errors made by the subject before a list of paired words was learned to a criterion level of performance. Compute the Pearson product-moment correlation coefficient. Interpret the sign and magnitude of the coefficient. Use the formula

$$r_{xy} = \frac{\Sigma XY - (\Sigma X)(\Sigma Y)/n}{\sqrt{\left[\Sigma X^2 - \frac{(\Sigma X)^2}{n}\right]\left[\Sigma Y^2 - \frac{(\Sigma Y)^2}{n}\right]}}$$

Subject	X Memory score	Y Verbal learning score
1	42	7
2	36	6
3	34	8
4	32	5
5	32	10
6	30	9
7	28	14
8	27	11
9	25	6
10	19	17

5 a Compute the correlation coefficient for the scores of the following sample of schoolchildren on a measure of scholastic aptitude and a measure of time spent with the child by the classroom teacher.

Child	Aptitude	Time (minutes/week)
Anne Marie	130	55
Michelle	122	42
Billy	114	38
Ruth	106	29
Andy	102	20
Helen	99	19
Carey	96	30
David	92	37
Johnny	90	43
Kristen	82	48

b Construct a scattergram for these scores and explain why the correlation coefficient was inappropriate as a measure of relationship in this case.

c If you were able to compute a valid measure of this relationship and found a rather high degree of relationship, how would you describe your results verbally?

6 The IQ of a randomly selected group of 50 students in a high school of 1500 students was measured. The scores are shown below. Find the mean and standard deviation of IQ in the sample. Use the stem-and-leaf technique to defend the argument that IQ is, or is not, distributed normally in the population of this high school.

128	159	112
135	129	130
158	133	113
119	164	126
143	111	135
125	129	122
124	136	129
148	100	126
104	128	118
132	119	134
123	140	148
121	132	127
114	129	138
147	135	121
128	121	130
112	123	128
134	129	

7 Can the population of scores for a test ever produce a smooth bell-shaped curve? What kinds of assumptions are we making?

8 Which of the following probably is normally distributed in the population?

a The height of adult American males

b Age at time of death of Americans

c Educational level of the world's adults

d Annual rainfall in Ethiopia

e The size of the annual budget of a country over the past 100 years

9 Convert the following raw scores on a mathematics test to z scores and T scores:

X	z	T
8		
4		
7		
6		
6		
5		
6		
7		

10 John scores 75 on a mathematics test and 80 on a history test. The class mean was 70 and the standard deviation 5 on the mathematics test. On the history test the mean was 85 and the standard deviation 10. The teacher decided that John was a better student in mathematics than in history. Can you tell why?

11 If the scores on the verbal subtest of the Graduate Record Examination are normally distributed, with a mean of 500 and a standard deviation of 100, what percentage of scores would be lower than 650? Why is a score of 750 considered very unusual?

12 Compute the covariance (S_{xy}) for the map-reading test and maze-tracing scores in Table 6-4. What does this value tell you? What can it not tell you? Now compute the correlation coefficient (r_{xy}) for the scores in Table 6-4. What does this value tell you that S_{xy} could not?

13 Construct scatter diagrams for data sets A and B. Why is a correlation coefficient an appropriate measure of relationship for the variables in data set A, but perhaps not for that in data set B?

Data set A		Data set B	
Reinforcements	Test score	Motivation level	Test score
11	10	13	8
10	9	12	8
8	7	11	7
8	8	10	8
7	5	10	8
5	5	9	8
3	2	8	5
3	3	7	4
2	2	7	3
1	1	6	2

REFERENCES

Draper, N. R., & Smith, H. (1981). *Applied regression analysis* (2nd ed.). New York: Wiley.

Edwards, A. L. (1979). *Multiple regression and the analysis of variance and covariance*. San Francisco: Freeman.

Hartwig, F., & Dearing, B. E. (1979). *Exploratory data analysis* (Sage quantitative applications in the social sciences series, university paper no. 16). Beverly Hills, CA: Sage.

Tukey, J. (1977). *Exploratory data analysis*. Reading, MA: Addison-Wesley.

Welch, W., Anderson, R. E., & Harris, L. (1982) The effects of schooling on mathematics achievement. *American Educational Research Journal, 19*, 145–153.

SUPPLEMENTARY READINGS

Berenson, M. L., Levine, D. M., Rindskopf, D. (1988). *Applied statistics: A first course*. Englewood Cliffs, NJ: Prentice-Hall.

Ferguson, G. A. (1981). *Statistical analysis in psychology and education* (5th ed.). New York: McGraw-Hill.

Glass, G. V., & Hopkins, K. D. (1984). *Statistical methods in education and psychology*. Englewood Cliffs, NJ: Prentice-Hall.

Hays, W. L. (1981). *Statistics* (3rd ed.). New York: Holt.

Pedhazur, E. J. (1982). *Multiple regression in behavioral research: Explanation and prediction*. New York: Holt.

Velleman, P. E., & Hoaglin, D. C. (1981). *Applications, basics, and computing of exploratory data analysis*. Boston: Duxbury Press.

7

MAKING INFERENCES WITH STATISTICS

In the last chapter we found that we could summarize data using measures of central tendency, dispersion, and correlation. Let's take a look at some typical situations in which descriptive statistics are used.

1 A company that conducts political polls prior to elections was hired by one of the state political parties to assess public opinion towards their candidates. In a sample of 100 voters selected randomly from the population of registered voters in the state, 55 percent favored the party's candidate, 40 percent favored the opposition, and 5 percent were undecided. On the basis of these data, the party's candidate was expected to win the election.

2 An educational researcher constructed a test to measure mathematics achievement. He gave the test to a random sample of 1000 students from the population of fifth graders in the United States. In the sample he found a mean of 45 and a standard deviation of 11.5. He assumed that if he had tested every child in the population, the values of mean and standard deviation would have been similar.

In both cases described above, values obtained in the samples were used to describe the populations from which the samples were drawn. This is a common use of statistics. However, the samples chosen may or may not resemble the population from which they are drawn. It is likely that the statistical values from the samples are close to population values, but occasionally samples (even random samples) produce poor estimates of parameter (population) values. Inferential statistics addresses this problem of drawing inferences about the population from samples.

Among the applications of inferential statistics is the testing of statistical hypotheses. To get a better understanding of what this means, consider the following data obtained in a research project designed to see whether students learn mathematics concepts better with a group lecture or an individualized teaching approach:

Lecture	Individualized
$n_1 = 25$	$n_2 = 30$
$\bar{X}_1 = 24.2$	$\bar{X}_2 = 27.8$
$S_1^2 = 81.0$	$S_2^2 = 64.0$

If a researcher were to repeat this study many times with different samples, the same means and variances would not be obtained each time. In fact, even though the lecture group had a lower mean this time, it could score higher than the individualized group the next time the study is done. What the researcher needs to know is the probability that in the population from which the sample was drawn, the group that is lectured will score higher than the group that is taught individually. In other words, inferential statistics is concerned with making inferences about populations from sample information. Another application of inferential statistics, called *interval estimation,* will not be considered at length here, although it is seen frequently in certain types of research. This involves estimating an interval of a particular size which probably contains the population value. For example, we could construct an interval around 24.2, the mean of the lecture group, using the size of the standard deviation to help us set the size of the interval. We would then be able to infer from the sample that the mean of the population would lie within this interval. Further, our inference could be made at a certain level of probability. In other words, we would be saying that the mean of the population lies between two values, and we are certain of this at a certain level of probability.

The basics of inferential statistics will be presented in this chapter. Before discussing these procedures, however, some fundamental concepts will be introduced. These include elementary probability, sampling and sampling distributions, and the foundations of decision making using statistical procedures. Our purpose in this chapter is not to teach how to analyze data or apply statistical procedures. That purpose is left to texts in statistics. Rather our purpose here is to help the reader understand the reasoning behind statistical inference and the meaning of certain analysis procedures and how they are used in research studies.

SETS AND PROBABILITY

In describing sampling, probability, and other topics in this chapter, the concepts of *set* and *elementary set operations* are useful. A *set* is simply a well-defined collection of objects or individuals. All the students currently enrolled in public schools in grades 1–12 in New York constitute a set. All enlisted personnel in the United States Army comprise another set. Sets are often named by using a roman capital letter. For example, the set A may be defined as the five children in a special reading group in the Garden Springs School. Particular objects or individuals within the set are called *members,* or *elements.* Thus, the children in the special reading group, Patty, John, Donna, Harry, and Bonnie, are the members of the set A. A way of defining a set is to list all its members. Thus,

$$A = \{Patty, John, Donna, Harry, Bonnie\}$$

constitutes a definition of the set A. Sets are often represented with a picture called a *Venn diagram.* Using this procedure, the set A is represented in the following way:

Several types of sets deserve special mention. A *universal set* is the totality of all objects or individuals from which a particular set is drawn; in other words, the *population.* Thus, all elementary-level teachers within a particular school district in California constitute a set. But the universal set in this case might be all elementary school teachers in the state of California. Using the Venn diagram we can show the set of teachers (T) in the school district and the universal set U of all teachers in California as follows:

Another special kind of set is the *null* or *empty* set. This set has no members. The empty set serves a function similar to the number zero, and will be useful in our discussion of probability. Still another type is the *subset,* which is a part of the original set. For example, one subset of the teaching staff of a particular high school would be the male teachers. The notion of a subset can be represented using the Venn diagram as follows, where B is the set of teachers and M is the subset of male teachers:

Two simple set operations are of considerable use to us. These are the *union* and *intersection* of sets. For example, let's consider a particular elementary classroom in which 10 students have brown hair, 12 have black hair, and 8 have blond hair. The set of all 30 students in the classroom is A. The three subsets of A are B (brown-haired students), C (black-haired students), and D (blond-haired students). The *union* of two sets or subsets forms a new set which contains all the members of the two sets. That is, the union of subsets B and C, consists of all students in the class who have brown or black hair. The set consisting of all students with brown or blond hair contains subsets B and D, and, of course, A is the union of subsets B, C, and D and consists of all students in the class. Figure 7-1 shows these unions.

The *intersection* of sets shows a different kind of property. The intersection of two sets contains all individuals who are members of both sets simultaneously. In the example just discussed, the intersection of the subsets B and C is an empty set because the intersection of sets B and C contains no elements. This is because each student is considered to have only one hair color. There are probably some intersecting subsets of students in the class, however. For example, two subsets of A might be E and F, where E is the set of 15 fast readers and F is the set of 15 slow readers. It might happen that 4 of the 15 slow readers have blond hair. Thus the intersection of D (blond-haired stu-

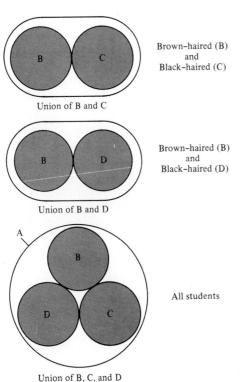

Union of B and C

Brown–haired (B)
and
Black–haired (C)

Union of B and D

Brown–haired (B)
and
Black–haired (D)

All students

Union of B, C, and D

FIGURE 7-1
Venn diagrams showing union of subsets to form new sets.

dents) and F (slow readers) contains the four blond-haired slow readers. This intersection of the subsets D and F is represented in the shaded area of the following Venn diagram:

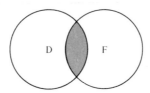

We saw that there were four children in the intersection of D and F. But how many are in the union of those two sets? Here we want to know the number of children who are either blond or slow readers. We said earlier that set D contained 8 blond-haired children and that set F contained 15 slow readers. However, four of the slow readers also have blond hair, so if we add the number of children in both sets, 8 + 15 = 23, we will have counted the children in the intersection twice. Therefore, we take the four children who are in the intersection away from the total of 23, and we have 19 children who are either blond or slow readers, or both blond and slow readers. The union of sets D and F is the shaded area in the Venn diagram in Figure 7-2.

Probability

Probability is very important to statistical inference. Sometimes the study of probability seems formidable to students in research methods courses. Yet it is encountered daily in our lives, and the concepts involved can be quite simple. For example, the forecast for tomorrow's weather might be "There is a 25 percent chance of rain." What this means is that when the conditions presently found have existed in the past, it has rained one out of four times, or 25 percent of the time. Or, to put it another way, when the set containing days in the past with the same conditions is examined, it is found that rain occurred on 25 percent of the days. This may also be expressed as ¼ or .25. This last way of indicating probability, the *proportion,* is used more than fractions or percentages, and is the method used in this text.

Those who are familiar with sports have surely seen many applications of

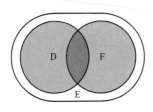

F = 15 slow readers

D = 8 blonds

Intersection of D and F = 4 blond slow readers

E = (15 slow readers) + (8 blonds) − (4 intersection of D and F) = 19

FIGURE 7-2
Venn diagram showing intersection of slow readers with blond students.

probability. The batting average of baseball players is a good example. A player who is hitting .300 has in the past hit the ball safely 3 out of every 10 times he has been at bat. Thus, assuming his batting skill remains the same, the probability that he will hit safely in his next turn at the plate is .30. In basketball we often hear the shooting percentage discussed. This refers to the number of shots taken at the basket which actually go through the hoop. That is, a player who is shooting 80 percent from the foul line can be expected to score 8 out of 10 shots from there, and the probability that he will make a single foul shot is .80.

Let's take an example from research of a situation involving probabilities. Suppose a psychologist claims to be able to look at a drawing made by a first-grade child and determine whether the child who drew it is a boy or a girl (the child's name does not appear on the picture). The psychologist proceeds to select one drawing at random and announces, "It's obvious that this picture was drawn by a boy." If she is correct this one time, does this mean that the psychologist can do as she claims?

To answer this question we need to determine the probability of guessing correctly who drew the picture. Stated another way, we would like to determine the probability that the psychologist was correct by chance alone. For any given child, the psychologist can be right or wrong in her response to the picture. If she is guessing randomly each time, she should be correct by chance about one time in two. Therefore,

$$p \text{ (correct decision)} = \frac{\text{correct outcome}}{\text{correct or incorrect}} = \frac{1}{2} = .5$$

and the probability of being correct is .5.

These ideas can be readily generalized using sets. We begin by defining *sample space* as a set that contains all possible outcomes of a simple experiment. In the experiment of guessing the sex of the student from a drawing, the sample space includes all answers (correct or incorrect) for all the pictures in the set. The sample space contains all the *sample points,* or *elements,* which are outcomes. A specific type of sample point, such as "correct" or "incorrect," is called an *event.* Thus, in general situations the probability of some event A occurring is

$$p \text{ (A)} = \frac{\text{number of sample points representing the event A}}{\text{total number of sample points in the sample space}}$$

The probability of A might be viewed as the proportion of outcomes that will result in event A over the long run. That is, if we repeated our experiment of determining the sex of the students from their drawings many times, we would expect the proportion of correct responses by chance alone to approach .5. But in a small number of trials, say four or five, the observed proportion of correct choices might be somewhat higher or lower than .5. To illustrate this idea, try flipping a coin. The probability of getting a head in any one flip of a coin is .5. Yet, we could flip a coin 10 times and only get 2 or 3 heads. If we flipped it a thousand times, however, we would be surprised if about half of the outcomes were not heads.

We can determine probabilities before or after the data are collected. Let's consider again the experiment in which the psychologist guesses the sex of the child who drew a picture. We know that the probability of being right strictly by guessing is .5 before we run the experiment because there are two equally likely outcomes, only one of which will occur each time. This kind of probability is called the *a priori* or *theoretical* probability. Now suppose we actually ran the experiment with 12 children and the psychologist was right 8 times and wrong 4 times. Based upon these data, we could compute another kind of probability, the *empirical* or *past performance* probability. From the results of the experiment with 12 children we would say that the probability that the psychologist would be correct in future trials is .67 if she is correct for 8 of 12 pictures. Weather forecasting probabilities, batting averages, and basketball shooting accuracy are examples of empirical probabilities.

Sets, Probability, and Inference in Research

We can use these relatively simple ideas to gain a perspective on how researchers make inferences. Let us consider a single question from a multiple-choice test in which there are five response options: *a, b, c, d,* or *e.* Only *d* is correct. We can see from the set of responses below that *d* is one of five choices in the set of all responses.

{*a b c d e*}

If a student who knows nothing about the subject makes a wild guess, the probability that the guess will be correct is only ⅕, or .20. If the student's response is correct, we therefore *infer* that the student knows the subject because the probability of guessing correctly is only .20. In other words, the probability of getting the item wrong is much greater (.80, to be exact) than the probability of getting it right. We could be wrong in our inference, but without the advantage of any additional information, our best guess must be based on probability.

To go back to our question about whether the psychologist can determine the sex of the student who drew a picture, we know that if the psychologist were guessing, each time she would have a .5 theoretical probability of being right. Over many trials she should be right about half the time. Therefore, we are not impressed by one correct decision. If she were correct much more than half the time, we might *infer* that the psychologist can do what she says she can do. We are able to make inferences using probability. In educational and behavioral research we attempt to make inferences about such things as instructional strategies, counseling techniques, instructional aids, and so forth, and to do this we depend on the concept of probability.

Another useful application of probability with interval or ratio data is to use

areas under the curve in a distribution. For example, if the scores on an aptitude test are distributed normally with a mean of 50 and a standard deviation
of 10, the resulting distribution looks like the one displayed in Figure 7-3.
Since the distribution of scores is normal, we know from Table B-2 in Appendix B that about 84 percent of the scores in the distribution fall below the score
60 (which is 1 standard deviation greater than the mean and equal to a z score
of $+1.00$). Thus the area under the curve between the lowest possible score on
the test and the score of 60 is about 84 percent and the area under the curve for
scores which exceed 60 is 16 percent. The probability that a randomly sampled
person from the group taking the test would have a score in excess of 60 is thus
.16.

Random Sampling

Samples from populations can be conveniently described using a set approach.
For example, in a study of a single year's graduates from a college of engineering, a sample of 75 out of the total of 150 graduates was chosen. The whole
population of 150 graduates comprised the universal set U, and the 75 in the
sample formed set G as represented in the following Venn diagram:

Drawing a sample such as this from a population can be done in a number of
ways. The first 75 students on a prepared list of graduates could be chosen, or
the graduates who remained in the state (and were therefore most accessible)
could be selected. Another method would be to take 75 of the students known
by a professor who wants to participate in the study. None of these procedures

FIGURE 7-3
Normally distributed aptitude-test scores.

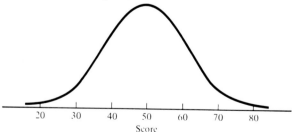

is entirely satisfactory because they all contain the potential for biasing the results of the study. The best way to avoid systematic bias in choosing a sample is to select a random sample.

A *random sample*, as we mentioned in Chapter 6, is one in which each member of the population has an equal probability of being chosen for the sample. Also, in a random sample, the selection of one member of the population does not affect the chances of any other member to be chosen. Random sampling is usually accomplished by doing the following:

1 Carefully define the population to be studied.

2 Make a list of all members in the population and number each member.

3 Randomly select a set of numbers sufficient for the desired size of the sample.

4 Determine membership in the sample by choosing individuals from the population list whose numbers have been selected randomly in step 3.

Of the four steps, step 3 requires elaboration. The most common way of accomplishing the third step is by using a table of random numbers like the one in Table B.1 of Appendix B. Random-number tables are specially constructed so that all numbers in them occur with equal probability. Thus, using this method, members of the population are selected into the sample with equal probability. Tables of random numbers may be used in the following way.

Step 1 Determine a method of reading numbers of the desired number of digits from the table. In the example where we must select 75 of the 150 graduate engineers, numbers between 1 and 150 are needed. Therefore, numbers of at least three digits must be selected from the table.

Step 2 Randomly choose a starting point in the table.

Step 3 Proceed in an orderly, predetermined fashion to extract numbers from the table for use in identifying the sample. Ignore numbers which are outside the range of those included on the population list.

Although we can reasonably expect that a random sample will be representative of the population, there is no guarantee that this will be true. It is possible to get an occasional random sample that gives a very biased view of the population. Yet in the long run random samples will tend to represent the population rather accurately, and fluctuations among sample estimates can be understood fairly well using some of the statistical techniques that we will discuss in this chapter.

PROBLEMS FOR THOUGHT AND DISCUSSION

1 Draw Venn diagrams to illustrate the following:

  a All men are mortal

    This is a man

    Therefore, this is a mortal.

b All fish in the sea

Some fish have scales

Some fish have gills

Some fish have gills and scales

Some fish have neither gills nor scales.

2 Indicate whether each of the groups listed below is an empty set, a universal set, or a subset.

a Teachers who are male in the population of teachers

b All cats who are also dogs

c Blond-haired policemen

d All mothers

e All students at a college

f History professors from the population of professors who teach at a particular college.

3 A recruiter for the Foreign Service is interested in hiring several employees who speak English and either French or German for a special assignment. There are 40 applicants for the positions. They are fluent in languages as follows:

A 17 speak French

B 21 speak German

C 20 speak English

Of those who speak French or German, 9 speak French and English, 8 speak German and English, 4 speak French, German, and English, and 1 speaks French and German only.

a Draw a Venn diagram showing population of applicants and the intersection of A, B, and C.

b How many applicants are in the intersection of A and B, A and C, and B and C?

c How many applicants are in the union of A and B, A and C, B and C, and A, B, and C?

d Name the set and tell how many applicants are actually eligible to hold the position in terms of language fluency.

e What is the probability that an applicant is eligible for the position in terms of the requirement that they speak English and either German or French?

4 In a recent mayoral election, there was a mix-up in the order of placement of names on the voting machine. Precinct workers could not remember whether the name of candidate A or Candidate B had been placed in the first position during the voting period. When the votes were totaled, the candidate whose name was in the first position on the machine had received 52 percent of the vote, and the second candidate had gotten 46 percent. The remaining votes had gone to a third candidate. In order to help solve the problem, a random sample of 50 of the 511 registered voters in the precinct who had cast their ballots on election day was surveyed. In the random sample, 27 said they had voted for A, 21 said they had voted for B, and the remaining 2 said their choice was C. On the basis of statistical inference and probability, who should have been declared the winner in the precinct? Why?

2 Which of the following would be biased samples of the population of college students at a state university? Why?

a A random sample of students buying tickets to see a movie presented by the student union

b A random sample of juniors voting for their class president

c A random sample of students registered for classes

d A sample of students leaving Gate D of the football stadium after a game

3 Randomly select a sample of 10 names from the 30 listed below using the table of random numbers (Table B.1) in Appendix B. If several samples of 10 names are chosen, should any one of the names be expected to appear on every list? Why? How many male and female names would be expected to occur on each list if half the names are male?

James	Alice	Len	Karen	Larry	Harry
Pete	Susan	Bill	John	Donna	Charles
Carol	Sandra	Patsy	Steven	Matt	Anne
Joe	Ellen	Sara	Marie	Robert	Donald
Fred	Mike	Joyce	Kate	Angela	Carolyn

SAMPLING DISTRIBUTIONS

Until now, when we referred to distributions we were talking about collections of individual scores. At this point we must develop ideas about another kind of distribution that is made up of *estimates.* For example, let us say that we are studying IQ scores in a population. We are interested in estimating the population mean (μ). To do this we select a random sample of 10 people from the population and administer the IQ test to each of them. Then we compute the mean of the sample and use it to estimate the mean of the population. We know that with this method our estimate will not be perfect, so just to make sure that we have done a good job of estimating, we take another random sample and compute another mean, and then we do it again, and again, until we have a large number of estimates of the parameter mean computed from samples of 10. This collection of means forms a distribution of estimators of the true population mean. Such a distribution of estimators is called a *sampling distribution.* We could also develop sampling distributions of other estimators such as variances and correlation coefficients.

The sampling distribution of the mean has some very useful properties. For example, no matter what the shape of the underlying distribution of scores, *the sampling distribution of the mean will tend to be a normal distribution with a mean of* μ. This tendency of the mean ($\overline{X}$) to form a normal distribution around μ, known as the *central limit theorem,* will apply when sample size is reasonably large. Using the curves in Figure 7-4 let us illustrate this property of estimates of the mean always to be normally distributed around the mean of the population. First, look at distribution 1. Imagine that we were taking several random samples from this population of scores. Our random procedure would lead us to take some scores from below the value of μ and some from above each time. The mean of each sample of 10 scores will sometimes fall above μ, other times below μ, but most of the time close to μ. Only rarely will values very much above or below μ be obtained. Therefore, our distribution of means ($\overline{X}$'s) around μ will tend to take on a bell, or normal, shape. You should be able to see that this would also be the case for the *rectangular* and *U-shaped* distributions of scores (distributions 2 and 3 in Figure 7-4).

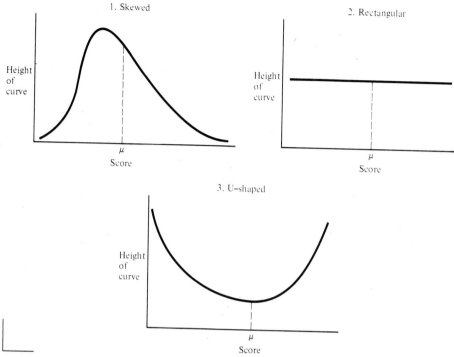

FIGURE 7-4
Three nonnormal population distributions of scores.

Another very useful thing to know about the sampling distribution of means is that the standard deviation of the distribution, called the *standard error of the mean,* is equal to the standard deviation of the distribution of scores divided by the square root of the sample size. Thus, if $\sigma_{\bar{x}}$ is the standard error of the mean, σ_x is the standard deviation of the distribution of X scores, and n is the size of the samples used to estimate $\bar{X}$, then

$$\sigma_{\bar{x}} = \frac{\sigma_x}{\sqrt{n}}$$

Now let us tie this all together using an example with scores on a test of verbal reasoning ability. The distribution of scores displayed in Figure 7-5 includes all the scores in the population. It is nearly normal, and has a mean of 25 and a standard deviation of 5. (In reality, we would typically not have all this information about the population, but it is included here for the sake of clarifying the discussion.) We randomly select a sample of 25 persons from the population and use the average of their scores to estimate μ. Then we select another sample, and another. Each sample yields a mean which is an estimate

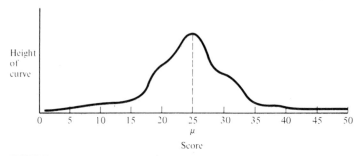

FIGURE 7-5
Population distribution of scores on a verbal reasoning test with $\mu = 25$ and $\sigma = 5$.

of μ. The means from these samples form the distribution pictured in Figure 7-6. Most of these estimates fall between 23 and 27. This is because the standard deviation of the sampling distribution equals 1.0. That is,

$$\sigma_{\bar{x}} = \frac{\sigma_x}{\sqrt{n}} = \frac{5}{\sqrt{25}} = 1.0$$

Since the distribution of these estimated means around a population mean is normal, the properties of the unit normal curve in Table B.2 in Appendix B are applicable. Therefore, 2 standard errors above and below the mean will include nearly all the estimates (about 95 percent of them), and that is why so many of the estimates of μ fall between 23 and 27 in Figure 7-6.

It should be relatively easy to see what would happen if we increased the size of the sample. Intuitively, it should be obvious that as more of the population is included in the sample, estimates should be closer to the population

FIGURE 7-6
Sampling distribution of means on the verbal reasoning test for samples of 25 individuals from a large population having a mean of 25 and a standard deviation of 5.0.

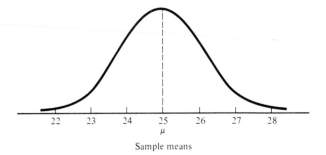

Sample means

value. Statisticians call this property *precision,* and more precise estimates come from larger samples. This property can also be seen by what happens to the standard error of the mean. As the sample size gets larger, the standard error of the mean gets smaller. For example, earlier we used a sample of 25 and computed the standard error of the mean to be 1.0 in the sampling distribution, based upon the population of reasoning scores depicted in Figure 7-5. If, instead, we had used samples of 100,

$$\sigma_{\bar{x}} = \frac{\sigma_x}{\sqrt{n}} = \frac{5}{\sqrt{100}} = .5$$

Since the standard error with a sample size of 100 is 0.5, about 95 percent of our estimates of the mean would fall between 24 and 26. Had samples of 10,000 been used, the estimates would have been even more precise. It should be clear from this that every sampling distribution refers to samples of a particular size. Thus, there is a sampling distribution for estimates based on samples of 5 scores, and another sampling distribution when 25 scores are used to estimate the parameter.

To this point we have been emphasizing $\bar{X}$ as an estimator of μ as if we knew the population mean and variance and the population standard error of the mean ($\sigma_{\bar{x}}$). However, usually we do not know the standard error of the mean in the population sampling distribution, nor do we know the standard deviation in the population of scores. A good estimate of $\sigma_{\bar{x}}$ in those cases is based upon the estimated standard deviation, as follows:

$$S_{\bar{x}} = \frac{S_x}{\sqrt{n}}$$

$S_{\bar{x}}$ is an estimate of $\sigma_{\bar{x}}$, the standard error of the mean in the population, and S_x is an estimate of σ_x, the standard deviation of scores in the population. The ability to estimate properties of sampling distributions of population is basic to inferential statistics.

STATISTICAL TESTS OF HYPOTHESES

Now we are ready to apply all we have learned about inference and probability to test hypotheses statistically. In Chapter 1, we discussed the difference between inductive and deductive reasoning. It is *inductive reasoning* that is used in the statistical testing of hypotheses—that is, reasoning from the specific to the general. More precisely, it is reasoned that the characteristics found in a sample reflect the characteristics of the total population. Thus statistical hypotheses are about parameters. (It might be a good idea to review the brief discussion of null and alternative hypotheses in Chapter 3 at this point.)

For example, consider the question of whether the average score on the verbal portion of the Graduate Record Examination (GRE-V) at State University is equal to the national average on the GRE-V of 500. A researcher wishes to test the hypothesis that the graduate students at State University average 500 on the examination. The null hypothesis, then, is that there is no difference between the average GRE-V score in the population and the average GRE-V at State University. It should be evident to the reader that this null hypothesis is really about the population of graduate students at State University, not just those in the sample that will be used to test the hypothesis. Therefore, the null hypothesis is stated as follows:

$$H_0 : \mu_s = 500$$

where H_0 is the symbol for null hypotheses, and μ_s is the mean of the population of graduate students at State University on the verbal portion of the GRE. The alternative hypothesis is stated statistically as

$$H_1 : \mu_s \neq 500$$

In the above, H_1 is the symbol for alternative hypotheses, and $\neq$ means "does not equal."

We test statistical hypotheses using estimates obtained from samples. To test our null hypothesis concerning the mean performance of students on the GRE-V at State University, we select a sample of 100 students from the population of students. We then compare the estimate of the mean obtained with the value of the mean if the null hypothesis is true (500) and decide whether to accept or reject the null hypothesis. We use the properties of the sampling distribution for the mean to make the decision.

Using Sampling Distributions in Hypothesis Testing

To visualize the sampling distribution of the mean, imagine that means are computed from several random samples of 100 students from State University. The resulting distribution of means obtained is the sampling distribution of the mean with a mean of μ_s. Most of the $\overline{X}$'s in the sampling distribution would be fairly close to μ_s. Only rarely would a value of a sample mean vary much from the parameter mean. Figure 7-7 shows the sampling distribution of the mean if the null hypothesis is true.

In our test of the null hypothesis that $\mu_s = 500$, we will not be taking a large number of random samples to form a sampling distribution. Rather, we compute a mean from only one sample, and we assume that since the means of most samples are close to the population mean, the mean of our one sample should likewise be close to the population mean. Of course, we could be wrong in making this assumption, but probably we are not. To carry this line of reasoning further, since our mean should be close to the population mean, if $\overline{X}$ is very far from 500, we will infer that μ_s is not equal to 500 and will consequently reject the null hypothesis.

We do not know, when we test it, whether the null hypothesis is true or not.

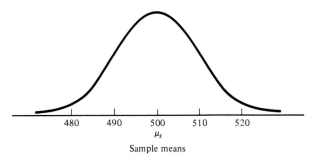

480   490   500   510   520

μ_s

Sample means

FIGURE 7-7
Sampling distribution of means from samples of 100 students
who took the GRE-V subtest.

If we did, we would not have to do the study. Furthermore, the assumption that our sample possesses characteristics similar to those of the population might be erroneous and might lead us to make inferences that are not correct. Figure 7-8 shows two cases, one where the null hypothesis is true and one where the null hypothesis is not true. For this example, let us change our null hypothesis slightly to say that the population mean at State University is less than or equal to 500 on the GRE-V. The alternative hypothesis would be that the population mean is greater than 500. We can say this symbolically as follows:

$$H_0 : \mu_s \leq 500$$
$$H_1 : \mu_s \hbar 500$$

where is read "is less than or equal to," and $\hbar$ is read "is greater than."
This will result in a directional hypothesis test because the relationship of the State University mean to the national mean is established beforehand and stated in the alternative hypothesis. Notice that in case 1 in Figure 7-8, the mean of the population sampling distribution is exactly 500, and means computed from random samples of that population will probably be fairly close to 500. Since the standard deviation of GRE-V scores is 100 and we are going to take a random sample of 100 scores from the population, we can substitute these values into the formula for the standard error of the mean as follows:

$$\sigma_{\bar{x}} = \frac{\sigma_x}{\sqrt{n}}$$

$$\sigma_{\bar{x}} = \frac{100}{\sqrt{100}} = 10.0$$

Using this information and the properties of the normal distribution, we can

Case 1. Null hypothesis that $\mu_s = 500$ is true.

null hypothesis
"no difference"

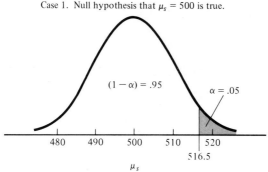

Case 2. Null hypothesis is not true; μ_s is really 520.

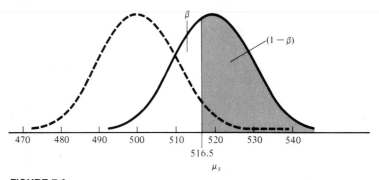

FIGURE 7-8
Two possible sampling distributions in which the null hypothesis is true (case 1) and false (case 2).

say, for example, that if we sampled repeatedly, about 68 percent of the randomly sampled means of GRE-V scores will fall between 510 and 490 when the sample size is 100.

To test the null hypothesis, we will choose a certain criterion value of $\overline{X}$. If our sample $\overline{X}$ is beyond that, we will reject the null hypothesis. Let us say that the criterion is that the sample mean must fall within the area that contains 95 percent of the sample means when the null hypothesis is true. If the sample means falls in the remaining 5 percent of the curve, we will reject the null hypothesis because such a sample would be unlikely from a population with a mean of 500. To set our criterion, we look up in Table B.2 the z score for which the area under the curve to the left of that score is .95, or 95 percent. We find that this z score is 1.65. Now, since 1 standard deviation in our sampling distribution is equal to 10.0, which was found by computing the standard error of the mean, 1.65 standard deviations is equal to

$$1.65(\sigma_{\bar{x}}) = 1.65(10.0) = 16.5$$

Therefore, 1.65 standard deviations above μ_s in our sampling distribution in case 1 shown in Figure 7-8 is 516.5, and any sample mean above that value would result in a rejection of H_0, while a sample mean below 516.5 would support H_0. Notice that in Figure 7-8, we have called the area under the curve representing the region of rejection α, and we have set it at .05, or 5 percent, of the total area. The region of acceptance is therefore $1 - \alpha$, or 95 percent, of the sampling distribution. We could have a sample value in the region of rejection even when the null hypothesis is true, but the probability of that happening is only .05.

Now look at case 2 in Figure 7-8, where the null hypothesis is not true. Most of our random sample estimates of μ would be greater than 500. In fact, they would cluster around 520. Therefore, most of our sample estimates of the population mean would lead us to reject the null hypothesis because the population mean is above 516.5. The critical value we have established upon which to base our decision about the null hypothesis is a z score of 1.65, which corresponds to a mean of 516.5. The region of the sampling distribution of $\bar{X}$ above the critical value of 516.5 is the area representing a correct decision. In case 2, we have identified this area as $1 - \beta$, which represents the probability of correctly rejecting the null hypothesis. Some samples would not lead to a correct decision. These samples would come from the region identified as β in case 2 of Figure 7-8.

Errors and Decision Making

We never know whether the null or alternative hypothesis is true in reality. If the null hypothesis is true, then we will have the situation depicted in case 1. If the null hypothesis is not true, case 2 illustrates the situation. In either case, we are likely to make the correct decision, but it is possible to be misled by our sample. The following four-cell table summarizes the four possible results for testing any hypothesis.

		Nature of reality	
		H_0 true	H_0 false
Decision about H_0	Reject H_0	Type I error (Probability $= \alpha$)	Correct decision (Probability $= 1 - \beta$)
	Accept H_0	Correct decision (Probability $= 1 - \alpha$)	Type II error (Probability $= \beta$)

If the null hypothesis is rejected, and it is true in reality, an error is made. The probability of making such an error is α. The incorrect rejection of the null hypothesis is known as a *Type I error*. If the null hypothesis is true and the sample statistic suggests not rejecting it, a correct decision is made. Furthermore, when the alternative hypothesis is true in reality and the sample leads to a rejection of the null hypothesis, a correct decision is made. We refer to the probability of making this correct decision as the *power* of the experiment. A *Type II error* occurs when the alternative hypothesis is true and the sample does not support a rejection of the null hypothesis. The probability of a Type II error is equal to β. Since we do not know the nature of reality, it is important to be aware, each time a decision is made about a hypothesis, that the decision might be incorrect. For example, when the null hypothesis is rejected, the decision could be correct, or a Type 1 error. On the other hand, if the null hypothesis is accepted, the decision could be a correct one, or a Type II error.

We can manipulate the probability of making a Type I error and power by changing the value of α. For example, if we make α larger by increasing it from .05 to .10, we will increase the probability of making a Type I error, but we will also increase power. This reduces β, the probability of making a Type II error. Figure 7-9 illustrates this relationship. Notice that when α is increased from .05 to .10, there is a decrease in the size of the area representing the probability of making a Type II error. The power can be increased and probability of

FIGURE 7-9
The effect on β of increasing α from .05 to .10. (*Note:* There will only be a real possibility of either α or β in any given investigation.)

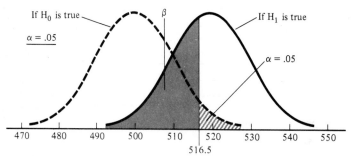

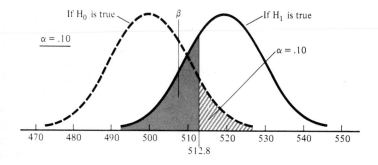

making a Type II error can be decreased by increasing the sample size. This is illustrated in Figure 7-10 with the population of GRE-V scores we have been discussing. It can be seen that when the size of the sample is 100, the size of β is smaller than with a sample size of 25. This is because the value of $\sigma_{\bar{x}}$ is smaller for a sample size of 100 than it is for a sample size of 25.

Since the researcher can establish the level of α and sample size, he or she has some control over the risk of making a Type I or Type II error in an experiment. Very often, especially when the sample size is not very large, α is set at the .05 level for hypothesis tests in the behavioral sciences and education. Occasionally, it is desirable to increase the probability of one type of error over the other, and in those situations the researcher alters the level of α to .10 or .01 or whatever value seems appropriate. For example, if treatment with a dangerous drug may cause relief of symptoms in terminally ill patients, the researcher might feel that to miss a potentially effective drug by making a Type

FIGURE 7-10
The effect on β of increasing sample size from 25 to 100. (*Note:* Either a Type I or a Type II will be a real possibility in any given analysis.)

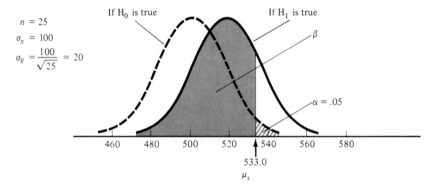

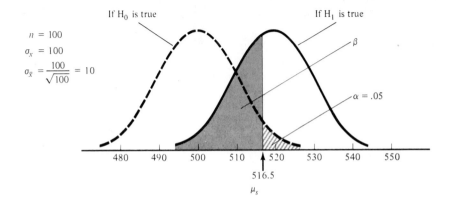

II error might be more undesirable than to attribute beneficial effects to the drug when there really are none by making a Type I error. In such a case, the researcher might increase α to as high as .10 or .15.

one tail *two tail*

Directional versus Nondirectional Tests

We have been discussing hypothesis tests as if all of α, the region of rejection, is in one tail of the sampling distribution. However, the more astute reader has probably realized that we have only been testing whether our sample statistic was very much above the parameter value to this point. Indeed, we had to write directional null and alternative hypotheses before the discussion could progress. But the GRE-V scores at State University could have averaged below 500 as well as above 500. To determine whether the mean was *either above or below* 500, the hypotheses should have been stated as

$$H_0 : \mu_s = 500$$

$$H_1 : \mu_s \neq 500$$

Directional hypotheses postulate that the size of the parameter will be in a specific direction from the value in the null hypothesis. In nondirectional hypotheses, no suppositions are made about the size of the parameters in the alternative hypotheses. Directional tests of hypotheses are made by putting α in one tail of the test distribution. This has been illustrated in Figures 7-8, 7-9, and 7-10. However, nondirectional hypotheses concerning one or two group means are generally tested using two tails of the sampling distribution, and α is split evenly between the two tails. This is illustrated in Figure 7-11 with the unit normal distribution. Since the point on the unit normal curve below which 2.5 percent of the distribution falls is found to be -1.96 in Table B.2, that becomes the point of decision (*critical value*) for low values of the test statistic. That is, any value of z less than -1.96 would result in a rejection of the null hypothesis. The point on the unit normal curve below which 97.5 percent falls

FIGURE 7-11
For a two-tail test when $\alpha = .05$; one-half of α is placed in the upper tail (.025) and one-half in the lower tail (.025).

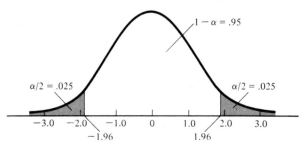

will have 2.5 percent above it in the tail of the distribution. This point is found to be +1.96. This should not be surprising because the unit normal distribution is symmetrical. It should be obvious to the reader that between −1.96 and +1.96 lies 95 percent of the area under the curve (because 97.5 − 2.5 = 95.0).

Most hypothesis tests in education and the behavioral sciences are nondirectional. Typical applications involve comparing a new treatment to a traditional one, or one group to another, and there is a possibility that the mean for one group could be higher or lower than for the other. Therefore, many applications of directional hypotheses and one-tailed tests are misdirected in these cases. It should be mentioned at this point, however, that some statistical procedures are designed to test nondirectional hypotheses using one-tailed tests. Some of these will be identified briefly in this chapter.

An Illustration of Hypothesis Testing

Now we are ready to test the null hypothesis we proposed earlier in this section that the mean GRE-V score at State University is 500. We stated this hypothesis as

$$H_0 : \mu_s \neq 500$$

and the nondirectional alternative is

$$H_1 : \mu_s \neq 500$$

where μ_s is the mean of the GRE-V scores in the population of university students on the test. Since the hypothesis test is nondirectional in nature, we are recognizing that μ_s could be less than, greater than, or equal to 500. We decide to test the hypothesis at the .05 level of α using the properties of the unit normal curve since we know that sampling distributions of $\bar{X}$'s around μ_s will be normal. We next decide to use a random sample of 100 scores to test the hypothesis, and this random sample has a mean of 521.4. The test publisher has reported that the standard deviation of the GRE-V test is 100, and we compute the standard error of the mean as follows:

$$\sigma_{\bar{x}} = \frac{\sigma_x}{\sqrt{n}} = \frac{100}{100} = 10$$

Furthermore, as has been illustrated in Figure 7-11, Table B.2 in Appendix B indicates that the area under the curve to the left of −1.96 standard deviations below the mean and to the right of 1.96 standard deviations above the mean comprises 5 percent of the total area under the curve. Therefore, any value of z below −1.96 or above +1.96 will result in rejection of the null hypothesis. Now we use the formula for z scores in a sampling distribution to tell us how far above or below the population mean our sample mean of 521.4 is. Thus

$$z = \frac{\overline{X} - \mu}{\sigma_{\overline{x}}} = \frac{521.4 - 500}{10} = 2.14$$

Since the z value of 2.14 is greater than 1.96, the value falls into the upper rejection region and we reject the null hypothesis. Therefore, we make the inference that it is not likely that the population of graduate students at State University averages 500. The alternative hypothesis that the students at State University have a different mean GRE-V score than the national mean is supported, and we say that the difference is *statistically significant*. By statistical significance, we mean only that the results would be unlikely to occur by chance if the null hypothesis were true. It does not mean that the result is important or noteworthy in any other sense. For example, with a large enough sample, a difference in IQ of a single point between two groups might be statistically significant. Yet such a small difference is not meaningful in terms of the way IQ scores are measured. A researcher might reasonably ignore such a statistically significant finding.

STEPS IN MAKING TESTS OF STATISTICAL HYPOTHESES

We shall summarize here the steps that are taken to test a statistical hypothesis. The reader would do well to relate these steps to the description of the test of the hypothesis in the last section.

Step 1 *State the null and alternative hypotheses statistically.* The hypotheses are stated using parameters. The hypotheses should be nondirectional unless there is good reason to believe that they should not be. Most hypotheses in the behavioral sciences and education are properly stated as nondirectional. Notice that statistical hypotheses may be stated about any parameter of a population. For example, it may be hypothesized that the variances of two different treatment groups are equal (i.e., $H_0 : \sigma_1^2 = \sigma_2^2$) or that the correlation between attitude toward school (X) and school achievement (Y) is zero for third graders (i.e., $H_0 : \rho_{xy} = 0$).

Step 2 *Identify the population for study and determine a procedure for obtaining a sample.* For most purposes, simple random sampling is best. At times, stratified or cluster samples may be used. However, since these are often not random samples from the entire population, caution must be used in interpreting the results.

Step 3 *Determine the appropriate statistical test to be used and set the level of α.* Various statistical tests are available to use for different types of hypotheses. Some are based on the unit normal distribution. Such tests may utilize z scores to test the null hypothesis. Hypotheses about *categorical data* (variables measured on a nominal scale) can be tested using the sampling distributions of χ^2 (read "chi square"). Chi-square tests are covered later in this chapter. Some of the distributions from the family of χ^2 distributions are shown in Figure 7-12. As the size of the problem being investigated becomes larger (that is, as the number of categories in the data increases), the *degrees of freedom*

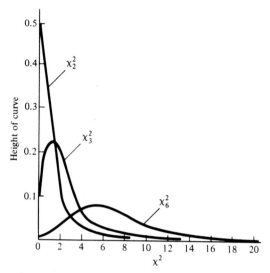

FIGURE 7-12
Curves from the family of chi-square distributions.

(df) increase. Notice in Figure 7-12 that as degrees of freedom increase, the chi-square distributions tend to look like normal distributions.*

Hypotheses concerning two means may sometimes be tested with z scores, but usually the family of t distributions shown in Figure 7-13 is used. Here, degrees of freedom are related to the sample sizes being used. Again, as degrees of freedom increase, t distributions tend to resemble a normal distribution.

Another family of curves commonly encountered in statistical inference is the family of F curves, some of which are shown in Figure 7-14. As with the t and the χ^2 curves, increasing the degrees of freedom changes the shape of the F curves. There are two types of degrees of freedom to be concerned about when using F curves. Specific formulas for F tests and degrees of freedom are again topics too involved for thorough coverage in this text. However, some illustrations of hypothesis testing using the F family of curves are included.

The choice of a statistic to be used for the hypothesis test depends on (1) the scale of measurement of the variables, (2) the parameter of interest in the hypothesis, and (3) the distributional and other assumptions that can reasonably be made about the data. No matter which sampling distribution is used, the testing procedure is identical. The total area under the curve is considered to represent a probability of 1.00. A portion of the area under the curve is desig-

---

* A classic source of information about chi square and other tests of categorical data is Siegel, S. 1956. *Nonparametric statistics for the behavioral sciences.* New York: McGraw-Hill.

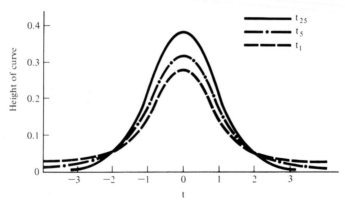

FIGURE 7-13
Curves from the family of *t* distributions.

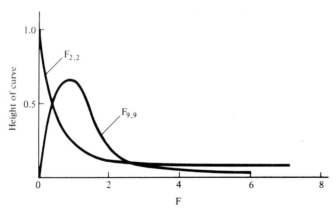

FIGURE 7-14
Curves from the family of *F* distributions.

nated a region of rejection for the null hypothesis, and a decision rule is stated which designates the critical values of the test statistic. The reader is referred to an introductory statistics text for more complete descriptions of the χ^2, t, and F families of curves and how to use them.

Step 4 *The sample data are collected* according to the sampling plan, and the value of the statistic is computed.

Step 5 The value of the statistic obtained is compared to the *critical values* of the statistic. If the sample value falls within the acceptance region, the null hypothesis is supported. If it falls into the critical region, the null hypothesis is rejected.

Illustrations of Hypothesis Tests about Group Means

Example 1

As part of a study of reasoning, a sample of male and female graduate students was given a test of conditional reasoning. Though more subjects were used in the experiment, a sample of 10 male and 10 female students is chosen here for purposes of illustration. The reasoning test consisted of 30 items that contained logical arguments. Subjects were asked whether or not the arguments were valid. The scores reported here represent the number of correct responses out of the 30 items. The null hypothesis to be tested in the study was as follows: Male subjects do not score differently from female subjects on a test of conditional reasoning. The corresponding statistical null hypothesis was

$$H_0 : \mu_M = \mu_F$$

where μ_M = the population mean of males
μ_F = the population mean of females

The alternative hypothesis, of course, was

$$H_1 : \mu_M \neq \mu_F$$

It was decided to set α at .05 and to use the following formula for t to test the null hypothesis:*

$$t = \frac{\overline{X}_1 - \overline{X}_2}{\sqrt{\dfrac{(n_1 - 1)S_1^2 + (n_2 - 1)S_2^2}{n_1 + n_2 - 2} \left(\dfrac{1}{n_1} + \dfrac{1}{n_2}\right)}}$$

where $n_1 + n_2 - 2$ = degrees of freedom, df

This formula is appropriate where the data are measured on an interval or ratio scale and are normally distributed in each population, where the subjects in the two groups are independent (not paired in some way), and where the variance of the scores is the same in both populations.

---

* For a more detailed discussion of this statistic see Glass: G. V., & Hopkins, K. D. (1984). *Statistical methods in education and psychology* (2nd ed.). Englewood Cliffs, NJ: Prentice-Hall, Chapter 12.

The data collected were as follows:

Male	Female
24	24
24	22
24	19
23	18
23	18
22	18
20	16
20	15
19	14
16	14
215	178

$$\bar{X}_M = 21.50 \qquad \bar{X}_F = 17.80$$

$$S_M^2 = 7.167 \qquad S_F^2 = 10.844$$

$$df = 10 + 10 - 2 = 18$$

Using Table B.3 we find that the critical value for rejection of the null hypothesis at the .05 level in a two-tailed test when $df = 18$ is ± 2.101.
Substituting in the formula for t, we find

$$t = \frac{21.5 - 17.8}{\sqrt{\frac{9(7.167) + 9(10.844)}{10 + 10 - 2}} \sqrt{\frac{1}{10} + \frac{1}{10}}} = 2.76$$

Since 2.76 falls beyond the acceptance region from -2.101 to $+2.101$, we reject the null hypothesis, and we therefore conclude that there is a *statistically significant* difference between the means of female and male subjects on the reasoning test.

Example 2

This study was done to see whether there was a difference in performance on the midterm and final examination in a course in elementary statistical methods. The null hypothesis was this: There is no difference in scores on the midterm and final examination in the statistics course. The statistical null hypothesis was

$$H_0 : \mu_1 - \mu_2 = 0$$

where μ_1 = the mean of the midterm
μ_2 = the mean of the final exam

The alternative hypothesis was

$$H_1 : \mu_1 - \mu_2 \neq 0$$

The scores of the 10 subjects on the two tests were as follows:

Subject	Midterm	Final	d	$(d - \bar{d})^2$
1	96	90	6	64
2	72	77	− 5	9
3	98	100	− 2	0
4	74	80	− 6	16
5	75	74	1	9
6	92	93	− 1	1
7	85	91	− 6	16
8	57	59	− 2	0
9	82	85	− 3	1
10	87	89	− 2	0
			− 20	116
			$\bar{d} = -2.0$	

where $\bar{d}$ is the difference between each student's midterm and final exam scores

Even though the hypotheses in examples 1 and 2 are similar, there is an important difference between the data in the two examples: In example 2, scores are paired. That is, there is a pair of scores for each student, one for the midterm and one for the final. In example 1, each student only had one score and there are no paired scores. Notice that in example 2, each of the scores in a midterm and final pair have something in common: They were obtained by the same student. (Paired scores can be obtained in other ways —for example, from twins, spouses, siblings, etc.)

When subjects are not paired, as in example 1, their scores are said to be *independent*. The formula for testing hypotheses about independent samples is the one for t which we used in example 1. Since the data in example 2 are paired, they are said to be *dependent*. A t test for dependent samples is therefore used when the variable is measured at an interval level and follows the normal distribution in both populations. This formula can be expressed as*

$$t = \frac{\bar{d}}{S_d / \sqrt{n}}$$

where $\bar{d}$ is the average difference between the pairs of scores, S_d is the standard deviation of the difference, and n is the number of pairs. The degrees of freedom for this statistic are $n - 1$. The difference between scores in each pair are shown in the columns to the right of the data. Since

* *Ibid.*

$\Sigma d = -20$, $\bar{d} = -20/10 = -2.0$. Using the formula for the standard-deviation-of-difference scores, we find

$$S_d = \sqrt{\frac{\Sigma(d - \bar{d})^2}{n - 1}}$$

$$= \sqrt{116/9} = \sqrt{12.89} = 3.59$$

Solving for t in the formula,

$$t = \frac{\bar{d}}{S_d/\sqrt{n}} = \frac{-2.0}{3.59/\sqrt{10}} = \frac{-2.0}{1.14} = -1.76$$

Let us assume that α is set at .05 for this example. From Table B.3, we find that for 9 degrees of freedom $t = \pm2.262$ for a two-tailed test at the .05 level (t values are obtained for the points below which 2.5 percent and above which 97.5 percent of the scores occur). Since our obtained value of t (1.76) is not less than -2.262 nor greater than $+2.262$, the null hypothesis is not rejected, and we conclude that the performance on the final examination is not different from that on the midterm.

Illustration of Hypothesis Test About Categories: The Two-Way Contingency Table

Assume that a researcher hypothesizes that there is a relationship between the sex of a teacher and the grade taught by the teacher. The researcher proceeds

TABLE 7.1
SEX-BY-GRADE-LEVEL CONTINGENCY TABLE WITH TOTALS IN THE MARGINS

	Grade level			
Teacher's sex	Elementary school	Junior high school	High school	Total
Males	15	19	20	54
Females	29	17	20	66
Total	44	36	40	120

to test this hypothesis by selecting a random sample of 120 teachers from a large metropolitan school system. These data are presented in Table 7-1.

A table containing the frequencies with which categories occur such as this is called a *contingency table*. In the study, individuals are classified according to sex and grade level taught. In the cells, or boxes, of Table 7-1 are recorded the frequencies with which each particular type of individual is observed to occur in the sample. These are called *observed frequencies*. Thus, in the sample, there are 15 male elementary school teachers, 19 male junior high school teachers, 20 male high school teachers, and so on. This particular table is called a 2 × 3 contingency table because there are two rows and three columns. Notice that the totals of each row and column are provided in the margins. These are called *marginal totals*. For example, the total number of elementary school teachers was 44, while the sample contained 36 junior high school and 40 high school teachers. Furthermore, 66 of the 120 teachers were women.

The null hypothesis for the study states that the sex of a teacher is unrelated to the grade level taught (or, to put it another way, sex of the teacher is independent of grade level). The alternative hypothesis is that there is a relationship between the two variables (they are not independent). How would the contingency table look if the null hypothesis were true? There is a simple formula for determining the cell frequencies when the null hypothesis is true. It is based on the marginal frequencies of the rows and columns. The formula is:

$$\text{cell frequency} = \frac{f_r f_c}{N}$$

where f_r = the maginal frequency of the row

f_c = the marginal frequency of the column

N = total total sample size

We call the frequencies we would obtain if the null hypothesis is true *expected frequencies*. Using the above formula, we can determine the expected frequency for the cell containing male elementary teachers in the following way:

$$\text{expected frequency of male elementary teachers} = \frac{(54)(44)}{120}$$

$$= 19.8$$

Table 7-2 shows all the expected frequencies computed using the above formula. The chi-square test is based on the differences between the observed and the expected cell frequencies. Now we are ready to test the hypothesis of independence.

TABLE 7.1
CONTINGENCY TABLE SHOWING INDEPENDENCE BETWEEN TEACHER'S SEX
AND GRADE LEVEL TAUGHT

Teacher's sex	Grade level taught			
	Elementary school	Junior high school	High school	
Males	19.8	16.2	18	54
Females	24.2	19.8	22	66
Total	44	36	40	120

Testing Independence Using Chi Square

The independence of sex and grade level can be tested by comparing the observed and expected frequencies for the six cells of the 2 × 3 contingency table. This comparison is accomplished using the chi-square (χ^2) test. To do this, we compute

$$\frac{[(\text{Observed frequency}) - (\text{expected frequency})]^2}{\text{Expected frequency}}$$

for each cell of the table. Then, we add together the six values to form the χ^2 statistic. Thus for the problem being considered,

$$\chi^2 = \frac{(15 - 19.8)^2}{19.8} + \frac{(19 - 16.2)^2}{16.2} + \frac{(20 - 18)^2}{18} + \frac{(29 - 24.2)^2}{24.2} + \frac{(17 - 19.8)^2}{19.8} + \frac{(20 - 22)^2}{22}$$

$$= 1.16 + .48 + .22 + .95 + .40 + .8$$

$$= 3.39$$

We take the same approach to making a decision about the significance of an χ^2 value as we did with a t value. That is, we determine the probability that an χ^2 value this large or larger would occur by chance if the null hypothesis were true. To do this, we refer to the χ^2 distribution. The χ^2 distribution is another statistical distribution (like z or t) for which a table has been developed to show the various percentiles of the distribution (see Table B.4 in Appendix B).

To use the table, we must first determine the degrees of freedom (*df*) associated with the χ^2 statistic we have computed. These degrees of freedom are computed by subtracting 1 from the number of rows in the contingency table and multiplying this quantity by 1 less than the number of columns in the table. Thus, in the example of teacher's sex and grade level, the degrees of freedom are found as follows:

$$df = (\text{rows} - 1)(\text{columns} - 1) = (2 - 1)(3 - 1) = 2$$

The chi-square distribution appropriate for this problem has 2 degrees of freedom.

Now we must set the significance level for the test and determine the critical value of the χ^2 statistic. If we set $\alpha = .05$, the critical value of χ^2 is the value which falls at the 95th percentile of the χ^2 distribution with 2 degrees of freedom. This value in Table B.4 is 5.991. Note that we use only one tail of the χ^2 distribution. We reject the null hypothesis only when the obtained χ^2 value exceeds 5.991.

The value of χ^2 obtained in our example is 3.39. Since this value does not exceed the critical value of the statistic, 5.991, we do not reject the hypothesis that the sex of a teacher is unrelated to the grade level taught.

Discussion of Chi-Square Tests for Contingency Tables

The study just described is fairly typical of applications of the χ^2 test of independence applied to contingency tables and illustrates some of the strengths and weaknesses of the method. On the positive side, the χ^2 test is appropriate in a great variety of research applications in which individuals are categorized in one or more ways according to a simple but well-defined process. Thus no elaborate measurement techniques are necessary and no complicated assumptions need be made about the scores of individuals (for example, that the scores follow the normal distribution). The scores are merely tallies from which frequency counts can be obtained for each cell of the contingency table.

Other factors tend to make the technique attractive. It appears to fit a great variety of research data, computation is fairly straightforward, and the interpretation of results seems simple enough. All one has to do is compute the χ^2, look up the critical value in the χ^2 table, and then, if the obtained χ^2 is significant, determine where the observed frequencies are higher or lower than expected by inspection of the contingency table.

However, the technique has some important limitations. Its very attractiveness and seeming universality encourage its application in situations where it is likely to yield little useful information. For example, it would have been difficult to determine the meaning of a significant chi square in the illustrative problem just presented if certain conditions were different. First, if sampling had not been random, the frequencies in the cells could have been the result of sampling bias. Second, if, instead of grade level taught, the ages of the students were given, we would necessarily have to lose some of this information in order to break down the data into categories of school (elementary, junior high, high school). Thus, the chi-square approach is not sensitive to degrees of differences in the independent variables. Further, a significant chi square will only tell us whether there are differences between some of the cells in terms of frequency. It will not reveal which cells are different from the others. This must be determined by additional analysis.

A Word about Nonparametric Procedures Including Chi Square

We mentioned that the chi-square procedure is used with categorical data and thus does not require an underlying normal distribution for the data. That is, the scores on the dependent variable need not be assumed to be distributed as a normal distribution. For this reason, χ^2 is considered a *sample-free* or *nonparametric* procedure.

A number of nonparametric procedures are designed for use with ordinal data. These procedures are particularly useful in situations where the appropriate measurement is at the ordinal level. Many researchers argue that measurements in the social and behavioral sciences and education are at best ordinal even though they are typically treated as interval. For example, it might be contended that intelligence, attitude, and personality scores may represent order within a group, but units of measurement for these variables would be difficult to identify. For that reason, nonparametric tests of order are often preferred by researchers. On the other hand, the *power* (i.e., the probability of detecting a difference or relationship where one exists) of nonparametric techniques tends to be lower than that of available parametric methods. For this reason, a larger sample size must be used to reduce the chance of making a Type II error. A large number of nonparametric techniques have been developed. Among the more commonly used are the median test, the sign test, the runs test, and the Kruskal-Wallis analysis of variance for ranked data. The reader is referred to texts such as Hays (1981), Siegel (1956), and Walsh (1962) for a more thorough treatment of these procedures. Before using these techniques, however, one should be aware of the strengths and limitations of each and the specific null hypothesis they were designed to test.

PROBLEMS FOR THOUGHT AND DISCUSSION

1 Imagine taking several random samples of size n and computing the mean ($\bar{X}$) for each sample from each of the population distributions that are graphed as follows. In each case, satisfy yourself that the resulting distributions of $\bar{X}$'s will approximate normal distributions.

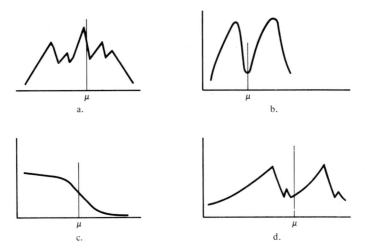

a.

b.

c.

d.

2 How can estimates of parameters be made more precise? Discuss this in terms of estimates of the population mean.

3 A researcher made repeated samplings of 36 scores from a population of scores which had a mean of 17 and a standard deviation of 6.

a What was the standard error of the mean in the resulting sampling distribution?

b What would be the boundaries which include the middle 50 percent of the estimates of μ? (Hint: use the formula for z scores. Find the values of z in Table B.2 in Appendix B which have 25 percent and 75 percent below them. Between them will be 50 percent of the z scores. Substitute the values of μ and the standard deviation of the sampling distribution in the z-score formula and solve for the values of $\bar{X}$ which include 50 percent of the scores.)

c What would be the boundaries which include 90 percent of the estimates of μ? Use the same procedures as in *b* above.

4 State the following hypotheses statistically:

a Men are taller than women.

b Boys' IQs correlate with the IQ scores of their sisters more than boys' IQ scores correlate with the IQs of their fathers.

c The variance of achievement-test scores is no greater for urban than for rural children.

5 On five 3 × 5 index cards, write the number 1; on three cards write 2, on four of the cards write 3, on three cards write 4, and on five cards write 5. Let the numbers on the cards represent the scores in a population of only 20 scores. The population distribution is

X	f
1	5
2	3
3	4
4	3
5	5

where X is the score and f is the frequency that a score occurs. What is the value of the population mean μ? Complete the graph of the population of scores below.

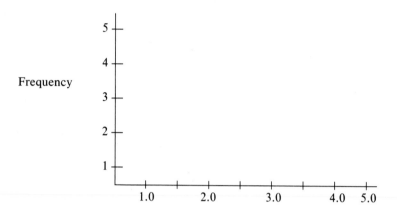

Now shuffle the 20 cards and place them in a container. Randomly select a sample of four cards. Find the mean of the sample and replace the cards in the container. Scramble the cards and select four more. Find the mean and replace the cards. Repeat this procedure 20 or 30 times. Now draw the graph of this sampling distribution of means in the space below:

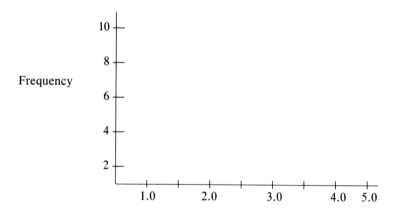

Do the means on the graph of the sampling distribution cluster around the value of μ and approximate a normal distribution? If they do not, can you suggest any reasons for this?

6 A researcher was interested in determining whether adolescent boys perform better academically when they are taught by teachers of the same or the opposite sex. He randomly selected 10 male students from the junior class in a high school to be subjects in the study. Five students were randomly assigned to a group that was taught all its courses by male teachers, and the other five were taught all courses by female teachers. The average grades for the semester are given below for the two groups.

Male teachers	Female teachers
90	71
85	89
80	87
87	94
69	75

a State the appropriate statistical hypotheses.
b Identify an appropriate test of the null hypothesis and set a level of α.
c Compute the value of the test statistic and make a decision about the null hypothesis.

7 From the literature in your own field of interest, find two studies that test hypotheses using statistics. For each article
a Write the statistical hypothesis (which may or may not be stated explicitly in the article).
b Identify the test statistic.
c What is the probability of making a Type I error?
d Can you say anything about the likelihood of a Type II error from the write-up?
e Are the conclusions appropriate based on the results of the statistical tests?

8 The importance of replication is stressed by researchers. Why is it important that statistical findings be replicated?

9 Ten pairs of identical twins raised in different homes were located for study. In each twin pair, one member was raised in a home of high socio-economic status (SES) while the other member was raised in a home of low SES. Since the twins were genetically identical but were raised in different environments, the question of interest was whether the different environments had an effect on the measured IQ of the subjects. The IQ scores were as follows:

Pair no.	Low SES	High SES
1	92	104
2	86	90
3	120	118
4	96	99
5	108	115
6	101	109
7	98	97
8	88	98
9	117	132
10	103	107

a State the appropriate statistical null and alternative hypotheses.
b Determine the appropriate statistical test. Set the α level.
c Compute the value of the appropriate statistic and make a decision about the correctness of the null hypothesis.

10 A researcher wished to learn whether there is a relationship between veteran status and voting patterns among college graduates. He selected a random sample of 90 male registered voters in a small town and identified voters as veteran or

nonveteran, and as registered Democrats, Republicans, or independents. He obtained the following data:

	Registration		
	Democrat	Republican	Independent
Veteran	19	10	14
Nonveteran	12	17	18

a Is there a relationship between veteran status and voter registration?
b What are some of the limitations of a study of this kind?

11 Cancelli, Bergan, and Jones (1982) used a chi-square approach to test hypotheses about how children solve complex subtraction problems. As part of a larger study, Cancelli et al. classified the responses of second-grade students (from two schools in Tucson, Arizona) on three different kinds of problems as representing one of three response patterns. This produced a response pattern by problem type contingency table. Then the researchers tested for dependence between type of pattern and type of problem. They found highly significant chi squares and concluded that the kind of response pattern a child used was to some degree determined by type of subtraction task.

a If this study were replicated, would the results be exactly the same?
b Do the significant chi squares found in this research tell us that children always solve the subtraction tasks in the patterns indicated by the results?
c Does the study tell us anything about how students solve subtraction problems whether presented verbally or numerically? (Tasks in this study were numerical.)
d To which population can this study be generalized?

HYPOTHESIS TESTING FOR COMPARISONS AMONG MORE THAN TWO MEANS

Let us suppose that a study is done to compare the attitudes of several groups towards using part of the day in public school for religious instruction. The groups represented are blue-collar, professional, and business persons from the community. The groups will be compared as to their attitudes towards religious education in the public schools. The dependent variable will be a questionnaire that allows individuals to indicate the degree to which they agree or disagree with 10 statements. When the responses to the 10 items are totaled, high scores will indicate a favorable attitude towards religious education in the public schools, and low scores will indicate an unfavorable attitude.

Assume that it was possible to measure the attitudes of all adult males in the urban area who are blue-collar workers, businesspersons, or professional persons. The population means on the attitude test are $\mu_1 = 40$ for blue-collar workers, $\mu_2 = 45$ for businesspersons, and $\mu_3 = 50$ for professionals. The population standard deviation σ_j in each group equals 10. Since these are population means, no hypothesis test is necessary, and we can conclude that the three groups differ in attitude.

Assuming that each group contains the same number of people, we can find the *grand mean* (μ) by taking the average of the group means as follows:

$$\mu = \frac{\mu_1 + \mu_2 + \mu_3}{3} = \frac{40 + 45 + 50}{3} = 45$$

Now suppose we want to set up a mathematical model to describe respondents' scores to the attitude questionnaire. We could use the grand mean for this purpose. Thus, to predict a person's score on the attitude instrument, we would use as a model

$$\hat{Y}_{ij} = \mu = 45$$

where $\hat{Y}_{ij}$ = the predicted attitude score
μ = the grand mean

This, of course, would be unsatisfactory because each person would have to get the same score. We already know that the population means for the three kinds of respondents were between 40 and 50, so there must have been scores that did not equal 45 in the population. In fact, by comparing each group mean to the grand mean, we could determine the *effect* of being in a particular group. For example, we could say that the effect of being blue collar was to lower the attitude score five units below the grand mean, while the professional group attitude was five units above the group mean. The business group mean was equal to the grand mean. This can also be said mathematically. Specifically, we define an *effect* as the difference between a group mean and the grand mean. Thus the effect for the *j*th group (where μ_1, μ_2, and μ_3 are represented in general by μ_j) is called α_j, and

$$\alpha_j = \mu_j - \mu$$

For example, the effect for the blue-collar worker group (α_1) is found by subtracting the grand mean from the mean of the blue-collar group. That is,

$$\alpha_1 = \mu_1 - \mu = 40 - 45 = -5$$

This value of -5 can be interpreted to mean that the effect of being a blue-collar worker is to reduce the attitude score by 5 units. It can be shown using the same procedure that the effect for the professional group is $+5$ and the effect for businesspersons is 0.

This new information about the effect of being in a group can be added to our model for each person's score. Thus we can propose the following expanded model:

$$Y_{ij} = \mu + \alpha_j$$

In the case of the blue-collar group for whom we computed $\alpha_1 = -5$, for example, the score of each person would be $45 + (-5)$, or 40. Using this equation, we would find the score for each businessperson to be $45 + 0 = 45$ and for each professional, $45 + 5 = 50$. Although this equation is better than using the grand mean alone, it suggests that we would get the same score for each person within a group, and this, of course, is unlikely. To allow for individual differences, we include a term we will call *error*. This error term (e_{ij}) is obtained by subtracting the Y score we get using the above equation from the actual Y score we get by giving the attitude test to a person. Thus the model for each obtained score (Y_{ij}) is best represented by the equation

$$Y_{ij} = \mu + \alpha_j + e_{ij}$$

We provide this discussion of the model for the data to develop a foundation for testing hypotheses about more than one mean. However, up to this point, the discussion has been about population parameters. In the next sections, we will expand our discussion to include sample values that would require testing hypotheses.

Testing Hypotheses about Sample Values

Suppose that we were actually to conduct the study of relationship between occupational type and attitude towards religious instruction in public schools. The population means and standard deviations would not be known. We first obtain a random sample of individuals. In this instance, we sample 30 individuals (10 from each of the three occupational strata). The scores for these individuals are presented in Table 7-3. As shown in the table, the group means estimated from the sample are not exactly equal to the parameter means

TABLE 7-3
SCORES FOR THE RELIGIOUS-INSTRUCTION ATTITUDE STUDY (*30 individuals*)

Individual	1 Blue collar	2 Business	3 Professional
1	33	50	62
2	48	45	47
3	38	40	52
4	63	45	62
5	33	35	72
6	28	25	57
7	38	50	32
8	28	65	42
9	48	55	52
10	33	40	52
Total	390	450	530
Group Mean ($\bar{Y}_j$)	39.0	45.0	53.0
Standard Deviation	11.01	11.06	11.25
Grand Mean	$45.67 = \bar{Y}_G$		

(which we would not know). The mean for the sample of blue-collar workers is 39.0, for the business group is 45.0, and for the professional group is 53.0. Although the means of each group differ, we are interested in knowing whether the population parameters they estimate are different. Thus we propose the null hypothesis* that the population means are equal, i.e.,

$$H_0 : \mu_1 = \mu_2 = \mu_3$$

One approach to testing this null hypothesis would be to use several t tests for independent samples, as described earlier in this chapter. But to do this, we would be required to make three separate null hypotheses, as follows:

$$H_0 : \mu_1 = \mu_2$$

$$H_0 : \mu_2 = \mu_3$$

$$H_0 : \mu_1 = \mu_3$$

This would result in three separate t tests, each of which contains an α probability of a Type I error. However, the overall probability of making a Type I error somewhere in the three tests would be greater than α. What is needed, then, is one overall test of the single null hypothesis

$$H_0 : \mu_1 = \mu_2 = \mu_3$$

We can make such a test using a procedure known as the *analysis of variance.* To employ this method, we make use of the model for representing Y_{ij}, the score of an individual that we just developed.

$$Y_{ij} = \mu + \alpha_j + e_{ij}$$

We can replace the parameters of this model with their estimates based on the data we have collected. The grand mean, μ, is estimated by summing together all 30 scores and dividing by the total number of scores. Thus

$$\overline{Y}_G = \frac{\text{the sum of all the scores}}{\text{the number of scores}}$$

$$= \frac{1370}{30} = 45.67$$

where $\overline{Y}_G$ is the estimate of the grand mean μ. The effect of membership in the jth group (α_j) is estimated by subtracting the sample grand mean $\overline{Y}_G$ from the mean of the jth group (represented by $\overline{Y}_j$). Thus α_j is estimated by $\hat{\alpha}_j$, where

---

* In this discussion, we have chosen to illustrate the procedure with an example using three groups. However, a larger number of means may be included. A more general null hypothesis, therefore, might be

$$H_0 : \mu_1 = \mu_2 \cdots = \mu_j$$

$$\hat{\alpha}_j = \overline{Y}j - \overline{Y}_G$$

Since we are estimating α_j, we use the symbol $\hat{\alpha}_j$. The error term in the model, e_{ij}, is obtained by subtracting the group mean from each individual's actual score (Y_{ij}). Thus

$$e_{ij} = Y_{ij} - \overline{Y}_j$$

Putting these estimates into the model, for Y_{ij}, each person's score, we obtain

$$Y_{ij} = \underbrace{\overline{Y}_G}_{} + \underbrace{(\overline{Y}_j - \overline{Y}_G)}_{} + \underbrace{(Y_{ij} - \overline{Y}_j)}_{}$$

$$\text{Score} = \begin{matrix}\text{grand} \\ \text{mean}\end{matrix} + \text{group effect} + \begin{matrix}\text{individual} \\ \text{error}\end{matrix}$$

Let us take a particular score in Table 7-3 to demonstrate the meaning of this equation. Individual 5 in group 3 obtained a score of 72. Therefore

$$\text{Score} = \underbrace{\begin{matrix}\text{grand} \\ \text{mean}\end{matrix}}_{} + \underbrace{\text{group effect}}_{} + \underbrace{\begin{matrix}\text{individual} \\ \text{error}\end{matrix}}_{}$$

$$72 = 45.67 + (53 - 45.67) + (72 - 53)$$

$$= 45.67 + \quad 7.33 \quad + \quad 19$$

Of course, this model can be used to represent the scores of all 30 persons in the sample. Recall that for a single sample, the estimated variance was given in Chapter 6 as

$$S_y^2 = \frac{\Sigma(Y - \overline{Y})^2}{n - 1}$$

In the analysis of variance, the numerator term $\Sigma(Y - \overline{Y})^2$ for the total variance (computed from all the scores treated as a single list) is partitioned into two parts. These parts represent variation *between the groups* and variation *within the groups* in the experiment. The quantity $\Sigma(Y - \overline{Y})^2$ is referred to as the *total sum of squares* (SS_T) and is partitioned as follows:

$$SS_T = SS_B + SS_W$$

where SS_B = sum of squares between groups
      SS_W = sum of squares within groups

This relationship can be shown algebraically by working from the equation for Y_{ij} summing across subjects' scores. Due to space limitations, this is another topic we will have to leave for texts specifically concerned with statistics. For our purposes, it will be sufficient to show the formulas for computing the total, between, and within sums of squares. These formulas are included in Table 7-4

TABLE 7-4
SUMS OF SQUARES FOR THE ATTITUDE STUDY

Source	Formula	Sum of squares
Between groups	$I \sum_{j=1}^{3} (\bar{Y}_j - \bar{Y}_G)^2$	986.67
Within groups	$\sum_{j=1}^{3} \sum_{i=1}^{10} (Y_{ij} - \bar{Y}_j)^2$	3330.00
Total	$\sum_{j=1}^{3} \sum_{i=1}^{10} (Y_{ij} - \bar{Y}_G)^2$	4316.67

with the values of the sums of squares for the busing-attitudes study.

Our strategy for testing the hypothesis is based on the partition of total variation (SS_T) into the systematic (between groups, SS_B) and the random (within groups, SS_W) components. As with the chi-square test, we must be concerned with degrees of freedom in the analysis-of-variance procedure. However, the explanation of degrees of freedom in the analysis of variance is too difficult to approach intuitively. For that reason, the degrees of freedom for SS_T, SS_B, and SS_W will be presented here without comment.

$$df_T = N - 1$$
$$df_B = J - 1$$
$$df_W = J(I - 1)$$

where df_T = total degrees of freedom
df_B = degrees of freedom for SS_B
df_W = degrees of freedom for SS_W
N = total number of subjects in the experiment
J = number of groups of subjects
I = number of subjects in each group

Using these formulas, the reader should readily see that $df_T = 29$, $df_B = 2$, and $df_W = 27$ for the busing study. The reader can verify that

$$df_T = df_B + df_W$$

When sums of squares are divided by their corresponding degrees of freedom, estimated variances known as *mean squares* are obtained. The between and within mean squares are the only ones in which we are interested. Sums of squares, degrees of freedom, and mean squares are usually presented in an *analysis-of-variance table* similar to the one shown in Table 7-5.

The null hypothesis that all the group means are equal can now be tested with an F statistic. This is computed by

$$F = \frac{MS_B}{MS_W}$$

where MS_B is the mean square between, and MS_W is the mean square within. Notice the computed value of F for the busing study is in the last column of the analysis-of-variance table in Table 7-5. Our mode of reasoning in testing the null hypothesis is identical to that of other statistical tests used so far. If the value of F computed from the sample is higher than the critical value, the null hypothesis is rejected.

The percentiles of the F distribution are given in Table B.5 in Appendix B. To look up the critical value of the F statistic for a particular test, we need to enter the table at the appropriate column and row. The appropriate column of the F table is determined from the degrees of freedom for MS_B, and the row of the table is equal to degrees of freedom for MS_W. For the attitude study, let's assume that we chose an α level of .05. The critical value for the F test (F with 2 and 27 degrees of freedom at the 95th percentile of the distribution) is approximately 3.35. Again, as with the χ^2 test, we need consider only one tail of the distribution. The obtained value of the F statistic in our example is 4.00, which exceeds the critical value of 3.35. Since the obtained value of F exceeds the critical value of F, we reject H_0. We conclude that the population group means are different; i.e., that blue-collar workers, businesspersons, and professionals differ in their attitudes toward religious instruction in the public schools.

What we have just discussed is referred to as a *one-way analysis of variance.* The analysis need not terminate at this point. There are procedures for determining precisely where the differences occur among the three groups included in the study. These procedures are beyond the scope of this presentation, and the reader is referred to texts such as Kirk (1982), Glass and Hopkins (1984), and Winer (1971). The reader is reminded that the analysis-of-variance procedure just described does not indicate which means are significantly different in a set of means. It only tests whether or not at least one mean is different from the others. Further, it must be remembered that the values of the mean squares will vary from sample to sample. They may mislead one to make a Type I or Type II error.

TABLE 7-5
ANALYSIS-OF-VARIANCE TABLE FOR THE ATTITUDE STUDY

Source	SS	df	MS	F
Between groups	986.67	2	493.33	4.00
Within groups	3330.00	27	123.33	
Total	4316.67	29		

Multiple-Classification Analysis Of Variance

Up to this point, we have been considering analysis-of-variance problems which involve a single classification variable. For example, the attitude study in the last section had only one classification variable, occupational group, which contained three levels of occupation, blue collar, business, and professional. But what if we were also interested in how age affected attitudes towards religious instruction in schools? We could divide subjects into two age groups, say 25- to 39-year-olds and 40- to 65-year-olds, and we would have a study with two classification variables.

Statisticians call the classification variables in analysis of variance *factors* and name statistical designs by the number of levels (categories) for each factor. For example, the age and occupation study would be called a 2 × 3 design because there are two levels of the first factor (age) and three levels of the second factor (occupation). Moreover, this design would be termed a *two-way* design because there are two factors. There might be three, four, or many factors. However, the larger the design, the more difficult the interpretation of results becomes. Rarely is a study conducted that is more than four-way.

Most of the characteristics of higher-order designs can be illustrated using a two-way example. To do this, we return to the attitude study with age and occupation as factors. Thirty new subjects are selected this time so that there are five in each cell. The means of each cell on the attitude test are given in Table 7-6.

The model for each score in a two-way analysis-of-variance model is similar to the one-way model discussed earlier but contains an effect term for each factor and a term for the interaction effect produced by both factors operating at the same time. That is, each score is considered to be influenced by its row, column, and cell. Effects due to column or row alone are called *main effects*. Effects due to row and column in combination are termed *interaction effects*. Thus the model for a score is

$$Y_{ijk} = \mu + \alpha_j + \beta_k + \gamma_{jk} + e_{ijk}$$

TABLE 7-6
SAMPLE MEANS FOR TWO-WAY ANALYSIS OF VARIANCE

| Age group | Occupational group | | | Age-group means |
	Blue collar	Business	Professional	
25-40	44	46	45	45.00
40-65	35	45	59	46.33
Occupation-group means	39.50	45.50	52.00	45.67

where Y_{ijk} = a person's score

μ = grand mean

α_j = effect of the jth age group

β_k = effect of the kth occupational group

γ_{jk} = interaction effect for the jkth cell

e_{ijk} = difference between group mean and a person's score

The above equation represents the model for a score in the population of scores. We can estimate effects in the model using an approach similar to the one used for one-way analysis earlier. However, the algebra is too involved to be appropriately included in the present text. The interested reader is referred to a source such as Kirk (1982, chap.8).

From the above equation, it should be apparent that with the two-way analysis-of-variance problem, three sources might cause means to vary systematically from the grand mean. These sources correspond to the three kinds of systematic effects identified in the model. Therefore, three hypotheses may be proposed as follows:

$$H_0 : \mu_j = \mu_j' \text{ for the two age levels}$$

$$H_0 : \mu_k = \mu_k' = \mu_k'' \text{ for the three occupational levels}$$

$$H_0 : \mu_{jk} = \mu + \alpha_j + \beta_k \text{ for each cell}$$

The computational formulas for the two-way analysis of variance are similar to those for the one-way design discussed earlier. They are based on partitioning the total variance into systematic and random components and then comparing the systematic with the random. In the case of the two-way design, there are systematic components attributed to each factor and the interaction, and random variance coming from individual differences within each cell. Again, we will leave the details of the specific formulas to an appropriate statistics text (e.g., Hays, 1981, or Kirk, 1982), while we concentrate on the meaning of the procedure as it is applied to hypothesis tests. The results of the two-way analysis of variance of the attitudes towards religious-instruction study are summarized in Table 7-7. In the table, there is a line for each of the hypotheses that can be tested in this study. The first null hypothesis corresponds to saying that there is no main effect due to age. Or, to put it another way, the two age groups will have identical test means in the population sampled. The second hypothesis is that there are no main effects due to occupation. The third hypothesis states that there are no interaction effects when a cell mean equals the grand mean plus the row and column effects. The meaning of the interaction hypothesis will be illustrated shortly.

The main effect of occupation is statistically significant beyond the .05 level. There is also a significant age-by-occupation interaction. Further, there is no significant difference in attitude between the older and younger members of the population. In other words, we do not reject the null hypothesis regard-

TABLE 7-7
ANALYSIS-OF-VARIANCE SUMMARY TABLE FOR THE TWO-WAY ATTITUDES STUDY

Source	SS	df	MS	F
Age (A)	13.33	$J - 1 = 1$	13.33	$MS_A/MS_W = .18$
Occupation (B)	781.67	$K - 1 = 2$	390.84	$MS_B/MS_W = 5.35^*$
$A \times B$ interaction	711.67	$(J - 1)(K - 1) = 2$	355.84	$MS_{AB}/MS_W = 4.87^*$
Within	1752	$JK(I - 1) = 24$	73.00	
Total	3258.67	$IJK - 1 = 29$		

$^*p \setminus .05$

ing age differences. However, the other two null hypotheses, concerning occupation and the interaction of age and occupation, are rejected at the .05 level of statistical significance. Our results suggest that the general model we gave for each score ($Y_{ij} = \mu + \alpha_j + \beta_k + \alpha_{jk} + e_{ijk}$) is incorrect because there was no support for the effect of age on attitude. However, the other effects included in the model were supported.

A Word about Interaction Effects

When there are significant main effects and interactions present in an experiment, the interpretation of the results is not as simple as may have been implied by the discussion so far. That is, an interaction might actually be the cause of the significant main effect. In such a case, it would not be appropriate to say that there were main effects, even though the existence of the main effect might be supported statistically. Let us use the means from four hypothetical studies displayed in Table 7-8 to shed some light on this.

The means in Table 7-8 have been graphed in Figure 7-15 by placing levels of A along the horizontal axis and values of the dependent variable along the vertical axis. These graphs help us observe the influence of the interaction effects. For example, in the figure depicting the means for study 1, the lines representing b_1 and b_2 are parallel, with b_1 always above b_2. This tells us that there is a main effect of B which is reflected by higher means in the b_1 cells than in the b_2 cells. Study 2, on the other hand, presents a different situation. Only one cell mean is different from the others. This causes the b_1 and b_2 lines in the figure to converge. When the lines in a graph are distinctly nonparallel, a significant interaction effect is probably present. Since only one cell is different, there appear to be significant main effects for both A and B factors. One can see that an effect exists only because of factor B under the a_1 condition and factor A under the b_1 condition. Therefore, only an interaction effect is present, and the main effects in this case are not meaningful. Thus, when there are significant interactions and main effects in the same study, the researcher must explore the interaction carefully before interpreting the significant main effect.

TABLE 7-8

MEANS FROM FOUR 2 × 2 ANALYSIS-OF-VARIANCE DESIGNS

Study 1

	b_1	b_2	
a_1	15	10	12.5
a_2	10	5	7.5
	12.5	7.5	

Two significant main effects,
no interaction

Study 2

	b_1	b_2	
a_1	20	10	15
a_2	10	10	10
	15	10	

Two significant main effects
and interaction

Study 3

	b_1	b_2	
a_1	20	10	15
a_2	10	20	15
	15	15	

Significant interaction only

Study 4

	b_1	b_2	
a_1	40	10	25
a_2	30	20	25
	35	15	

One significant main effect (B),
and interaction

Study 3 provides us with an example of a significant interaction with no main effects. Observe how the lines cross. Such an interaction is called *disordinal*. On the other hand, when the lines do not cross, an interaction is said to be *ordinal*. Study 4 had a significant main effect for factor B and a significant interaction effect. Is this a disordinal interaction? Before answering the question, redo the graph using the levels of B on the horizontal axis and draw the lines formed by the a_1 and a_2 means.

Probably one of the most common errors in research using analysis of variance with two or more factors is failure to interpret significant main effects with respect to significant interactions. Usually, enough data are reported in research articles in professional journals for a careful reader to make a correct interpretation even if the author did not. Graphs such as those found in Figure 7-15 are considered a useful aid for interpreting interactions. Can you interpret the interactions reported in Tables 7-6 and 7-7?

Research Applications of Analysis of Variance

Examples of research using the analysis of variance abound in the current professional literature. Many of the applications go beyond the fundamental pro-

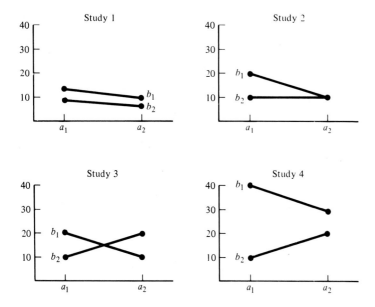

FIGURE 7-15
Graphs of the cell means of the four studies depicted in Table 7-8.

cedures just discussed. However, the basic features—the analysis-of-variance model, partitioning of the sums of squares, computing F ratios, and so on—are recognizable even in complex applications of analysis of variance. We have chosen two research studies to illustrate applications of one-way and two-way analysis of variance.

An Application of One-Way Analysis The first study, by W. Robert Kennedy (1975), concerned the relationship between the grade received in a freshman English class and students' ratings of quality of the instructional methods. The subjects were 467 first-semester college students. The dependent variable was the score on a 15-item rating scale designed to measure the students' ratings of instructional methods of the faculty member who taught their section of the course. For the independent variable, students were classified according to the grade they received. The null hypothesis tested was that there was no difference in mean ratings of instructors among students who received A, B, C, or D as a grade.

The results of the analysis of variance are presented in Table 7-9. They were reconstructed from the information given in the article since the actual analysis-of-variance table does not appear. If $\alpha = .01$, the value of F obtained was significant. Thus the null hypothesis that the mean ratings of instructors are equivalent across the grade groups was rejected, and the alternative hypothesis that these means differ (i.e., that grades received in courses are related to ratings of instructional methodology) was accepted.

TABLE 7-9
ANALYSIS-OF-VARIANCE TABLE FOR THE KENNEDY STUDY

Source	SS	df	MS	F
Grade group	2,721.51	3	907.17	9.67*
Within	43,435.39	463	93.81	
Total	46,156.90	466		

*$p \setminus .01$.

An Illustration of Two-Way Analysis Our illustration of two-way analysis of variance is based on a study by McCollister, Burts, Hildreth, and Wright (1986) in which computer-assisted was compared with teacher-assisted instruction. The sample consisted of 53 kindergarten children. Based on a pretest, the children were divided into three skill levels. Level 1 consisted of children who could recognize and count less than 70 percent of the numbers from 1 to 5. Level-2 children were able to recognize and count less than 80 percent between 1 and 10 but more than level-1 children, while level-3 children were able to count and recognize 80 percent of the numbers between 1 and 10 but less than 80 percent between 11 and 20. Children in levels 1 and 2 were given instruction in counting and recognizing with numbers from 1 to 10. Level-3 children received the same kind of instruction, but they dealt with quantities and numbers from 11 to 20. Children in each level were randomly assigned to be taught by a computer or a teacher. After instruction, each child's numerical recognition was assessed. The study was analyzed with a 3×2 (levels-by-treatments) analysis of variance. The results of the analysis of variance of the numerical recognition scores are summarized in Table 7-10. Table 7-10 shows that the effects of treatment and of level were statistically significant.

TABLE 7-10
ANALYSIS OF VARIANCE FOR NUMERICAL RECOGNITION

Source	df	MS	F
Treatment	1	53.3	4.82*
Level	2	944.6	85.49†
Treatment X level	2	26.6	2.41
Error	47		

Source: McCollister, T. S., Burts, D. C., Hildreth, G. J., & Wright, V. L. (1986). Effects of computer-assisted instruction and teacher-assisted instruction on arithmetic task achievement scores of kindergarten children. *Journal of Educational Research, 80,* 121–125. By permission of Helen Dwight Reid Educational Foundation, published by Heldref Publications, Washington, D. C. 20016. Copyright © 1986.
*$p \setminus .05$
†$p \setminus .01$

Since the analysis of variance was significant for the treatment and level factors, we can interpret these results further by looking at the means in Table 7-11. It appears that the computerized instruction produced higher numerical-recognition scores than the teacher-assisted instruction for the second- and third-level children but not for the first-level children. The lack of significant interaction might be taken to suggest that the finding for level 1 might be due to chance or other technical considerations regarding the analysis of variance. It would be possible to carry the analysis further with additional significance testing of selected pairs of means. However, post-hoc analysis (after the analysis of variance) is another topic we will leave for a text more specifically dedicated to statistical concepts (e.g., Hays, 1981, and Kirk, 1982).

Additional Points regarding Analysis of Variance

Analysis of variance is one of the most popular tools for statistical analysis in educational and behavioral research. In addition to the one-, two-, and three-way designs previously described, a wide variety of other designs exists. The reader interested in gaining more information about the various configurations of analysis of variance is referred to texts such as Kirk (1982) and Winer (1971).

The independent variables or factors one encounters in applications of analysis of variance can be classified into two kinds. The first is called *fixed* factors. These are factors that contain all levels of classification of interest. The factors we looked at in the previous three studies were all fixed factors. The other kind is called *random* factors. They contain only a random sample of the levels of a factor being studied. For example, suppose that we are interested in differences in social climate among the 150 elementary schools of a city. To obtain data from every school would be expensive. Therefore, we might randomly select a sample of 20 schools to study intensively. If we find differences among the sample schools, we will be able to generalize the finding to all 150

TABLE 7-11
MEANS OF NUMERICAL-RECOGNITION SCORES

Level	Computer-assisted		Teacher-assisted	
	n	X	n	X
1	7	2.1	8	3.5
2	8	7.5	5	4.4
3	13	17.8	12	14.4

Source: McCollister, T. S., Burts, D. C., Hildreth, G. J., & Wright, V. L. (1986). Effects of computer-assisted instruction and teacher-assisted instruction on arithmetic task achievement scores of kindergarten children. *Journal of Educational Research, 80,* 121–125. By permission of Helen Dwight Reid Educational Foundation, published by Heldref Publications, Washington, D. C. 20016. Copyright © 1986.

schools because the sample of schools was random and therefore can be considered representative of the population of schools. Occasionally fixed and random factors appear in a single experiment. Such a design is called a *mixed-effects* design. An analysis-of-variance design which contains only fixed factors is called a *fixed-effects design,* while one which contains only random factors is called a *random-effects design.* There are differences in computations of the F tests between experiments which involve fixed and those which involve random factors. Again, the interested reader is referred to one of the appropriate texts to pursue this further.

Another point to emphasize in analysis of variance is that the procedure discussed here tests only overall effects. It provides no information about which means or combinations of means are different when the null hypothesis is rejected. The procedures for exploring these differences are called a priori or *planned comparisons* when they precede the analysis of variance and a posteriori or post hoc, as mentioned earlier, when they are used after a significant F ratio has been found.

Analysis-of-variance techniques can also be applied to situations in which there is more than one dependent variable. In a later section, we will consider this kind of application. In view of the diversity and flexibility of analysis of variance, it is little wonder that the procedures are used extensively. At least two other developments have contributed to the popularity of the method in recent years. First, with the advent and increasing availability of computers, the effort involved in the computations has been minimized. Second, the preference of many modern researchers for controlled experimentation using comparison groups and random assignment of subjects led to a natural increase in the use of analysis of variance. When well-conceived and executed experimental designs (such as the posttest-only control-group design described in Chapter 4) are analyzed with appropriate analysis-of-variance procedures, causation may be inferred (but not proved). Since much research is conducted to increase our understanding of causal relationships, investigators have naturally been attracted to analysis of variance.

Although the analysis of variance has great potential for the educational and behavioral science researcher, certain limitations deserve mention. First, the analysis of variance is a complex and sophisticated tool. It can easily be misused or misinterpreted, especially by someone with inadequate training. The selection of a proper analysis-of-variance design is often difficult. Additional problem areas for researchers utilizing the analysis of variance are the improper identification of hypotheses, the use of groups whose scores are not independent (common in designs using pretests and posttests), and serious violations of the underlying statistical assumptions.*

---

* These assumptions are given in many statistics texts. The analysis-of-variance procedure is generally quite insensitive to anything but extreme violations of assumptions. An excellent source on this topic is Sheffé, H. (1959). *The analysis of variance.* New York: Wiley.

Analysis of Covariance

Analysis of covariance is similar to analysis of variance, but it also uses the regression concepts that we covered in the last chapter. It may be used to increase the power of the F test or to control extraneous influences in an experiment. To illustrate how analysis of covariance is used, consider an experiment in which three ways of teaching problem solving to undergraduate students are compared. In the first method, called the *integrated approach,* students are given problems and learn to write computer programs to solve them. In the second treatment group, students are taught computer programming in the first half of the semester and then are given problems to solve on the computer using the programming skills they have learned. In the third approach, problem-solving strategies are taught in classroom lectures, and students are encouraged to practice these strategies, using software previously developed in a computer laboratory. Subjects are randomly assigned to treatments, and the experiment is conducted over the course of one college semester. The dependent variable in the experiment is a final examination in solving problems administered at the end of the semester.

So far, this research seems to be the kind for which a one-way analysis of variance to test the null hypothesis that the means of the three groups on the final examination are equal would be appropriate. However, the researcher foresees a problem in that the students are taking the same course for credit on the same college campus. She reasons that this could create threats to internal validity, such as compensatory equalization and diffusion or imitation of treatments (see Chapter 4) even though the students are randomly assigned to treatments and are told not to study or do homework assignments with students in other sections of the same course. To control for this problem, the researcher creates a measure called *opportunity for collaboration.* This measure is based on information the students provide in a 10-item questionnaire concerning things such as academic major; membership in fraternities, sororities, and campus clubs; location of dormitory rooms; etc. The more pairings on these items that a student has with students in other treatments, the greater the probability of some sort of collaboration that might affect the purity of the treatments. The number of pairings for each student are totaled by computer and transformed into a more manageable number (since for some students, the total could be very large) using an appropriate transformation procedure.

One would expect the opportunity-for-collaboration variable to be correlated to the amount of actual collaboration across treatments. Further, the opportunity variable should also be correlated to performance on the final examination if the students do get together on class assignments during the year. On the other hand, opportunity should not be correlated to the treatment because the students were randomly assigned. The researcher would like to remove the effects of collaboration across treatments from the final exam scores by predicting final exam scores with the opportunity scores. The relationship between opportunity and final exam scores is shown with the Venn diagram in Figure 7-16. The darkly shaded area represents the amount of the variance in

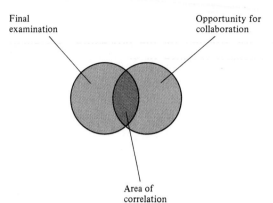

Final examination

Opportunity for collaboration

Area of correlation

FIGURE 7-16
The relationship between opportunity for collaboration and final examination test score.

final examination that is common with the opportunity variable. In other words, this area represents the correlation between the two variables. The lightly shaded area to the left is unique to the final exam and is the part of the dependent variable that the researcher considers a "purer" measure of the effects of the treatment (if there are any effects). An analysis of variance done on the portion of the dependent variable remaining after the effects of the extraneous variable is removed (the lightly shaded area) is an analysis of covariance. The variable that is removed is called the *covariate*. It is possible to have more than one covariate in a single analysis.

Catterall (1987) used analysis of covariance in a study of the effects of group counseling on 157 low-achieving high school students. Of the subjects in the study, 120 volunteered to participate in a four-day workshop designed to improve their academic performance. One hundred students actually attended the workshop; the remaining twenty served as controls. A second control group consisted of eligible students who did *not* volunteer for the workshop. A variety of pre- and posttest measures (such as teachers' grades, work habits, students' attendance in class, etc.) were used in the study. Analysis of variance of each of the posttest measures indicated no significant differences between the treatment group and the two control groups on all measures except grade-point average. The author then used the pretest measure of each variable and sex as covariates and performed one-way analyses of covariance in order to increase the power of the analysis. In this case, it was found that the values of F for the analysis of covariance (ANCOVA) yielded a similar pattern of results. Only the grade-point average approached significance in the covariance reanalysis.

The procedures and calculations in the analysis of covariance are too involved to go into here, and interested readers are again referred to a source more directly concerned with statistical analysis (e.g., Kirk, 1982). However, the example of the study of teaching students to solve problems helps to illustrate certain points. First, ANCOVA can provide a statistical method of controlling extraneous influences in an experiment. Second, it is a way to make a statistical test of a hypothesis more powerful, theoretically because only random and extraneous influences are affected by the procedure. Systematic treatment effects should be unchanged because of an assumption that the covariate is correlated to the dependent variable but not to the treatment variable.

The potential for misuse of the analysis of covariance can be great. For example, it is often used to equalize nonrandom treatment groups. The reasoning behind this is that by removing the effects of extraneous differences between the groups, the equivalence of the treatment groups is established. The fallacies in this approach are rather difficult to explain, but one obvious problem with this kind of thinking is that people can differ in more ways than would be feasible to covary in a single experiment. Thus, if IQ score is used as a covariate in a learning experiment, there might still be a problem with such nuisance variables as learning style, prior experience with the subject being learned, and so on. Good sources on the use and misuse of ANCOVA are the Evans and Anastasio (1968), Elashoff (1969), and Glass, Peckham, and Sanders (1972) references at the end of this chapter.

MULTIVARIATE ANALYSIS IN RESEARCH

Thus far we have been discussing statistical techniques involving a single dependent variable. For example, in the section on χ^2 analysis, the dependent variable was the classification of a subject to a cell in a contingency table. The dependent variable in the analysis of variance was a single interval measurement. Studies of the effect of one or more independent variables on a single dependent variable are common. They are known as *univariate* studies. However, many of the phenomena researched in the behavioral sciences and education are so complex that they are difficult to represent meaningfully by just one dependent variable. For example, it would be overly restrictive to characterize constructs like intelligence, personality, and achievement as single variables. Usually measures of these constructs contain several different kinds of items and subtest scores. A class of statistical procedures has been developed for use with several dependent variables and one or more independent variables. These procedures are referred to as *multivariate* analyses. The computational formulas and the origins of multivariate procedures are far too involved for coverage in the present text; appropriate references are cited in the discussion of each procedure for the interested reader.

Multivariate Analysis of Variance

The first multivariate procedure we will discuss is the multivariate analysis of variance.* Most of the concepts of analysis of variance we discussed previously apply here. Instead of having one score for each person, however, there

---

* See Johnson and Wichern (1988) for a description of this technique.

are scores on two or more dependent variables. To illustrate, we will describe a study by DeVries and Edwards (1973) of the effects of learning games and student teams on classroom procedures. Subjects were 110 seventh-grade students in a mathematics class. The three independent variables were task (games, quiz), reward (teams, individual), and achievement (low, middle, high). Thus, the design was $2 \times 2 \times 3$. Tasks included (1) learning games that required use of knowledge or skill in competition with others and (2) biweekly teacher-made quizzes. Reward conditions involved the assigning of grades or other less formal rewards to individuals based on their performance or to groups based upon the performance of all (or a subset of) team members. Students were assigned to low-, medium-, or high-achievement groups based on prior achievement in the subject matter. The dependent variables were four scales on the "Learning Environment Inventory" (Difficulty, Competition, Satisfaction, and Cohesiveness), plus a parallel measure constructed by the authors to measure mutual concern.

In a multivariate analysis of variance, the study of main effects and interactions is similar to the univariate analysis. But they are not studied separately for each of the dependent variables because testing effects over and over again would increase the probability of making a Type I error. The procedure begins by considering the dependent variables (all five in this case) as a set and testing the hypotheses on all variables simultaneously. A commonly used statistic for this is the multivariate F. The computation of this statistic is far too complex for this text, but the results of the DeVries and Edwards study presented in Table 7-12 do serve as a useful illustration.

The multivariate F tests are significant for the main effects of task and reward and the task-by-reward interaction. The F ratios for the other main effects and interactions were not significant. These are general results that apply to one or several of the dependent variables. The next task in the multivariate analysis of variance is to determine precisely which dependent measures are affected by the three sources of variance that provided significant effects. Probably the simplest of a variety of techniques available is to look at the univariate F ratios (for task, reward, and task-by-reward) for each of the five dependent variables. These F ratios, obtained for each variable separately, are presented in Table 7-12. As the table shows, the univariate F ratios for task are significant for the ratings of difficulty, satisfaction, and competition. The F ratios for reward are significant for competition and mutual concern, and the F ratios for the task-by-reward interaction are significant for competition and cohesiveness. Also, it is indicated from the results presented in Table 7-12 that difficulty shows a significant effect of achievement. Based on the analysis, the authors were able to make conclusions regarding the effects of the task and reward conditions upon the dependent variables of difficulty, satisfaction, competition, mutual concern, and cohesiveness by considering the differences between the treatment means where effects were significant.

To summarize, the DeVries and Edwards study was done to assess the effects of three independent variables representing task, reward, and prior student

TABLE 7-12
MULTIVARIATE RESULTS FOR THE DEVRIES AND EDWARDS DATA

| | Multivariate | | | Univariate F ratios | | | | |
Source	df	F	df	Difficulty	Satisfaction	Competition	Mutual concern	Cohesiveness
Task (A)	5,94	7.14‡	1	14.92‡	13.00‡	6.03*	3.25	<1
Reward (B)	5,94	4.86†	1	1.19	1.34	6.61*	12.74‡	3.37
Achievement (C)	10,188	1.76	2	6.00†	1.31	<1	<1	<1
A × B	5,94	2.81*	1	<1	<1	3.98*	<1	6.24*
A × C	10,188	<1	2	1.81	<1	<1	1.30	1.31
B × C	10,188	1.26	2	2.10	<1	2.06	1.30	1.32
A × B × C	10,188	<1	2	<1	<1	<1	<1	<1
Error			98					

*$p < .05$.
†$p < .01$.
‡$p < .001$.

Source: DeVries, D. L., and Edwards, K. J. (1973). Learning games and student teams: Their effects on the classroom process. *American Educational Research Journal*, 10, p. 314. Copyright 1973, American Educational Research Association, Washington, D.C.

achievement upon five separate dependent variables representing the learning environment. The design was thus a three-way multivariate analysis of variance. A comprehensive understanding of the effects of the independent variables was possible through a consideration of the multivariate F tests, univariate F tests, and the size of the appropriate treatment means for the significant effects.

When a significant multivariate F is obtained, it means that there is a significant effect on the group of dependent variables. It does not provide specific information about which of the dependent variables contributed to the significant effects. As was seen in the DeVries and Edwards study, significant multivariate effects may be explored further using univariate tests. In the DeVries and Edwards study, the univariate analysis of variance was used to test null hypotheses for each dependent variable separately. These univariate analyses of variance are interpreted similarly to the univariate analysis-of-variance procedures discussed earlier in this chapter.

Another approach to exploring the nature of significant multivariate effects is to order the variables by importance using some logical or theoretical basis. Then tests for significance are applied sequentially. First a univariate F test is made on the first dependent variable. Then a univariate F is calculated for the additional effect on the second variable. Then the third and so on until the full set of variables has been included. Using this *stepdown* method, a researcher can start with a variable that is considered the most important in the set and study the additional effects (over and above those explained by prior variables) for each of the dependent variables in sequence.

The interpretations that we can make from hypothesis tests in the multivariate analysis of variance are similar to those we can make from univariate tests. However, the procedures involved are more complex, as are the problems which multivariate procedures can handle. The potential for misuse of these procedures is great for the researcher not well trained in the area.

Discriminant Analysis

A statistical procedure related to regression and multivariate analysis of variance is *discriminant analysis.** It is used primarily to study the classification of subjects into groups based upon a number of predictor variables. For example, let us say that we have six scores for each student who attends a small college. Using these scores, we hope to be able to identify the region of the country from which the student comes. The prediction variables are all interval-scale scores, such as attitudes towards political figures, personal values, academic grade-point average, height, weight, and number of years of driving experience.

When we are considering only two groups, discriminant analysis is really a special case of regression analysis where the criterion, membership in one or the other group, is coded 1 or 0 and is predicted from the independent vari-

---

* See Tatsuoka (1988) for a description of this procedure.

ables. When there are more than two groups, the analysis becomes more complex. The discriminant-analysis procedure produces a set of weights which, when multiplied by the scores on the set of variables, allows for maximum differentiation among the groups.

A good illustration of an application of discriminant analysis is reported in a study by Suzuki (1975). The research concerned ratings of narrative descriptions of children with learning or behavior problems. As part of a larger project, teachers in training from different countries rated the severity of the problems depicted in behavioral descriptions of mentally retarded children. The mean ratings of severity for the items describing mentally retarded children are indicated in Table 7-13, with lower means indicating more severe ratings. An overall test performed on the data which is analogous to an analysis-of-variance test was statistically significant beyond the .05 level.† This was interpreted to mean that the teachers did not rate the items equally from one country to the next and suggested that the country from which a teacher came could be identified to a degree by the ratings of severity given to the items. The analysis can be extended by applying univariate statistical tests to each variable to detect which particular means are different across the countries.

Factor Analysis

A third example of a multivariate analysis involves no independent variables but several dependent variables. This approach searches for "structure" among a set of dependent variables. For example, imagine a psychologist who has six tests, each purporting to measure a different aspect of mental ability: vocabulary, computational speed, verbal reasoning, numerical computation,

†Wilk's Lambda = .170; F = 10.065; df = 90,1120.

TABLE 7-13
MEAN RATINGS OF SEVERITY OF PROBLEMS IN DESCRIPTIONS OF
BEHAVIOR OF MENTALLY RETARDED CHILDREN IN FOUR COUNTRIES

Item	U.S.	Colombia	Taiwan	Scotland
1	2.706	2.351	2.696	2.360
2	2.860	2.857	2.964	2.567
3	2.490	2.182	2.294	2.227
4	2.056	1.441	1.991	1.653
5	2.391	2.091	2.196	1.973
6	2.049	1.584	1.500	1.560
7	1.804	2.558	2.313	1.840
8	1.391	1.558	1.357	1.333
9	1.203	1.403	1.134	1.027
10	1.063	1.260	1.089	1.027

Source: Adapted from Suzuki (1975).

numerical problem solving, and verbal comprehension. The researcher might suspect that the six tests represent overlapping traits and that a smaller number of variables can be used to represent mental ability. In the Venn diagrams in Figure 7-17, three of the variables—vocabulary, verbal reasoning, and verbal comprehension—overlap to form a cluster. The darkened area which all the variables touch represents the portion of the three variables that is common. That area has been designated as factor 1. Similarly, the three factors relating to numerical skills overlap, and the portion of overlap has been labeled factor 2. Because of the way the variables are related to the factors, we might say that factor 1 represents verbal abilities and factor 2 numerical abilities. Notice in the diagrams that the tests of verbal skill do not overlap (correlate) with the numerical tests. Also, each of the six variables overlaps with one of the factors to some extent and helps to define it. In addition, there is a portion of the variance of each variable which it does not share with either factor. The procedure is to partition the total variance for a variable into that part which is shared with one or more factors (common variance), and that part which is not shared with any factor (unique variance).

The mathematically sophisticated procedure for identifying the underlying common factors, referred to as *factor analysis,* is described in such texts as Harman (1976) and Gorsuch (1983). For our purposes, it is sufficient to say that the procedure is based upon correlation. Initially in factor analysis, the correlations of each variable with every other variable in the set are obtained. Statistical procedures are then applied which result in the

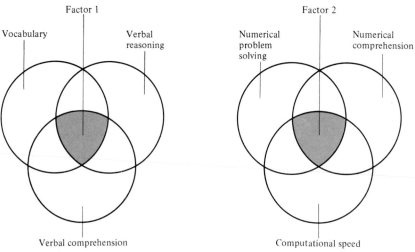

FIGURE 7-17
Two factors formed by the common variance of six variables.

correlations of the variables with the common factors. These correlations are called *factor loadings* and allow for the interpretation of the factor structure.

A study by Tamir (1975) includes a factor analysis of four cognitive preference variables. These variables represent the different modes in which an individual can attend to scientific information.

1 *Recall*—acceptance of scientific information for its own sake;

2 *Principles*—acceptance of scientific information because it exemplifies or explains some fundamental scientific principle or relationship;

3 *Questioning*—critical questioning of scientific information for completeness, general validity, or limitations;

4 *Application*—acceptance of scientific information in view of its usefulness and applicability in a general, social, or scientific context.

These variables were measured as they apply to the area of biology using the 40-item Biology Cognitive Preference Test (BCPT). The subjects were 989 Israeli twelfth-grade biology students. The data were factor-analyzed to determine the underlying structure of the test. This was done to determine (1) the number of underlying factors needed to explain the variance of the set of variables and (2) the optimal definition of these factors. The number of underlying factors needed in the problem was found to be two.

The final result of these procedures was the factor matrix shown in Table 7-14. The matrix shows the correlations of each of the original variables with the two factors defined through the factor analysis. From these correlations, it is obvious that factor 1 involves the recall or principles modes of attending to scientific information whereas factor 2 involves the questioning and application modes. The percentages of common variance accounted for by these factors are 65 percent for factor 1 and 35 percent for factor 2. Factor 1 accounts for a larger portion of the scores than factor 2. The result of this analysis is reduction of four modes of attending to scientific information into two general modes.

TABLE 7-14
FACTOR MATRIX FOR THE TAMIR DATA

Cognitive preference variable	Factor 1	Factor 2
Recall	.75	− .26
Principles	.64	.14
Questioning	− .35	.65
Application	.13	.57
Percent of variance	65%	35%

Source: Tamir, P. (1975). Relationship among cognitive preference, school environment, teachers' curricular bias, curriculum, and subject matter. *American Educational Research Journal, 12,* 244. Copyright 1975, American Educational Research Association.

META-ANALYSIS

Although the body of research literature is constantly expanding, a large number of studies on a single topic can provide a confusing picture in terms of findings. For example, Kulik, Kulik, and Schwab (1983) reviewed 60 studies designed to evaluate the usefulness of special programs to help college students who had been identified as having potential for academic difficulty. Some of the studies suggested that these programs were valuable; others suggested that they were not. Many of the studies showed the effects of the special programs to be slight. Therefore someone who was interested in developing a similar program should have difficulty interpreting the conflicting findings in the literature.

Glass (1977) suggested a way to use statistics to analyze the results of tests of similar hypotheses across many studies which he called *meta-analysis*. One of the primary tools in a meta-analysis is effect size (ES), which is defined as

$$ES = \frac{X_t - X_c}{S_c}$$

where X_t = the mean of the treatment group
X_c = the mean of the control group
S_c = the standard deviation of the control group

The reader should readily see from the equation that if ES is positive, then the treatment effect outweighs the control. Similarly, a negative ES would indicate a higher control group mean. If there were no difference between the effects of the treatment and control, then ES would be close to or equal zero. The procedure calls for identifying every available study that tests the effects of interest. Then effect sizes are computed for every study. Finally, statistical analyses are applied to the effect sizes to determine overall effects for the set of experiments.

Kulik et al. (1983) used meta-analysis in their study of evaluations of the effects of supportive programs for high-risk students. On the basis of a meta-analysis of 60 studies that had been conducted in different settings under varying conditions and with different subject groups, Kulik et al. were able to conclude that high-risk students who enrolled in special programs stayed in college longer and achieved better grades than did control-group students.

It has been argued that meta-analysis procedures emphasize the quantitative aspects of data rather than broader interpretation of the findings (Eysenck, 1978; Slavin, 1984). Further, the procedure has been criticized for combining things that are different and therefore cannot be combined. For example, in the Kulik et. al. study, results were combined from studies that had been done at a variety of different kinds of institutions (e.g., private universities, urban community colleges, etc.), using differing kinds of program support (e.g., tutoring, counseling, etc.) and differing student populations, criteria, and measurement techniques. Whether a general effect can be surmised from such diverse information seems to be a basis for some conflicting opinions regarding meta-analysis (e.g., Gallo, 1978; Wortman, 1983). Another concern involves the way a researcher establishes criteria for inclusion of studies in a meta-analysis. There might be a tendency to exclude studies that do not support certain effects or conclusions of interest to the researcher. In addition, the pool of research literature for various reasons tends to favor findings that are statistically significant. Nonsignificant findings do not seem to get published as readily.

Meta-analysis does have its advantages (Cooper, 1982). One of the favorable aspects of meta-analysis generally cited is that the procedure tends to be less subjective than the traditional practice of classifying studies in a "box-score" format (e.g., those supporting positive effects, those not supporting effects, those supporting negative effects). Further, meta-analysis provides a method for exploring the external validity of the findings of a group of studies which, if taken individually, might not have defendable external validity. Despite the controversies about it, meta-analysis appears increasingly in the research literature, and it may contribute to procedures for interpreting research literature (Slavin, 1984). However, the application of meta-analysis requires objectivity and considerable sophistication in research. Several sources of information about meta-analysis are indicated in the references and supplementary readings at the end of this chapter.

SUMMARY

Inferential statistics provides methods for using information about samples to draw conclusions about the characteristics of populations. Statistical inference depends heavily upon concepts in probability. A representative sample is of primary importance in inferring characteristics of the population because any bias in the sample could increase a probability of an incorrect inference. Random sampling is the best method of obtaining a representative sample. However, random sampling will occasionally result in the selection of an unrepresentative sample.

Statistical hypotheses often concern parameters of one or more populations. Using the information provided by one or more sample estimates, a decision is made regarding the truth of a null and an alternative hypothesis. The decision is made based on the probability that the obtained sample result could occur by chance if the null hypothesis were true. This probability is determined by referring to a sampling distribution of the statistic for the parameter estimate. The decision is made with the understanding that an error of one of two types may have been made. A Type I error occurs when the null hypothesis is rejected when in reality it is true. A Type II error occurs when the null hypothesis is not rejected when in reality it is false. *Power* is the probability of not making a Type II error. Through the choice of α and sample size, the experimenter has some control over the probabilities with which Types I and II errors occur.

Since research in education and the behavioral sciences is largely inductive, proceeding from the specific to the general, inferential statistical procedures are especially important in these fields of research.

Procedures for several types of hypothesis tests regarding the mean of one or more groups using the unit normal and t distributions were discussed briefly in this chapter with illustrative examples.

The χ^2 procedure was included as an example of nonparametric or distribution-free techniques. These techniques do not depend upon rigorous assumptions about the distribution of the dependent variables. However, they are typically less powerful than the corresponding parametric techniques.

One-, two-, and three-way analysis-of-variance procedures were discussed. The analysis of variance is perhaps the most popular statistical technique in educational and behavioral science research today because of its precision and flexibility. One of the most important features of the method is its ability to deal with the main effects of independent variables and their interactions.

Multivariate methods were discussed briefly. The main advantage of these methods is that they allow the researcher to study multiple inputs and multiple effects. For example, in comparing a new educational program with its predecessor, a researcher can compare the programs using multiple measures of cognitive and affective achievement rather than a single measure of achievement. The results obtained from a multivariate analysis may be more valid than consideration of each dependent variable separately. Alternatively, using multivariate procedures such as factor analysis, researchers are able to understand sets of dependent variables better through determining more general variables that essentially explain the variance of a larger set of variables.

Multivariate procedures can lead to much more thorough understandings of educational phenomena. However, the sophistication needed to apply and interpret the results of these procedures correctly is much greater than that needed for univariate statistical procedures, and the potential for misapplication or misinterpretation is accordingly much greater. These procedures are being used more and more frequently in educational and behavioral science research as the statistical sophistication of researchers increases.

With the proliferation of research literature in education and the social and behavioral sciences, methods for combining research results across studies are needed in order to develop more generalizable statements about empirical tests of hypotheses. Meta-analysis is a procedure for combining effects across many studies that is being used increasingly. The procedure has been criticized for the basis on which studies are chosen for inclusion. There is some question also as to whether it makes sense to combine data from widely differing studies. However, proponents argue that meta-analysis is more rigorous and objective than alternative approaches.

PROBLEMS FOR THOUGHT AND DISCUSSION

1 From your own field of interest, find examples of research studies that use analysis-of-variance or regression analysis.

2 A researcher is interested in studying the relationship between the ability to solve a problem in logic, speed in performing a manual task, and score on a standardized test of English vocabulary. Suggest some appropriate questions which might be asked as a basis for investigating these variables. Suggest an analysis appropriate to answer the questions you have asked.

3 It has been suggested that analysis of variance permits causal interpretation of research. From what you know about research design and threats to validity in experiments, under what conditions would this be true? Can you find examples of true experimental studies and nonexperimental studies that used analysis of variance? Which seems more important, the research design or the statistical analysis, when making inferences about causation?

4 Look at examples of multivariate procedures reported in the research literature. Do the statistical methods employed allow for consideration of more complex problems and constructs?

5 Is factor-analytic research more like experimental or descriptive research?

6 A researcher reports that in a meta-analysis of 68 studies on the effects of psychotherapy on adolescent drug abusers, it was found that psychotherapy was significantly effective in lowering the incidence of school-related problems. Discuss some questions about this finding and the meta-analysis that you might pose to the researcher.

REFERENCES

Cancelli, A. A., Bergan, J. R., & Jones, S. (1982). Psychometric and instructional validation approaches to the hierarchical sequencing of learning tasks. *Journal of School Psychology, 20,* 232–243.

Catterall, J. S. (1987). An intensive group counseling dropout prevention intervention: Some cautions on isolating at-risk adolescents within high schools. *American Educational Research Journal, 24,* 521–540.

Cooper, H. (1982). Scientific guidelines for conducting integrative reviews. *Review of Educational Research, 52,* 291–302.

DeVries, D. L., & Edwards, K. J. (1973). Learning games and student teams: Their effects on classroom process. *American Educational Research Journal, 10,* 307–318.

Elashoff, J. D. (1969). Analysis of covariance: A delicate instrument. *American Educational Research Journal, 6,* 383–401.

Evans, S. H., & Anastasio, E. J. (1968). Misuse of analysis of covariance when treatment effect and covariate are confounded. *Psychological Bulletin, 69,* 225–234.

Eysenck, H. J. (1978). An exercise in mega-silliness. *American Psychologist, 33,* 517.

Gallo, P. (1978). Meta-analysis—A mixed meta-phor? *American Psychologist, 33,* 515–517.

Glass, G. (1977). Integrating findings: The meta-analysis of research. In Shulman, L., (Ed.), *Review of research in education.* Itasca, IL: Peacock.

Glass, G. V., & Hopkins, K. D. (1984). *Statistical methods in education and psychology* (2nd ed.). Englewood Cliffs, NJ: Prentice-Hall.

Glass, G. V., Peckham, P. D., & Sanders, J. R. (1972). Consequences of failure to meet assumptions underlying the fixed effects analysis of variance and covariance. *Review of Educational Research, 42,* 237–288.

Gorsuch, R. (1983). *Factor analysis.* Hilldale, NJ: Erlbaum.

Harman, H. (1976). *Modern Factor Analysis.* The University of Chicago Press.

Hays, W. L. (1981). *Statistics* (3rd. ed.). New York: Holt.

Johnson, R. A., & Wichern, D. W. (1988). *Applied multivariate statistical analysis* (2nd ed.). Englewood Cliffs, NJ: Prentice-Hall.

Kennedy, W. R. (1975). Grades expected and grades received—their relationship to students' evaluation of faculty performance. *Journal of Educational Psychology, 67,* 109–115.

Kirk, R. E. (1982). *Experimental design: Procedures for the behavioral sciences* (2nd ed.). Belmont, CA: Brooks/Cole.

Kulik, C. L. C., Kulik, J., & Schwab, B. (1983). College programs for high-risk students: A meta-analysis of findings. *Review of Educational Research, 53,* 397–414.

McCollister, T. S., Burts, D. C., Hildreth, G. J., Wright, V. L. (1986). Effects of computer-assisted instruction and teacher-assisted instruction on arithmetic task achievement scores of kindergarten children. *Journal of Educational Research, 80,* 121–125.

Siegel, S. (1956). *Nonparametric statistics for the behavioral sciences.* New York: McGraw-Hill.

Slavin, R. E. (1984). Meta-analysis in education: How has it been used? *Educational Researcher, 13*(8), 6–15.

Suzuki, M. G. (1975). Cross-national comparison of educational programming preferences, ratings of severity, and classification of learning or behavioral problems. Unpublished doctoral dissertation. Lexington: University of Kentucky.

Tamir, P. (1975). The relationships among cognitive preference, school environment, teachers' curricular bias, and subject matter. *American Educational Research Journal, 12,* 235–264.

Tatsuoka, M. M. (1988). *Multivariate analysis: Techniques for educational and psychological research* (2nd ed.). New York: Macmillan.

Walsh, J. E. (1962). *A handbook of nonparametric statistics* (2 vols.). New York: Van Nostrand.

Winer, B. J. (1971). *Statistical principles in experimental design* (2nd ed.). New York: McGraw-Hill.

Wortman, P. (1983). Meta-analysis: A validity perspective. *Annual Review of Psychology, 34,* 223–260.

SUPPLEMENTARY READINGS

Bray, J. S., & Maxwell, S. E. (1982). Analyzing and interpreting significant MANOVAS. *Review of Educational Research, 52,* 340–367.

Huberty, C. J. On statistical testing. *Educational Researcher, 16* (8), 4–9.

Hunter, J. E., Schmidt, F. L., & Jackson, G. B. (1982). *Meta-analysis: Cumulating research findings across studies.* Beverly Hills, CA: Sage.

Light, R. J., & Pillemer, D. B. (1984). *Summing up: The science of reviewing research.* Cambridge, MA: Harvard.

Pedhazur, E. J. (1982). *Multiple regression in behavioral research: Explanation and prediction.* New York: Holt.

Pruzek, R. M. (1971). Methods and problems in the analysis of multivariate data. *Review of Educational Research, 41,* 163–190.

Stock, W. A., Okun, M. A., Haring, M. J., Miller, W., Kinney, C., & Ceurvorst, R. W. (1982). Rigor in data synthesis: A case study in reliability in meta-analysis. *Educational Researcher, 11*(6), 10–14, 20.

CHAPTER 8

OBSERVING AND MEASURING

One of the major contributions of observation and measurement to research is *objectivity*. That is, using measurement scales and systematic observation, the researcher is able to remove at least some degree of his or her own biases and feelings from the data. Objectivity is essential in scientific research because it is necessary that others be able to understand and replicate a finding before it is considered dependable. Since it facilitates communication and promotes objectivity, the role of observation and measurement in research cannot be underestimated. Indeed, many feel that progress in science depends almost totally upon the ability to observe and measure objectively and well.

There would surely be very little communication among researchers if there were no objective observation or measurement. For example, assume that a researcher was studying the relationship between anxiety in a child and the child's performance in class. The researcher designated the children she felt were anxious and then developed a sense of their classroom performance by talking to them. After this, she claimed she had a better feeling about the performance of children who were not anxious. The problems with a non-objective measurement approach to research such as this are obvious.

In earlier chapters, we discussed designing research and analyzing data without giving much thought to the nature of the variables and the operationalization of constructs. Many well-designed and well-analyzed research investigations suffer because of improper or inadequate attention to observation and measurement of dependent and independent variables. In this chapter, we will discuss some of the fundamental principles of measurement that are important in research. We will review reliability, validity, errors of measurement, and other fundamentals of measurement. In addition, we will look at the group of instruments known as *standardized tests*. Our purpose here is to make the reader aware of the role of measurement in research and of some of the concepts involved.

Chapter 4 emphasized the internal and external validity of experimental studies. In many ways, measurement or observational validity is even more basic in research because this kind of validity applies to all forms of research—qualitative, experimental, descriptive, and evaluative. No matter how well a study is conceived or conducted, if observations and measurements are not objective, clear, appropriate, and valid for the intended purposes, the study cannot provide dependable information.

THE IMPORTANCE OF MEASUREMENT AND OBSERVATION

To illustrate the importance of measurement to research, we shall consider the problem of selecting an appropriate dependent variable for an evaluation of the effectiveness of a training program in decision making for business executives. The training program stressed the application of inductive and deductive reasoning to executive decision-making situations. After the training program was completed, its effectiveness was evaluated by four different industrial psychologists, who compared executives who completed the program with a control group. Although each researcher used an identical posttest-only control-group design to assess the effectiveness of the program, each measured the dependent variable differently.

Table 8-1 shows the results of each researcher's evaluation of the treatment. The first researcher reasoned that the program should have made the participating executives smarter and that this should have led to "swelled heads" among them. Therefore, he used hat size as a dependent variable. Of course, such training programs do not affect hat size, so this researcher found no difference between the two groups and concluded that the training program was not useful. The second researcher decided to use judges' ratings to assess the effectiveness of the training program. Executives who had received the training and those who had not were ranked by judges according to their decision-

TABLE 8-1
RESULTS OF EVALUATIONS OF THE SAME TRAINING PROGRAM USING FOUR
DIFFERENT CRITERION MEASURES

Researcher and criterion	Treatment-group posttest mean	Control posttest mean
1 Hat size	7¼	7¼
2 Judges' ratings	8	8
3 Commercial reasoning test	78	73
4 Executive decision test	38	28

making ability. Since there were 15 executives in each group who received ranks from 1 to 15, the average rank had to be 8 in each group and no differences could be found. The third researcher used a commercially available test of reasoning ability. He felt that since there was a relationship between executive decision making and reasoning ability, effects of the training program should be observable in the scores on the reasoning test. The fourth researcher also measured reasoning ability, but he did it differently. He developed a test of executive decision making for use in the evaluation of the training program. Items in the test were based upon the lesson objectives of the training program. Since the test related highly to the course content, the executives who had undergone the training performed best on it. It should be evident from this example that what is measured and how it is measured are critical issues in a research study. The dependent and independent measures used must be appropriate to the concepts under study and the purpose of the research.

FUNDAMENTAL PRINCIPLES OF MEASUREMENT

In Chapter 6, we defined *measurement* as "the assigning of numbers to objects according to a set of rules." Further, we identified four kinds of measurement scales—nominal, ordinal, interval, and ratio—and discussed their impact upon the selection of procedures for statistical analysis. However, we have not yet related these scales to research applications.

In general, we can say that the kind of measurement scale used should reflect the purpose of the measurement. For example, when a nominal scale is used, the purpose of measuring is to classify. Thus, although we assign numbers as names of categories (such as 1 = black students, 2 = white students, and 3 = other groups of students), it is clear that we mean to use the numbers only as labels. On the other hand, ordinal scales have more of a comparative purpose. Objects, events, or persons are ordered based upon the degree to which some characteristic is present in them. Another example of the use of measurement scales is illustrated by a scheme used to evaluate the distance an athlete can throw a football. The scale is marked off in standard units of equal length, such as feet. The purpose of the scale is not just to order the athletes in terms of how far they throw the football but also to be able to know the difference in distance between tosses. That is, a toss of 20 feet is 10 less than one of 30 feet, which is 10 less than one of 40 feet, and so on. This kind of measurement scale is interval. Since this interval scale has a real zero point, it also happens to be a ratio scale.

The Nature of What Is Measured

In the natural and physical sciences, units of measurement and constructs are better identified than in the behavioral sciences and education. For example, there is little dispute concerning whether length, weight, and time exist and can be measured in the physical sciences, although there may be theoretical or practical questions concerning these constructs under certain conditions. In behavioral and educational research, however, the problems of measurement are much more difficult. Three questions with which researchers in these sciences must constantly be concerned are

1 Does the construct being measured exist?
2 How can the construct be operationally defined, and what is the best kind of scale and units to measure it?
3 If the construct exists and can be measured, is it important to include it in the research?

The first problem is probably clear enough to the reader. No one really knows whether constructs such as intelligence, personality, and motivation really exist in the ways they have been conceptualized. If everything possible to be known about human behavior were known, it might be found that these are not useful constructs. However, in the absence of such complete knowledge, we make educated guesses about them.

The second problem is just as perplexing. Even if we accept the definition of a construct, the measurement of it does not always follow directly. For example, even if we accept the definition offered by the psychologist Lewis Terman (1916) that intelligence is the ability to think in abstract terms, we do not know very much about how to measure intelligence because psychologists would doubtless disagree among themselves over what constitutes abstract thinking.

The third problem is also compelling for the researcher. If a construct is generally agreed to exist and there are some generally recognized techniques available to measure it, is the variable an important one for the research questions being asked? This is a problem in all kinds of research. For example, in designing research to assess the effects of preschool programs, researchers often have a problem determining appropriate measures to use because the focus and goals of programs tend to be diffuse—e.g., emotional and social development, concept development, improved health—so that suitable measures of the whole range of the objectives are difficult to find. Measures that do not reflect the emphases of the program cannot be entirely satisfactory.

We should stress at this point that although we say that we measure something, what we really measure are attributes of that thing. For example, we do not measure a child when we administer an IQ test. Rather, we measure the characteristics of the child which the IQ test is designed to measure. Although we call what the IQ test measures ''intelligence,'' in reality the general meaning of the word may not correspond perfectly with what the test measures. A measurement technique is useful only when it reflects the existence of the trait or attribute in reality. For example, we might use hair length as a measure of physical strength and say the longer the hair, the stronger the person. However, we would not find the measure dependable, for there probably is little correspondence between hair length and physical strength.

A measure should not only reflect reality, it should do it accurately. Thus a measure should convey notions of quantity or quality dependably. To illustrate this point, the height of horses is measured in units called *hands*. If *hand* were defined as "the distance across the palm of an adult person's hand," obviously the height of a horse would depend upon who is doing the measuring. People with small hands would have taller horses. This kind of measure does not give an accurate picture of the trait or attribute. In the case of measurement of height in hands, the standard width of a hand has been set at 4 inches. Thus a horse that is 18 hands tall is 72 inches, or 6 feet, tall, and 18 hands is a measure that communicates how tall the horse really is.

Constructs May Not Be Measured Directly

In the social and behavioral sciences and in education, constructs often cannot be measured directly. For example, we may speak of measuring personality, achievement, concept development, intelligence, or mechanical ability, yet, in fact, we do not measure the construct directly. Rather, we identify some behaviors or characteristics we feel represent a construct and then assume that a person possesses the qualities of the construct to the degree that he or she demonstrates these characteristics or performs the behavior. Consider for a moment what is done when intelligence is measured using an instrument like the Wechsler Intelligence Scale for Children—Revised (WISC-R) (Wechsler, 1974) or the Stanford-Binet Intelligence Scale (Thorndike, Hagen, & Sattler, 1986). The child is asked a variety of questions requiring different kinds of mental processes and responses. For example, the child might be asked to name the seasons or to recognize the similarities in two objects or ideas that are somehow abstractly related. The child's responses are scored according to standardized criteria based upon a large number of children who have taken the test. The problems with this approach are illustrated using the actual responses given by a young boy from a rural area. When asked to describe the similarities of two different kinds of fruit, he responded, "They are two things we never get to see around here!" and when asked to name the seasons of the year, he replied, "Squirrel, deer, possum, and partridge." Since he did not give the generally accepted answers, his intelligence score was reduced. But we cannot be sure that he was really less intelligent than someone who answered the questions more typically. We are forced to measure most things indirectly in this way in the behavioral sciences. Researchers must always recognize the limitations of their measurement methods and not overinterpret scores.

METHODS OF MEASURING

When we speak of measurement in the behavioral sciences and education, we usually include a variety of activities. Traits may be measured using a standard scale, or behavior may be observed and classified. Furthermore, questioning techniques such as open-ended interviews conducted to determine how people feel about political candidates or consumer products allow researchers to obtain information which might be difficult to obtain with more formal methods. However, the analysis of this kind of data is more difficult than data obtained using more structured measurement techniques.

In educational and behavioral science research, tests are the primary measurement tool. In other sciences, devices such as weight scales, columns of mercury, and voltmeters are used for measurement. For our purposes here, a *test* may be defined as "a systematic procedure for obtaining observations of performance." Although paper-and-pencil tests predominate in research on human behavior, other methods of testing are frequently used. For example, one way to see how much a sea captain knows about navigation would be to give him a paper-and-pencil test containing questions about navigation. Another method would be to observe him performing at the helm of a ship under various conditions. Although it might be easier to obtain a numerical score on the first kind of test, the second test would probably give us a better idea of the captain's navigational skill.

Because measurement in educational and behavioral research is generally indirect and because specific measurement techniques may not be available to meet the exact needs of the researcher, it is sometimes difficult to select the most appropriate method of measurement to use in a research study. The researcher must carefully select or design the best measurement technique that is available. To do this, the validity and reliability of the measures must be considered.

VALIDITY

Probably the single most important characteristic of a test is its validity.* Other characteristics are important, but if a measuring instrument is not valid, it is useless. *Validity* can be defined as "the degree to which a test measures what it is supposed to measure." There are three fundamental approaches to the validity of tests and measures. The first, *content validity,* concerns the degree to which the test items represent the domain or universe of the trait or property being measured. The second, *construct validity,* concerns the degree of relationship between the measure and the construct being measured. The third approach, *criterion-related validity,* concerns the ability of the test to predict or estimate a criterion. We shall now discuss each of these three approaches to validity more extensively.

Content Validity

To understand content validity, let us assume that we are interested in measuring social studies achievement in high school students. To do this, we must

---

* Although it is more traditional in texts to present validity after reliability, we chose to cover validity first because of its relative importance and to discuss the relationship between the two concepts later. As we shall see, reliability is necessary but not sufficient for validity.

identify the universe of content of high school social studies. Then, by randomly sampling items from this universe, we should obtain a group of items for our test that is representative of the content of high school social studies. Figure 8-1 shows the relationship of the item sampling to the universe of items.

Unfortunately, establishing the content validity of a test is not as simple in practical situations as has just been suggested because it is usually not a simple matter to identify the universe of content. Therefore, typically it is not possible to sample items randomly from the universe of content. This problem is usually handled by having expert judges identify a content area. For example, in the case of our social studies test, a group of recognized high school social studies curriculum experts would be asked to identify the area for which the test is to be developed. Then a group of items would be designed to be representative of the content identified by the judges. Finally, the judges would be asked their opinions about how well the items reflect the content area. Thus the determination of content validity usually depends considerably upon judgment rather than mathematical procedures and is, accordingly, subject to the beliefs, values, and biases of the judges.

There are other problems in establishing content validity. Many of the concepts or traits studied in education and the behavioral sciences cannot be identified very specifically. Consider, for example, mathematical ability, emotional status, attitudes, values, and school achievement. For many of these complex traits, the more specifically the universe of content is defined on a test, the less the test will resemble the trait. To illustrate this problem, let us consider a test to measure achievement in an undergraduate psychology course. We might begin to develop the test by defining certain objectives, such as "the student knows the meaning of reinforcement in learning." However, we find that there are many ways to observe or test knowledge. The student could be asked to define *reinforcement*. Another approach would be to ask for examples of reinforced behavior. On a more theoretical level, students could be asked to

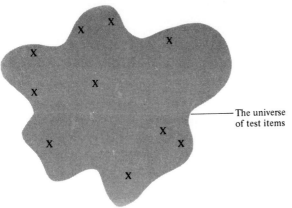

FIGURE 8-1
Ten items, indicated by *X*'s, selected randomly from the universe of items in high school social studies.

The universe of test items

compare Skinner's ideas about reinforcement with those of Thorndike. It is possible that a student could give examples of reinforced behavior without knowing the definition of *reinforcement*. On the other hand, being able to give the definition of *reinforcement* does not assure that the principles can be applied. With this in mind, it becomes evident that to specify the universe or domain of the unit in a psychology course on reinforcement beyond the "knowledge" level is fraught with difficulty. We must first decide what we mean by the term "knowledge." Then we decide which aspects to emphasize. A content-by-objectives grid, similar to the one discussed in Chapter 13, may be useful for such purposes (see Figure 13-1).

Besides the difficulties already mentioned, an item may require more or different traits than it was designed to measure if it is to be answered correctly. To understand this point better, read and answer the test item in Figure 8-2. The item asks a child to place an X on the thing that is a toy. Clearly, the duck on the right looks most like a toy. But a bright child who knows about telephones might notice that there are only 9 holes on the telephone dial where there should be 10 and therefore that the phone must be a toy also. Furthermore, the airplane might be considered a picture of a toy plane. The drawing does not show that it is undoubtedly a real one. So the brighter, more aware child who knows a great deal about the concept of *toy* might answer haphazardly on such an item because each of the choices appears to be correct. Such an item might at first glance *appear* to have content validity. Yet when it is studied more carefully, the content validity should be questioned because the item does not dependably test the content it was designed to assess.

Construct Validity

Earlier (Chapter 3), the role of constructs in research was discussed. Construct validity concerns the degree to which the test measures the construct it was designed to measure. It is probably evident to the reader that variables such as mechanical ability, introversion, numerical reasoning, and attitudes towards

FIGURE 8-2
A sample item from a test of concept learning.

Instructions

Place an X on the thing that is a toy.

school clearly involve constructs, and tests of them would require construct validation. However, it is less obvious that tests of skills and school achievement also concern the measures of constructs and require evidence of construct validity. This point has often been ignored in educational achievement testing in favor of emphasis upon content or other forms of validity.

There are two parts to the evaluation of the construct validity of a test. First and most important, the theory underlying the construct being measured must be considered. Second, the adequacy of the test in measuring the construct is evaluated. For example, let us suppose that we are interested in measuring a personality trait that we have called "airiness," which we have defined as "open, sprightly, and active." We have based this upon our own observations. We then ask experts, psychologists, psychiatrists, and social workers to evaluate our construct of airiness. The experts whom we query cannot agree that our definition is the correct one for *airiness,* nor can they agree upon an alternative definition. Furthermore, assume we cannot find evidence in the research literature to support the existence of the airiness construct as we have defined it. On the basis of such information (or the lack of it), the validity of the construct itself can be questioned. However, even in view of such information, it is difficult to state emphatically that airiness as we have described it has no meaning.

But assuming that the construct being measured is a meaningful one, we must examine the adequacy of the test used to measure it. There are two basic approaches to this, and both should be used to investigate construct validity. The first approach involves gathering data concerning the trait being measured using some established method and comparing decisions based upon these data to those based upon the test being assessed. The decisions based upon the different sources should be similar. This is known as *convergence.* That is, if interpretation of data from various other sources is convergent with interpretations from the test, construct validity of the test is supported.

The second major approach which must be taken to evaluate the construct validity of a test is known as *discriminant validity.* This involves demonstrating that the construct may be discriminated from other constructs that may be somewhat similar or entirely different. For example, assume that we had identified the construct "readiness to begin to attend first grade" and had made a test of it. We could determine convergent validity by correlating our test with another one designed to measure readiness for school and by comparing the interpretations of scores made on our test to judgments made by experts in early-childhood education. On the other hand, discriminability might be studied by correlating the test to variables from which we would hope it could be differentiated, such as sex and age of the child and education of the mother and father.*

* See, for example, Hayes, M., Mason, E. J., & Covert, R. (1975). Validity and reliability of a simple device for readiness screening. *Educational and Psychological Measurement,* 35, 495–498.

Construct Validity by Factor Analysis   One of the primary tools for studying construct validity is the complex statistical procedure known as *factor analysis,* a brief discussion of which was provided in Chapter 7. *Factor analysis* is a method of identifying sets of variables that correlate highly among themselves but not with other variables. The sets of variables identified are called *factors,* and the factor structure found in a collection of variables helps to determine the structure of the concept.†

Let us consider the study of the validity of a form used by college students to evaluate their instructors (Covert and Mason, 1974). The form consisted of 17 items upon which ratings were made according to a 5-point scale. Based upon previous research in the area of student evaluations of teachers, the rating form was developed to reflect three areas of concern: the qualities of the instructor, classroom and class assignments, and other variables such as students' expectations for grade and difficulty of the course, pace of the course, and student workload. Factor analysis of a large number of students' ratings of their teachers on the 17 items supported the existence of the three factors which the assessment instrument was designed to measure. Specifically, a factor was identified which was composed of teacher and teaching characteristics (i.e., clarity of presentation, availability to students, responsiveness to class, etc.). A second factor contained a group of items which related to student expectations or perceptions of the course. The third group of items correlated rather highly with what might be called *course characteristics,* such as quality of textbook, quality of assignments, examinations, and discussions. The factor analysis was considered to support the construct validity of the evaluation form because the items formed factors representing the three areas which the instrument was designed to measure. Furthermore, items did not seem to correlate highly with more than one factor. For example, items which related highly to the teaching factor did not correlate highly with the student perceptions or the course characteristics factors.

Construct Validity by Multitrait-Multimethod Analysis   Campbell and Fiske (1959) suggested what might be an ideal approach to determining discriminability and convergence in construct validity. This approach recognizes that in the measurement of a trait, scores are influenced by characteristics of the method of measuring as well as the trait. With the multitrait-multimethod approach, more than one method is used to measure more than one trait. Then a matrix of correlations is formed in which each measure of a trait is correlated with other measures of the same trait and with measures of at least one other trait using the same method. For an illustration of this idea, assume that we wish to measure three traits: mathematical ability, vocabulary, and compulsiveness in a group of children. We measure each trait in two ways. First, we ask the classroom teacher to judge the children in our sample on each

†A readable discussion of factor analysis for those who need some understanding of the method but do not have enough preparation in statistics to handle the sophisticated procedures involved is provided by Dennis Child (1970) in *The essentials of factor analysis.* New York: Holt.

trait, using a 10-point scale. Then, we ask the children to take paper-and-pencil tests designed to measure each of the traits.

Before looking at the multitrait-multimethod matrix in Table 8-2, let us think about what we expect to see if our construct measures of the three traits are valid. First, should we expect a reasonably high correlation between scores to be obtained by the two different methods of measuring the same trait? Second, do we expect two different traits to correlate highly when measured by the same methods? The answer to the first question is "yes," to the second is "no."

For an illustration, turn now to the matrix in Table 8-2. The block of particular interest is in the lower left-hand corner showing the correlation between scores obtained by the two methods of measurement (in boxes). Notice that the first question can be answered affirmatively. That is, the correlation between the two methods is moderately high for each trait (.59, .63, .68). The values in the diagonals within parentheses are called *reliability coefficients* and are covered later in this chapter. They represent the correlation between scores on the same trait measured with the same method. Notice that these coefficients are higher than when the same traits are measured by different methods. Also notice that in the off-diagonal elements of the lower-left quadrant, the correlations between different traits measured with different methods are quite low (.29, .18, .09, .27, .11, .12). Furthermore, the correlations between the different traits measured using the same methods (.40, .31, .29, .37, .25, .18) are lower than they are for the same traits measured by the different methods. The findings depicted in Table 8-2 therefore support the convergent and discriminant validity of the measures.

It is desirable to use the multitrait-multimethod matrix whenever studying construct validity of a measure. This is not always feasible because of unavailability of alternative methods or economic considerations. However, there is little doubt that the approach should be more widely used than presently is the case.

TABLE 8-2
MULTITRAIT*-MULTIMETHOD† MATRIX

	Traits	Method 1			Method 2		
		A_1	B_1	C_1	A_2	B_2	C_2
Method 1	A_1	(.77)					
	B_1	.40	(.81)				
	C_1	.31	.29	(.92)			
Method 2	A_2	.59	.27	.11	(.71)		
	B_2	.29	.63	.12	.37	(.78)	
	C_2	.18	.09	.68	.25	.18	(.83)

*Traits are (A) compulsiveness, (B) mathematical ability, and (C) vocabulary.
†Methods are (1) teacher judgment and (2) students' test performance.

Criterion-Related Validity

What makes criterion-related validity different from content and construct validity is that it concerns the relationship between a test and a criterion rather than a construct or domain. To illustrate, assume that we wish to devise a test to identify psychologists who are exceptional at dealing with problems of adolescents. We begin by having impartial experts determine from a large group of counseling psychologists those whom they judge to be best at handling adolescent clients. We then construct 587 items to which counseling psychologists are asked to reply "yes" or "no," such as "I believe it is important to wear shoes" and "I like to do things alone."* We then go through the responses and select the items which the good counselors answered one way and the remainder answered the other way. Assume that this process produces 107 items, which we put together to form what we shall call the Test of Effectiveness in Counseling Adolescents (TECA).

We feel this test will identify good counselors for adolescents. The criterion of interest here is ability to counsel adolescents. We might explore further the criterion-related validity of TECA by administering it to a new group of counselors that has previously been divided into those who are effective with adolescents and those who are not. Then we could determine how well the test identifies the group to which each counselor is assigned.

Thus criterion-related validity is concerned with detecting the presence or absence of one or more criteria considered to represent traits or constructs of interest. There are two types of criterion-related validity. *Predictive* validity concerns the ability of the measure to forecast the presence or absence of the trait in the future, and *concurrent* validity involves the capability of the measure to reflect the present status of the criteria. The Graduate Record Examination is expected to have predictive validity because it is used to help identify students who will perform well in graduate studies. On the other hand, the Minnesota Multiphasic Personality Inventory (MMPI) would be expected to have concurrent validity because it is used to identify the kinds of personality characteristics people now have.

An illustration of a study of predictive validity is provided by Zytowski (1976). A sample of 882 men and women who had taken the Kuder Occupational Interest Survey in high school or college were located 12 to 19 years later. At the time of the follow-up study, 51 percent were employed in an occupation that would have been suggested by the test. Furthermore, better prediction was achieved when the occupation was one of those named on the profile. Such data are interpreted as supporting the predictive validity of the instrument.

A point often ignored when criterion-related validity is considered is the importance of construct and content validity. For example, suppose that we are interested in selecting people for leadership positions within a large corpora-

---

* Notice that the items need not correspond in an obvious way to the trait being measured.

tion. We may begin by trying to find items which predict leadership ability, but we would quickly find that we must first decide what is meant by *leadership*. This, of course, is a construct-validity problem. Content validity would become important if we wished to sample the items from the domain of leadership.

RELIABILITY

Validity is concerned with how well a test measures what it is supposed to measure. *Reliability* involves the consistency, dependability, or stability of the test score. That is, if we used the measure many times with the same person and the test was reliable, we would get approximately the same score each time. However, if the test were not reliable, there would be a great deal of variability in the scores across several administrations. This variability would be due to chance or random conditions. To use a simple analogy, imagine two people hitting a nail with a hammer. One is not being very accurate and many of his swings miss the nail. The other hits the nail each time. In terms of hitting the nail, the first person is not reliable, but the second one is.

Observed Scores and Reliability

To understand reliability in terms of measurement, we will begin with the notion of *obtained,* or *observed,* score. This is the score that someone gets on a test or measurement. It is, for example, the IQ score on an IQ test, number of items answered correctly on an ability or achievement test, or number of times a type of behavior is observed on a behavior-recording scale. The observed score may be thought of as the result of two different components. One component reflects the true amount of the trait possessed and is called the *true* score. It is not influenced by random or external conditions such as fatigue of the respondent, noise outside the room, or any other variables that might affect the observed score. The other component reflects the effects of these external chance conditions and is called the *error* score. Observed score is the sum of the true and error scores. Thus, if X_0 represents the observed score, X_t the true score, and X_e the error score, then

$$X_0 = X_t + X_e$$

True scores are theoretical because we never really know the value of an individual's true score. However, if it were possible to do so, we could take a group of observed scores and break each one down into true score and error, and we would find that occasionally the error component raises the observed score, and at other times lowers it. In the long run, over a large number of test administrations to a single person, the positive and negative error scores should total zero because they are due to chance influences. Table 8-3 shows the hypothetical relationship among observed scores, true scores, and error scores for 20 students on a test of mechanical skills. We could find the mean,

TABLE 8-3
OBSERVED SCORES, TRUE SCORES, AND ERROR SCORES OF 20
STUDENTS ON A TEST OF MECHANICAL SKILLS

Student	Observed score	=	True score	+	Error
Joe	17		18		− 1
Laura	21		19		+ 2
Alan	33		28		+ 5
Jay	18		21		− 3
Jill	35		32		+ 3
Joan	41		35		+ 6
Peter M.	35		37		− 2
Albert	29		29		0
Ellen	21		26		− 5
Steve	25		23		+ 2
Peter K.	36		39		− 3
Fred	33		31		+ 2
Sue	34		38		− 4
Linda	22		25		− 3
Ken	37		33		+ 4
John	18		25		− 7
Sandra	21		22		− 1
Becky	28		26		+ 2
Robert	30		29		+ 1
Cindy	32		30		+ 2

variance, and standard deviation of each kind of score relatively easily following procedures discussed in Chapter 6 when we have a table like this. In reality, true scores and error scores are never known.

As we just stated, true scores are not known in real situations, and the data
in Table 8-3 are hypothetical. Yet we can illustrate the meanings of certain
terms using these data. Specifically, the variance of the error column is called
the *variance error of measurement*. The variance of true and observed scores
can also be obtained. Although we do not know the actual component values,
we can estimate these quantities statistically using observed scores.

Reliability is defined as "the ratio of variance in true scores to variance in
observed scores," or

$$r_{xx} = \frac{\sigma_t^2}{\sigma_0^2} = \frac{\sigma_t^2}{\sigma_t^2 + \sigma_e^2}$$

where r_{xx} = reliability
σ_t^2 = variance in true scores
σ_0^2 = variance in observed scores
σ_e^2 = variance of error

Let us say, for instance, that in a certain population of observed scores
$\sigma_e^2 = 25$ and $\sigma_0^2 = 100$. Since

$$\sigma_o^2 = \sigma_t^2 + \sigma_e^2$$

we can easily find the true score variance σ_t^2 by subtracting σ_e^2 from σ_0^2, or

$$\sigma_0^2 - \sigma_t^2 = \sigma_e^2$$
$$100 - 25 = \sigma_t^2$$
$$75 = \sigma_t^2$$

Then, applying this to the formula given above for the reliability, we find

$$r_{xx} = \frac{\sigma_t^2}{\sigma_0^2} = \frac{75}{100} = .75$$

Therefore, it can be said that 75 percent of the variance in the observed scores is attributable to true score variance.

In Chapter 6, we saw that the squared correlation coefficient was theoretically equal to the proportion of variance in Y that could be accounted for by predicting Y from X. Thus, if $r_{xy} = .80$, we would say that 64 percent of the variance in Y was common with the X variable. This leads us to another interpretation of reliability. If we let r_{xx} represent reliability and $r_{x_ox_t}$ represent the correlation of true scores and observed scores, then r_{xx} is the squared correlation between observed and true scores, as follows:

$$r_{xx} = r^2_{x_ox_t}$$

Since the maximum value of a correlation coefficient is $+ 1.00$, it can be readily seen from the above relationship that the maximum reliability coefficient is 1.00 and the minimum is 0.0.

Computing Reliability

A number of techniques have been developed for estimating reliability from the observed test scores or item responses. Generally, the higher the reliability, the less the effect of chance upon a measure. The lower the reliability, the more the measure reflects chance factors. Four approaches have been developed to estimate reliability. The first, *stability,* involves administering the test to a group, waiting a period of time, then readministering the test to the same group, and finally correlating the scores obtained on the two testings. The procedure yields a reliability estimate known as a *stability coefficient.* If individuals perform similarly on the two tests, the correlation will be high and so will reliability. A major problem with the stability approach concerns the length of time between administrations of the test. If it is too short, performance on the second test might be affected by people remembering the test from the first time. On the other hand, waiting too long might result in the sample of respondents changing—that is, getting older and undergoing critical or otherwise important experiences—so that they will actually be a different group by the second test administration. Furthermore, there is a natural tendency for lower reliability estimates to be obtained in the stability method the longer the time between test administrations.

A second approach is known as *equivalence*. In this method, two equivalent forms of the test are formulated and administered to the same persons during a single time period. The correlation between the scores on the two forms is considered an estimate of reliability.* The major problem with this method, of course, is in developing two tests that are perfectly equivalent. Although some standardized test publishers claim equivalence between two or more forms, rarely are the tests fully interchangeable.† The less parallel the two test forms are, the lower the correlation between them, and consequently the lower the estimated reliability will be. Another problem with the equivalence approach is the length of time it takes to administer two tests. During that time, subjects can become bored, tired, or uninterested, all of which can affect reliability estimates.

A third approach to the investigation of reliability involves combining *stability and equivalence*. In this combined method, two parallel forms of the test are administered to a group of respondents over a period of time. The problem of subjects being influenced by the first testing in the stability method is of less importance with this method. Furthermore, the problem of fatigue setting in during the long time needed to administer two forms of the same test in the equivalence method is overcome. However, the problems of finding equivalent forms and determining the optimal time period between test administrations remain.

Internal consistency, a fourth approach to reliability, is frequently used because it provides an estimate of reliability with only one administration of a test. This approach involves looking at the consistency or stability of performance among test items. There are several methods for computing estimates of reliability using the internal consistency approach. Among the most common are the split-half approach utilizing the Spearman-Brown formula, the Kuder-Richardson formula 20, and the coefficient alpha.

The Spearman-Brown reliability formula requires splitting a test into halves, usually by dividing the total test score into scores on the odd items and scores on the even items. Then the following formula may be used:

$$r_{xx} = \frac{2r_{0e}}{1 + r_{0e}}$$

where r_{xx} = reliability

r_{0e} = the correlation between scores on the odd and even items

---

* This correlation has been shown to be algebraically equivalent to the proportion of observed score variance that is true score variance. For a simple proof of this see Knapp, T. R. (1971). *Statistics for educational measurement*. Scranton, PA: Intext, pp. 82–83.
†For a discussion of equivalent forms, see Anastasi (1982, pp. 111–113).

This formula emphasizes differences between items rather than between respondents. Furthermore, for tests in which a time limit is provided, this formula is not appropriate. Finally, the longer the test, the more reliable it will generally be.

To illustrate use of the Spearman-Brown reliability formula, imagine that we gave an intelligence test to a large sample of children. Then we determined the number of odd items and the number of even items each child answered correctly. Next, we correlated the odd and even scores and obtained a correlation coefficient of .89. Using the Spearman-Brown formula, we would then find the reliability as follows:

$$r_{xx} = \frac{2r_{0e}}{1 + r_{0e}} = \frac{2(.89)}{1 + .89}$$

$$= \frac{1.78}{1.89} = .94$$

A reliability of .94 suggests that 94 percent of the variance in observed scores is due to true score variance. This is high reliability for a test in education or the behavioral sciences. Generally, reliabilities above .90 are considered acceptable for most behavioral science and education applications. However, there are no hard-and-fast rules about acceptable levels of reliability. For some screening devices, acceptable reliability might be as low as .70. It should be remembered, however, that the less reliable a test, the less dependable its scores.

The Kuder-Richardson formula 20 provides an estimate of the average split-half reliability for all possible splits in a test without requiring actually splitting the test. The data used are individual item responses. The formula for this method can be written

$$r_{xx} = \frac{k}{k - 1} \left(1 - \frac{\Sigma pq}{S_o^2} \right)$$

where r_{xx} = estimated reliability
     k = number of items on the test
     p = the proportion of people who respond correctly to each item
     q = $1 - p$
     S_o^2 = observed score variance

This formula, as with other methods, will generally give higher reliability estimates when the test is lengthy, and it is designed to be used with untimed tests.

To illustrate the use of the Kuder-Richardson formula 20, we will use the data depicted in Table 8-4. The mean number of items answered correctly was 9.6, and the variance was 7.83. Substituting in the Kuder-Richardson formula 20,

TABLE 8-4
PROPORTION RESPONDING CORRECTLY
AND INCORRECTLY ON 15 TEST ITEMS

Item	Proportion correct (p)	Proportion incorrect (q)	pq
1	.53	.47	.249
2	.79	.21	.166
3	.47	.53	.249
4	.60	.40	.240
5	.44	.56	.246
6	.33	.67	.221
7	.40	.60	.240
8	.28	.72	.157
9	.37	.63	.233
10	.49	.51	.250
11	.44	.56	.246
12	.33	.67	.221
13	.40	.60	.240
14	.16	.84	.134
15	.42	.58	.244
			$\Sigma pq = 3.336$

$$r_{xx} = \frac{k}{k-1}\left(1 - \frac{\Sigma pq}{S_0^2}\right)$$

$$= \frac{15}{14}\left(1 - \frac{3.336}{7.83}\right)$$

$$= 1.07(.573) = .61$$

Thus the internal reliability of the test is estimated to be .61. This means that according to the estimate, only 61 percent of the variance in observed scores is true score variance.

The coefficient alpha (Cronbach, 1951) is an internal consistency index designed for use with tests containing items that have no right answer. An attitude test in which respondents indicate the degree to which they agree or disagree with statements on a 5-point scale is an example of a test for which items are not scored as right or wrong. The formula for the α coefficient is

$$\alpha = \frac{k}{k-1}\left(\frac{S_0^2 - S_i^2}{S_0^2}\right)$$

where k = the number of items on the test
S_i^2 = the variance of each item
S_0^2 = the variance of all scores on the total test.

Interpretation of coefficient α is the same as other internal consistency reliability coefficients (i.e., from 0.0 to 1.0, with higher reliability closer to 1.0).

There are a number of other methods for computing reliability. Furthermore, the topic of reliability is a complex one. Readers interested in a more complete discussion are referred to texts designed specifically to deal with measurement, such as Nunnally (1978), Jackson and Messick (1967), Allen and Yen (1979), and Lord and Novick (1968).

The Standard Error of Measurement

Refer back to Table 8-3 for a moment. We said that the variance of the error score column was called the *variance error of measurement*. The square root of this is called the *standard error of measurement*. Although it can be estimated directly using an analysis-of-variance approach, it is usually more convenient to estimate the standard error using reliability by applying the following formula:

$$SEM = S_o\sqrt{1 - r_{xx}}$$

where SEM = the estimated standard error of measurement
      S_o = the standard deviation of observed scores
      r_{xx} = the estimated reliability obtained using one of the methods described above

Thus if the reliability of a set of scores having a standard deviation of 10.0 is .75, the standard error of measurement may be found as follows:

$$SEM = 10.0\sqrt{1 - .75}$$
$$= 10.0\sqrt{.25}$$
$$= 5.0$$

The standard error of measurement is very useful in the interpretation of scores. Since the error components of scores influence obtained scores in a random fashion, occasionally they will result in observed scores being higher than true scores. Other times, errors will cause obtained scores to be lower than true scores. Over a great number of test administrations for one person, the error components will be normally distributed, with a mean of zero. Furthermore, the standard deviation of the distribution of a person's observed scores around the true score is the standard error of measurement. To understand this, look at Figure 8-3, where the normal distribution of obtained scores for one person has been drawn around the true score of 110. The standard error of measurement is 5.0. Notice that about 68 percent of the time, the obtained score will be within ± 5.0 of the true score of 110; and about 95 percent of the time, obtained scores will fall within ± 10.0 of the true score of 110.

As said before, we never really know the value of true scores. What we re-

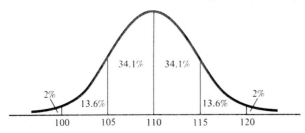

FIGURE 8-3
Normal distribution of obtained scores around an individual's
true score of 110 when standard error of measurement is 5.0.

ally are doing is assuming that the obtained score represents the true score. Then we use a hypothetical normal distribution, with a mean equal to the obtained score, and an estimated standard error of measurement to set limits which probably include the true score. Our reasoning goes like this:

1 The true score must be as far from the obtained score as the obtained score is from the true score.

2 It is probable that the obtained score is within ± 1 standard error of measurement of the true score since the area between − 1*SEM* and + 1*SEM* of the true score contains 68 percent of the obtained scores.

3 Therefore there is a 68 percent probability that the region bounded by ± 1 *SEM* around the obtained score includes the true score.*

See whether you can follow this reasoning in Figure 8-4. Notice, in this example, that the observed score is 114 and the true score is 110. A hypothetical curve has been drawn with dotted lines. If we move 1 *SEM* above and below the observed score, we develop an interval from 109 to 119, which would include the true score of 110 and would be assumed to include 68 percent of the observed scores. The standard error of measurement is important to consider in selecting a measurement for research investigations. The larger the standard error of measurement, the less precision there is in the measurement. Thus the *SEM* is related to reliability. Tests with higher standard errors of measurement are less reliable.

The Relationship between Reliability and Validity

It has been shown statistically that in practice, the squared validity coefficient cannot be greater than the reliability coefficient.† That is, validity is at its maximum when the validity coefficient squared, r^2_{xy}, equals r_{xx}, the reliability co-

---

* Actually, we would probably use values other than ± 1 *SEM*, which was chosen to simplify this discussion.

† For a discussion of this, see Allen and Yen (1979).

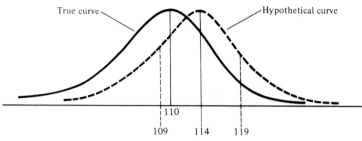

FIGURE 8-4
Hypothetical normal curve around an individual's obtained score of 114 and
the true normal distribution of obtained scores around his true score of 110
with an estimated standard error of measurement equal to 5.0.

efficient. Thus reliability affects validity: the lower the reliability, the less validity a test can have.

On the other hand, the reliability of an instrument may be high but the instrument may have no validity. For example, assume that we used an adult's
shoe size as an indication of ability to learn mathematics. Obviously, shoe size
has nothing to do with ability to learn mathematics and consequently would
have no validity for that purpose. However, nearly every time we measure an
adult's shoe size, we get the same score. Thus our measure is highly consistent
and, consequently, highly reliable. Researchers must be careful to identify
both the reliability and the validity of their measurement techniques.

VALIDITY AND RELIABILITY SPECIFIC TO RESEARCH INVESTIGATIONS

Most of what we have said so far about validity and reliability apply to testing
in general. When a test is designed for some clinical or educational application
in education, psychology, or some related field, the validity and reliability are
determined in terms of the intended use of the test. However, when this established test is then used in research, the application, setting, or purpose
might change the test, resulting in a need for studying the reliability and validity in the context of the research. To illustrate, consider the case of the researcher who asks teachers to indicate which items on a mathematics test they
think a particular child would pass in a study of students' success or failure on
tests as a function of teachers' expectations. The mathematics test may be one
of recognized reliability and validity when it is used as a measure of students'
achievement. On the other hand, the test's validity and reliability have not
been demonstrated for its use as a measure of teachers' expectations of student performance.

Even in situations where an instrument is being used in the manner in which
it was designed to be used, problems with validity and reliability may arise.

Researchers will often use parts of established tests—for example, the vocabulary subtest of the Wechsler Intelligence Scale for Children—Revised (WISC-R) (Wechsler, 1974). The vocabulary subtest requires the child to give definitions of words that are presented orally. It was intended by the test designers to be given at a certain point in the WISC-R testing session. When the subtest is not given at that point, it is not clear how test performance might be affected. The principle concern in this case might be the reliability of this subtest when it is administered alone and not as part of the larger battery.

Another problem might arise if the researcher intends to use the WISC-R vocabulary subtest as an index of something other than general vocabulary as intended by the test designers. For example, if the intention was to use the test as a measure of verbal fluency or academic skill (neither of these uses was intended when the WISC-R was designed), the validity of this new application of the subtest should be determined even though the subtest has already been shown to be valid as a general vocabulary test.

PROBLEMS FOR THOUGHT AND DISCUSSION

1 Three psychologists were asked to develop tests for the air force to use to select candidates for flight training. The first psychologist gathered a sample of 50 items from other tests which recruits normally take when they enter the military service and compared responses on the items by pilots and nonpilots. The second psychologist systematically analyzed a construct which he called "readiness for pilot training." Based on the scientific literature available to him on the topic, he devised a model of the construct and sampled items from the domain represented by his model which formed the basis of his test. The third psychologist contacted 30 pilots and asked them to tell him "the three most important items a pilot needs." He analyzed all the responses that he received and, based upon them, developed a 30-item multiple-choice test. Thus each of the three psychologists proposed a different paper-and-pencil test to measure the same thing.
   a Discuss the validity of each approach.
   b Discuss the relative merits of each.
   c Might there be other ways to select candidates for pilot training?
2 Discuss the kinds of validity that it would be most important for each of the following tests to have:
   a Group intelligence test
   b Test of personality characteristics
   c Test of attitudes towards ethnic minority groups
   d Diagnostic reading test
   e Visual-motor coordination test
   f Mechanical ability test
   g Test of academic achievement in mathematics
   h Test of ability to learn mathematics
3 One farmer measures the quality of his tomatoes by their size, another by the number of bushels he brings to market, and a third by the number of ribbons awarded his tomatoes at the state fair. Discuss the validity of each measure.
4 A researcher used as his dependent variable a test that was too easy. Subjects answered nearly all of the items on the test correctly. Another researcher used a test

which gave wide variability of scores among the subjects. Which probably had greater reliability? Why? Which test had greater validity? Why?

5 For the following scores, the test was split into halves using odd- and even-numbered items, and half scores were recorded. Estimate the reliability of the test and the standard error of measurement, and interpret them in terms of true and obtained scores.

Student	Total score	Odd score	Even score
A	75	35	40
B	83	40	43
C	62	31	31
D	71	36	35
E	59	27	32
F	98	47	51
G	87	45	42
H	76	38	38
I	85	43	42
J	92	48	44

6 A school board wants to determine whether individualized or group recognition for performance in the classroom leads to more effective learning. To accomplish this, it designs a study in which the same curriculum will be followed with each approach. Twelve fourth-grade classrooms in a medium-sized suburban school district will be randomly assigned to follow the individualized or the group-oriented method for one full academic year. The essential difference between the two kinds of treatments will be that children will be rewarded on an individual basis for their performance in the individual setting, while in the group setting, rewards will only be given when everyone in the class has attained a designated level of performance. Teachers will be trained in adapting the existing instructional materials and texts to the group or individual approach as appropriate. In addition to other observations that will be made during the course of the year (classroom tests, behavioral observations, interviews with teachers), a final achievement test will be given at the end of the school year in order to determine how much each group actually learned.

a What kind of validity would it be most important to verify for the final achievement test?

b How is the validity of the final achievement test affected by the sample of students, purposes of the research, and curriculum of the students?

7 Using the formula for the standard error of measurement ($SEM = S_0\sqrt{1 - r_{xx}}$), find the value of SEM when the reliability of a test is 1.0. Then, find the SEM for a test with no, or zero, reliability. What can be said about the maximum and minimum values of the SEM?

8 Look at the manuals of several published tests. Is information given about reliability, validity, and standard error of measurement? Is this information adequate to determine the usefulness of the test for research purposes?

STANDARDIZED TESTS

Imagine the chaos that would result if each researcher used measurement techniques that only he or she understood. Suppose, for instance, two researchers are studying physical growth rates in children. One uses the length of his thumb as a unit of measurement, the other uses a stone she found on a camping trip. When they make known the results of their research, one describes the number of thumbs grown, the other reports growth in stones. Obviously, they are not communicating with each other or their general audience since the length of the thumb and the stone used in the studies were not generally accepted standards. To obviate this difficulty is the purpose of standardized tests. Standardized tests are designed so that people using them will obtain scores which can be interpreted meaningfully by others.

Three characteristics identify standardized tests. First, a standardized test contains clear, concise instructions for administration. Second, each respondent is given standard material or tasks to which to respond. Finally, procedures for scoring are clearly described. Instructions, materials, and scoring are developed so that different people administering and scoring the test will obtain similar results. A well-designed standardized test administered in the prescribed manner will result in ensuring maximum reliability and validity of the scores.

When a researcher uses a previously used or published measurement instrument, standardization of materials, administration, and scoring may already have been established. However, in the case of instruments designed specifically for a particular research investigation, the burden of standardization rests with the researcher. A useful guideline to follow in developing standardized measurement procedures for research purposes is that materials, administration, and scoring should be sufficiently described to enable anyone who wants to replicate the research to apply exactly the same measurement. It is recommended that researchers who develop new measurement devices for their research make these instruments available to others along with complete instructions for administration and scoring. One way to do this is to submit the material to a document bank such as ERIC or the National Auxiliary Publications Service.*

NORMATIVE- AND CRITERION-REFERENCED TESTS

For the most part, the tests and measurements we have been discussing so far can be termed *normative-referenced:* that is, the scores obtained on such tests are interpreted according to norms. For example, if we use an achievement test which has a mean of 75 and a standard deviation of 15, then the student who obtained a score of 90 can be said to have scored 1 standard deviation above the mean. When we say this, we are really comparing the student who scored 90 to the mean. However, often such a score is not sufficiently informative. In the case of achievement tests, for example, comparing a score to a

---

* ERIC was described in Chapter 3. The National Auxiliary Publications Service (NAPS) is operated by the American Society for Information Science (ASIS). Information about NAPS may be obtained from ASIS or a research librarian.

norm conveys no information about how well a student knows the subject; it only tells where he or she scored in relation to others who took the test. There might actually be very little difference between the knowledge of the highest scoring student and that of the lowest one. Also, we should know the characteristics of the norm group. When the norm group is markedly different from the group to which a test is administered, normative-referenced scores can be misleading. Some examples of normative-referenced tests, such as the Iowa Test of Basic Skills, the Stanford Achievement Test, and the Graduate Record Examination, are discussed in Chapter 9.

Criterion-referenced tests were designed to meet the need for specific information about performance. These tests are referenced to specific objectives, or *criteria*. On such tests, a score of 90 percent means that 90 percent of the material tested has been mastered. From this comes the notion of *mastery*. An individual is said to have reached mastery when he or she can perform a certain percentage, typically about 90 percent, of the objectives the test measures.

There are some obvious problems with designing criterion-referenced tests. The selection of criteria is no easier than in a normative test. Furthermore, the selection of objectives within a trait to be measured is subject to the perceptions and biases of the test designer. For example, consider a criterion-referenced test developed to assess mechanical skills; one test designer might emphasize manual dexterity items, another might emphasize problems dealing with mechanical devices. Furthermore, constructs such as achievement in history or mathematical problem-solving skills are often inadequately represented by a list of criteria to be tested. Making the list longer may make the test appear more adequate, but usually complex tasks require complex objectives that do not always translate into simple test items. However, carefully designed criterion-referenced tests can be more useful in identifying the amount of skills mastered than normative-referenced tests not designed for that purpose. For a more thorough discussion of criterion-referenced testing, the reader is referred to references such as Bloom, Hastings, and Madaus (1971), Popham and Husek (1969), and Guskey (1985).

Reliability of Criterion-Referenced Tests

Reliability is a desirable quality of all tests. However, the study of reliability of criterion-referenced tests gives us some difficulty because formulas for computation of reliability are based upon variance. Yet criterion-referenced tests tend to minimize variance because respondents are expected to meet the criterion of mastery, for example, correct on 90 percent of the items. This complicates the reliability picture considerably. As yet, no simple solution to this problem has been agreed upon. However, Berk (1980) recommended a method in which the test is administered twice and then reliability is estimated from the proportion of individuals who consistently reached the criterion score. The

Berk article provides a good review of the issues involved in reliability of criterion-referenced tests.

Validity of Criterion-Referenced Tests

Criterion-referenced tests usually measure a content area, as in achievement testing. For that reason, content validity is usually the primary validity concern, although construct validity should be considered as well because variables being measured, such as mathematics achievement, are constructs. Procedures for determining the content and construct validity of a criterion-referenced test are similar to those discussed for normative-referenced tests earlier in this chapter.

LATENT TRAITS—A DIFFERENT APPROACH TO THE MEASUREMENT OF TRAITS

The normative measurement approaches we have discussed are based on the premise that the construct being measured is normally distributed in the population of people who take the test. Scores actually represent the relative position of a person with regard to a normative group. For example, if a student gets a score of 80 on an achievement test that has a mean of 70 and a standard deviation of 10, the 80 reveals that the student's score is 1 standard deviation above the mean. However, it does not tell us very much about how much of the academic program the student has actually mastered. In fact, the 80 is a sort of rubber yardstick in this regard because if the normative group were changed (i.e., the test renormed using a higher achieving group), the student would get a different score for the same performance, placing the estimate of achievement at a different place relative to the normative group. Figure 8-5 shows the distributions of scores on the same test normed with two different groups. In each case, the mean is designated as 70 and the standard deviation as 10. Notice that the same level of performance (raw score of 10 correct out of 15 items) results in different scores depending upon which normative group is used as a basis.

Latent-trait theory is a relatively new development in testing that represents an attempt to get around the relationship between the normative group and the test score. It assumes that an underlying concept or trait (*latent trait*) can be measured on a scale that represents amount of the trait analogous to the way a ruler measures length. Latent-trait theory (also known as *item-response theory*) is rather complex, and a complete discussion of it is beyond the scope of the present text. Our purpose here is to explain the approach enough so that when it is encountered in the literature, it will be recognized. Readers interested in learning more about latent-trait measurement are referred to the supplementary readings at the end of this chapter.

The approach is based on the item characteristic curve. To illustrate this curve, look at Figure 8-6, in which curves from three test items are drawn. Notice that the horizontal axis represents ability (amount of that trait), while the vertical axis shows probability from 0.0 to 1.00. The ability scale is a concept that is more statistical than psychological or educational because it is based on mathematical models that are applied to the data.

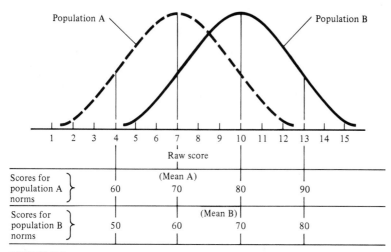

Scores for population A norms		60		(Mean A) 70		80		90	
Scores for population B norms		50		60		(Mean B) 70		80	

FIGURE 8-5
Raw scores normed on two different groups.

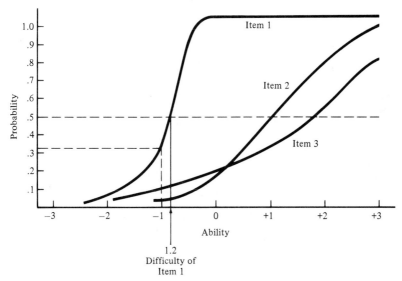

FIGURE 8-6
Item characteristic curves for three test items.

The characteristic curve of each item, somewhat S-shaped, is formed by plotting the proportion of people with a certain ability who responded correctly to the item. To illustrate, consider the curve for item 1 in Figure 8-6. Approximately 33 percent of the people at ability level −1 responded successfully to item 1, while at ability level +2, 100 percent responded correctly. Two properties are used to characterize the item characteristic curve. The first is *difficulty,* defined as the point on the (horizontal) ability scale identified by a perpendicular drawn from the point on the curve where it crosses the .5 proportion. Using this definition, the difficulty of item 1 is shown as 1.2 in Figure

8-6. Notice that items passed more frequently by those at the lower ability levels have lower difficulties by this definition. The second property of an item characteristic curve is *discrimination*. Item discrimination refers to how useful the item is in distinguishing between respondents at different ability levels. Generally, the steeper the slope, the better the item is at discrimination because the probabilities of passing the item differ more between the low abilities and the high abilities. Of the three items in Figure 8-6, item 1 has the highest discrimination because of its steep slope, and item 3 has the lowest.

Latent-trait theory approximates the item curves, using mathematical functions applied to item scores. As we said earlier, the procedure is complex and requires numerous calculations. Therefore, computerization of the analysis is essential for application of this procedure. Theoretically, the procedure produces tests that are less dependent on the character of the normative sample than is the case with traditional normative sampling (Lord, 1970). It also provides a basis for comparing tests because the scale is considered to be based on latent ability rather than on the normative sample. However, in practice, the realization of these benefits is not always readily obvious (see Kolen, 1981; Holmes, 1982). Yet the approach shows considerable promise for many applications in testing and research in the future.

MEASURING GAINS

Measurement of change over time is a particularly attractive idea to researchers, especially in applied settings and in evaluation of programs. This is because it seems obvious that the effects of a program or an experimental treatment would be reflected in the difference between pre- and posttest scores. However, measuring change does not turn out to be a simple matter. Furthermore, the interpretation of change scores can be quite misleading.

Suppose we wanted to see how much a young child grows over a 2-year period. We measure the child's height initially and then at the end of 2 years. We find that the child was originally 41 inches tall and, in 2 years, grew to a height of 48 inches. Thus we would say that the child grew 7 inches, and we identify 7 inches as his *gain score*. Since there is not a great difference between the observed score (X_0) and the true score (X_t) in measuring height, the interpretation of the gain score is rather straightforward. Now let us turn our attention to a common situation in educational research. An observed score is obtained from several subjects on a pretest. Then the treatment condition is applied to them. Finally, a posttest measure is obtained. Naturally, the observed scores for the pretest (X_{01}) and for the posttest (X_{02}) are used as estimates of the true scores of the two tests (X_{t1} and X_{t2}). Gains can be identified by subtracting X_{t1} from X_{t2}. However, we never know the true scores. The observed scores X_{01} and X_{02} serve as estimates of the true scores but are not equal to them. The error components X_e serve to randomly depress or elevate observed scores around the true scores. Therefore, the difference between observed scores might be due to chance error rather than gain. To illustrate this point, consider two observed scores in which the true scores are identical, but error has served to elevate the second observed score. When X_{o1} is subtracted from X_{02}, the positive result suggests a gain although there really was none. The average gain in a group of individuals might reflect change, but there are problems analyzing pre- to posttest change, some of which were discussed in Chapter 4, such as regression towards the mean. Other problems can arise if the test is too difficult or too easy. In such cases, gains will be difficult to show. In addition, the reliability of change scores tends to be lower than the reliability of the test taken once (Allen & Yen, 1979). Several methods have been suggested to deal with the problem of gain scores, but none is fully satisfactory. It is recommended that before an analysis of gain scores is attempted, a statistician or measurement expert who is familiar with the problems be consulted.

SUMMARY

Measurement is important in research because it provides objectivity and standards for specifying variables. The selection of procedures for specifying measurement of variables must be appropriate to the questions being asked in the research investigation. In education and the behavioral sciences, constructs may not be measured directly. However, degrees of traits or attributes may be inferred, based on behavior.

Validity concerns the degree to which an instrument measures what it is supposed to measure. There are three principal approaches to establishing validity. Construct validity refers to the degree to which the test measures the constructs under consideration. Content validity concerns the representativeness of the items in the test of the universe or domain of items. Finally, criterion-related validity involves the ability of the test to predict or estimate a criterion such as achievement or intelligence. Although one form of validity may be emphasized in a particular situation, all tests should have construct validity.

Reliability refers to the consistency of a measurement. It may be defined as "the ratio of true score variance to observed score variance." There are four approaches to the study of reliability. The first, stability, involves the correlation of test scores over two administrations of the same test. In the second, equivalence, the scores on two equivalent tests are correlated. A third approach, stability and equivalence, involves administering equivalent forms of the test at two different times. Finally, internal-consistency reliability is computed using a single administration of the test. It may be based on split-half methods or item reliability.

The standard error of measurement is the standard deviation of observed scores around the true scores. It is estimated using the following formula:

$$SEM = S_0\sqrt{1 - r_{xx}}$$

where SEM = the standard error of measurement
   S_O = the standard deviation of observed scores
   r_{xx} = the estimated reliability coefficient

The greater the reliability, the lower the standard error of measurement.

Measurements and observations must be valid for the purposes for which they are used in research investigations. A test that is validated for one clinical, diagnostic, or educational purpose is not necessarily valid for another application in a research setting. Further, instruments designed specifically for use in a research setting should also be of demonstrated validity and reliability. A researcher can say little about the results of a study when the meaning of the observational or measurement techniques cannot be established.

Standardized tests have well-established procedures for administration and scoring and have standard materials. Normative-referenced tests provide scores which are interpreted in terms of norms. Criterion-referenced tests provide scores which are interpreted in terms of objectives, or criteria. Reliability of criterion-referenced tests presents special problems. Latent-trait scales are based on a theoretical latent ability which can be measured through statistical procedures applied to item scores. Gain scores have special problems that stem from the relatively large standard error of measurement of the tests and measurement techniques used in educational and behavioral science research. Furthermore, the reliability of gain scores is less than the reliability of either of the scores from which they are derived.

PROBLEMS FOR THOUGHT AND DISCUSSION

1 Obtain two or three published articles reporting research in your field of interest. Review the validity and reliability of the measurements used in the investigations. Do the measurement techniques seem reliable? Do they seem valid? Is the type of validity reported appropriate for the conditions under which the measurement is used? How can these conditions affect results and the interpretation of research data?

2 Assume that you have been asked to evaluate the effectiveness of a shop safety training program in a tire factory. Discuss some of the measurement issues which would be of concern to you in designing such a study.

3 The school principal asks you to help her design a study of the effects of two different approaches to teaching science in the elementary school. The principal would like you to administer some tests to groups of students after they have been taught a unit with each method. Would you use a normative- or a criterion-referenced test to measure the effects? Why?

REFERENCES

Allen, M. J., & Yen, W. M. (1979). *Introduction to measurement theory*. Monterey, CA: Brooks/Cole.

Anastasi, A. (1982). *Psychological testing* (5th ed.). New York: Macmillan.

Berk, R. A. (1980). A consumers' guide to criterion-referenced test reliability. *Journal of Educational Measurement, 17,* 323–349.

Bloom, B., Hastings, J., & Madaus, G. (1971). *Handbook on formative and summative evaluation of student learning.* New York: McGraw-Hill.

Campbell, D. T., & Fiske, D. W. (1959). Convergent and discriminant validation by the multitrait-multimethod matrix. *Psychological Bulletin, 56,* 81–105.

Covert, R. W., & Mason, E. J. (1974). Factorial validity of a student evaluation of teaching instrument. *Educational and Psychological Measurement, 34,* 903–905.

Cronbach, L. J. (1951). Coefficient alpha and the internal structure of tests. *Psychometrika, 16,* 297–334.

Guskey, T. R. (1985). *Mastery learning.* Belmont, CA: Wadsworth.

Holmes, S. (1982). Unidimensionality and vertical equating with the Rasch model. *Journal of Educational Measurement, 19,* 139–147.

Kolen, M. (1981). Comparison of traditional and item response theory methods for equating tests. *Journal of Educational Measurement, 18,* 1–11.

Lord, F. M. (1970). Some test theory for tailored testing. In Holtzman, W. H. (Ed.), *Computer-assisted instruction, testing, and guidance.* New York: Harper & Row.

Nunnally, J. C. (1978). *Psychometric theory* (2nd ed.). New York: McGraw-Hill.

Popham, W. J., & Husek, T. R. (1969). Implications of criterion-referenced measurement. *Journal of Educational Measurement, 6,* 1–9.

Terman, L. M. (1916). *The measurement of intelligence.* Boston: Houghton Mifflin.

Thorndike, R. L., Hagen, E. P., & Sattler, J. M. (1986). *Guide for administering and scoring the Stanford-Binet Intelligence Scale* (4th ed.). Chicago: Riverside.

Wechsler, D. (1974). *Manual for the Wechsler Intelligence Scale for Children—Revised.* New York: Psychological Corp.

Zytowski, D. G. (1976). Predictive validity of the Kuder Occupational Interest Survey. *Journal of Counseling Psychology, 23,* 221–233.

SUPPLEMENTARY READINGS

Baker, F. B. (1985). *The basics of item response theory.* Portsmouth, NH: Heinemann.

Fiske, D. W. (1971). Is measurement knowledge? *Contemporary Psychology, 16,* 126–127.

Guilford, J. P. (1954). *Psychometric methods* (2nd ed.). New York: McGraw-Hill.

Gulliksen, H. (1950). *Theory of mental tests.* New York: Wiley.

Jackson, D. N., & Messick, S. (1967). *Problems in human assessment.* New York: McGraw-Hill.

Knapp, T. R. (1971). *Statistics for educational measurement.* Scranton, PA: Intext Educational Publishers.

Lord, F. M., & Novick, M. R. (1968). *Statistical theories of mental test scores.* Reading, MA: Addison-Wesley.

Newmark, C. S. (1985). *Major psychological assessment instruments.* Boston: Allyn and Bacon.

Sattler, J. M. (1988). *Assessment of children* (3rd ed.). San Diego: Sattler.

Yen, W. M. (1986). The choice of scale for educational measurement: An IRT perspective. *Journal of Educational Measurement, 23,* 299–325.

CHAPTER 9

METHODS OF MEASURING
AND OBSERVING
BEHAVIOR

In the present chapter, we will consider some of the techniques used to measure and observe in the behavioral sciences and education. Specifically, we will briefly discuss achievement, aptitude, and personality testing; construction of tests and test items; and observational instruments, scaling, questionnaires, and projective testing. Finally, we will review the essentials of choosing a measurement technique for use in a research investigation. Although a complete discussion of all instruments used to measure or observe is not possible here, the approaches and techniques presented should serve as a sufficient introduction.

It should be kept in mind that the measurement delimits the variable. For example, in a study of compensatory education, we might wish to measure intelligence. Yet when we use the Stanford-Binet IQ score as a measure of intelligence, we narrow our concept of intelligence to what the Stanford-Binet test measures. This is true whenever a complex construct is measured. Then there is a problem of sampling which occurs with observation techniques. When utilizing behavior rating scales, for example, we only record or rate the behavior to which the scale is sensitive. This was illustrated in a conversation between an experimental psychologist and his research associate. The psychologist was complaining that he could see their laboratory animals were developing several behavioral peculiarities which did not show up in the data they had collected. "But there is no place on the form to record 'neck stretch' and 'bird yawning,'" the research associate responded. Consequently, the effects of the treatments, which were apparent to the researchers, were not evident from the observations they were making.

SOME APPLICATIONS OF TESTS

In the last chapter, we discussed the validity and reliability of tests. We also looked at normative-referenced and criterion-referenced testing. In the following section, specific tests of achievement, aptitude, ability, and personality will be considered.

Achievement Tests

An achievement test assesses the extent to which a person has attained, accomplished, or mastered certain information or skills. Some achievement tests are standardized and are available on the commercial market, such as the Stanford Achievement Test, Iowa Tests of Basic Skills, and the California Achievement Test.* Researchers occasionally cannot find commercially available standardized achievement tests appropriate to their needs, however. For example, a researcher might be asked to evaluate the achievement of students attending a postgraduate professional training session for dentists. If there is no standardized achievement test available, the researcher might design a test. However, the researcher would then be responsible for indicating the characteristics of the test, including reliability and validity, when reporting the results of the study.

Achievement tests may be designed to be administered to an individual or to a large group. They can be designed to assess general achievement or achievement in some specific area, such as mathematical problem solving, the anatomy of a frog, or the operation of the internal combustion engine. Researchers must be selective in choosing the proper tests for their needs.

Cautions in Selecting Standardized Achievement Tests One common error made by the neophyte researcher concerns the kind of scores obtained from tests. Commercial standardized tests often have a number of different scales that are used to report scores. The least useful for research purposes is the *grade-equivalent* or *grade-placement* score because of its lack of meaning. A grade-equivalent score is the median score (the mean is used on some tests instead) obtained by children at a certain grade level. For example, if the median of students in the second month of fifth grade who take a particular achievement test is 38 correct items, then a score of 38 correct items is assigned a grade-equivalent score of 5.2, representing fifth grade, second month. However, grade-equivalent scores cannot be interpreted the same way across tests and subtests. For example, a grade score of 6.7 on a subtest might correspond to a percentile rank of 79 for a fifth grader while on another subtest of the same examination, 6.7 might correspond to a percentile rank of 92. Another problem with grade equivalents is that they do not correspond to subject

---

* More detail about tests mentioned in this chapter may be found in the test anthologies listed at the end of the chapter.

matter. Thus a second grader who has a grade equivalent of 5.2 in reading does not necessarily read as well as a fifth grader who scored 5.2 on the test. This is because the grade equivalent of 5.2 for the second grader was obtained statistically based on the number of items the student and second-grade classmates answered correctly in the form of the test designed for second graders. This test probably included little or no fifth-grade curriculum. The fifth grader who scored 5.2, on the other hand, obtained this score on a test designed for use at the fifth-grade level. Consequently, the fifth grader scoring 5.2 and the second grader scoring 5.2 may not be performing at the same level despite their identical grade-equivalency scores.

Other methods of reporting scores can also cause problems. Percentiles, percentile ranks, and stanines are common methods used to report achievement-test results. All these methods are appropriately considered to be ordinal rather than interval scales. The more powerful techniques of parametric statistics may not be appropriate for these kinds of scores. Although questions can also be raised about the application of parametric techniques to data based on standard scores, standard scores are generally most useful to the researcher. (Standard scores were discussed at some length in Chapter 6.)

Fitting the Test to the Research Purpose Another common problem in using achievement tests in research concerns whether the tests are normative- or criterion-referenced. As we saw in the last chapter, normative-referenced test scores are interpreted with regard to the scores of other people who took the test, whereas criterion-referenced tests are interpreted in terms of tasks or objectives upon which the test is based: For example, consider a student who had a standard score of 72 on a standardized normative-referenced test which had a mean of 50 and a standard deviation of 10. That student's score is interpreted as an extremely good one, since it is more than 2 standard deviations above the mean. Yet the student may not have mastered much of the material upon which the test was based. Can you explain the conditions under which this would be true? It should be evident that when a test is too difficult, standard scores may be high even when mastery is not. On the other hand, criterion-referenced scores only indicate how much of the stated objectives was mastered and not how well a person performed in relation to others. Thus, in research requiring conclusions concerning the amount of material learned, criterion-referenced tests should be used. It is a common fault of research evaluating the effectiveness of educational programs that normative-referenced assessment is used when criterion-referenced testing is more appropriate.

Aptitude and Ability Tests

Aptitude tests are designed to measure a person's potential for performance of a task, skill, or occupation. They are used mostly for predictive purposes. Graduate students are familiar with the Graduate Record Examination (GRE), which measures verbal and quantitative ability. Schools that use GRE scores in their admissions procedures feel that the scores are predictive of successful completion of a graduate program.

Educators, counselors, and psychologists often use multifactor or general-aptitude batteries, which assess a number of abilities. The Differential Aptitude Test (DAT) is one example. This test contains eight subtests: verbal reasoning, numerical ability, abstract reasoning, clerical speed and accuracy, mechanical reasoning, space relations, and language usage. The test can be administered in grades 8 through 12 and is considered useful in academic and career counseling of students. Such a test might be used by a researcher to evaluate the effectiveness of a program designed to prepare students for careers in engineering. Can you see how? A number of these general aptitude tests are commercially available. Researchers can find them listed in the *Mental Measurements Yearbooks* and other test review sources at the end of this chapter.

Perhaps the most commonly used tests of ability are the intelligence tests. We have considered some of the problems inherent in intelligence testing earlier in our discussion of validity. The major difference between multifactor aptitude tests, such as the DAT, and intelligence tests concerns the nature of the constructs measured. Intelligence is generally seen as a basic or general trait, whereas aptitudes are more specific—for example, musical aptitude, mechanical aptitude, verbal aptitude.

A wide variety of aptitude and ability tests is available from test publishers. Some are individual; others are group tests. Most of these are paper-and-pencil tests, although practical tests of aptitudes and abilities are also used. For example, the road test necessary to obtain a license to drive an automobile in most states is an aptitude test because it is administered to determine a driver's ability to control the vehicle, follow safe procedures, obey traffic laws, and not cause accidents. It is a test that predicts the kind of driver one will be.

Personality Tests

Actually, the word "test" may be inappropriate when describing an instrument that measures personality traits because it implies an examination or evaluation in which the respondent is expected to perform in a way that reflects maximum capabilities. This is not the case with personality assessment at all. Rather, personality tests are used to identify behavioral tendencies or characteristics. For this reason, instruments that measure personality are often identified as inventories rather than tests.

There are three general kinds of personality tests. One is the *checklist of behaviors or problems*. The Mooney Problem Checklist is an example of this kind of personality instrument. It consists of a list of problems. The person simply reads through the list and places a check next to each item that describes his or her situation.

A second kind of personality instrument is the *structured test of general adjustment*. The Minnesota Multiphasic Personality Inventory (MMPI) is an example of this kind of instrument, which requires people to respond to a number of items on a scale indicating how much each item is like them, how important they think it is, or some other way. Personality characteristics are ascribed based on patterns of responses.

The third kind of personality assessment technique is known as *projective testing*. In projective testing, the individual is presented with ambiguous stimuli and asked to "project" his or her feelings and personality onto the stimuli. In this way, it is assumed that the individual's inner feelings, needs, and personality can be explored. An example of this kind of approach is the Rorschach test, which requires the individual to tell what he or she sees in ten ambiguous inkblotlike stimulus plates. This kind of testing relies heavily upon the interpretations made by the examiner, and consequently there are many problems involved with using it in empirical research. We will look at projective techniques in more detail later in this chapter.

Other Kinds of Tests

Other characteristics commonly measured by paper-and-pencil-type assessment instruments include interests, creativity, readiness, social development, and attitudes. Many of these tests are listed in test anthologies, such as the *Mental Measurements Yearbook,* published by Buros Institute of Mental Measurements. In these anthologies, tests are listed by category and reviews are provided. In addition, for the tests considered, relevant literature is referenced.

TEST CONSTRUCTION

Researchers try to avoid making new tests because procedures for demonstrating reliability and validity can be time-consuming and expensive. However, a completely suitable measurement device might not be available for a given situation, and the researcher may have to develop an instrument to suit existing needs. Therefore, researchers must know something about test construction. Also, and more importantly, understanding how tests are made enhances the researcher's conception of the meaning of test scores and the research findings based on them.

Test construction must begin with the purpose of the test and the kind of validity it is to have. One approach is to develop a table of specifications, or content-by-objectives grid. Chapter 13 discusses this concept further in the context of program evaluation. The table should depict the domain of traits or behaviors from which items will be sampled. An example of a table of specifications for a test of attitudes towards cigarette smoking is shown in Table 9-1. The researcher determined the categories of content and the proportions of representation according to the needs of the research, and the test items reflected these priorities. Such an approach helps to ensure the validity of the

TABLE 9-1
SPECIFICATIONS FOR A TEST OF ATTITUDES TOWARDS SMOKING
CIGARETTES

Content area	Proportion of emphasis	Number of items
Personal experience with cigarettes	.20	4
Knowledge of effects	.15	3
Availability to person	.20	4
Knowledge of pertinent health facts	.15	3
Peer-group usage of cigarettes	.10	2
Personal view of relationship of smoking to health	.20	4
	1.00	20

measure. However, validity and reliability, as we discussed in the last chapter, must be demonstrated.

Test items are designed with two approaches to scoring in mind. The first leaves nothing to the judgment or imagination of the person doing the scoring. In fact, the rules for scoring these tests are so clear-cut that computers often do the scoring. These tests are called *objective* tests because the scoring is not subject to personal biases, perceptions, or interpretations of the scorer. The other approach to scoring is called *nonobjective*. In this kind of testing, the views, values, and perceptions of the scorer come into play in varying degrees. A degree of objectivity can be injected into the scoring of such items by the structure of the items and the clarity of the scoring criteria. In the following sections, we will consider the design of objective and nonobjective test items.

Objective Test Items

Objective test items are simple to respond to and simple to score. The four most common types—true-false, multiple-choice, supply, and matching—will be discussed in this section.

True-False Items   The simplest kind of test item is a declarative statement which the respondent must indicate as being true or false. An example of a true-false item is as follows:

Books have pages.   (True)   (False)

The respondent would check True because the statement is obviously true. However, many true-false questions are not that straightforward. Consider the following illustration:

Men are taller than women.   (True)   (False)

There are two ways to interpret this question. The first, "*All* men are taller than *all* women," would naturally make the statement false. On the other hand, the question could be understood as "Men are taller *on the average* than women," which is true. This kind of ambiguity is difficult to avoid in true-false questions, but when the items are worded carefully, the problem can be minimized.

Another difficulty with true-false questions concerns the bipolar nature of the possible responses. To illustrate this, consider the following item from a personality inventory:

I feel good about myself.   (True)   (False)

People who feel good about themselves all the time, or do not feel good about themselves all the time, are rare. A respondent might be likely to wish that there were some alternative to true and false in this case. The person forced to make a choice between true and false may not feel he or she is answering truthfully whichever choice is made. Thus, for some statements, true and false may not provide sufficient option for the respondent.

Designers of true-false tests sometimes (with limited success) try to clarify items by adding phrases or by making the sentence longer, as in the following:

I usually feel good about myself.   (True)   (False)

It would be unusual for a person to choose False. Here, the problem is social desirability. That is, society expects people to feel good about themselves, at least sometimes. People tend to respond to these items as they are "supposed to" respond to them. In fact, the social desirability problem occurs with all strategies of human assessment but becomes especially pervasive in tests of personality, interests, and attitudes.

Another problem with adding words or phrases to qualify a true-false item is that the qualification sometimes does not make the item true or false. Consider the following:

People who cook French food are French.   (True)   (False)

The item developer realized that not all those who cook French food are French, and consequently that the item is neither true nor false. He tried to repair the item by inserting a qualifier as follows:

Often people who cook French food are French.   (True)   (False)

Now the question can be true or false. Often those who cook French cuisine are French, and often they are not.

True-false tests often appeal to researchers because of their simplicity. But it is not very easy to construct good items, and the bipolar nature of the responses limits the kind and quality of information that can be obtained. In addition, a great many of these items must usually be used to investigate a topic. This makes such tests lengthy, and boredom can become a problem.

Multiple-Choice Items   The multiple-choice format is by far the one most often used in educational and psychological tests. A multiple-choice test item consists of a question or incomplete statement followed by a number of possible responses. The respondent chooses the one that best completes the sentence or answers the question. The following is an illustration of a multiple-choice item that might appear in a test of physics knowledge:

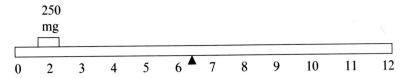

In the above diagram, in order to balance the bar, another 250-mg weight would have to be placed with its center at the _____ point on the bar.

a 8
b 9
c 10
d 11
e anywhere between 7 and 12

The multiple-choice type of question is popular because it is easy to score and is easily adaptable to a number of different kinds of needs. Moreover, recording of responses on specially designed printed sheets will allow scoring and tabulating of test performance by computer.

Much has been written about the construction of multiple-choice test items (for example, Cunningham, 1986; McMorris, Brown, Snyder, and Pruzek, 1972). The reader is referred to any of the many introductory measurement books in education and psychology—for example, Anastasi (1982), Sax (1980), or Thorndike and Hagen (1986)—for a more complete discussion of construction of multiple-choice items.

Some problems frequently occur in designing multiple-choice questions. First, response choices are not always easy to find nor is it easy to arrive at suitable wording. They should all be plausible. Each response option should be in the same grammatical form and should be written to be appropriate as a response to the item. To illustrate this problem, consider the following item:

Near the mouth of the river that Henry Hudson explored, _____ was established.

a dam
b New York City
c farming center
d school for Indian children

Notice that all the incorrect responses (*a, c,* and *d*) need to be preceded by a definite or indefinite article (a, the, one, etc.). Only the correct response, *b*, would fit without modification. This of course would give an unfair advantage to a student proficient at grammar who did not know history very well.

Another problem with multiple-choice items is that the responses should be clearly different so that a choice can be made but not so different that one of the choices stands out clearly as the best or worst. Consider the following item from a test in research methods:

The best research design for use in the behavioral sciences and education is

a a true experimental design.
b the posttest-only control-group design.
c the pretest-posttest control-group design.
d any of the experimental or quasi-experimental designs which would facilitate investigation of the complex nature of the variables with which these sciences deal.

The first three choices are very similar. If one chooses *a*, then one assumes *b* and *c* are also correct because they are examples of experimental designs. Also, there is room for the expression of personal bias in a question like this. A researcher who does most of his work under highly controlled conditions in a laboratory or other structured setting might prefer *b*. A researcher who uses field and action research techniques or who does evaluation might prefer *d*. Furthermore, a person who knows nothing about research, or who has no particular point of view, might choose *d* simply because of its length.

Multiple-choice items are usually used in achievement and aptitude testing. However, the multiple-choice format is also frequently used to obtain the descriptive characteristics of subjects who participate in a study. An example of this application is shown in Figure 9-1. The multiple-choice format is also found in other types of tests. For example, an item on an interest inventory might be the following:

I most like to

a go hiking with my friends.
b go driving in the country alone.
c read mystery stories.
d play cards for money.

Notice that in this application there is no correct answer in the same sense that items on a multiple-choice achievement or ability test have a correct answer. For this reason, most discussions of multiple-choice items do not include such applications, although many of the guidelines for preparing and dealing with such multiple-choice items are similar to those for ability- and achievement-test applications.

Subject No. _____

Demographic Survey

Check the choice that is most appropriate in each of the following items:

1. Sex
   a. Male
   b. Female

2. Age
   a. 20-24
   b. 25-29
   c. 30-35
   d. 36-45
   e. 46-55
   f. above 56

3. Highest educational level
   a. High school graduate, some college
   b. College diploma (bachelor's degree)
   c. Bachelor's degree and some graduate school
   d. Master's degree
   e. Master's degree and some additional graduate training

4. Marital status
   a. Unmarried
   b. Divorced or separated
   c. Married
   d. Widow/widower

FIGURE 9-1
A set of multiple-choice items for collecting demographic data from a sample of
subjects in a research investigation.

Supply Items Supply items are common in achievement and personality
testing. They are simply statements or sentences in which a part has been deleted. The respondent provides the missing portion to complete the sentence
or provides the answer to the question.

The major problems with supply items are that they are often difficult to
score and subjects' responses can be difficult to quantify. The following items
are typical of those in a supply-type personality test:

I feel best when my friends _____ .
When I was a child I liked _____ .
I get very sad when _____ .

These items are open-ended and have the advantage of allowing the respondent freedom to reply in his or her own way. However, objective scoring standards are difficult to establish. When achievement is being tested, this problem
is reduced. This is illustrated by the following items:

Parallel lines never _____ .
Perpendicular lines are at _____ angles to each other.
The side opposite the right angle in a triangle is called the _____ .

In the first item, several words may be supplied to convey the same idea. Thus
"meet," "touch," "cross," or "go through the same point" could all have

been given to convey the same idea and should all be credited as correct. However, there is an element of judgment here that cannot be avoided. What if a student answered that the missing word was "overlap"? If the student meant that parallel lines do not cross each other when he said overlap, then his answer must be considered correct.

Good supply items can be difficult to construct. In achievement applications, the word or phrase to be supplied must be clearly the only one that is appropriate or scoring becomes a problem. Furthermore, the part to be supplied should reflect some aspect of the content domain and not just a word deleted from a sentence. For example, the following item would be a poor one:

Elephants are mammals who _____ in the jungle.

The author meant the missing word to be "live." However, there are a lot of things elephants do in the jungle—eat, sleep, reproduce, fight, run, swim, herd together, and so on. Any of these answers must be taken as correct.

In projective or personality applications, the major problem in the construction of supply-type items is selecting the part of the sentence to delete that will elicit the best response. If not enough of a sentence stem is included, there will not be enough information to guide the subject's response. For example, the item:

I _____ .

obviously does not direct the subject towards very much. If an association with the word "I" is wanted, the item seems reasonable. On the other hand, if the response is supposed to elicit the degree of the person's involvement with a job, the item is clearly deficient.

Matching Items Matching items are common in achievement tests because they emphasize recall of information. They require matching elements from two separate lists. For example, one list might contain the names of famous people, the second occupations, with the respondent required to match the name of each person with his or her occupation. Matching items can be difficult to construct. Also, there are limitations on the kind of knowledge these items can assess. Cunningham (1986) and Gronlund (1985) are two good references for obtaining suggestions about improving matching-test items.

Nonobjective Test Items

Nonobjective test items have the advantage of allowing the respondent to supply any answer deemed appropriate. The price paid for allowing the subject increased freedom in responding is decreased precision of scoring. This does not mean that scoring is completely subjective and arbitrary. The scorer must formulate guidelines for interpretation and scoring.

Examples of nonobjective test devices are essays, open-ended interviews, and projective personality tests. These devices pose special problems for the researcher because the characteristics of the scorer can influence the score assigned in this kind of test. Some research questions are best investigated using these instruments. In these cases, however, the researcher must take great pains to demonstrate that there was a minimum of subjectivity in scoring. There are several ways to do this. One of the most common is to develop clear guidelines or criteria for scoring responses based on the table of specifications, or content-by-objectives grid. In addition, more than one rater should be used. A high degree of agreement between raters is essential.

Selecting Test Items

After items have been written, they must be administered to a sample of subjects, and the responses must be analyzed to explore the strengths and weaknesses of the items. This investigation of the items is called *item analysis*. The principle upon which item analysis is based is that each item should contribute to the test score in a manner consistent with what the test was designed to measure.

Several different techniques are used in item analysis. To some extent, the techniques used depend upon the purpose of the test and the type of item. For example, in normative-referenced achievement tests, the level of difficulty and the ability of items to discriminate between better and poorer students would be two important considerations. On the other hand, in an ability test designed to predict performance, the concern might be that an individual's score on each item should correlate with the total test score. If this is true, then it can be assumed that the item contributes to the total score. The intricacies of item analysis are too great to go into here. Those who are interested should consult any of the several textbooks on tests and measurements in the References and Supplementary Readings lists at the end of this chapter.

Final Steps in Test Construction

After the best items have been selected according to an item analysis, the test designer must return to the table of specifications, or content-by-objectives grid, and further select items that will correspond to the original intentions of the test. Then the test should be tried with a sample of individuals from the appropriate population to see how it works. Scoring should be clarified and scoring criteria determined. Directions, materials, and conditions must be carefully described so that the test will meet the criteria of a standardized instrument. If the test is to be normative-referenced, then scoring interpretation in terms of the objectives must be provided.

It should be evident that a researcher who decides to develop his or her own measurement instruments assumes a considerable burden. Not only must the test be designed and items written, but the items must be tested, and the test standardized. Then the researcher must show that the instrument is reliable and valid. To avoid the effort involved in designing tailor-made tests, most researchers prefer to try to find existing instruments suitable for their purposes. Although compromises may be required, the researcher must be certain that the measuring instrument finally selected is appropriate for the research hypotheses. For example, a graduate student was interested in measuring the amount of sharing that pairs of children will exhibit in an experimental situation. She discovered a test in which children were required to cooperate in order to be successful. Although the research was purported to be a study of sharing, it was really an investigation of cooperation because of the measurement that was used.

OTHER METHODS OF MEASURING AND OBSERVING

Most of our discussion to this point has concerned tests. We now turn to techniques not usually classified as tests, such as observation, scaling, the semantic differential, interviewing, projective methods, and sociometry.

Observation

As with so many terms used in research, *observation* has a special meaning to the researcher, one much more restricted than our everyday use of the term. Let us take, as one example, a teacher's observation of a child's behavior in class. "John's behavior is terrible. He is always out of his seat. He calls out to the other children, and he disturbs the class." This might be taken to describe how John behaves in class. Yet to the researcher, it is not specific enough. The researcher might ask, "What does it mean that he is '*always* out of his seat'?" "How often does he call out to other children?" "How does he disturb the rest of the class?" Moreover, the researcher might ask whether the teacher is an accurate and dependable observer: "Would other observers interpret John's behavior the same way?"

Researchers use a wide variety of observational techniques to record behavior. Three that are common are the categorical rating scale, the numerical rating scale, and the graphic rating scale. The following categorical-scale item is from an instrument designed to observe and record the behavior of a teacher:

This teacher seems to be _____ .
extremely enthusiastic
moderately enthusiastic
mildly enthusiastic
somewhat unenthusiastic
extremely unenthusiastic

This item could easily have been written as a numerical scale by assigning numbers to the categories. For example:

How would you characterize this teacher?

1 extremely enthusiastic
2 moderately enthusiastic
3 mildly enthusiastic
4 somewhat unenthusiastic
5 extremely unenthusiastic

Notice that the numbers reflect order of degree of enthusiasm. The same item could also have been written in graphic scale form as follows:

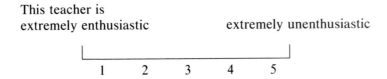

This teacher is
extremely enthusiastic   extremely unenthusiastic

    1   2   3   4   5

To respond to this type of scale, the rater marks the point on the scale from 1 to 5 which reflects the degree of enthusiasm perceived in the teacher.

These three methods of recording observations are very similar. However, they have certain differences that make one type more useful than another in particular research situations. When a total score is appropriate, the numerical scale is most useful because it provides a number score for each item. When the degree of the trait is important, then the graphic scale is most useful because the scale can be considered continuous, and the rater can indicate values between the points on the scale. The section on scaling contains relevant points to consider when using such ratings. In addition, there are other observational instruments which utilize behavior checklists and frequency counts.

Sampling Behavior One of the major decisions a researcher must make when using observational techniques concerns how to sample behavior. This can be done on a time-related or a behavior-related basis. To further complicate matters, when using a time-related basis, the researcher can make periodic or continuous observations. Periodic observations are those in which the behavior of the subject is observed and recorded at specific time intervals and for specific durations of time. For example, the behavior of a person might be observed periodically at 20-minute intervals for 5 minutes each time. On the other hand, in continuous observation the person might be observed continuously for an hour.

Another somewhat related problem concerns the question of what constitutes a single item of behavior. This is particularly bothersome when using behavioral checklists or inventories, although it can also be present with other types of observation instruments. For example, let us say that a classroom behavior checklist requires an observer to record every instance of several kinds of behavior that a child is seen exhibiting. Among those listed is the category "aggression toward other pupils." The observer notes that at one point, the pupil calls the boy sitting next to him an "idiot." As he does that he rises out of his seat, hits the boy three times, and scribbles on the boy's desk with a crayon. Since all this occurred together, it might all be recorded as one act of aggression towards another child; yet the offending pupil called the other boy a name, hit him, and wrote on his desk. Should these be considered three acts? Also, the boy was hit three times in succession; each blow might be considered a separate act of aggression. Obviously, guidelines for the definition of a single behavior must be developed when such instruments are used.

Sometimes, behavior is not observed directly; instead, videotapes or films are made and are analyzed later. This offers several advantages. First, it can provide a precise record of what actually occurred. Second, it facilitates independent review by several observers so that impressions can be compared. Third, it may facilitate nonobtrusive recording. That is, often the mere presence of an observer will alter the quality or quantity of behavior displayed by those being observed. Modern videotape recording equipment can be set up in a room and left. Those being observed, after a period of adjustment, often forget that the camera is present. However, there are some disadvantages to filming or videotaping. For example, people being observed, especially children, may act differently than they normally would if a camera were not present. Also, with most of the videotape equipment commonly used for recording observational data, the cameras and microphone cannot follow all the action in a classroom. Often the event that precipitated some behavior that was observed was not recorded on the videotape because of the angle of the camera. Furthermore, there are problems with equipment compatibility between manufacturers and between models for a single manufacturer. A researcher who plans to use videotape equipment should be sure that all components of the system are compatible and operational.

Validity and Reliability Validity and reliability are just as important with observational procedures as with other measurement techniques. Problems about the validity of this type of data are not unique. Construct validity is of primary importance in observational instruments. The objectivity of the observer can affect validity. Usually, research studies which utilize observational data include observer training to try to ensure that observations are done as objectively and consistently as possible.

The reliability of observational instruments has one problem not common to other measurement methods; that is, rater reliability. The reliability of the instrument may be studied using some of the standard methods. Rater reliability is a new concept, however. It concerns the consistency of observers in recording behavior. Typically, rater reliability is investigated by comparing ratings among several observers. If each observer records behavior similarly, then the observers are recording consistently and rater reliability is said to be achieved. Usually, raters must be trained to use an instrument before rater reliability will be realized.

Observation in Qualitative Research The measurement and observation methods we have considered to this point are primarily quantitative in nature;

that is, information about the observations is represented in numerical or categorical terms. Other methods may be more suitable for research dealing with whole issues and concepts within a natural setting (e.g., ethnographic field studies, qualitative evaluation, etc.).

For example, a researcher might be interested in determining what happens in a school when children from different ethnic and cultural backgrounds are placed together in the same learning environment. The quantitative researcher might use a series of scales designed to measure attitudes towards other ethnic and cultural groups and also give a number of achievement tests. Further, a quantitative researcher might do some observing in the playground that would enable him to make statements like "The average student spoke to a child of the same ethnic group seven times but only four times with someone from another group in a 45-minute period." Although this is all useful information, it does not paint an integrated picture of how instructional and classroom processes are affected by ethnic diversity in the student group. Qualitative observation would be directed towards developing a more integrated view, one in which the researcher unobtrusively observes and records, in essence becoming, herself, the observational instrument.

The range of qualitative observational procedures does not seem great at first glance. Three methods seem to predominate in much of the qualitative research in the social sciences and education: direct observation, interviews, and document study.

Direct observation is done in natural settings, with contexts undisturbed by the observational procedure. Further, observation is usually recorded in some way (e.g., with notes, videotapes, audiotapes, photographs, etc.). Contrast this with the observational record a more quantitatively oriented researcher might keep (e.g., behavioral checklists in which a behavior is checked every time it is observed within a specified time period). In addition, the interviews used by a qualitative researcher tend to be more open-ended than the structured multiple-choice approaches common in research with a more quantitative emphasis. A qualitative researcher might use an outline or a list of questions, but he would be more flexible and willing to explore issues as they arise during an interview. Document exploration is also done differently by qualitative and quantitative researchers. Documents (e.g., minutes of meetings, letters, the administrative files of an agency, the archives of an institution or library, etc.) may be used in a variety of ways by the qualitative researcher in order to gain insight into the context and social processes underlying events. For example, documents might be explored for any implicit and explicit messages they might contain. They might be looked at in the context of other messages, events, or information. Further, they might be analyzed chronologically to study relationships within a temporal perspective.

Although the qualitative researcher seeks to provide ecologically valid observational data, maintaining objectivity when collecting and interpreting qualitative data is more difficult and complex than it is when collecting quantitative data. This is because the qualitative researcher plays an active role in interpreting the data as it is recorded; and the researcher's background, theories, knowledge, values, and perspectives are therefore more likely to become part of the observational instrumentation. Special skills and training are therefore required for qualitative research. Wolcott (1981), in recognizing the difficulty of preparing a potential qualitative researcher to be an effective observer, offered four suggestions. First, observe and record everything. Second, observe, but look for nothing in particular. These first two strategies, taken together, suggest the researcher should be ready to observe and take note of the elements of the scene rather than become distracted by expectations or predispositions about aspects of what should be found. The third strategy is to look for paradoxes or inconsistencies. For example, one paradox in education occurred in the early 1980s. Many federal agencies were concluding at that time that because of rapidly developing innovations in technology, education in the United States had to be upgraded and improved if the country expected to compete effectively in the world. Yet at the same time, federal support for education was diminishing (Congress of the United States, 1982; National Commisson on Excellence in Education, 1983). Exploration of such paradoxes can lead to insight about underlying conflicts and processes in a natural setting. The fourth strategy suggested by Wolcott was to identify the central problem facing the group being studied. For example, the central problem of a class in physics methods might be to pass the final examination in order to satisfy the requirements for a degree, rather than to become a competent researcher. Recognizing this as the central focus will help reveal social processes and other aspects of the class, such as how assignments are done and the quality of interaction between the teacher and the class.

While we make distinctions between qualitative and quantitative approaches to observation, in reality, the domains of the two kinds of observational approaches are less distinct. For example, a researcher using an achievement test to make a quantitative assessment of an instructional innovation might make videotapes of classes using the instructional materials in order to gain some sense of how the students and teachers related to and used the materials in the classroom. In addition, she might make qualitative interpretations of the test data, such as inferences about the quality of knowledge represented by those achievement test scores. On the other hand, a qualitative researcher who is interested in school climate might also recognize that quantitative achievement data was necessary in order to document an aspect of the overall scene that is being studied.

Scaling

Scaling techniques are used to measure attitudes, judgments, opinions, and other traits not easily measured by tests or other measurement techniques. A number of scaling techniques have been developed over the years, but in this section we will consider only three of the better known methods: the Likert, the Thurstone, and the Guttman methods.

Likert Scales Likert scales are sometimes called *summated rating scales*. Each item is assumed to represent a different aspect, but to possess the same quantity or magnitude, of the trait. Furthermore, it is assumed that each item represents the construct being measured. Likert-scale items consist of a statement or characteristic towards which the respondent indicates degrees of intensity. For example, on the Likert-type item "Politicians are basically honest," the respondent uses the following scale:

a strongly agree
b agree
c undecided
d disagree
e strongly disagree

The same 5-point (strongly agree to strongly disagree) scale would be used to record the individual's response to every other item as well. Responses on each item would then be quantified by assigning a value of 5 to "strongly agree," 4 to "agree," 3 to "undecided," 2 to "disagree," and 1 to "strongly disagree." The responses would be summed (and possibly averaged). If each item is written so that higher scores reflect more positive attitudes, then the higher the total (or average), the more positive the attitude towards politicians.

Likert scales are commonly used in educational and behavioral research. They allow for assessing differences in degree or intensity on a trait and are less difficult to construct than some other kinds of scales. Furthermore, the assumption that each item has a similar value in regard to the single characteristic being assessed is one that is apparently not difficult for researchers to make. However, the assumption may not be justified in all cases.

Thurstone Scales Thurstone scales can be used in most of the same situations as Likert scales. They are sometimes called *equal-appearing interval scales* because of the scaling procedure. The Thurstone scaling method involves developing a large number of items, or statements, relating to the construct. Then judges rate these items on a scale which contains 9 points or more (most often 11 points are used). This scale is designed so that the judges can rate the items with respect to the degree of the construct that they contain. Finally, the items are ranked according to the median ratings assigned by the judges, and a small number of items are selected which are spaced more or less evenly across the scale of the trait according to the judges' ratings.* Thus, in the Thurstone procedure, the items themselves are ordered to form the scale. An individual's score on the attribute is determined by the number of items with which that individual agrees.

Thurstone scales probably would be more widely used if they were easier to

---

* See Shaw and Wright (1967), pp. 21–22.

TABLE 9-2
THURSTONE SCALE DESIGNED TO MEASURE ATTITUDES TOWARDS SCHOOL

Weight	Item	Statement
1.2	1.	School is important.
2.5	2.	To get any benefit from school, one must work hard.
4.0	3.	School provides useful knowledge.
5.1	4.	It is important to get good grades.
6.5	5.	Teachers are fair.
8.3	6.	I have friends at school.
9.8	7.	School is a good place to meet other people.
11.0	8.	School is fun to attend.

construct. However, many researchers find the procedure, which involves getting responses from a large number of judges to develop the scale and then applying the scale to a sample to study reliability and validity, to be too time-consuming. Thus, unless there is a Thurstone-type instrument already existing to measure the attribute in question, a researcher would probably prefer some other procedure. An example of a Thurstone scale is shown in Table 9-2. It was designed to measure attitudes towards school in junior high school students. The items were chosen from a large pool of items because they seemed to be equally distant from each other in terms of attitude towards school to a group of judges. The student is asked to place an X next to the three items that he or she feels are most true about school. The attitude score is usually the median of the weights, which in this case reflect the median ratings assigned by the judges to the items on an 11-point scale. Thus a student who agrees most with items 1, 3, and 7 will have a Thurstone-scale score of 4.0 since 4.0 is the median of the weights of those items (1.2, 4.0, 6.5).

Guttman Scales The assumption underlying the Guttman procedure is that when an individual responds correctly to an item, the individual would also respond correctly to all items which are ranked below it on the scale. Thus, if we know an individual's total score, we should be able to predict that person's score on each item. To illustrate, consider a scale measuring knowledge of monkeys made up of the following three items:

1 All monkeys are animals.   (Yes)   (No)
2 All mammals are monkeys.   (Yes)   (No)
3 Capuchins are monkeys.   (Yes)   (No)

Anyone who answers number 3 correctly (Yes) would probably also be correct on 1 and 2. Anyone who is correct on number 2 (No) would probably also respond correctly to the first item. The following diagram illustrates these response patterns, where 1 means answering the item correctly, 0 means getting it wrong.

Respondent	Item	1	2	3	Total Score
1		1	0	0	1
2		1	1	0	2
3		1	1	1	3

It can be seen that a person's performance on an item can be predicted perfectly from the total score. This scale is called *unidimensional* because only one trait is represented by the scale. Each item reflects an increasing degree of that trait.

Guttman scales are rather difficult to construct, and there are problems with their use too complex to be discussed here. The interested reader may consult texts on attitude scaling for a more complete discussion (e.g., Edwards, 1957; Shaw and Wright, 1967).

The Semantic Differential

The semantic-differential technique was devised to measure and compare the meaning of concepts based upon Osgood's notion of semantic space (Osgood, Suci, and Tannenbaum, 1957). It is founded on the idea that the meaning of a concept can be described using coordinates on a three-dimensional graph, the dimensions having been identified by factor analysis.

Osgood conducted research on many scales and reported on the factor loading of each scale with respect to the three dimensions of activity, potency, and evaluation. These scales are made up of pairs of polar adjectives, such as hot-cold, rough-smooth, and good-bad. Typically, the adjective pair is arrayed at each end of a 7-point scale. The points may be numbered from 1 to 7 or -3 to $+3$. Thus a hot-cold scale would look like this:

Hot   1   2   3   4   5   6   7   Cold

Respondents would mark an X in the space that represents their choice. A number of these scales would be used to rate a single concept. Figure 9-2 shows a semantic differential for the concept *teacher*. The concept to be rated

FIGURE 9-2
Semantic differential for rating the concept *teacher.*

fast	_____ _____ _____ _____ _____ _____ _____	slow
strong	_____ _____ _____ _____ _____ _____ _____	weak
clean	_____ _____ _____ _____ _____ _____ _____	dirty
active	_____ _____ _____ _____ _____ _____ _____	passive
large	_____ _____ _____ _____ _____ _____ _____	small
beautiful	_____ _____ _____ _____ _____ _____ _____	ugly

appears above the scales. The scales have little, if anything, directly to do with the concept being studied. Furthermore, the scales were chosen to represent the three dimensions of activity (fast-slow, active-passive), potency (strong-weak, large-small), and evaluation (clean-dirty, beautiful-ugly).

There is no one established way to analyze semantic differential data. The procedure produces a tremendous amount of data. Without computerized scoring and analysis, interpreting semantic differential data can be quite tedious. Osgood suggested a method of studying the geometric distance between the points plotted in three-dimensional space. Others suggested alternative procedures. For example, Kubinec (1970) used factor analysis and discriminant analysis to analyze ratings of self-concept using the semantic differential.

The semantic differential has been widely used in research. It is attractive to researchers because it permits a comparison of connotative as well as denotative meanings of concepts, and it has been shown by Osgood and others to be fairly valid and reliable even across cultures. However, analysis and interpretation of semantic-differential data is not easy. On a practical level, it is difficult to know what is meant when a concept such as *school* is more smooth than rough, more wet than dry, and more hot than cold. Because of this, the technique may give one the feeling that one's feet are firmly planted in the air. This is not to say that the semantic differential is not useful. Rather, when *semantic differences* in concepts are to be investigated, the method is well suited to the task. However, the relationships between semantic scales and the other constructs that educational and behavioral science researchers investigate need to be better understood. Inexperienced researchers often try to use the method to do things it was not designed to do and cannot do. They collect large amounts of semantic differential data and then find that they are unable to analyze it using traditional procedures.

Sociometry

Sociometry is a technique for studying interaction patterns among peers in a group. It is simple enough to be used with young children, yet sophisticated enough to use for studying complex patterns among adults. Depending upon the questions asked of respondents, a number of aspects of social interaction may be investigated. The following are examples of questions that might be asked in a sociometric investigation:

1 Which child in the class would you *most* like to sit next to you?
  Which child in the class would you *least* like to sit next to you?
2 Which child in the class would you *most* like to do a project with?
  Which child in the class would you *least* like to do a project with?
3 Which child in the class do you like the *most*?
  Which child in the class do you like the *least*?
4 Who in the class is the *best* leader?
  Who in the class is the *worst* leader?

There are several ways to analyze the response to sociometric instruments. Probably the easiest to understand and one of the most widely used in behavioral science and educational research is the matrix approach. Figure 9-3 shows a matrix of sociometric responses to the questions "Who in the group do you like most?" and "Who in the group do you like least?" for a group of five people. From the matrix, we can see the choice that each person made by reading across each line. By reading down each column, we can tell who was chosen most frequently as least and most liked. By summing the five columns, we find that John's total is 3. No one else had as high a total, so John seems to be the most liked person in the group. Joyce's total, −3, makes her appear to be the least liked person in the group.

Another way to analyze sociometric data is the *sociogram*. Figure 9-4 shows a sociogram for the question "Who in the group would you choose to be leader of the group?" The arrow indicates the choice of a person. Thus Pete, Cindy, and Alice chose Fred, while John chose Alice. Thus it would appear that Fred would make the best leader in the eyes of the group. Notice also that John, Pete, and Cindy were not chosen at all. The sociogram is easy to construct and interpret. But empirical methods of data analysis are not as easily applied to sociograms as to matrices.

The validity of sociometric techniques is related to the interpretations which are made from the data. If, for example, one wanted to know who was considered most attractive in a group, the question of who would make the best leader would not be appropriate. In addition, the reasons for choices cannot be inferred from a sociometric study. Before interpreting responses to the question of who would make the best leader, the researcher must assume that all group members know one another.

The reliability of sociometric instruments must also be established. The usual method is to correlate nominations of group members obtained at two different times. The interpretation of reliability of a sociometric instrument is somewhat more complex than reliability of a test. The problems involved have been summarized by Gronlund (1959).

Sociometry is a useful technique for studying social interaction. However, there is a tendency to overinterpret the data. Characteristics of the respondents and their motives cannot often be inferred from the responses. Furthermore, a person may be a consistent choice among the members of one group

Person	Choice				
	Mary	John	Fred	Joyce	Bob
Mary		1		−1	
John	1			−1	
Fred		1		−1	
Joyce			1		−1
Bob		1	−1		

FIGURE 9-3
Sociometric matrix of a group of five people, where 1 means "like the most" and −1 means "like the least."

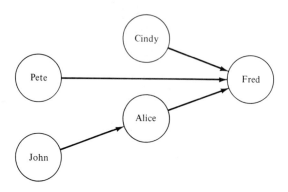

FIGURE 9-4
Sociogram of responses to the
question "Who would you choose to
be leader?"

but not another. Thus one who is designated a leader, or most liked, may not be so chosen in a different group. Although the sociometric technique seems intuitively simple, a researcher planning to use it would be wise to become familiar with the strengths and limitations of the procedure by reading a thorough treatment of the topic (for example, Gronlund, 1959).

Sociometry has been proposed as a method for studying the behavior of groups. For example, Fox, Luszki, and Schmuck (1966) and Barclay (1966) suggested use of the method to diagnose social relations in the classroom. Barclay (1983) developed a method for using sociometric ratings for studying classroom climate and developing treatment interventions for learning and behavior problems in the classroom. The approach has been used extensively as a dependent variable in research as well (Barclay, 1974).

Interviews and Questionnaires

Interviews and questionnaires are similar in many ways. They are both used to measure some of the less observable characteristics of people, such as values, goals, opinions, attitudes, preferences, and so on. An *interview* can be defined as a verbal discussion conducted by one person with another for the purpose of obtaining information. We have all participated in interviews at one time or another. For example, a physician taking a patient's medical history is conducting an interview. Similarly, psychologists, social workers, lawyers, clerics, and police officers regularly interview in the course of their work. Questionnaires, on the other hand, do not involve face-to-face interaction between the person asking the questions and the respondent. Usually, questionnaires are distributed by mail or in some other impersonal way and are self-administered.

Interviews The interview method of data collection is quite flexible and can be easily adapted to a variety of situations. The main reason for the flexibility of the method is the presence of the interviewer, who can explore responses with the person being interviewed, ask additional questions to clarify points, and, in general, tailor the interview to the situation.

Interviews may be *structured* or *unstructured*. Structured interviews include specific, set questions to which a response is sought. The respondent is provided several acceptable answers and must choose one. For example, consider the question:

> Do you feel that corporal punishment should be allowed in the public schools?

If the question is part of a structured interview, the respondent will be given some choices, such as "yes," "no," and "undecided" from which to choose a response. However, if the interview is unstructured, the respondent will be allowed to express his or her views and feelings in his or her own words. Furthermore, probing questions such as "How do you mean that?" "Can you explain further?" and "Why do you feel that way?" might be put in an unstructured questionnaire to allow for a more complete answer. Obviously, the interviewer relinquishes some objectivity in scoring as well as uniformity of the interview schedule when using unstructured techniques. However, the greater flexibility of unstructured methods may offset this loss in some situations. The researcher must determine which method is more appropriate in view of the objectives of the research, the cost involved, the skill of the available interviewers, time considerations, and other factors.

Interview schedules must be shown to be reliable and valid. In addition to the interview questions themselves, which may influence reliability and validity, the interviewer also plays a crucial role. The biases, perceptions, and opinions of the interviewer can influence the questions that are asked, the way that they are asked, the responses that are given, and the way those responses are recorded and interpreted. These influences could have a profound effect upon the validity of the interview. Validity can also be influenced by reluctance on the part of the respondent to discuss some topics face to face with the interviewer. For example, a respondent might be reluctant to express his or her personal choice of a political candidate when the interviewer seems to favor another candidate. Reliability can be affected by the interviewer as well as by the items of an interview schedule. Interviewers must be trained to ask questions in a consistent manner and to record all the data they get objectively. While attempting to reduce interviewer unreliability, the researcher must also consider the reliability of the interview schedule itself and the questions it contains. This can be investigated using methods similar to those used for other measurement instruments.

Difficulties with the Interview Method Although the interview method may seem relatively simple and straightforward, there are problems that should be recognized. For example, the questions asked are subject to interpretation. The interviewer might think that one question is being asked, and the respondent might interpret it differently and answer another. To illustrate, the question asked might be "Have you ever had to get counseling for family problems?" The interviewer might have been interested in psychological or marriage counseling. Yet, the respondent could easily interpret the question as meaning financial counseling or consulting with a physician regarding children's growth rates, diet, or illness. Furthermore, the question could be answered affirmatively by a respondent who helped obtain family counseling help for someone else! For example, if the respondent were a social worker whose job is to help people find services in their community, the response could have been "yes" even though the person never had to seek counseling for his or her own family. This type of problem can be detected and corrected more readily in an unstructured interview.

In addition to the problem of interpretation, the structure of a question is very important. That is, the way the question is asked may cue the respondent to a desired response. This is more likely to occur in a structured interview or in an unstructured interview with an untrained interviewer. Furthermore, subjects must be motivated to respond to the questions honestly and appropriately. If they are not, the validity of the interview must be questioned.

As was mentioned earlier, interviewers must be trained so that the data they collect will be both reliable and valid. They must be trained to recognize when a response is complete and when to ask for clarification or qualification. In addition, training should include methods for keeping the respondents on the topic without telling them how to respond. Interviewers must also be able to record responses quickly and accurately. They should not use nonstandard shorthand methods that might lead to incorrect interpretations later. Sometimes, to avoid this problem, tape recorders are used. However, this presents another difficulty because often respondents are reluctant to be candid when they know their responses are being recorded.

Finally, the more unstructured the interview, the more difficult the scoring and interpretation becomes. Although unstructured interviews allow for greater flexibility in gathering data, the lack of structure increases the necessity for objectivity and skill in the interviewer. Furthermore, the lack of structure often makes for difficulty in identifying trends or consensus among respondents.

Questionnaires Questionnaires are very similar to interviews. However, instead of the items being administered and responses being recorded by someone else, a questionaire is self-administered. The questionaire offers certain advantages over the interview. Specifically, a larger sample can be reached economically and greater anonynmity can be provided to the respondents. The first advantage increases the generalizability of the data. The second can result in people being more willing to respond openly and honestly to the questions.

However, with these advantages also come disadvantages. Specifically, questionnaires tend to be less flexible and adaptable than interviews. The advantage of having an interviewer present who is capable of adapting to the situation and the subject's responses is lost. Thus one assumes that the respondent is able to provide the appropriate information in response to the questions. Yet, if he or she cannot read or write well enough to do this, the assumption is false and the quality of data is affected. In addition, because no interviewer is present, the motivation and commitment of the respondent cannot be assessed. Finally, although a larger group may be sampled, getting enough returns for a representative sample can be a problem. People who respond to questionnaires that are distributed by mail may not be typical of the population. That is, they may have some specific point of view about which they feel very strongly. Persons not as committed to a position might not feel as motivated to respond, thus creating a systematic bias in the data. Researchers who use questionnaires usually find it necessary to have a plan for prodding respondents to answer. And rarely can researchers expect more than 70 percent of those sampled to respond. The remaining 30 percent might have a point of view that if included in the data, would have resulted in interpretations considerably different from those actually made.*

Projective Methods

Have you ever looked at a painting or sculpture and felt that you knew something about the personality or emotions of the artist? Have you ever felt the mood of the composer from the music he or she wrote? In a sense, this is the essence of projective measurement. Projective techniques are used primarily by psychologists studying the personalities of their clients or patients. Using these methods, interpretations may be made by a trained examiner who is sensitive to the meanings of the observed behavior. Projective techniques are based on the notion that people tend to *project* their values, attitudes, needs, emotions, personality, and motivations upon external objects. For example, the young child who "punishes" a doll or teddy bear for something the child itself had done could be considered to be projecting its own past onto the toy.

Projective devices usually consist of relatively unstructured stimuli. The more ambiguity in the stimuli, the more latitude the person has to involve himself or herself in the stimuli. Furthermore, although an individual is not asked to talk about himself or herself when taking a projective test, a trained examiner can detect much from the responses.

All the projective devices available require considerable expertise and training on the part of the examiner before the data they provide can be meaningfully interpreted. One of the most popular projective devices is the Rorschach technique. It consists of 10 cards that resemble inkblots or smears. The person is asked to respond to each card by telling what is seen in the blots. Responses are scored according to location, size, form, shading, color, content, and other characteristics, using certain scoring methods that have been devised (e.g.,

---

* See Madge, J. (1965) *The tools of social science.* Garden City, NY: Doubleday Anchor. Chapter 4 contains a relatively thorough discussion of the interview and questionnaire and includes a discussion of sample bias.

Beck, 1952, Klopfer and Kelley, 1942; Piotrowski, 1965). The scoring of the Rorschach is quite complex, and considerable training and practice is required for proficiency.

A number of projective devices utilize pictures as stimuli. Among the most popular are the Thematic Apperception Test (TAT) and the Children's Apperception Test (CAT). These techniques utilize ambiguous pictures about which the respondent is asked to tell a story. The content, theme, and various aspects of the stories are then interpreted to reveal the personality and emotional characteristics of the respondent.

Drawing is also commonly used as a projective device. Subjects are asked to draw their family, themselves, or some other person or object, and the drawings are scored objectively. Other projective devices include word-association techniques, toys and games, role-playing situations, unstructured interviews, sorting tasks, and sentence-completion tasks.

Projective techniques have certain distinct advantages over other methods of personality assessment. Perhaps the most impressive is that they are very difficult to fake. That is, knowledge of the test, the test items, and the objectives of the test usually do not invalidate the results. The themes and quality of responses are more significant than what is actually said by the subject. With other methods of assessment of personality, values, motivation, and the like, people may tend to respond in ways they feel will impress the examiner, which makes accurate interpretation of personality traits difficult. However, with projective methods, this is less of a problem.

A second advantage of projective devices is that their ambiguity does not limit the kinds of qualities that may be investigated. Even very rare personality characteristics or unusual motivations may be detected by these devices. More objective methods would require specific items sensitive to those personality characteristics or motivations to detect them. In addition, projectives assess a broad range of characteristics, such as self-concept, sex-role identification, personality type, interpersonal style, values, and other aspects of personality and emotion. An individual test would be required for each of these characteristics with a more objective or structured instrument.

There are disadvantages to projective techniques, however. The lack of structure that gives the method its strength is also a source of weakness. Because of differences in stimuli and scoring that each respondent may be subject to across administrations, generalization can be difficult. The ambiguity also leads to subjectivity in scoring and, thus, great difficulty in demonstrating reliability and validity. To complicate the issue further, scoring is dependent not only on the perceptions of the scorer but also on the theoretical orientation to which the scorer subscribes.

Further, the use of projective methods in research is controversial. Besides obvious problems with reliability and validity, there may be problems concerning invasion of privacy because they are broad-range instruments. Although the person who administers the instrument may be interested in only one aspect of personality, the instrument reveals a wide range of personality facets.

Some of the information uncovered might not be appreciated by the person taking the test (a more complete discussion of ethical issues and the right to privacy appears in Chapter 14). Because of the limitations regarding objectivity of scoring, reliability, validity, ethical problems, and the difficulty in quantifying responses, projective techniques should be used with care only by qualified examiners. It would be wise to investigate alternative methods of assessment before deciding that projective techniques are appropriate for use in a research study.

CHOOSING A MEASUREMENT TECHNIQUE

The researcher should select from among the variety of procedures available those most supportive of the research objectives. Figure 9-5 contains 15 considerations applicable to selecting a method for measurement in a research study. It is usually a good idea to explore several existing measurement instruments before selecting one or designing a new one to use in a research investigation. When selecting an instrument, however, the investigator should be aware that when a construct is operationalized using a specific test, the construct may become redefined into something that was not intended in the hy-

FIGURE 9-5
A form listing considerations for selecting a test to use in a research study.

A. Evaluation of a measurement instrument for _____
(constructs being measured and purpose(s))

B. Test title: _____ Author: _____

C. Criteria for Selection	Appropriateness			Comments
	Very appropriate	Adequate	Not appropriate	
1. Construct(s) measured by tests				
2. Reliability (types and coefficients)				
3. Validity (degree and types)				
4. Standardization group(s)				
5. Reading level				
6. Complexity and adequacy of instructions				
7. Complexity of administration				
8. Ease of scoring				
9. Norms provided				
10. Time required for administration				
11. Description of test construction				
12. Characteristics of items				
13. Availability of equivalent forms				
14. Comments of reviewers (e.g., in Buros's *Mental Measurements Yearbook*				
15. Match between research needs and test				

potheses. The research purposes should contribute to the selection of the measurement technique and not vice versa. Unless the research is designed specifically to evaluate the measurement instrument, the hypotheses or objectives should be stated before the measurement instrument is selected.

STANDARDS FOR TESTS

Much of what was covered in this and the last chapter regarding standards for tests is widely accepted by researchers in the social and behavioral sciences and education. A good overview of these standards may be found in a document titled *Standards for Educational and Psychological Testing* prepared by a joint committee of the American Educational Research Association, the American Psychological Association, and the National Council on Measurement in Education (1985). The report covers validity, reliability, test development, scaling, and the publication of tests. It also includes sections on the use of tests in clinical, educational, vocational, and other applications.

SUMMARY

Researchers in education and the behavioral sciences measure constructs such as achievement, personality, aptitude and ability, behavioral tendency, interests, and values. Researchers generally prefer to utilize existing measurement instruments. However, if no existing ones are appropriate, researchers will construct instruments to meet their needs, using a plan such as a table of specifications. In addition, they will necessarily determine the reliability and validity of their tests.

Tests may be objective or nonobjective. The objectivity of a test is determined by the amount of judgment a scorer must use in grading the test items. Objective test items require little scorer judgment. Each item has only one correct answer. True-false, multiple-choice, matching, and supply items are considered to be relatively objective, whereas essay and open-ended interview items are considered relatively nonobjective.

In addition to paper-and-pencil tests, researchers use observational ratings, scales, sociometry, interviews and questionnaires, and projective devices for observation and measurement. With these techniques as with tests, reliability and validity must be considered. Researchers should be aware that they define a variable by operationalizing it using a specific measurement device. Therefore, the nature and purpose of the research should help determine the measurement instruments that are used.

PROBLEMS FOR THOUGHT AND DISCUSSION

1 A researcher designed a study to investigate creativity in young children. He was primarily interested in whether exposure to a wide variety of experiences as part of a highly enriched school program led to greater creativity. His design required comparison of first-, third-, and fifth-grade children who were attending an enriched

school program with a similar group of students in a more traditional program. Consider each of the following choices that he has for a dependent variable. Which would you choose if you were the researcher? Why?

a A test of creativity designed by the researcher himself

b A standardized test of creativity which has internal reliability estimates of .74 and .79 and was considered a valuable instrument for measuring ability to solve problems creatively by a previous researcher.

c A standardized test of academic achievement.

d A personality test which measures creativity on one of its subtests.

e A test of artistic ability.

2 Often intelligence tests are used as dependent variables in studies of the effectiveness of educational interventions. Consider the following hypothetical example of this:

Mothers of disadvantaged low-socioeconomic-status children were given child-rearing instruction by the faculty of a medical school. In addition, medical and dental needs of the children were met by the program. Nutritional guidance and information was provided by a traveling public health nurse. At the end of a year in the program, each child was administered the Stanford-Binet Intelligence Test to determine the effectiveness of the program. It was found that the average score of children in the program was four IQ points higher than that of a similar group who did not participate in the program.

a Do you think the program was effective according to the criterion of intelligence? Why?

b Was intelligence the proper criterion to use in this case?

c Can you think of some other criteria for evaluating such a program?

3 Develop several examples of supply, multiple-choice, and true-false items. Then carefully read the items and critique them. Would you change any of the items after having reread them? If possible, have someone else read your items and discuss them with you.

4 Select two empirical studies from the research literature which use measurement or testing methods discussed in this chapter. Do the measurement methods serve to delimit the definition of what is measured? Can the variables be measured differently? Suggest some alternative methods for measuring the same constructs and variables.

5 In the literature, locate at least two methods of measuring each of the following constructs:

intelligence
creativity
learning style
leadership style
academic achievement
mechanical ability
reading achievement
socioeconomic status
group cohesiveness

In each case, discuss how the meaning of a score is affected by the measurement technique used.

REFERENCES

American Educational Research Association, American Psychological Association, & National Council on Measurement in Education (1985). *Standards for educational and psychological testing*. Washington: American Psychological Association.

Anastasi, A. (1982). *Psychological testing* (5th ed.). New York: Macmillan.

Barclay, J. R. (1966). Sociometry: Rationale and technique for effecting behavior change in the elementary school. *American Personnel and Guidance Journal, 44,* 1067–1076.

Barclay, J. R. (1974). *Some notes on research with the Barclay Classroom Climate Inventory.* Lexington, KY: Educational Skills Development.

Barclay, J. R. (1983). *Barclay Classroom Assessment System.* Los Angeles: Western Psychological Services.

Beck, S. J. (1952). *Rorschach's test.* New York: Grune & Stratton.

Congress of the United States, Office of Technology Assessment (1982). *Informational technology and its impact on American education.* Washington, D.C.: Office of Technology Assessment.

Cunningham, G. K. (1986). *Educational and psychological measurement.* New York: Macmillan.

Edwards, A. L. (1957). *Techniques of attitude scale construction.* New York: Appleton-Century-Crofts.

Fox, R., Luszki, M. B., & Schmuck, R. (1966). *Diagnosing classroom learning environment.* Chicago: Science Research.

Gronlund, N. E. *Sociometry in the classroom.* (1959). New York: Harper & Row.

Gronlund, N. E. (1985). *Measurement and evaluation in teaching* (5th ed.) New York: Macmillan.

Klopfer, B., & Kelley, D. M. (1942). *The Rorschach technique.* New York: Harcourt, Brace & World.

Kubinec, C. M. (1970). The relative efficacy of various dimensions of the self-concept in predicting academic achievement. *American Educational Research Journal, 7,* 289–305.

McMorris, R., Brown, J. O., Snyder, G. W., & Pruzek, R. M. (1972). Effects of violating item-construction principles. *Journal of Educational Measurement, 9,* 287–295.

National Commission on Excellence in Education (Apr. 1983). *A report to the nation and the Secretary of Education.* U.S. Department of Education.

Osgood, C., Suci, J., & Tannenbaum, P. (1957). *The measurement of meaning.* Urbana: The University of Illinois Press.

Piotrowski, Z. A. (1965). *Perceptanalysis.* Philadelphia: Ex Libris.

Sax, G. (1980). *Principles of educational measurement and evaluation.* Belmont, CA: Wadsworth.

Shaw, M. E., & Wright, J. M. (1967). *Scales for the measurement of attitudes.* New York: McGraw-Hill.

Thorndike, R. L., & Hagen, E. (1977). *Measurement and evaluation in psychology and education* (4th ed.) New York: Wiley.

Wolcott, H. F. (1981). Confessions of a trained observer. In Popkowitz, T. S., & Tabachnick, B. R. (Eds.), *The study of schooling: Field based methodologies in educational research and evaluation.* New York: Praeger.

SOURCES OF INFORMATION ABOUT TESTING

1 The Buros Institute of Mental Measurements. Lincoln: University of Nebraska.

 The Buros Institute, founded by O. K. Buros, has been publishing anthologies of test information since 1938. After Buros' death, responsibility for the Institute and its publications was assumed by the University of Nebraska at Lincoln. The publications of the Institute are among the most useful collections of information about tests available. The publications include editions of *Mental Measurements Yearbook (MMY), Tests in Print, Personality Tests and Reviews, Intelligence Tests and Reviews, and Vocational Tests and Reviews.*

2 Sweetland, R. C., & Keyser, D. J. (Eds.) (1983). *Tests.* Kansas City, MO: Test Corporation of America.

Contains brief descriptions and summaries of tests and their publishers and cost.

3 Newmark, C. S. (Ed.) (1985). *Major psychological assessment instruments.* Boston: Allyn & Bacon.

Contains thorough descriptions of 11 of the major psychological instruments used for applied needs as well as research. Covers validity, reliability, research data, clinical interpretation, and other issues.

4 *Journal of Educational Measurement.* National Council on Measurement in Education (NCME).

Contains research, technical reports, test reviews, book reviews, and other issues related to testing.

SUPPLEMENTARY READINGS

Covin, T. M. (Ed.) (1974). *Classroom test construction: A sourcebook for teachers.* New York: MSS Information Corp.

Cronbach, L. J. (1970). *Essentials of psychological testing* (3rd ed.). New York: Harper & Row.

Edwards, A. L. (1957). *The social desirability variable in personality research.* New York: Dryden.

Embretson, S. E. (Ed.) (1985). *Test design: Developments in psychology and psychometrics.* Orlando, FL: Academic.

Lyman, H. B. (1971). *Test scores and what they mean* (2nd ed.) Englewood Cliffs, NJ: Prentice-Hall.

Merwin, J. C. (1973). Educational measurement of what characteristic of whom (or what) by whom and why. *Journal of Educational Measurement, 10,* 1–6.

Plake, B. S., & Witt, J. C. (Eds.) (1986). *The future of testing.* Hillsdale, NJ: Erlbaum.

Samuda, R. J. (1975). *Psychological testing of American minorities.* New York: Dodd, Mead.

Sattler, J. M. (1988). *Assessment of children's intelligence* (3rd ed.). San Diego: Sattler.

Shoemaker. D. M. (1974). Toward a framework for achievement testing. *Review of Educational Research, 45,* 127–147.

Thorndike, R. L. (1975). Mr. Binet's test 70 years later. *Educational Researcher, 4(5),* 3–6.

Torgerson, W. (1958). *Theory and methods of scaling.* New York: Wiley.

CHAPTER 10

COMPUTERS AND RESEARCH

Computers are so widely used today that most people spend at least part of the day interacting in some way with them. For example, automatic computerized teller machines enable customers to perform bank transactions even after closing hours. Bills are paid, telephone surveys are conducted, and manufacturing processes are monitored by computers. *Word processors*—computers programmed to process language symbols—have largely replaced typewriters. Computers have even become the tools of artists and musicians. In fact, the list of applications of computer technology in modern society is virtually endless.

Just as computers have become indispensable in other areas of human activity, they have profoundly influenced the research field. Some research that would not have been possible or could only have been done at great cost and with huge investments of human time and effort is now done routinely and instantly with computers. For example, some advanced statistical analysis procedures, like factor analysis, discriminant analysis, and multivariate analysis of variance, procedures that once required a year or more for several workers to compute, are now done in seconds with modern high-speed computers. In this chapter, we will explore various ways in which the computer is used as a tool by the researcher.

WHAT IS A COMPUTER?

A *computer* is an electronic machine that can perform simple operations rapidly and accurately. These simple operations involve numbers and arithmetic and logical processes that can be organized into more complex procedures, such as statistical analysis, word processing, telecommunications, monitoring of other machines, data management, and so on. A computer as most users know it is really a system consisting of many components, each of which performs some unique function. Some components are input devices, used to transport information into the computer. Other devices are for *output*; that is, communicating from within the computer to the outside. Most of us are familiar with input devices such as keyboards and game paddles and output devices like printers and visual display screens. In addition, a computer system usually includes some form of data storage device, such as a magnetic tape or disk, or other equipment designed to store data.

All of the components of a computer system mentioned so far are part of what is called *hardware*. Hardware includes all the physical equipment of a computer system (e.g., disk drives, printers, microchips, keyboard, visual display screen, central processor, etc.). The hardware components of a basic computer system are diagrammed in Figure 10-1. This equipment is made operational by the *software* (or programs). Software consists of the instructions to the computer that tell it what it is supposed to do. Some software is etched permanently into electronic microchips within the computer system itself. Other software is read into the computer every time the computer is used for a particular purpose. It is software that gives computers their versatility. One type of software, called the *operating system,* provides the basic instructions the computer needs to perform its functions and to run programs.

Generally, the computers researchers use can be divided into three size categories. Microcomputers are the smallest, followed by minicomputers and mainframes. However, computer size is determined more by the speed and capability of the computer than by the physical size of its components, so it is difficult to attach specific significance to the physical size of the computer. Further, as technology advances, small computers become more capable without increasing in size. In fact, many of the microcomputers that one sees on desk tops today are more capable than the large mainframe systems of just 20 years ago, even though those mainframe computers sometimes occupied several large rooms. Further, the largest of today's mainframes, the supercomputers, are many times more capable than were their predecessors, even though they are not appreciably larger.

In the recent past, researchers used microcomputers mostly for control of experiments, stimulus presentation, and word processing. Large-scale data processing and statistical analysis tended to be done on mainframes and minicomputers. However, as microcomputers become more capable, many more data-analysis tasks are being done on microcomputers. A large computer system is still preferred for large analyses and for dealing with very large data sets, however.

COMMUNICATION TO AND FROM A COMPUTER

An array of devices and methods for communicating with a computer exists. In the old days of computing (not so very long ago), the principal mode of com-

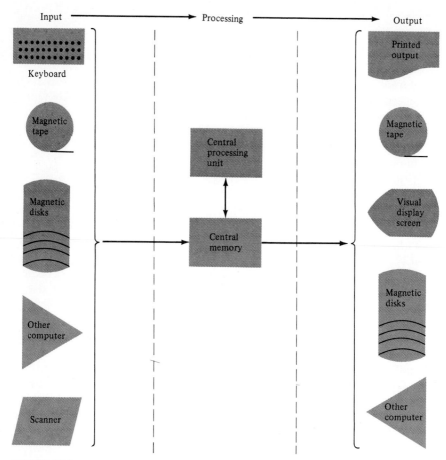

FIGURE 10-1
Hardware components of a typical computer system.

munication with computers was with cards in which holes were punched. One line of instructions was placed on each card, which had room for 80 characters. A character could be a number, a letter, or a symbol (e.g., *, &, $, @, etc.). (See Figure 10-2.) However, most researchers now communicate with computers, whether large or small, by way of terminals with keyboards and visual display monitors. Remnants of the card method of input are that the screen displays on monitors are often 80 characters (or columns) across and the tendency of many computer users to refer to a line of data or instructions on the screen as a "card."

Languages and Programming

Computers process instructions and data using a very elementary code based on binary numbers (1s and 0s). Figure 10-3 shows how the numbers 1 to 10 are

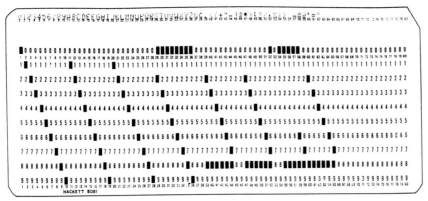

FIGURE 10-2
An 80-column card, showing punches for letters, numbers, and symbols.

Number		Binary
0	=	0000
1	=	0001
2	=	0010
3	=	0011
4	=	0100
5	=	0101
6	=	0110
7	=	0111
8	=	1000
9	=	1001

FIGURE 10-3
Binary equivalents up to nine.

depicted in binary numbers. This code, known as *machine language,* is quite cumbersome for people to learn and use. For this reason, higher-level languages—languages that are more like English—have been developed for use when programming a computer. Figure 10-4 shows two programs written in these higher-level languages to add two numbers and then find the average. One is written in BASIC (Beginner's All-purpose Symbolic Instruction Code) and the other in Pascal. Notice that the instructions in the two programs are different. Despite the similarity to English, either of these languages requires study if one wishes to program with it. Further, the programs shown in Figure 10-4 are short and simple; but programs can become very long, sometimes up to several thousand lines, when the instructions involve complex processes. In addition, the computer must have been programmed to translate statements in these higher-level languages into machine language.

Most researchers do not need to learn how to program because a great many computer programs are already available. Researchers who are not able to find the appropriate program or who require special programs to meet their

A. Pascal

```
PROGRAM AVERAGE;
    VAR
        I : INTEGER;
        SUM, AV, X1, X2 : REAL;

    BEGIN
        SUM := 0;
        FOR I := 1 TO 2 DO
            WRITELN ('TYPE IN FIRST NUMBER:');
            READ (X1);
            WRITELN ('TYPE IN SECOND NUMBER:');
            READ (X2);
        SUM := X1 + X2;
        AV := SUM/2;
    WRITELN ('THE AVERAGE OF 2 NUMBERS IS:', AV)
END.
```

B. BASIC

```
10   REM  AVERAGE OF 2 NUMBERS
20   PRINT "THE FIRST NUMBER IS"
30   INPUT A
40   PRINT "THE SECOND NUMBER IS"
50   INPUT B
60   SUM = A + B
70   AVRG = SUM / 2
80   PRINT "THE AVERAGE IS:  ";AVRG

90   END
```

FIGURE 10-4
Programs written in Pascal and BASIC for getting the average of two numbers.

needs can either learn to write programs in one of the high-level languages or employ an experienced programmer to do their programming. However, not all languages are equally suited to all computers and tasks. Some languages (e.g., BASIC and Pascal) are designed for all-purpose programming; others are designed to emphasize particular types of applications (e.g., LISP and PROLOG for artificial intelligence and list processing, COBOL for business applications, FORTRAN for scientific applications, etc.). Thus a researcher who requires special programs not only has to decide whether or not to hire a programmer but also which programming language is most suitable for the applications being contemplated. The advice of a computer professional can save the researcher costly errors and delay.

Preexisting and Packaged Programs

The effort required to use a computer is considerably reduced when preexisting programs are available or when packaged programs can be used. A *packaged program* is a generalized program written so that it can be used by anyone with a proper set of instructions and the necessary computer equipment. For example, there are a number of packaged programs that graph or perform statistical analysis. All that is usually needed to use these programs is that the data and the necessary instructions be put into the computer. In a large research facility, such as a university, regional laboratory, or research institute, the computer center staff will maintain programs and manuals and make them available to users. In addition, many packaged programs can be purchased for use on microcomputers, thus expanding the possibilities for sophisticated data processing techniques beyond the large research institutions. Among the more popular packaged programs available for mainframe and smaller computers are the Statistical Analysis System (SAS Institute, Cary, NC) and the SPSS series (SPSS, Inc., Chicago). Both of these packages go beyond statistical programming to include a number of related tasks, such as graphing, data management, report writing, and other kinds of programs. However, since statistical analysis remains the central purpose of these packages, we will look at them later in the section on statistical analysis.

USES OF COMPUTERS IN RESEARCH

As you probably realize by now, computers can do a great many things for the researcher. They can be tireless observers and recorders and extremely accurate and rapid data handlers. With the proper programming and peripheral devices, computers can be indispensable research assistants, capable of speeding the research process and, at the same time, making possible more sophistication in research design and analysis. In this section, we will explore some of these specific uses.

Computers in Data Collection

Before the advent of computer technology, data collection from large samples posed many problems. For example, each item of a measurement instrument had to be scored by hand. Then a list had to be made of all the scores for further analysis. Machines can now grade test responses rapidly and transfer the information directly to a computer for more extensive analysis. With this technology, respondents use answer sheets similar to the one shown in Figure 10-5. The test items are printed on separate sheets and thus may be reused. Responses are recorded on the answer sheet by darkening the appropriate spaces. Completed forms are read by a device called a *scanner,* which reads the marks made on the sheet. Most scanners can be programmed with a scoring key of correct answers to provide a total score as well as item scores. The item and total scores can then be sent to a computer for analysis and reporting. Such a system greatly enhances test design and research by providing information about performance on each item as well as on the whole test. Scanning devices are currently available within the price range of microcomputers and are becoming commonplace in schools, research settings, and testing centers.

Coding and Preparation of Data for Analysis   When answer sheets are used with scanning and data are entered directly into the computer, data prepara-

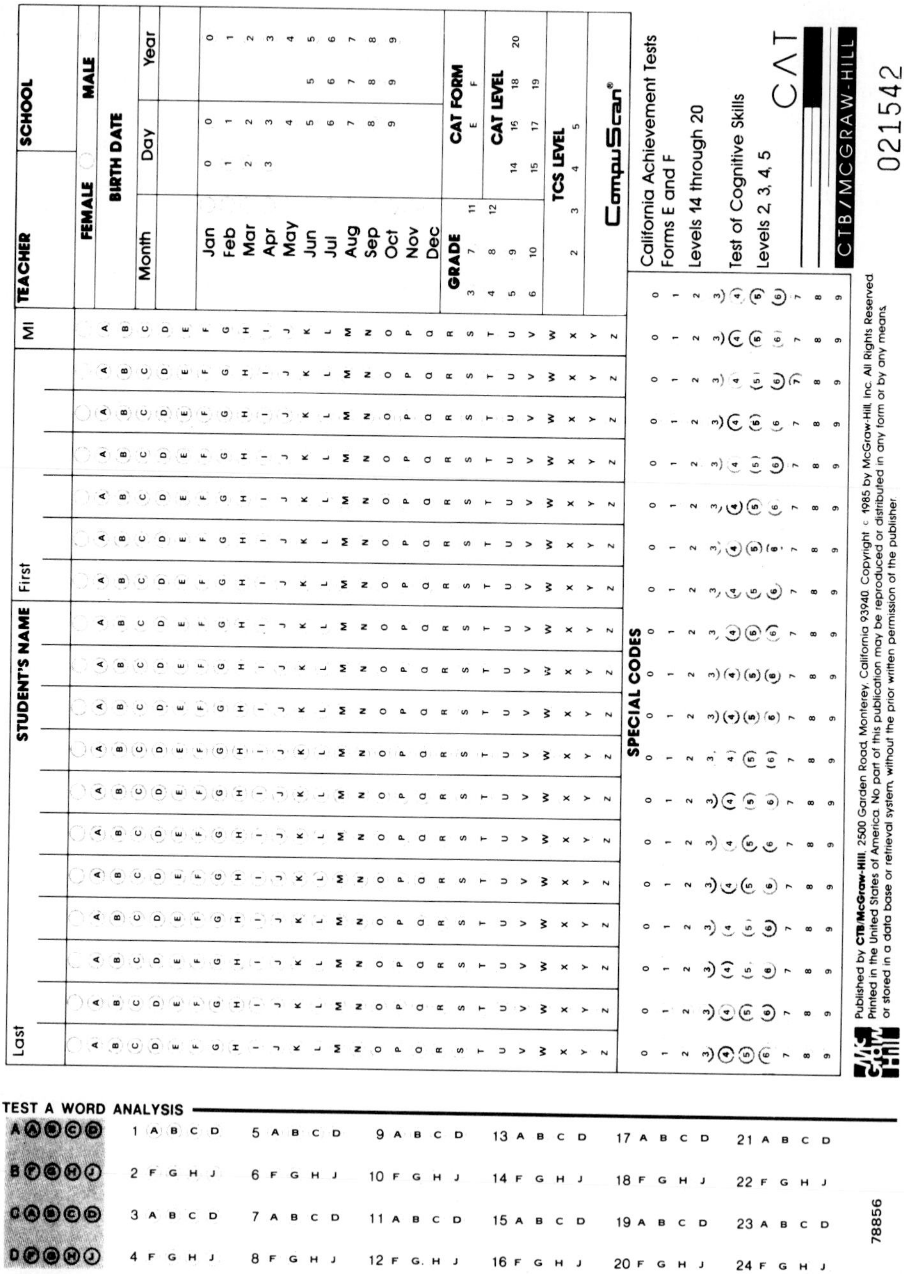

FIGURE 10-5
A standard answer sheet used for electronic scanning of responses.

tion requires little special attention. However, the researcher should be mindful of how data files are read by computers when a specific computer program package is to be used. The data must be put in an organized format so that all the information can be processed correctly. Therefore, it is recommended that before preparing a data file, a researcher consult the appropriate manuals and, if necessary, seek advice from someone who is familiar with data processing and the programs that will be used.

Before data are entered by hand, a roster of the data should be prepared. A *roster* is actually a sheet on which data are written in columns. Usually programming sheets or large accounting ledgers are used for rostering of data. Figure 10-6 shows data in rostered form. In the roster, each piece of data is placed in specified numbered columns. This requires that the researcher determine how much space an element of data will need. For example, IQ scores usually range from about 55 to about 155. Since the highest IQ scores contain three digits, three spaces must be reserved for each IQ score. Data may be rostered in a fixed format, which means that variables will be assigned to specific columns (as shown in Figure 10-6), or in freefield format, in which the order of listing is important rather than the specific column. Thus, for example, if each subject in the study will be represented by three scores, then every three scores will be read as a set of three scores (usually separated by spaces) and column location will not be important. Further, each set of three scores must be entered in the same order; that is, the same variable must always be in the first position, the second position, and so on. It is harder to read or find specific entries in a freefield format than in a fixed format, but the roster tends to be more compact in freefield. In freefield data input format, missing data can cause problems because without the same number of scores for each subject, the computer loses count. Before deciding on a format, however, a researcher must determine the preferred method of data organization for the statistical program package that will be used.

Rostering data serves a couple of purposes. First, it facilitates keyboarding data into a file at a computer terminal. Second, it provides a "hard copy" of all the data that could prove useful if an electronic disaster of some sort (e.g., power failure, lightning storm, blown fuse, etc.) caused the electronic file in the computer system to be lost or damaged.

Another issue to consider when preparing data is coding. To make for more efficient rostering or to reduce the size of data lists, it is often desirable to code data. For example, the words "experimental group" would require 18 spaces in a roster if spelled out. If the experimental group is assigned a single letter or number (such as *E* or 1), no information is lost and the entry process is facilitated. Codes can be given to categories of any type, including ordinal categories (e.g., the first 10 percent of the class in terms of grade-point average is assigned the number 1, the next 10 percent is assigned the number 2, and so on).

The following sequence describes the collection and tabulation of data in preparation for computer analysis. The first three steps should always be fol-

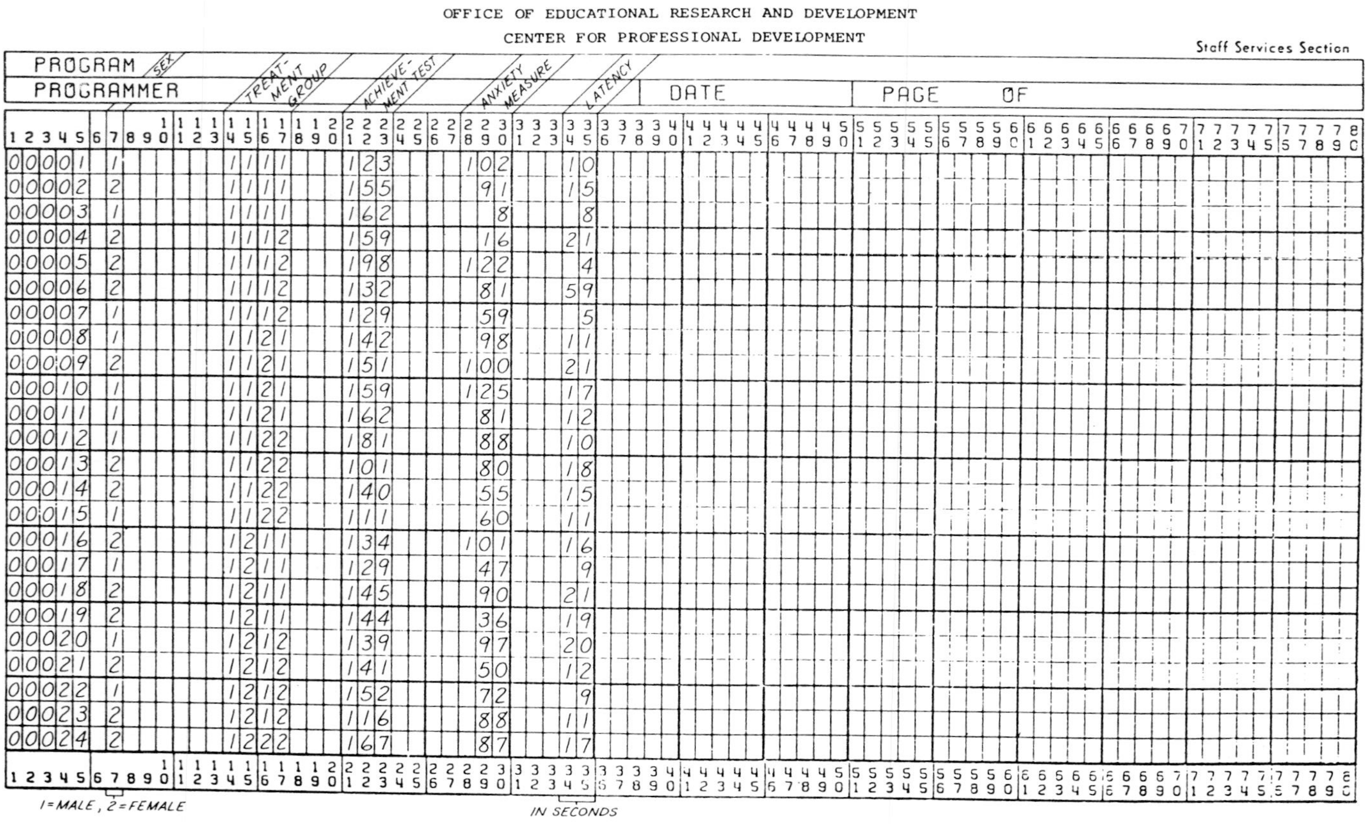

OFFICE OF EDUCATIONAL RESEARCH AND DEVELOPMENT

CENTER FOR PROFESSIONAL DEVELOPMENT

Staff Services Section

PROGRAM

PROGRAMMER

DATE   PAGE   OF

LATENCY   ANXIETY MEASURE   WHITE TEST   PERM'T GROUP   SEX

IN SECONDS

1 = MALE, 2 = FEMALE

FIGURE 10-6
A data roster.

lowed, even when computer analysis is not planned, for they will facilitate analyzing data by hand or calculator.

1 Collect data according to predesignated procedures.

2 Complete any coding of the data that is necessary. For example, if the data are in nominal form, it might save time and writing effort to assign numbers to categories. Thus, if political party affiliation was studied, Democrats might be assigned 1, Republicans 2, and Others 3. Ordinal or interval data may also be coded. This is usually done to reduce the range of scores. For instance, assume that 100 subjects in a research study ranged in age from 11 to 75 years. The researcher could divide the age range into categories and then assign numbers to represent the categories, as follows:

Age	Category
11–20	1
21–30	2
31–40	3
41–50	4
51–60	5
61–70	6
71–80	7

3 Place the data for all subjects on a roster or list. Usually large accounting or graph paper is useful for the construction of a roster, or, as shown in Figure 10-5, a program coding sheet may be used. Notice that all the scores for each subject are placed on one line and that columns are labeled with the names of the variables.

4 Type the data at a computer terminal (or microcomputer). The organization of instructions and data for computer analysis using various statistical packages is discussed below.

Collecting Data, Monitoring, and Controlling Experiments Small computers are often used in laboratory and other research settings because of their ability to collect data and monitor and control experiments. For example, microcomputers can be used to monitor physiological data generated from experiments in physical or psychological stress. These data could include temperature, motor activity, eye movement, minor electronic potentials across the surface of the skin, and other measures. However, most of these measures require continuous readings (*analog*), and computers are *digital* (use discrete units) in their operations. The continuous data from temperature reading, for example, must be turned into digital form for computer processing. This is done with a device between the computer and the temperature sensor called an *analog-to-digital converter* (or a/d converter). While the details of a/d devices (and also d/a converters that do the reverse; i.e., convert from digital to analog) and how they work are beyond the scope of this text, the transformation of the data that occurs as a result should be mentioned. An illustration of this kind of transformation is shown in Figure 10-7, where a continuous signal sampled at a specified time is changed to a digital signal for computerized processing.

Using other specialized data-collection devices, it is now possible to track children with serious handicaps 24 hours per day or to study physical changes that may occur while students are learning, sleeping, solving problems, or engaging in other activities. In the psychological laboratory, stimulus pictures can be displayed, responses recorded and timed, and other elements of experimental control can be achieved. As the technology develops, more computerization in the laboratory can be expected.

The Computer as a Tool in Statistical Analysis

Computers have many obvious advantages in data analysis. Their ability to perform high-speed arithmetic operations on large amounts of data has resulted in virtual elimination of the drudgery of computations required in complex univariate and multivariate statistical procedures. Packaged statistical programs are available at most computer centers to meet most of the statistical analysis needs of the users, and additional programs can be developed to meet specific needs.

Most computer programs for statistical analysis packaged for use on large computers are also available in microcomputer versions. However, we

FIGURE 10-7
Analog data transformed to digital.

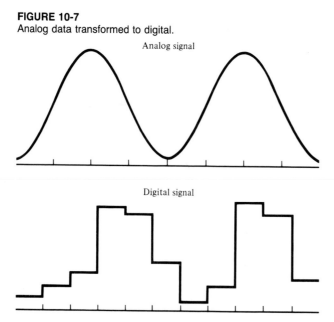

will limit our discussion to the setup and running of these programs on large computers. Similar procedures would be used with the microcomputer versions of these packages.

Using Packaged Programs Figure 10-8 shows the general layout of a data-analysis job using the Statistical Analysis System (SAS) on a large computer to produce descriptive statistics of two variables (knowledge and attitude) for two groups (experimental and control). The procedure will also do *t* tests of the difference between experimental and control groups, first using knowledge as the dependent variable, then attitude. The lines of instructions and data shown in Figure 10-8 are typed into the computer from the terminal. The first three lines provide information that is required by the system. This information includes identification of the user, the account number, the packaged program being used, and other information the computer system will need to run the job. There is some variation from one computer installation to another and between types of computers regarding the exact format of the system instructions required. Further, some packages are run in interactive mode at some installations, which means fewer system instructions are required. (The SPSS[x] example in Figure 10-9 for the same analysis is shown in interactive mode.) Following the systems instructions, the next set of lines are instructions required by the SAS program package. They tell the computer which set of programs in the package will be used to complete the present analysis. As shown in Figure 10-8, the data follow these instructions.

FIGURE 10-8
Lines of instructions and data for an SAS job.

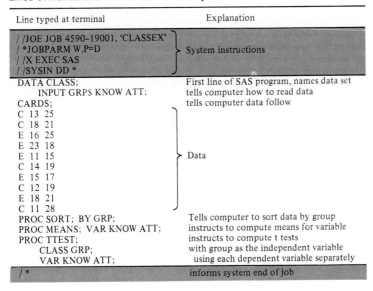

Line typed at terminal	Explanation
//JOE JOB 4590-19001, 'CLASSEX' / *JOBPARM W,P=D / /X EXEC SAS / /SYSIN DD *	System instructions
DATA CLASS;	First line of SAS program, names data set
INPUT GRP$ KNOW ATT;	tells computer how to read data
CARDS;	tells computer data follow
C 13 25	
C 18 21	
E 16 25	
E 23 18	
E 11 15	Data
C 14 19	
E 15 17	
C 12 19	
E 18 21	
C 11 28	
PROC SORT; BY GRP;	Tells computer to sort data by group
PROC MEANS; VAR KNOW ATT;	instructs to compute means for variable
PROC TTEST;	instructs to compute t tests
CLASS GRP;	with group as the independent variable
VAR KNOW ATT;	using each dependent variable separately
/*	informs system end of job

Line typed at terminal	Explanation
LINKTO SPSSX	Tells system SPSS^X is needed
TITLE EXPERIMENTAL VS	
CONTROL ON KNOWLEDGE AND	Title of job
ATTITUDE	
DATA LIST FIXED/1 (A) GRP 1 KNOW 3-4 ATT 6-7	
RECODE GRP (E=1) (C=2)	
T-TEST GROUPS=GRP/VARIABLES = KNOW ATT	SPSS^X instructions
BEGIN DATA	
C 13 25	
C 18 21	
:	
:	
:	Data
:	
E 18 21	
C 11 28	
END DATA	
FINISH	Program instructions

FIGURE 10-9
Lines of instructions and data for an SPSS^X job.

Notice that the instructions for the two analyses shown in Figures 10-8 and 10-9 are different. Both packages are capable of similar analyses and have a wide variety of applications in statistics, but there are differences in how things are done with each package and people who do statistical analysis tend to prefer one or the other. Output from the SAS analysis is shown in Figure 10-10. The SPSS^X output is similar. Two other widely used program packages are Minitab (Minitab, Inc., State College, PA) and BMDP (University of California, Berkeley).

The publisher of each program package publishes a set of manuals describing the program in the package and how to use it. In addition, the staff of the computer facility often provides manuals and instructions explaining local processing procedures. A user of a program package should obtain the manuals that contain the directions for setting up the data and the program. Manuals and publications for some of the more frequently used statistical program packages have been listed at the end of this chapter.

Spreadsheets *Spreadsheets* are programs that turn the computer into enormous ledgerlike electronic data sheets. Data can be assigned to rows or columns, and arithmetic and logical procedures can be applied to them. In addition, columns, rows, and cells can be made dependent upon other columns, rows, and cells. In other words, spreadsheets are like extremely flexible data rosters that permit users to design the analysis that will be done to the data set as it is entered into the spreadsheet. Spreadsheets are also unique in that as data are added to the spreadsheet, all of the other cells are updated.

```
                                                     SAS                        11:08 WEDNESDAY, MARCH 23, 1988    1

VARIABLE      N        MEAN        STANDARD      MINIMUM       MAXIMUM      STD ERROR       SUM        VARIANCE        C.V.
                                   DEVIATION      VALUE         VALUE        OF MEAN

KNOW         10    15.10000000   3.78447119   11.00000000   23.00000000   1.19675487  151.00000000  14.32222222     25.063
ATT          10    20.80000000   4.07703596   15.00000000   28.00000000   1.28927197  208.00000000  16.62222222     19.601


                                                      SAS

                                                TTEST PROCEDURE

VARIABLE: KNOW

GRP      N          MEAN        STD DEV      STD ERROR       MINIMUM        MAXIMUM     VARIANCES         T        DF   PROB > |T|

C        5   13.60000000     2.70185122     1.20830460   11.00000000    18.00000000     UNEQUAL      -1.3007       6.6       0.2369
E        5   16.60000000     4.39317653     1.96468827   11.00000000    23.00000000     EQUAL        -1.3007       8.0       0.2296

FOR HO: VARIANCES ARE EQUAL, F'=     2.64 WITH 4 AND 4 DF     PROB > F'= 0.3692
---------------------------------------------------------------------------------------------------------------------------------
VARIABLE: ATT

GRP      N          MEAN        STD DEV      STD ERROR       MINIMUM        MAXIMUM     VARIANCES         T        DF   PROB > |T|

C        5   22.40000000     3.97492138     1.77763888   19.00000000    28.00000000     UNEQUAL       1.2852       8.0       0.2347
E        5   19.20000000     3.89871774     1.74355958   15.00000000    25.00000000     EQUAL         1.2852       8.0       0.2347

FOR HO: VARIANCES ARE EQUAL, F'=     1.04 WITH 4 AND 4 DF     PROB > F'= 0.9710
```

FIGURE 10-10
Sample of output from SAS job in Figure 10-8.

For example, a school superintendent planning the budget for the following year might use a spreadsheet to determine whether the cost of hiring more teachers might be partially offset by the reduced insurance cost resulting from smaller classes and, thus, added supervision. With a spreadsheet, the superintendent could put average class size in one cell and then use an equation provided by the insurance company to calculate rates in another cell after it is computed based on information in other cells of the spreadsheet (e.g., playground and gym equipment, history of accidents, injuries, and lawsuits in the district, presence of a nurse in the building, etc.). This would permit the superintendent to try several class-size scenarios and get results virtually immediately. This kind of application opens numerous possibilities for policy researchers and evaluators of programs in which data are collected daily affecting decisions that must be made on the basis of those data. Arithmetic and statistical formulas and equations and logical conditions (e.g., IF CLASS $\hbar$ 35 THEN RATE = 6500) may be built into the spreadsheet as needed by the user.

In addition to their potential for flexible ongoing analysis of data, many spreadsheet programs have built-in graphing or reporting capabilities. Others are designed to be compatible with database, graphics, project planning, and word processing programs. These additional capabilities make spreadsheets extremely valuable for many research tasks. However, spreadsheets have some disadvantages. They require a computer with a considerable amount of memory and speed if they are to be used with large data sets or for complex analyses. Further, an error in one of the equations or data entries may be difficult to recognize and even more difficult to find and correct. Finally, because they are so flexible, setting up an analysis on a spreadsheet requires a considerable amount of planning, skill, and effort. For these reasons, many researchers prefer to use statistical packages for data analysis.

Other Useful Computer Applications in Research

In addition to enhancing data collection and analysis, computers help researchers in a number of other ways. In Chapter 3, the value of computerized library searching and how it has made it easier and faster to locate background information on a topic was discussed. To this list of jobs done by computers, we now add database management, communications, word processing, computer-based learning and testing, and artificial intelligence.

Database Management *Database Management* is the process of storing, retrieving, and maintaining information in files and records. Sophisticated packaged programs exist for maintaining databases on all sizes of computers. However, large data sets, such as those created by the Census Bureau, require the power of very large computers. Databases can be established for many purposes (e.g., for keeping track of people—such as patients in a hospital, clients of a mutual fund company, students in a school system, or holders of credit cards—or for storing other kinds of information). The information stored in a database may be used for the purpose of describing the populations represented or to aid in decision making. The computerization of a database permits more sophistication in researching and reporting about its contents. It also saves time. For example, if a public health researcher wishes to know how many elementary school students in the local school district have been exposed to the mumps and the data are in computerized form, he can sample the health records of the whole district in minutes. However, if he must review the files by hand, the question could take weeks to answer. Further, with a computerized database, the researcher could easily determine which students live in homes with siblings who were exposed to the disease. This information would be much more difficult to locate manually.

Database research has raised a number of ethical questions regarding the individual's right to privacy and other rights guaranteed in a free society. Basically, the questions revolve around whether the people about whom the data were compiled should be given an opportunity to approve the research and, further, who should be given access to the information in the database. Most schools, institutions, and other agencies that maintain databases have policies and guidelines governing protection of the information.

Communications Communication among researchers has been greatly facilitated by networks that link computer systems. One example is BITNET, a network that connects many of the major research institutions worldwide. Using communications systems such as these, researchers can send and receive "mail" and communicate more rapidly and efficiently than they can by traditional mail or telephone. Data files and results of research can be transmitted quickly over these lines. ARPANET (Advanced Research Projects Agency NETwork) is a governmental computer network linking governmental agencies, research centers, universities, and other agencies. Other networks exist for similar purposes. Most campuses and research agencies provide methods for communicating between researchers and transferring data and information for research purposes.

Word Processing The use of word processors to prepare reports, test materials, and questionnaires is widespread. However, computers are being used as word processors in novel ways to aid in research. For example, in the area of linguistic or literary analysis of text, word processors can help put text into computerized files for analysis by other programs, can count words and phrases in long text, can measure length of text, or, in concert with other programs such as databases, can determine qualities of style or compare characteristics with other texts (Thury, 1988). Thus word processing capabilities are resulting in computers becoming involved to an unprecedented degree in research in the humanities.

Computer-Based Learning and Testing   Computers can present instructional material and administer tests to individuals (Bramble & Mason, 1985). Their ability to present tasks to individual students, time and record their responses, and evaluate their errors opens new dimensions for psychologists and educators to study learning. Instructional experiences can be tailored to individual performance on previous tasks. Further, the computer can keep records (called *audit trails*) of individual performance within an instructional sequence. These records can be studied by researchers to provide insight into learning styles, mastery, task complexity, and other issues. Further, computers can use realistic simulations of complex events, thus permitting greater realism in laboratory research. For example, a researcher interested in how problem-solving skills are used in real-life settings can simulate a small business, the controls of an airplane, debate in a congressional committee, or a chemistry laboratory experiment to study how individuals solve problems under realistic conditions.

Artificial Intelligence (AI)   Our discussion only scratches the surface of how computers can be used in research in education and the behavioral and social sciences. One of the most exciting uses of computers is in the area of artificial intelligence (AI). *Artificial intelligence* is a field dedicated to the creation of machines that will respond in a manner similar to the responses of cognitively sophisticated human beings (Yazdani, 1986). Although still in its infancy, AI shows promise of becoming a powerful research tool, permitting investigation of old, unresolved questions in new ways. For example, a researcher could test a theory of cognitive development by designing an AI program that would respond to moral arguments as a child at different ages would be expected to respond according to the theory. The responses obtained from the AI program could then be compared with the ways that real children responded to the same arguments. This could provide a more sophisticated test of the theory than a series of hypothesis tests in the traditional manner because the program becomes a more complete rendition of the theory than would otherwise be the case in a controlled laboratory study. However, the ability to do this kind of research is still rather remote. Robotic devices for teaching and providing assistance to handicapped learners in areas such as speech, hearing, and vision also are beginning to appear in research settings. As new developments in the field of technology and computing appear, they will continue to reveal new and promising areas and methods of research in education and the social sciences.

LIMITATIONS

As important as computers currently are to researchers, they have certain limitations that can affect how they are used in research. The a/d converter's effect on continuous data was already mentioned. A similar subtle change in the character of data may occur from coding. For example, it may be convenient, in a particular situation, to process age data by grouping the ages into categories (e.g., 5 to 7 years old = 1, 8 to 10 years old = 2, and so on), but this coding scheme would not permit the study of changes that can occur within categories (for example, between 5 and 6 years of age). To further illustrate, it might be important to know that a certain group of subjects came from Sweden, but this information would be lost if the subjects' origin were coded as 1 = European, 2 = African, and 3 = Other. Another problem is the insensitivity of computers. Computers do not have feelings, intuition, or other human qualities, even when they are programmed with artificial intelligence. Further, despite the speed and accuracy of their operations, their output does not always show the correct solution. More precisely, when computers contain errors in their programming or data, they make errors in output. In addition, the theory and procedures used in designing the program might not be correct or might involve wrong assumptions, thus leading to incorrect solutions. Computer professionals use the acronym GIGO (garbage-in garbage out) to refer to the problematic solutions that can result from erroneous processing of data. Researchers should keep in mind that computers, despite all their usefulness, are, after all, machines, and their infallibility is dependent upon how they are programmed and used.

SUMMARY

Computers have had profound effects on research. Practically all research involves computers at one stage or another. Devices that scan marks on an answer sheet when paired with a computer can greatly facilitate data entry for computerized analysis. Large and small computers are routinely used by researchers to collect and analyze data. Researchers can write custom software, using high-level programming languages like BASIC or Pascal, or they can use preexisting or packaged programs. Two of the more comprehensive program packages are SAS and SPSS^x. The Minitab and BMDP packages are also frequently used for statistical analysis. Spreadsheets are like huge flexible electronic data rosters and can be used for data analysis. The ability to update all calculations whenever new data are entered makes spreadsheets particularly useful in evaluation and decision-oriented research. In addition to statistical analysis, computers are used for literature searches, for monitoring and controlling experiments, in managing databases, for communication, and for word processing. Artificial intelligence (AI) is a developing field that holds much promise both as an area for research and as a research tool.

PROBLEMS FOR THOUGHT AND DISCUSSION

1 List all the research applications that you can for computers. Where possible, give examples of these applications from the research literature.
2 Discuss the following applications of computer technology in terms of feasibility and usefulness.
   a Controlling presentation of stimuli to experimental animals and recording their responses.

  b Maintaining records of transactions in a small hardware store.
  c Locating reference materials in a library.
  d Comparing means of five experimental groups, each having 12 subjects, using the analysis-of-variance technique.
  e Finding the average score for a sample of 10 students on an ability test.
  f Maintaining records of patient treatment needs in a hospital.
3 Discuss the appropriateness, including economic considerations, of using the computer for each of the following:
  a Finding the average educational level of the adult population of the state of Connecticut from census information.
  b Finding the mean and standard deviation of scores on a quiz in a college mathematics class of 11 students.
  c Randomly selecting a sample of subjects to participate in a market research study from a population of credit-card holders.
  d Randomly assigning 12 subjects to one of three treatment groups.
4 Discuss the various uses that have been found for computers in modern civilization. Discuss the implications of these for researchers.
5 Obtain instructions for using a computer that is available to you to run the programs listed in Figure 10-4. The computer must be capable of running Pascal or BASIC. Further, the instructions in the list may require certain changes for the version that is available.
6 If a computer is available with SPSS or SAS, try running the program listings in Figures 10-8 or 10-9. Be sure to use the system instructions appropriate for the computer system you are using. Also, the program instructions may require some change, depending on the version of the package that is available.

REFERENCES

Bramble, W. J., & Mason, E. J. (1985). *Computers in schools*. New York: McGraw-Hill.

Thury, E. M. (1988). Scholars working with "found objects": Humanities research projects. *Academic Computing, 2*(4), 6–9, 57–61.

Yazdani, M. (1986). *Artificial intelligence: Principles and applications*. New York: Chapman & Hall.

PACKAGED COMPUTER PROGRAMS

Most computer centers that support research activities have a number of data-analysis packages available for users. Those listed below are among the more generally available, but check with the program librarian at a particular center to identify the packages available.

1 BMDP: Biomedical Computer Programs. Berkeley: University of California. (User manual: Brown, M. B., Engleman, L., Frane, J. W., Hill, M. A., Jennrich, R. I., & Toporek, J. D. (1981). *BMDP statistical software*. Berkeley: University of California Press.)

  Provides a wide range of statistical programs, plotting, and other programs.

2 Two major mainframe software packages are:

Statistical Analysis System. Cary, NC: SAS Institute. (User manuals: *SAS user's guide: Basics* and *SAS user's guide: Statistics* (1982).)

SPSS: Statistical Package for the Social Sciences. Chicago: SPSS. (User manual: *SPSS[x] user's guide* (2nd ed.) (1986). Chicago: SPSS).

Both the SAS and the SPSS packages contain programs with a wide variety of applications, including descriptive statistics, graphing, plotting, statistic inference and hypothesis testing, correlation, regression, and multivariate analysis. They also offer reporting, data management, and other capabilities. In addition, both are available in versions that will run on large computers and microcomputers.

3 Minitab. State College, PA: Minitab. (User manual: Ryan, B. F., Joiner, B. L., & Ryan, T. A. (1985). *Minitab handbook* (2nd ed.). Boston: Duxbury.)

Minitab's statistical-analysis offerings are a bit different from the above packages. They were designed for use by students in math and statistics courses. Some of the routines in Minitab are not as powerful as the ones available in other packages, but Minitab has more exploratory data analysis programs than many of the other packages. Also, the package is easy to learn and to use.

SUPPLEMENTARY READINGS

Collyer, C. E., & Enns, J. T. (1986). *Analysis of variance: The basic designs*. Chicago: Nelson Hall. (Describes the analysis of variance with BMDP, SAS, and SPSS[x].)

Norušis, M. J. (1983). *Introductory statistics guide SPSS[x]*. Chicago: SPSS.

Norušis, M. J. (1986). *The SPSS guide to data analysis*. Chicago: SPSS.

Ryan, B. F., Joiner, B. L., & Ryan, T. A. (1985). *Minitab: handbook* (2nd ed.). Boston: Duxbury.

Spencer, D. D. (1986). *The illustrated computer dictionary* (3rd ed.). Columbus, OH: Merrill.

PART THREE

THREE

APPLYING THE TOOLS
OF RESEARCH

Now that all the elements of a research study have been presented, we turn to using them together in research activities. The first chapter in this section (Chapter 11) focuses on designing, doing, and evaluating research. In addition to a discussion of these activities, practical guidelines and checklists are provided for setting up and evaluating research studies; the ethical and legal responsibilities of researchers are also covered. Chapter 12 covers writing about research; it emphasizes proposals and reports but addresses other topics as well. Chapter 13 depicts evaluation as a relatively new and wide-open field of application of all manner of research skills and techniques in applied settings. Evaluation has a different slant on information than does other kinds of research. It emphasizes who the information is for, how it will be used, and the political and contextual analysis of it. The final chapter (Chapter 14) presents a discussion of the social and political aspects of research in education and the behavioral sciences in the United States and provides a brief look at future trends in research.

CHAPTER 11

PUTTING IT ALL TOGETHER— DESIGNING, DOING, AND EVALUATING RESEARCH

For both the practitioner and the researcher, skills in dealing with research are essential. In this chapter, we will consider how to integrate and use the various aspects of research we have studied. For the sake of simplifying the presentation, each topic has been discussed as if it existed in isolation. For example, we discussed experimental design, statistics, and measurement in separate chapters. In the present chapter, we will first see how to integrate these topics to produce a useful research study. Then we will consider the process of conducting a research study. Finally, we will review procedures for evaluation of research investigations.

SELECTING THE RIGHT STUDY

One of the most difficult aspects of doing research, particularly for the new researcher, is determining what to investigate. Part of the reason for this is that good research topics are rarely obvious and have to be ferreted out of what is already known, believed, understood, or suspected. Finding the right study to conduct should begin with one's background and awareness of a field of knowledge, the literature, or with one's own observations. Following determination of the topic comes narrowing the topic to a specific aspect, formulating the research problem, reviewing current knowledge relevant to the problem, proposing hypotheses or research expectations, and, finally, specifying the study that will be done. Each of these facets of identifying the study that will ultimately be done are discussed below.

Establishing a Background

Background for research includes all one's formal and informal training and experiences. Background provides an awareness of the topic as a potential research field and also contributes to a perspective. One's background relative to a research area can be enhanced by reviewing the research literature. The kind of extensive reviews provided in the *Encyclopedia of Educational Research* (H. E. Mitzel, 1982, New York: Free Press) and the annual volumes of *Review of Educational Research,* published by the American Educational Research Association, can be useful resources. Both contain summaries and analyses of research topics. In addition, journals that publish reviews of research in specific areas, such as *Psychological Bulletin,* published by the American Psychological Association, and *Review of Educational Research,* published by the American Educational Research Association, can be of great assistance in the development of background. Other journals and annuals that review current research and thought on specific topics can be found in most academic libraries.

Choosing a Topic

Once the researcher's background in a field has been established, interest and feasibility become primary concerns. Interest will help sustain the kind of protracted effort, persistence, thoroughness, and objectivity required to do research. Feasibility involves time, personnel, equipment, the skills of the researcher, and other potential needs. It also entails the status of available knowledge and technology in related fields. A researcher who is interested in discovering what is occurring in the cells of the nervous system when a person is learning to speak a second language, for example, will find such research very difficult to design because of deficiencies in our knowledge about the nervous system and the technology of studying the activities of nerve cells in living subjects.

The importance of the background and commitment of the researcher cannot be overemphasized. Many new researchers make the error of not addressing their own strengths and interests. Rather, they direct their research efforts towards problems they think will be perceived as difficult or prized by others. Topics currently in vogue also seem to be attractive to many new researchers. Choosing a topic to satisfy others may have the benefit of ensuring a community of researchers who are investigating similar questions and can provide mutual support. However, a research topic chosen on the basis of personal interest will elicit greater commitment than one chosen for other reasons.

Feasibility of a study may involve cooperation from others. For example, a study might necessitate gaining permission from a school board or obtaining funds from a private foundation. It might require cooperation with other researchers in order to obtain equipment or space. In the early stages of thinking about a research area, some concern should be given to feasibility in terms of one's access to needed resources and one's personal background and skills (knowledge and skills in statistics, computer programming, developmental psychology, or other areas might be required, for example). If the requisite background or resources are lacking, then the probability of a successful study is low. To illustrate, one graduate student became interested in how computers could be used to teach number concepts to preschool children. His interest emerged from his observation that young children appeared to enjoy playing certain games on a computer and that many of these games involved numerical or quantitative concepts. He developed a research proposal from his idea. However, he did not consider feasibility issues early in his planning (he had no group of children to sample and no computer programming skills; he did not have access to computers or to the required software). When time came to do the study, the student found all these unforeseen needs had to be met all at once. This proved too much of a barrier, and he eventually dropped the idea, despite his interest.

Students who are preparing to do research in their graduate programs and are looking for suitable research problems often vacillate between topics because they view certain areas as not feasible. However, when basic needs (e.g., sample of subjects, equipment, etc.) are recognized early, meeting these requirements becomes less difficult. Although some consideration of feasibility and interest is necessary in the early planning stages, the specific solutions to many problems can come later, when the planning is further along and the research has been more clearly specified.

Formulating the Problem

Formulating and stating the problem to be researched is one of the most difficult aspects of doing research. The best research problems are usually not the obvious ones. Often neophyte researchers lack the confidence, patience, or background to analyze what is known in order to identify the problem. Two criteria for a "good problem" are

1 There is a basis for the problem statement (e.g., previous research, experience, archival support, etc.).

2 The problem is researchable (it suggests operational hypotheses or research expectations).

To gain some insight into the process of clarifying a problem, consider the example of a graduate student who was interested in the suitability of various counseling approaches in different cultural settings (an example of such a study is Lin [1986]). From literature he had read concerning counseling theory and approaches and anthropological work in comparative cultures, he sensed that certain counseling methods might not be as appropriate in some settings as in others. After spending some time considering what might be a good problem in this area, he decided on the following:

How acceptable are different counseling approaches in different cultural settings?

However, in considering this question, he began to feel that the problem was too broad. There are many different approaches to counseling; some have a scientific basis, others are founded on philosophical or religious beliefs and values. Further, the meaning of *culture* is not specific enough. Culture may be defined as "the concepts, habits, skills, arts, instruments, institutions, etc., of a given people in a given period" (*Webster's New World Dictionary of the American Language,* 1957). However, by such a definition, a culture might be a racial group, a city, a country, a religion, or other entity. The notion of *acceptability* presented additional problems. The student tried to narrow his problem further.

How acceptable are counseling theories and techniques developed in the United States to professional counseling psychologists in Taiwan?

Notice that the problem has been limited to two countries with rather different cultures. Further, the concept of counseling approaches has been limited to theories and techniques developed in the United States. Because of the increased specificity, it would appear easier to design a study for the second problem than for the first.

Reviewing the Literature

The review of the literature should serve to clarify the problem and give a justification for the study that will be done. While reviewing the literature, the researcher must often consider a wider array of published and unpublished works than will actually be used in the written report. Most researchers develop their own way of compiling literature during the review. For example, some summarize what they read on index cards in a manner similar to the one described in Chapter 3. Others place the information in their own electronic database using a microcomputer. What is important is not how the information is stored but that it is systematically reviewed and analyzed in terms of implications for the study being proposed.

Because this phase of development in a study is called *reviewing the literature,* the new researcher may provide too strict an interpretation to the kinds of information sought. The guiding principle in a literature review should be the location of information relevant to the study. For this reason, information that is not necessarily "literature" per se, should be considered. For example, the information contained in unpublished reports circulated informally among researchers and unpublished documents listed in the ERIC system might be useful in documenting a research problem. In addition, preliminary studies, carefully described observations made by researchers and practitioners, and published information that suggests support for relevant relationships might be useful in developing background for the study. Finally, expert opinions and speculations, theory, and theoretical perspectives can all contribute to the basis for the study.

The amount of literature to be reviewed really depends on the problem.

Comprehensiveness is more important than amount. As far as possible, all views, theories, arguments, and research findings should be represented. For example, if a researcher is interested in the problem of how parents' level of education affects their children's academic performance and some research suggests that these two phenomena are independent of each other while other findings suggest a high correlation between them, both kinds of studies should be reviewed. Analysis of disparate information in the literature can often provide new insight and be the source of real creativity in research.

Stating Hypotheses or Research Expectations

Once the literature has been reviewed and the researcher knows the problem well, she or he is ready to make some "educated guesses" about the resolution of the problem. These guesses might take the form of hypotheses or expectations for the outcome of the research. Generally, hypotheses imply some sort of experimental or comparative study. However, some problems require descriptive or exploratory studies for which expectations for research outcomes might be more appropriate than hypotheses. For example, if a problem calls for determining the attitudes towards political conservatism in midwestern college students, the expectation for the study would be that the political attitudes of the students would be described by the study. Whether a study is based on hypotheses or research expectations, the support for the design comes from the review of the literature.

The mechanics of stating the various kinds of hypotheses (e.g., substantive hypotheses, statistical hypotheses, null hypotheses, alternative hypotheses,) has been covered elsewhere (Chapter 3). For this reason, we will concentrate in the present discussion on the origin and use of hypotheses in research. However, much of our present discussion also applies to research expectations where they are more appropriate than hypotheses.

In Chapter 3, we defined a *hypothesis* as "...a tentative declarative statement about the relationship between two or more variables." The relationship should be based on the problem, the literature that was reviewed, previous research, prior observations, preliminary studies, and other pertinent information. For example, one researcher was interested in the general conditions that lead teachers to view a consultant as an expert. Research in social status and role expectations (e.g., Miller & Morgan, 1983) suggests that in interpersonal relationships, when higher status is perceived, greater competence is expected. This line of reasoning led to the question: What determines status in teacher consultant relationships? for which the following hypothesis was proposed:

A consultant in school testing who is thought to hold a doctor's degree in psychology will be rated as more expert by teachers than one who is thought to have a master's degree in psychology or a master's degree in adult education.

The *dependent variable* (the variable that is measured or observed) in this hypothesis is a rating of perceived expertise. The independent variable is represented by three social-status conditions (two types of master's degree and a doctorate). The hypothesis suggests that the status conditions will affect the ratings of expertise. A third kind of variable, the *intervening* (or nuisance) variable, although not mentioned in the hypothesis, is nonetheless of concern to the researcher. Intervening variables threaten the internal validity of an experiment (see Chapter 4 on internal validity). Some intervening variables that might be of particular concern in testing the above hypothesis could be the gender of the consultant and the teachers doing the rating, the age difference between the teacher and the consultant, prior experiences with psychologists and testing experts, etc.

As they are represented in the hypothesis, the independent and dependent variables are not sufficiently specified. Terms like "consultant," "more expert," and "is thought to have" are not sufficiently self-explanatory. For example, is an expert consultant one who is widely recognized through publications, creative contributions to the literature, and practical experience; or is anyone with a doctoral degree in psychology perceived to be an expert? More important, how will the expert consultant be described to the subjects in the study? This description has important implications for the meaning of the results.

Once terms and variables have been defined, they may be further operationalized for the study. The researcher might specify the term "expert consultant" with the following description for the study:

Dr. Tester, author of four books and over fifty articles on psychological testing in schools, received his doctoral degree in psychology from State University with a specialization in psychometrics.

Perceived effectiveness would be operationalized with a rating scale devised by the researcher. This scale would include items pertaining to perceived competence, personal warmth and empathy, and ability to explain complex material.

Designing a Research Study

It is surprising how many critical decisions have already been made about design by the time hypotheses or research expectations are stated. For example, in the hypothesis about the effect of consultant status on the ratings of expertise given, ratings of a consultant described as having a doctoral degree will be compared to ratings of a consultant thought to have a master's degree in psychology or adult education, thus suggesting a comparison of experimental groups. Details of the procedures of the study still must be made explicit. After the hypotheses or research expectations have been determined, the specific research design should be formulated.

The Research Design We have seen that the hypotheses or research questions suggest the type of study to be done. One more illustration of this point will be made with the research question: What are the effects of restructuring organizations on internal staff relationships? This question can be addressed in many ways. One approach to this question would be to design a descriptive longitudinal study in which school personnel are observed and interviewed over a period of time, perhaps two years immediately before and after a merger of two districts. On the other hand, the study could be designed as an experiment to test the hypothesis that female employees adapt more readily to new administrative structures than do males. We discussed threats to internal and external validity in Chapters 4 and 5 and pointed out that while much of that discussion was geared towards the testing of hypotheses in experiments and quasi-experiments, some of the threats might also apply to interpretations of descriptive results. Validity is a major concern of the research designer.

Designing a research study should not be viewed as a simple series of steps. The researcher begins with a tentative design; then he or she analyzes the design's validity, makes any changes that seem to be needed, and checks the validity again in a repetitive process until an acceptable design is attained. Sometimes the changes that improve the validity of the design also change the study so that the original hypotheses are no longer addressed by the research. In such a situation, the researcher must decide to go with the new version of the hypotheses or change the study again.

A Study as a System of Interrelated Elements   Because of the number of issues that must be considered in designing a valid research study, many scientific investigators prefer to think of the research process as a system composed of a series of interdependent elements or functions. The functions of this system can be diagrammed to display the relationships among them. Figure 11-1 shows the elements of a research design. This figure might be viewed as a generic model for the design of a research study.

The model in Figure 11-1 is admittedly a simplification of what might occur in reality. However, going through this diagram in sequential fashion ensures systematic consideration of the various facets of a research project. Furthermore, the arrows and diamond shapes show how considerations that are revealed later in the design process might cause reconsideration of what came earlier.

Figure 11-2 shows how a researcher used the diagram in Figure 11-1 to develop an investigation of the effects of the gender of an examiner on the students' test performance. The action taken in the first six steps is summarized next to the appropriate functions of the model. Notice that the first six steps culminated in the research proposal.

Development of the Research Proposal

A research proposal is a written exposition of the reasoning that goes into the design and development of a study; it explains the basis for the research and the procedures that will be followed. Proposals are often written to permit other researchers to evaluate the research before it is done. For example, a

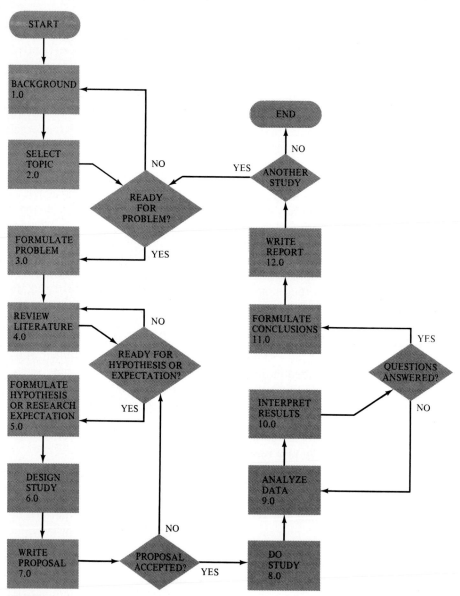

FIGURE 11-1
The system of elements of a research study.

graduate student may present a proposal to the faculty committee that will supervise his or her research or a research scientist may send a proposal to the review committee of a funding agency. In addition, a proposal can serve as a guideline for monitoring an ongoing study to insure that it is conducted as it was designed.

SYSTEM

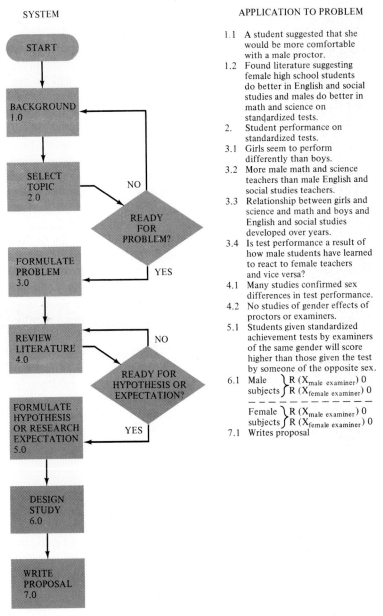

APPLICATION TO PROBLEM

1.1 A student suggested that she would be more comfortable with a male proctor.
1.2 Found literature suggesting female high school students do better in English and social studies and males do better in math and science on standardized tests.
2. Student performance on standardized tests.
3.1 Girls seem to perform differently than boys.
3.2 More male math and science teachers than male English and social studies teachers.
3.3 Relationship between girls and science and math and boys and English and social studies developed over years.
3.4 Is test performance a result of how male students have learned to react to female teachers and vice versa?
4.1 Many studies confirmed sex differences in test performance.
4.2 No studies of gender effects of proctors or examiners.
5.1 Students given standardized achievement tests by examiners of the same gender will score higher than those given the test by someone of the opposite sex.
6.1 $\text{Male subjects} \begin{cases} R\ (X_{\text{male examiner}})\ 0 \\ R\ (X_{\text{female examiner}})\ 0 \end{cases}$

$\text{Female subjects} \begin{cases} R\ (X_{\text{male examiner}})\ 0 \\ R\ (X_{\text{female examiner}})\ 0 \end{cases}$
7.1 Writes proposal

FIGURE 11-2
Application of system in Figure 11-1 to a study of effects of examiner's gender on students' test performance.

A written proposal is organized to reflect the systematic thinking that went into the development of the research (see Figures 11-1 and 11-2). Usually, a proposal will have two major sections. The first will contain a description of the problem area, an identification of the problem, and a review of the literature. Based on this review, hypotheses or research expectations will be proposed. The second section will contain a description of the methodology that will be used to achieve the goals established for the research. There will typically be discussions of the subjects from which the sample will be drawn; the materials, equipment, and techniques that will be used; and the procedures that will be followed to collect and analyze the data. In addition, time schedules, plans for funding, and procedures for gaining approval for subjects' participation (e.g., parental consent forms) might also appear in the second section.

The amount of detail put into a proposal depends upon the audience for which it is intended. Faculty committees that approve master's theses or doctoral dissertations require considerable detail. Federal research funding agencies also require considerable specification. However, for certain audiences and purposes, shorter and less detailed proposals are appropriate. For example, a school board might require a proposal from a researcher who plans to do research in the district. However, the school board is usually neither interested in nor prepared to analyze the technical adequacy of the proposal. Its interest in the proposal is limited to its wish to be certain that the research will not cause harm to children, require an inordinate amount of time that would otherwise be spent learning in the classroom, involve additional duties for teachers in violation of any contract agreements, and so on. In addition, they will want assurance that the research is worthwhile. Thus, for some audiences, certain aspects of a proposal will be emphasized more than others. Chapter 12 discusses, in greater detail, the actual writing of proposals.

The Researcher in the Proposal Process

From the discussion thus far, it should be fairly obvious that the researcher is making decisions all the time that a research proposal is being formulated. Many of these decisions depend on the researcher's own values and perspectives rather than on hard-and-fast rules about designing research.

For example, a doctoral student was interested in the change in children's understanding of number concepts as development occurs from first grade through twelfth grade in school. She knew from the literature (e.g., Gelman & Gallistel, 1978) that understanding of the concept of *number* changes from very simple relationships of numeration (e.g., the number "1" paired with one thing, "2" with two things, etc.) to more complex concepts concerning sequence, quantity, and inclusive relationships (e.g., "3" is included in "5"). The researcher also found that the literature suggested differences between boys and girls in terms of when these concepts develop. However, the study was already becoming very large. It included a total of 18 different treatment combinations—independent variables included grades (six odd-numbered grade levels from first to eleventh), and task (three kinds: sequential, quantitative, and inclusive). For this reason, the researcher decided not to include the gender factor in the study. To do so would have required doubling the number of subjects (so that there would be enough male and female subjects at each grade level). This would have increased the time and costs required to do the study. Further, it would have added complications to the analysis. Thus the decision to eliminate the gender variable was made for practical, not scientific, reasons. However, the researcher did plan to record subjects' gender in the data file in order to analyze it separately.

Another aspect of researcher influence on the design of a study concerns how the researcher reasons and makes decisions from the available information. Much of the reasoning used in designing a study is inferential rather than deductive. The differences between these two kinds of reasoning were discussed in Chapter 1. A researcher tries to fill gaps in knowledge by making inferences.

The effects of a researcher's inferences on research can be profound. For example, one investigator noticed that students who are very anxious before taking an examination do less well then do students who do not experience such anxiety. He knows about research results suggesting that college students who feel they have not studied sufficiently before a major examination are more anxious about the exam than are those who feel their preparation was adequate. He therefore infers a relationship between the number of hours a student spends studying for an examination and anxiety, concludes that poor preparation causes test anxiety, and proposes research to cure test anxiety by helping a student learn to study for a test. However, the reasons for test anxiety are known to be more complex. In fact, some students are overanxious about their performance, prepare thoroughly for examinations, and then perform poorly because they become upset when they feel challenged. Thus a treatment condition based on this researcher's inference would be inappropriate. Researchers cannot avoid being influenced by their values, background, and perspectives as they make inferences in the design of their research. However, they should be aware of these influences and how they can affect the design process.

DOING THE STUDY

Once a proposal has been accepted and decisions about how to implement the design have been made, all the planning that went into the proposal is put into practice by doing the research. The purpose of the investigation is to find truth. Subtle biases or extraneous influences should be avoided when possible.

Many researchers find it useful to design a checklist to follow during the data-collection period to insure that the research plan is followed. Such a checklist is shown in Figure 11-3. Using a checklist will help the researcher avoid undue influence from the subjects or conditions of the research. For example, a researcher who is interested in studying the effectiveness of a method

CHECKLIST FOR CONDUCTING RESEARCH STUDIES

Title of study: _____

Purpose: _____

Hypostheses or research questions: _____
_____
_____

Consideration	Time period	Person responsible	NOTES

1. Selection of the sample
   a. Identify population to sample
   b. Develop sampling strategy
   c. Select sample
   d. Obtain consent from subjects or their representatives

2. Contexts and environments
   a. Identify setting for the study
   b. Design script or written scenario for experimenter to follow
   c. Determine unique needs or requirements for the setting (one-way mirror, electrical outlets, etc.)
   d. Visit site
   e. Obtain permission for use of facility, if necessary

3. Methods and materials
   a. Identify measurement instruments and validity and reliability of them (might involve pilot study)
   b. Identify equipment that will be used (e.g., microcomputers, video equipment, text materials)
   c. Arrange for equipment to be available when needed
   d. Train experimenters and aides in procedures and experimental conditions
   e. Do pilot trial of procedures
   f. Fine-tune procedures based on results of trial
   g. Make sufficient copies of forms
   h. Arrange for data collection (hire aides, obtain equipment, set schedules, etc.)
   i. Arrange for subjects to be brought to, or to be in site of, study at appointed time
   j. Arrange for computerized analysis of data, if necessary (set up account, data base, obtain necessary computer programs)
   k. Identify statistical or other consultants, if necessary

4. Collection of data
   a. Ensure that those who will collect data are present
   b. Observe conditions for duration of study to ensure procedures are followed as outlined
   c. Data coding
   d. Data storage
   e. Data entry
   f. Adjustment in data collection required by field setting

5. Data analysis
   a. Statistical analysis
   b. Computer programs or packages
   c. Other forms of analysis
   d. Addressing hypotheses

6. Logistical concerns
   a. Funding
   b. Personnel
   c. Schedules
   d. Space
   e. Transportation
   f. Training
   g. Printing and copying
   h. Proposal writing
   i. Reporting
   j. Equipment and supplies

FIGURE 11-3
Checklist for conducting research.

of mentoring vocational education students on the job might be influenced by the difficulty of traveling between sites and thus seek shortcuts to collect the data. One such shortcut might be to have local supervisors make the observations. However, this would violate the proposed procedures and would introduce a source of variation that the research was not designed to control, that due to different (and untrained) observers. Further, site supervisors might have more of a vested interest in reporting a good situation than would an impartial observer.

Checklists help to keep research from wandering. It should be no surprise that researchers possess many qualities occurring naturally in humans, qualities like curiosity, boredom, and anxiety. These qualities can sometimes lead to unintentional changes during the course of a study. For example, an investigation designed to explore group problem solving on school boards became a study in salary disputes when the researcher became more interested in the issue being considered than in the processes involved in the discussion. Many good studies originate in the course of other studies, but because new variables are being studied and different data will be collected, a new proposal and design should be prepared. The purposes of neither the original study nor the new one will be served by haphazard changes made during the course of a research investigation.

Finally, a checklist helps the researcher conduct the study in a systematic manner. There is a greater chance that all steps and procedures will be followed in the proper sequence when they are listed clearly. A study that is managed with the assistance of a well-designed checklist will be less likely to be vulnerable to unforeseen validity problems later. The researcher should adapt the checklist shown in Figure 11-3 to suit the particular study that is planned. It should be based on the description of the methods and procedures in the proposal. Each major element of the checklist is discussed below.

Selection of Sample

Generally, it is crucially important that the sample and the population from which the sample came be clearly identified. The sample must be designed to be representative of the population if the results are to be generalized beyond the group studied. For example, if a study is done with a randomly selected group of undergraduates on a university campus, the sample would be considered representative of the population of undergraduates on that campus. However, if only full-time students living in the dormitory were included in the sample, then the group studied could not be considered representative of the whole campus because of the number of students who live off campus or who attend the university only part time.

The researcher should identify not only the population to be sampled but the strategy for sampling. For example, will a simple random-sampling strategy or a cluster-sampling method be used? In addition, the researcher has ethical obligations to the subjects that require attention at the time the sample is asked to participate in the study. The ethical concerns of the researcher are discussed in the next section. The time and place the sample was taken should be identified as specifically as possible because people, attitudes, customs, language, and values can change over time and these changes can influence research outcomes. Further, descriptive information about the sample can help specify its composition. This information is normally collected at the end of the study by way of a demographic questionnaire. A sample demographic questionnaire from a study of political attitudes of school board members is shown in Figure 11-4.

Contexts and Environments

The researcher should plan the environment in which the study will take place. For example, if the study will involve group observation and video-recording

FIGURE 11-4
Example of a demographic questionnaire to provide information about sample of subjects.

BACKGROUND QUESTIONNAIRE

You are requested to answer the following questions to assist in interpretation of the data. You will not be identified by your response. All analyses will be based on grouped data.

1. Please check the box below that represents your sex:

   ☐ Male   ☐ Female

2. In the space below, please write your age (in years):

   _____

3. Place a check in the box that best represents the amount of your formal education:

   ☐ less than eighth grade
   ☐ between eighth and twelfth grade, but not a high school graduate
   ☐ graduated from high school
   ☐ some college, but not a four-year degree
   ☐ graduated from a four-year college program
   ☐ some postgraduate studies but no graduate or professional degree
   ☐ completed graduate or professional studies

4. Check the box below that best represents your employment status:

   ☐ Employed full-time   ☐ Employed part-time
   ☐ Unemployed   ☐ Full-time student
                      ☐ Other (explain)_____

5. Check the box below that reflects your current political registration status:

   ☐ Registered Democrat   ☐ Registered Republican
   ☐ Registered, but unaffiliated ☐ Not registered
                      ☐ Other (explain):_____

THANK YOU!

equipment will be part of the setting, the researcher should recognize the effects of the presence of this equipment and the process of obtaining permission to tape. If necessary, plans should be made to minimize these effects. Further, the researcher should be able to specify or control the conditions of the environment sufficiently to insure the validity of the study.

Methods and Materials

All methods and materials should conform to the proposal. Those assigned responsibility for collecting the data should be trained. Tests, measures, and observation instruments should be used as proposed. Any deviation should be fully explained and taken into account in the interpretation of the data.

Collection of the Data

The data should be collected according to the procedures detailed in the proposal. If the method section was done carefully, there should be few major problems at this stage. However, unforeseen circumstances do arise, and the researcher must be prepared to deal with them. For example, equipment may not work properly, trained assistants may become unavailable because of personal problems, people may not arrive on time, and so on. Most experienced researchers, aware of Murphy's law that "If anything can go wrong, it will," build back-up procedures into their studies to deal with the unexpected. Further, if an experiment is to be conducted over a period of time, as with a field experiment to test a curriculum innovation, daily logs should be kept. In these logs, researchers should note changes or irregularities in the experimental conditions as they occur. These logs can be useful when seeking explanations or interpreting unexpected or unusual results later.

Data Analysis

The data analysis should be planned during the proposal stage. Once the data are collected, the analysis may require modification because of unexpected events that occurred during the data collection. However, regardless of any changes in the planned analysis, the data should be analyzed in the manner that best answers the questions and addresses the hypotheses of the study.

Logistics

Logistics involves the time, personnel, and other resources necessary to accomplish the study. Logistical concerns should be thoroughly addressed in the proposal. Poor use of resources can result in a marred or even an incomplete study.

Using a checklist like the one in Figure 11-3 will help insure that the study proposed is the one that is done. In addition, knowing what happened at each stage of the study will help in interpretation and generalization of the findings. Several suggestions for keeping the unexpected from having too great an influence on the results are listed below. Most of these suggestions come from experience and fall into the category of common sense.

1 Do not try to do too much in one study. Before beginning the proposal, look at what past researchers in the field have covered in a single investigation. Try to scale your efforts realistically in view of the available time and resources.

2 Avoid test-retest experiments unless they are absolutely necessary to test your hypotheses. Very often, researchers plan to use a pretest only to determine whether randomization worked; that is, to see whether the treatment groups are equivalent on the dependent variable. But randomization should work most of the time, and the posttest-only control-group design is preferred in such situations because (a) data collected under this design are easier to analyze and more easily interpreted, (b) subjects are more likely to participate in the whole experiment if they are only required to take one test, and (c) this design tends to have greater external validity.

3 If the pretest-posttest approach must be used, the longer the time between tests, the greater number of influences there are in addition to treatment effects. Moreover, the longer the time between pretesting and posttesting, the fewer original subjects will be available for posttesting. This is a common problem in evaluation of educational interventions in schools. For example, one researcher attempted to evaluate novel special-education programs in an urban setting. She began by pretesting about 60 retarded children in different settings at the start of the school year. By the end of the year, nearly half the children had moved from the district or had been placed in residential settings. Another large group of children was still available but had been placed in several different settings during the semester by teachers who were interested in seeing each child receive the optimum experience. Only nine of the original children remained in the original setting throughout the academic year. Thus what began as a fairly substantial project to evaluate these special classes ended in disaster.

4 Avoid using complex, esoteric, or novel equipment or media if it is not needed. It may make the research more exciting to use special equipment, but these devices often break down or do not work as well as desired. A good example of this kind of problem was observed when a student used complex equipment in a research project. The student planned to present stimulus material over closed-circuit television to several classrooms simultaneously. The material included pairs of objects that had similar characteristics, such as size and color; and the experimental task required subjects to group them according to these characteristics. The student arranged to have over 100 people sitting in four classrooms to participate in the study. Unfortunately, the closed-circuit TV system he was planning to use was not working on that day. The experiment could have been conducted by having aides present the materials live to smaller groups of subjects, by using one small videotape recorder in each room, or in some other way. But because of the technical problems, the experiment was not completed as planned, and a large number of people were inconvenienced.

5 Avoid making unusual or unpleasant demands of subjects. Try to design experiments that minimize boredom. Subjects who lose interest or feel that they have been "used" or "manipulated" inappropriately may refuse to co-operate, which can have a major effect upon the study and the researcher's ability to complete it.

6 When it is appropriate and possible, use objective measures that can be machine-scored. This will reduce scorer error and scorer bias and ease data preparation for computerized statistical analysis.

7 When raters must be trained, as in situations where behavior rating scales are used, train a couple of extra raters in case they are needed. Also, if assistants are used to help collect the data, have extras who may be called upon in the event that they are needed.

8 Avoid measurement and statistical-analysis techniques you do not understand. Many errors made in research arise from the use of techniques not well understood by the researcher.

This list does not include all possible problem areas, but it does touch upon many of the difficulties that arise during the data-collection stage of investigations in education and the behavioral sciences. The researcher must take great pains in attending to details to minimize the effects of these problems when they do occur and, when possible, prevent them from occurring.

ETHICAL AND LEGAL CONCERNS IN RESEARCH WITH HUMAN SUBJECTS

A class of students is told that an experiment will run during the semester and that they are expected to participate. What rights does (or should) a student have in this situation? To whom is the researcher responsible? Who will be told about the results? Does the researcher have any special obligations to the subjects? Do subjects have any rights in a research study? They do, but this was not always recognized. Early researchers in education and the behavioral sciences did not have their responsibilities concerning the welfare or rights of their subjects clearly delineated. This was true in psychology, for example, as recently as 1967, when the *Casebook of Ethical Standards for Psychologists* (American Psychological Association, 1967) was published. Principle 16 of these standards, the only one dealing with ethics in research, stated simply that "The psychologist assumes obligations for the welfare of his research subjects, both animal and human." There was little recognition at that time that what one research psychologist might consider to be looking out for the welfare of his subjects, another might not.

Researchers themselves have been considering the problem of ethics for some time. There was some fear among researchers in medical, psychological, sociological, educational, and other fields with human subjects that if laws or regulations were developed concerning ethical responsibilities, some research might be prevented. For example, if there were a law which stated that only volunteer subjects could be used in research projects, then results could only be generalized to volunteers. Operating that way, we would never learn very much about the population at large. Others pointed out that by avoiding the issue, the behavioral research professions were actually forcing society to protect people's rights by imposing restrictive legislation (Schwitzgebel, 1967; Thomson, Chodosh, Fried, Goodman, Wax, & Wilson, 1981; Walter, 1969).

Agencies that fund research began to make recommendations about the ethics of research in the 1960s. For example, in 1967, the Office of the Surgeon General of the United States issued guidelines for projects funded by the Public Health Service. These provisions emphasized (1) confidentiality of information about subjects, (2) the need to obtain "informed consent" from subjects who were told the purpose of the study, the dangers involved, and the tasks inherent in participation, and (3) the researcher's responsibility for subjects' health and physical welfare (Surgeon General, 1967). These directives placed responsibility for monitoring government-funded research upon the sponsoring institution and the federal government.

As the public became more sophisticated about the need to protect subjects in new fields of research such as behavior modification, psychosurgery, and psychopharmacology, certain trends began to emerge. Among these were positions taken by agencies such as the National Institute of Mental Health and other federal research agencies that fund research requiring ethical review of funded projects. Currently, all agencies under the Department of Health and Human Services and the Department of Education require that research organizations (e.g., universities, research laboratories, etc.) have an Institutional Review Board (IRB). The purpose of the IRB is to review research proposals to guarantee protection of the rights and welfare of human and animal subjects in research. These reviews must be completed for all biomedical and behavioral research proposals submitted for funding. Many research institutions require that all studies, whether funded or unfunded, be reviewed by the IRB. Moreover, professional organizations such as the American Psychological Association now offer more detailed guidance to researchers ("Ethical Principles," 1982).

Obviously, some research poses a greater threat to subjects than does other research. Subjects in an experimental surgery procedure are exposed to greater risk than are those in a study of toothpaste preferences. IRB review procedures at many institutions recognize these differences and put research projects into categories according to the kind of risks they present. Generally, the greater the risk, the greater the demands of the IRB and the responsibility placed on the researcher. However, the general principles for protection of human subjects are the same for all types of research. Some of the more generally recognized principles which appear in most of the guidelines provided to date are summarized in the following sections.

The Research Should Have Value

Most research is clearly more valuable to some people than to others. For example, research in music appreciation is typically more highly prized by the musicologist than by the dietitian. This principle does not refer to value in that sense. Rather, the research should be considered in terms of its usefulness in contributing to the advancement of human knowledge. This principle is fundamental to all the rest. If the research has no purpose, it should not be done. Can you think of an example of research having no value or purpose whatsoever?

The Researcher Is Responsible for His or Her Subjects

This principle is considered valid with respect to all types of research using human subjects. Even research as innocuous-seeming as a market survey for coffee-brand preferences requires that subjects' rights not be violated. If a subject prefers not to participate or prefers that it not become general knowledge that he uses a particular brand of coffee, this preference should be respected by the researcher. Furthermore, the researcher is not to be considered omniscient in determining ethical responsibilities. Advice and consultation should be sought from peers, Institutional Review Board, and supervisors. Indeed, if the research is to be funded by a government agency, such consultation may be required.

The Investigator Is Responsible for His or Her Own Actions and Those of His or Her Aides

The use of graduate assistants or research assistants does not free the investigator of responsibility for the protection of the rights and welfare of the subjects. Research in school settings provides some interesting illustrations of this principle. Consider, for example, a graduate student representing a university faculty member who collected data concerning the prediction of reading achievement in two kindergarten classes. When she had all her data, she made a chart showing each child's IQ and predicted reading score and posted a copy of it on the bulletin board in each classroom. Several parents complained that this was a violation of the children's privacy and was instrumental in affecting the teacher's expectancies for their children. The activity of the aide is the researchers' responsibility.

Subjects Must Provide Informed Consent

Subjects should be willing to take part in the study after being informed of all aspects of the research that might influence their decision. Subjects should have all the information about the study that they need to make a decision about participating. They should not be misled.

Of course, certain types of investigations with human subjects would be impossible to conduct when subjects are entirely aware of everything about the experiment. For example, in a study of the effects of certain drugs upon behavior, it would be difficult to tell whether any observed changes in the behavior of subjects were the result of drug effects or subjects' knowledge that their behavior was supposed to change as a result of the drug. We see the same problem in studying the teacher-pupil relationship. If teachers are told that the purpose of an investigation is to see if the expectations they have for a child in their class influence the way they behave towards that child, it would be impossible to know whether any effects noted were the results of expectations or of the fact that teachers knew about the nature of the study.

Another problem is that when subjects decide to leave the sample group after being informed about the purpose of the study, the research may be conducted on a sample that is no longer representative. Consider, for example, an attractive young sociology student who performs an interview survey on the sex habits of college students. After being informed of the purpose and nature of the study, it is possible that many of the college students sampled would refuse to give that kind of information to a peer, and the few who respond to the survey would represent a very special group of people.

When, for various reasons, it is not possible to do meaningful research and get informed consent from the subjects at the same time, the investigator has the responsibility to provide the subjects with as much information as can be given without ruining the experiment. This should be sufficient for the subjects to decide whether to participate. When this procedure is followed, the weight of the researcher's responsibility to protect the subjects' welfare and rights during the conduct of the experiment and afterward is increased. After the data are all in, subjects should be given the information that was withheld as soon as possible.

Obtaining informed consent from children who participate in studies as subjects presents special problems. Specifically, even if one could be sure of the children's ability to determine for themselves whether or not to participate, the legality of their decision is questionable.

The general practice in working with children is to send a letter to the parents. The letter should state that the children have an opportunity to participate in a research project in school. It should also include a description of the purpose of the research, tell what the children will do, and assure the parents that the results will be kept confidential and the child's school program will not be affected in any way by participation in the research. Further, the parents should be told that they can elect, without penalty, not to have their children participate in the study. The letter should give the names, addresses, and phone numbers of the principal investigator and the person to contact if more information is desired. Many letters also include a form to return if the parents do not wish their child to participate. Lack of a response would be considered implied informed consent. Again, it would seem the researcher must assume additional responsibility for protection of subjects in such cases. Institutional Review Boards often have recommended procedures and form letters for obtaining parental consent for use when children are involved in research. It is probably a good idea to ask the IRB to review a proposal when children are subjects in the study even when funding is not a prospect.

The Experimenter Protects Subjects from Harm, Danger, or Discomfort

The researcher assumes this responsibility even though he or she has obtained informed consent and the subject is aware of the risks. Thus a curriculum specialist who is devising educational technology to enhance student comprehension is responsible in the field testing of the equipment for ensuring that there is no shock hazard with exposed wires. Under this principle, unnecessarily tedious or boring tasks should be avoided. Furthermore, lasting psychological effects of treatments should be avoided. For example, if part of the experimental treatment involved telling the subject something that could adversely affect his or her self-concept, the effects of this information should be removed after the completion of the study.

Anonymity and Confidentiality

Subjects have the right to insist that their anonymity as participants in the research will be observed. They should be assured that they will not be identified by their performance or the nature of their participation. This is usually accomplished by using numbers to identify subjects and by analyzing the data on a group rather than an individual basis.

Often, researchers collect data which subjects prefer not to become generally known. The researcher has the responsibility of ensuring that information about the subjects and their responses remains confidential and that it is used for no purpose other than the experiment for which it was intended. This would mean, for example, that a researcher who had conducted an experiment in a third-grade class designed to identify the better mathematics students could not discuss the performance of individual students with the teacher. To do so would be a violation of the confidentiality of the subjects. Or a researcher who collected personality data to correlate with learning styles could not discuss the personality scores with the school principal for the purpose of recommending certain students for psychological counseling, even though their scores suggested a need for counseling. To do this, the researcher would first have to secure release from his or her obligations for confidentiality from the subjects.

Subjects Must Not Be Coerced

Subjects must not be coerced to participate in the research. This principle had been violated consistently before ethical codes for researchers were formalized. For example, coercion would be forcing prisoners to participate in behavior-modification research as a precondition of their parole. This obviously represents the use of coercion. Another example was represented by a psychology instructor who required that any student receiving an A in his courses must have been a subject in at least two psychology research projects during the semester.

Responsibility after the Investigation Is Completed

After the completion of the experimental procedures, the investigator has additional responsibilities towards the subjects. If any incorrect information was given as part of the experimental treatment, subjects should be told the truth as soon as possible after the data are collected. Furthermore, if the subjects' state of being was changed at all during the course of the study, these effects should be removed. For example, if, in a study of the effect of anxiety on test performance, subjects in the high-anxiety group were told that failing the test would result in suspension of their driver's licenses, the subjects would have to be told after the data were collected that their performance really had nothing to do with their driving privileges. Furthermore, the experimenter should ensure that any anxiety caused by the experiment is allayed.

In summary, the final responsibility for the welfare of subjects in behavioral research with human participants lies with the researcher. The rights of the subjects as well as their health and comfort should be considered by researchers as they design their studies. Moreover, these concerns apply to nonexperimental research, such as surveys, as well as to experimental investigations.

EVALUATION OF RESEARCH

Determining what is good research is essential for both researchers and users or consumers of research. Researchers must be able to judge the quality of their own work and that of others in order to form conceptualizations of the fields they are studying. In evaluating research, all aspects of research that we have been considering are brought to bear.

The concept of "good research" is a difficult one. High technical quality in a study may not guarantee its acceptability to the research community. A well-designed and well-executed study may not address the proper question. For example, an administrator of a school district who wants to know what kinds of incentives would best enhance a teacher's sense of success would probably find a poorly conceived study of teachers in a school district more useful than a technically sound study in experimental psychology dealing with enhancement of chimpanzee problem-solving performance.

In addition, what might be a good and accepted method in one discipline would seem questionable, at best, in another. Such might be the case, for example, with a study done as part of the evaluation of a training project. Even though the study involved a fairly tight experimental procedure with randomly assigned subjects, the problem being addressed is based on a practical need for information and is not designed to become part of the body of experimental literature. A theory-oriented researcher might be very skeptical about the quality of this research, despite a lack of technical criticism of the study. Thus in seeking to judge the quality of any research, one cannot ignore the values and perspectives of the person doing the evaluating. However, the discussion here will emphasize the technical, rather than the personal, aspects of research, while recognizing that personal perspectives and values can be an important element in the evaluation of any research study.

Two fundamental approaches to determining what good research is are stressed here. The first concerns the validity of the procedures used in the conduct of the study itself: the research questions, the methodology used to address those questions, the research design, the data collected, and the analysis of the data. The second approach concerns the meaning, interpretation, and conclusions drawn from the analysis. The two approaches have been integrated into the research evaluation checklist shown in Figure 11-5.

Figure 11-5 rates the handling of each of the major aspects of a research investigation on the following scale:

5 = very satisfactory
4 = satisfactory
3 = weak
2 = no support—inadequate
1 = not considered in the study—inadequate
0 = not applicable

The ratings for all the items may be totaled. Studies with higher scores will tend to be better research. Another way to view the evaluation would be to use a profile based on the ratings. The ratings within a category may be summed and averaged for the number of items used (excluding those not applicable). A sample profile is shown in Figure 11-6. In this figure, it can be seen immediately that even though the total score is relatively high for this study (it averages about 3.6 for the 29 items rated), low scores in the construct validity area would render the validity of the conclusions suspect. Such a rating would probably reflect problematical measurement procedures.

In evaluating research, we sometimes tend to look more favorably on research that agrees with our own point of view. This tendency can affect our objectivity. A robust skepticism in viewing and evaluating research is encouraged, even when the research was done by the reviewer or a close colleague with a similar perspective. In this discussion, our focus has been on the design and execution of the research. Another aspect of evaluating research—the way it is communicated through the research report—is covered in the chapter on writing about research (Chapter 12).

SUMMARY

A research investigation begins with a question or problem that emerges or is developed from the researcher's knowledge, background, and experience. Hypotheses are proposed as educated guesses to answer the problem or question. Previous research findings, theory, prior observations, and existing literature on the topic can all contribute to the formulation of the hypotheses. In descriptive studies in which experimental hypotheses are not appropriate, research expectations may be developed. Many of the major decisions about the re-

CHECKLIST FOR EVALUATION OF RESEARCH STUDIES

Factor	Answer (yes/no)	Explanation and notes	Rating 1-5

Background for the study

1. Is purpose clear?
2. Are research questions and/or hypotheses supported by literature, theory, or observations?
3. Are research questions or hypotheses implicitly or explicitly stated?
4. Are research questions or hypotheses operational?
5. Does the logic of the approach seem sound?

Validity of research design
(Review Figure 4.11)
A. If the study is experimental or quasi–experimental, diagram the design (if not, go to B):

6. Does the design provide for equivalence of comparison conditions before the treatments are applied?
7. Can it be verified that treatment conditions remain constant for the duration of the study?
8. Can the results of the study be plausibly explained as effects of the treatments? (i.e., What are the threats to internal validity?)
9. Can alternative explanations be provided that are also plausible?

B. Determine whether or not the study is experimental:

10. Were the conditions under which the study was done identified clearly?
11. Is the design appropriate for the purposes hypotheses or research questions addressed by the study?
12. Can the study be replicated by another researcher?
13. Was the population represented an appropriate one for the purpose of this study?
14. Was the sample determined appropriately?
15. Can the results be generalized to the intended population?
16. Are the subjects appropriate for the intended purposes of the study?
17. Were the measures appropriate for the population of subjects studied?

Validity of the operationalization of constructs

18. Were independent and dependent variables clearly defined?
19. Were independent and dependent variables representative of underlying constructs?
20. Were the measures valid and reliable for the purposes for which they were used in the research?
21. Were intervening variables measured or observed effectively as necessary?
22. Did the operationalization of the variables permit an objective study?

Validity of the analysis of data

23. Are statistical analyses appropriate to answer the questions or test the hypotheses?
24. Are statistical procedures appropriate for the data?
25. Do analyses satisfy the stated purposes of the study?
26. Were statistical tests and decision rules established?
27. Was the sample large enough to overcome random or irrelevant influences?
28. Do the conclusions and interpretations follow from the data and the analysis?
29. Were the appropriate units of analysis used?

FIGURE 11-5
Checklist for evaluation research studies.

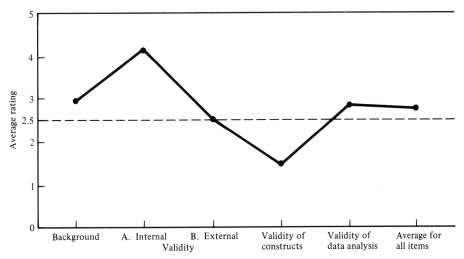

FIGURE 11-6
Profile of average ratings for each category.

search design have been made by the time the hypotheses or research expectations are expressed. Sometimes it helps research designers to think of a study as a system in which several components act together to produce a valid study. Proposals are written to make review of the thinking behind the design of a study available to others for review and criticism.

In doing a study, the researcher should adhere to the design and methods proposed. A checklist can help the researcher keep a study on track and manage the activities and tasks required to complete it. Researchers have an ethical obligation to protect their subjects' rights, welfare, and privacy. Subjects must give their informed consent to participate in a study and must not be coerced. Parents of children should be contacted in writing to obtain informed consent. Confidentiality of data must be provided as well. Most funding agencies, research institutions, and universities have Institutional Review Boards (IRBs) and peer-review procedures to ensure that subjects' rights are not violated in research investigations.

Research is evaluated on the basis of the methodology used, the value of the findings, and personal perspectives. A technically competent study is not necessarily an important one for a specific need. Both consumers of research and professional researchers should be able to evaluate research in their field. Consumers of research must be able to recognize good research in order to aid their understanding and decision making. Researchers should be able to select research that can help provide a sound basis for their own work.

PROBLEMS FOR THOUGHT AND DISCUSSION

1 Select a topic you would like to research. Find a study in the research literature dealing with that topic. Then use that study as the basis for your own study. Use the steps outlined in Figure 11-1 to design your research.

2 For the study that you designed for the problem above, make a checklist for completing the research similar to the one in Figure 11-3.

3 Design a demographic form for collecting data that will help define the sample and provide potential variables for secondary analysis of the data. What variables should be included in the demographic form? Why?

4 The following two studies are considered by many to be classic research in education and psychology. Consider each one in terms of the responsibilities of the researchers to their subjects.

Example A

Rosenthal, R., & Jacobson, L. (1968). *Pygmalion in the classroom.* New York: Holt.

At the beginning of the school year, students in a school were administered group IQ tests. The tests were actually *Flanagan's Test of General Ability* (TOGA), but teachers were told that the test was the "Harvard Test of Inflected Acquisition," which was designed to locate the children who would "bloom" academically during the school year. After the test was scored, a random 20 percent of the students in each grade were reported to their teachers as "potential bloomers." At the end of the year, the children were all retested with the TOGA. Since the children in the lower grades who were randomly identified as *bloomers* had higher IQ gains than their peers on the second testing, the researchers concluded that teacher expectancy was operating as a self-fulfilling prophecy.

a If you were the parent of a child who took part in this experiment, might you have any concerns about your child's participation? What might they be?

b As a teacher in this school, might you have any misgivings about taking part in this research?

c As a researcher, are there any concerns about the rights of the subjects or the responsibilities of the researcher you might raise?

Example B

Milgram, S. (1963). Behavioral study of obedience. *Journal of Abnormal and Social Psychology, 67,* 371–378.

In discussions of ethical and legal problems in research using human subjects, the Milgram studies are often mentioned. In this research, subjects were recruited from the adult population of New Haven, Connecticut, through a newspaper ad offering $4.00 an hour plus carfare for participating in a "study of memory." The purpose of the research was actually to investigate the point at which subjects would refuse to cooperate with the experimenter. The subject was initially brought into a room where there was someone who was dressed as a technician and a middle-aged man who was a confederate of the experimenter but who appeared to be a subject. This man and the subject drew lots to determine the roles each would play in the experiment. The lots were rigged so that the confederate was always the "learner" and the real subject was always the "teacher." They were then led to another room, where the "learner" was seated in a chair and told to learn a list of word pairs. His arms were strapped into the chair and electrodes were attached to his wrists through which electric shocks would supposedly be administered whenever he made an error. The real subject, or "teacher," was then taken to another room and seated in front of an electronic control panel. He or she could see the learner through a window placed between the two rooms. The control panel had switches for administering shocks to the subject in 15-volt increments up to 450 volts. The teacher-subject was told to administer increasing levels of shock each time the learner made an error. The man in the learner role was actually an actor who received no shocks at all.

Subjects began to indicate conflict when the learner began to show discomfort. When the subject seemed reluctant to administer a shock, the experimenter ordered him to continue. The results of the experiment were impressive. Although many subjects were very emotionally affected by the task, a significant number continued to administer shocks to the highest level. Some of the subjects continued to show signs of stress long after the experimental conditions were over.

d What are some of the ethical problems with a study such as the one described above?

e Could Milgram have obtained informed consent from his subjects?

f Should research like the Milgram studies be done? Why, or why not?

REFERENCES

Ethical principles in the conduct of research with human participants (1982). Washington: American Psychological Association.

Gelman, R., & Gallistel, C. R. (1978). *The child's understanding of number.* Cambridge, MA: Harvard.

Lin, C. H. (1986). *Chinese and American perceptions of Rogers', Perls', and Ellis' approaches to psychotherapy.* Unpublished doctoral dissertation. Lexington: University of Kentucky.

Miller, S. I., & Morgan, R. R. (1983). *An introduction to the social psychology of education: Implications for learning and instruction.* Cambridge, MA: Schenkman.

Thomson, J. J., Chodosh, S., Fried, C., Goodman, D. S., Wax, M. L., & Wilson, J. Q. (1981). Regulations governing research on human subjects. *Academe, 67,* 358–370.

SUPPLEMENTARY READINGS

Adair, J. G., Dushenko, T. W., & Lindsay, R. C. L. (1985). Ethical regulations and their impact on research practice. *American Psychologist, 40,* 59–72.

Isaac, S., & Michael, W. B. (1981). *Handbook of research and evaluation.* San Diego: Edits.

Locke, L. F., & Spirduso, W. W. (1976). *Proposals that work: A guide for planning research.* New York: Teachers College.

CHAPTER 12

WRITING ABOUT RESEARCH: PROPOSALS AND REPORTS

Probably the most important way that researchers communicate is through their writing. For this reason, writing about research is as critical as any other part of the research process. The base of knowledge in science and research depends on communication of ideas and results to others. In this chapter, we will discuss writing about research. Specifically, we will cover proposing and reporting about studies and critically reading written reports about research.

STYLE

A number of misconceptions about the writing style of researchers persist. One is that research writing should be murky, complex, and incomprehensible. This view seems to stem from the idea that research is supposed to be so complex, it defies comprehension. In fact, good research writing is simple, clear, objective, unobtrusive, and understandable. Anyone familiar with a field should be able to read, understand, and evaluate a well-written research report in that field.

Another misconception is about the word "style" itself. Style of expression is central in creative writing and literature. A famous author's writing style is almost like a signature. It is unique and recognizable. For example, consider the following phrase, "...long ago, there was a small town with a mysterious past, a black stain under a purple sky." (Wiesel, 1973, p. 3). We sense from those few words that the author is not describing a happy or frivolous place. The style of this author creates in the reader a mood, feelings, and a sense of atmosphere.

Style in scientific or research writing has a different function. The purpose of research writing is to focus attention on the events and conditions of the study and to describe those events in clear, objective, and unequivocal terms. In other words, while in literary writing, the major focus is on style, in research literature, the focus is not on style but on subject matter. In scientific writing, there is a generally accepted style that everyone follows. The creativity of a researcher should be found in the conceptualization, design, and execution of the study, not, to any great extent, in the writing style of the report.

Researchers must use words precisely. Each word in a research report has a specific meaning, and sometimes that meaning is not the same as in everyday parlance. For example, a researcher who sees something unusual in the laboratory might turn to an aide and say "That's interesting!" meaning that it is unusual, unexpected, or noteworthy. Since the word "interesting" has other meanings (e.g., intriguing, curious, attention-focusing, etc.), the same researcher would probably not refer to the finding as "interesting" in a research report. Many researchers (more through tradition and practice than through formal agreement) use the word "remarkable" to mean unusual and noteworthy in research writing. Yet this word would sound strange if used that way in daily conversation. Similarly, words like "clever," "huge," "small," and "fine" are not often seen in research literature because their meanings are not specific enough. They are replaced by words whose meaning has been specified for the research field (e.g., "remarkable"), by words denoting exact quantities and measurements, and by standard phrases. In addition, the conventional meaning of a word in one field may be different from its meaning in another field. For example, to a mathematician, the word "integration" refers to a mathematical procedure; to many psychologists, the word is used as a goal of therapy or counseling and corresponds to improved self-concept.

Research writers should also avoid wording that is vague, emotional, or confusing. Everyday wording is acceptable so long as it meets the criteria for clarity and objectivity. Consider, for example, the following sentence from a graduate student's research proposal: Higher order abstractions can be resolved into componential symbols which can then be enthusiastically made subjective to the investigative processes. Few people, even researchers in the field, would be capable of interpreting that sentence! What the student meant to say was clearer in the following revised version: Complex ideas can be analyzed and broken down into components, which can then be studied further. Although it sounds less impressive, the second version is clearer and, therefore, better. Also notice that as the student who wrote the sentence said, "the enthusiasm was removed" from the revised version. This is because the word "enthusiasm" suggests the values and standards of the researcher and thus violates the tone of objectivity that should prevail in research writing.

Several guides for writing about research and other scholarly work are available. In education and the behavioral sciences, the *Publication Manual* of the American Psychological Association is a widely used standard of research writing. It addresses not only writing style but also format of the research report. The supplementary reading list at the end of this chapter includes several of the style manuals widely used in education, psychology, and related fields. These style manuals provide guidance for all kinds of research and scholarly writing for professional audiences, including proposals, journal articles, and final reports. Later in this chapter, we mention some of the differences in style and format between some of the guides. It is recommended that the student become familiar with the style manual most appropriate for his or her discipline.

THE PROPOSAL

In the last chapter, we discussed the reasoning and planning processes that go into developing a proposal. Now we turn our attention to the written description of those processes and the plan to do research that is a result of them. A written proposal is a blueprint, or plan, for the research investigation. In a sense, it is like a business contract because it depicts the work to be done in order to achieve a result, which is the ability to make a decision about hypotheses. Research proposals are written for theses and dissertations. They are also commonly written to obtain funds for research from governmental and private agencies. Occasionally, they are written to describe a project so that permission to use a population may be obtained. For example, a researcher interested in studying the relationship of alcohol use to participation in violent crime might wish to conduct a survey of a prison population regarding their drinking habits prior to incarceration. In order to be allowed to ask the prisoners to participate in the investigation, the researcher must get permission from the warden. Typically, a proposal that describes the purpose, methods, and procedures to be used would be required before permission would be granted in such a situation.

Although there are several different purposes for writing proposals, they each have a considerable amount in common. No matter whom it is written for, the proposal defines and delineates the project to be undertaken. Furthermore, the structure of all proposals is basically similar. Proposals written for different purposes will differ only in the placement of emphases in the various sections. For example, in the proposal written to obtain permission from the warden to use prisoners as subjects, the description of the methods of data collection and analysis would be emphasized so that there would be no question about how prison regulations, routines, and policies would be affected. On the other hand, a proposal written for a master's thesis research would require more detail in the documentation and development of the problem and hypotheses. There would also be a need to clearly identify data-collection and analysis procedures, but the influence of these procedures upon the daily lives of the subjects would not be expected to be spelled out as clearly as in the proposal written for the warden. Finally, proposals for research grants tend to be fairly detailed and also usually require that a budget be attached.

Here we will emphasize the format of the research proposal but omit any discussion of budgets. This is because the nature and format of the budget section of a proposal depends greatly upon the requirements provided by the funding sources. The reader is referred to publications and instructions provided by funding agencies regarding the preparation of budget sections of proposals.

A proposal has three distinct sections: the title, the introduction, and the method section. Although the three sections are found in almost all proposals, the organization and content of the sections may vary according to personal preference and local tradition. The descriptions of the sections given below are fairly standard, but the purpose and audience for the proposal and practices of the professional field should be considered.

The Title

The title should act as a summary of the proposal itself. It should give information about the variables in the study, the relationships considered, and the population from which a sample was drawn and studied. For example, consider the following title:

The Relationship of Learning Style and Personality to Ethnic Background in Urban 10-Year-Old Children

Reading it, one is readily able to identify the variables and the target population of the study. Can you tell which are the independent and which the dependent variables in this study? Do you think it is experimental, quasi-experimental, or descriptive?

The title should be as short as possible. Furthermore, when the study is to be included in an index or catalogue, such as ERIC or *Dissertation Abstracts International*, wording is important because studies are often indexed according to key words in the title. To keep a title short without eliminating essential words, unnecessary terms such as "A study of...," "A systematic consideration of..." or "The effects of..." should be omitted. Moreover, details of method or procedure can be eliminated because they are available in the text. Thus, the title

A Research Investigation of the Hypothesis That There Is a Relationship between Compulsive Personality and Child-Rearing Practices in Urban and Rural Parents

can be reduced to the following:

Compulsiveness and Child-Rearing Practices in Urban and Rural Parents

The second version clearly is improved by its brevity. The purpose of the study is more evident, and so is the relationship among the variables studied.

The Introduction

The introduction acquaints a reader with the background of the problem, provides a statement of the problem, and reviews previous research. A theory, or model, which represents a conceptual approach to the problem may be included. The specific hypotheses, definitions, and a discussion of the importance of the proposed study should also be in the introduction. A suggested outline of the introduction for a proposal is shown in Figure 12-1. The order of presentation of the sections may vary.

The length of the introduction depends upon what is needed to make a convincing argument for the research. Some introductions might only require six or eight pages of typed text; others might require three or four times that. In general, it is to the researcher's advantage to keep a proposal as short as possible so that the primary points and arguments are as clear as possible.

The Background of the Problem In Chapter 11, we discussed how background in a research area is developed through experience, observation, training, and reading of the relevant literature. In the introduction, the background that led to the recognition of the problem is summarized. As an illustration of this, we look at a reading teacher in a multilingual school in the southwestern United States who became concerned that a large proportion of the children with delayed reading skills came from homes where a language other than English was spoken. After doing some library research, the teacher realized this phenomenon had been noted by others. Further, he learned that researchers had approached the topic in a variety of different ways. Armed with this knowledge, the teacher proposed to test some innovative reading-curriculum ideas that might reduce the reading problems some of the multilingual children were experiencing. Thus, with a background based on training, personal experience, and awareness of the literature, the teacher was introduced to an area of research.

A Statement of the Problem The problem may not occupy a separate section in the introduction. Often, the statement of the problem is integrated with

Suggested Outline for Introduction

I. Background of the problem
    A. How the problem came to be recognized
    B. Factors contributing to the problem
II. Problem
    – A question about a relationship among two or more variable
III. Review of previous research
IV. Theoretical or conceptual formulation
V. Specific hypotheses, research questions, or expectations
VI. Definition of terms
VII. Importance or significance of the study

FIGURE 12-1
Suggested outline for the introduction section of a proposal.

the background, hypotheses, or other parts of the introduction. Generally, a problem is a question arising from the theoretical positions, experience, background, and observations. Statement of problems was discussed in Chapters 3 and 12.

Previous Research on the Problem In the introduction, the scope of the literature and background information supporting the study should be narrowed to relate specifically to the proposed research. Thus a broad concern about how leadership style affects group behavior should be narrowed to the effects of leadership behavior on students in the classroom or workers on a production team. The library is probably the best place to locate information on previous research. We have already discussed such useful resources as ERIC, *Psychological Abstracts,* and *Education Index.* These can be of assistance in locating pertinent research. Many research libraries now have these indexes available on computer terminals, permitting rapid search by topic, author, and subject.

Often a worthwhile research problem has not been thoroughly investigated, and relevant literature is thus difficult to locate. This was the case when microcomputers first appeared on the educational scene. Researchers interested in investigating the effectiveness of presenting instruction by microcomputer compared to other media approaches found little in the literature to support their inquiry. However, a wealth of literature on related topics did exist which could serve quite well. For example, since much of the early computer-assisted instruction (CAI) functioned very much like programmed instruction (Alessi & Trollip, 1985; Bramble & Mason, 1985), research on programmed materials contributed to the development of much research on computer-based learning. Further, since computerized instruction generally was presented on a monitor that was similar to a television set, some of the TV-learning literature was also useful. Even though there is not much previous research to draw on for a specific question, therefore, research in closely related areas can sometimes help to substantiate the reasons for doing a particular study. With this in mind, however, any researcher has the responsibility to see that his or her problem is adequately documented to justify the investigation.

A literature review should not read like a shopping list. Information identified to support the research problem should be integrated and presented in an organized way rather than just listed in alphabetical order. A conceptual perspective or theory can be used to give structure to the presentation of this material. Researchers sometimes provide structure by organizing previous research in terms of the variables used or the measurements employed.

Theoretical or Conceptual Perspective A researcher's perspective is often apparent in how the problem is presented. For example, we might say that a particular piece of learning research was "Skinnerian" or "Piagetian" because it is organized according to the views of the well-known behavioral psychologist B. F. Skinner or Jean Piaget, the developmental researcher and theorist (Bower & Hilgard, 1981). Much educational and social science research has been designed to reflect well-known theoretical perspectives such as these.

Another approach is to create a structure or model specifically for the research. This is commonly done in evaluation research. For example, consider the county school administrator who proposes to the school board that a research investigation be done to help the board determine whether split-session and smaller classes or single sessions with larger classes are a better way to deal with overcrowding in the county high school. The administrator cannot find any specific literature dealing with a comparison of the two types of sessions. However, she does find considerable literature on the effects of class size. She also finds numerous studies on the effects of split sessions. From this literature, she is able to determine that although there is a tendency for smaller classes to produce better learning, there is also a tendency for split sessions to produce a whole array of difficulties, including more discipline problems; increased costs for transportation, heating, and maintenance; and a rise in scheduling complaints. Using these findings, the administrator pieces together a model that includes input variables (e.g., number of students assigned to the high school, number of hours the school can be kept open for classes, budget, number of teachers available in each subject, etc.) and output variables (class size, achievement-test results, frequency and type of discipline problems, etc.). This model provides her with a structure for organizing the studies found in the research literature.

Specific Hypotheses, Research Questions, or Expectations As we saw in Chapter 3, *hypotheses* are declarative statements designed to answer a question posed in the problem statement. *Research expectations* are more like objectives to guide descriptive research design. For example, using the split-session problem described above, the administrator might have proposed a descriptive study of attitudes of principals whose schools are currently on split sessions. The research expectation would be that these attitudes can be assessed by way of a mail survey.

Many different research approaches and hypothesis statements are possible for any problem. In the case of the split-session and class-size study described above, some potential hypotheses would be

• Students in small classes (fewer than 18 students) perform better on end-of-semester achievement tests than do students in large classes (more than 27 students) in the same academic subject.

• Students in split-session programs perform as well as do students in regular-session classes in all subjects on the end-of-semester examinations.

• In split-session programs, students in morning classes score higher on end-of-semester examinations than do students in afternoon classes.

These hypotheses are stated so that each gives an idea about how the study will be done (e.g., comparisons between groups based on final examinations).

Definition of Terms Any term to be used in the study that does not have a well-accepted definition in the field must be defined. For example, "split session" might mean different things in different school districts. In one district, it might mean students come to school in two sessions, the first beginning at 7:30 a.m. and continuing until 12:30 p.m., the second starting at 12:30 p.m. and continuing until 5:30 p.m. In another district, the times might be different, the two sessions might overlap, or there might be a third session. The precise meaning of "split session" in the particular study should be given. "Class size" has already been defined in the hypothesis above, but this also could have been done in a section containing definitions.

Significance of the Study The introduction section of the proposal generally contains a discussion of the significance of the study. Most studies have at least one justification; that is, to increase knowledge. Other reasons for the importance of doing the study should refer to its purpose. This purpose might be to test a theory that has been proposed. Or the reasons for doing a study might be more pragmatic, such as contributing to a base of information for policy planning.

To avoid confusion, it probably should be mentioned that the significance we refer to here should not be confused with *statistical significance* (which has to do with the probability that the results could have been obtained by chance if the null hypothesis were true in the population; see Chapter 7 for a discussion of statistical significance). It is possible, in fact, for a result to be statistically significant and, at the same time, not very important. For example, in a large enough sample, a 1 point or less difference in IQ score (e.g., between 111.0 and 111.87) might be statistically significant, but it is obviously not very important.

The Method Section

In newspaper reporting it is considered essential to answer five questions: Who? What? Where? When? and How? The same five questions should be addressed in the method section of a research proposal. It should describe subjects, materials, procedures, research design, and data analysis. A typical outline for a method section of a proposal is included in Figure 12-2.

Subjects The subjects section, usually about a paragraph or two in length, contains a description of the population of interest. The approximate size of the sample to be used in the study is mentioned. Furthermore, characteristics of the sample that will be identified are listed.

Materials Everything that will be used to establish the experimental or research conditions and measure and define the variables is included in the materials section. Thus tests or measures which operationalize the dependent and independent variables, equipment used to present stimuli or record responses,

Method

I. Subjects
   A. Population to be sampled
   B. Approximate sample size
   C. Demographic characteristics of sample
II. Materials
   A. Instrumentation and tests
      1. Validity and reliability
      2. Pilot studies
      3. Description of tests and measures
   B. Apparatus – each piece of equipment
III. Procedures
   A. Data collection
      1. Assignment/identification of groups
      2. Administration and portrayal of experimental conditions
        or context of data collection
      3. Time frame for data collection
   B. Research design
   C. Analysis of data – tests of hypotheses
   D. Logistics
      1. Sources of materials
      2. Time schedule of research projects
      3. Letters of compliance with ethical standards, etc.

FIGURE 12-2
Outline of the method section of a
research proposal.

special rooms, and any machines or devices, such as tape recorders or computers, which actually monitor and control the conditions of the research should be described. In addition, any available information about reliability, validity, data from pilot studies or other sources should be included, particularly when the proposed procedures or measurement instruments are not standard. Furthermore, when a special piece of equipment is used, such as a random-access slide projector or a computer-assisted instruction (CAI) system, the manufacturer and model numbers are commonly included.

Procedures The procedures include what is actually done in the research study. Specifically, data collection, design, and analysis of data are clearly described, along with any special concerns, such as sources of materials, funding, and the time frame for the completed research.

The description of the data-collection procedures includes assignment of subjects into groups, specific plans for definition of the groups, and measurement of dependent and independent variables. A step-by-step description of the conditions under which the data are to be collected must be included. It should be a complete portrayal of the experimental or research conditions or the context under which the data will be collected in a field of study. The time frame within which data collection will be completed is also specified. For example, a researcher who is proposing a study of values among adolescent boys and girls in a summer-camp setting might propose to collect data during the first 2 days of camp. Over a period of time in a camp setting, youngsters tend to adopt group values because they spend a great amount of time participating in group activities. Therefore, the timing of the study of values in such a situation is critical and must be specified.

The research design must be identified in the procedures section. When an experimental or quasi-experimental design is to be used, it should be identified. This will help the researcher describe the strengths and weaknesses of the design. If the study is to be a descriptive survey, a historical search, or some other format that does not conform to the experimental or quasi-experimental situation, it should also be identified and described.

The analysis and research design must provide for testing the hypotheses stated in the introduction. Procedures of data analysis should be described, but only in general terms since the researcher has no way of knowing what difficulties will arise that will require adaptation of the analysis. For example, although the researcher fully intends to have a certain number of subjects in each cell of the analysis of variance, subjects could be absent, refuse to cooperate, fall asleep during the treatment condition, or, in some other way, cause conditions that would reduce the number of subjects in one or more cells.

Finally, the logistics of the proposal must be considered. This involves identification of sources of materials and equipment; time schedule for completion of the whole research project, including the writing of the final report; and any letters that may be necessary to obtain a sample, ensure compliance with ethical standards (see Chapter 11), regulations, or other guidelines, and ensure availability of equipment and resources. This last section is often minimized or ignored, and yet it is crucial to the successful completion of the study because it deals with matters that are often taken for granted. A number of examples in our experience will serve to highlight the importance of these circumstances.

1 A doctoral student had planned for months to collect data for his dissertation. On the day he arrived at the school with all his equipment and materials and four paid assistants, he found the school closed for an administrative holiday.

2 A researcher planned to use an opaque projector to present visual materials to groups of children in an after-school center. She was assured that the school had an opaque projector which she could use. However, the after-school center staff did not have access to it, and when she arrived to run the study, she found she had no projector to use.

3 A researcher made several videocassette tapes to use in training subjects in an investigation of group processes. However, when he arrived at the site, he found only a brand of videocassette player that could not play his tapes.

REPORTING COMPLETED RESEARCH

After an investigation is completed, it must be communicated to others so that the findings can be evaluated and considered in the context of other research, theories, and existing knowledge about the topic. Researchers usually report the findings of their investigations to the field in at least one of three ways. The first is the detailed and comprehensive research report. Thesis and dissertation research is usually presented to the faculty in the form of a detailed report so that all aspects of the problem, procedures, and findings may be scrutinized by the examining committee. Agencies that grant funds to support research usually receive detailed reports from researchers when their studies are completed.

The kind of research report that is published in professional journals is a more condensed version of the above. This is because of the expense involved in publishing and the fact that few researchers have time to read every report related to their field of research in detail. Thus journal publications usually are long enough to convey the essential information about the purpose, methodology, findings, and conclusions of the study. If more detail is required, the author of the study may be contacted at an address that is usually included with the article.

The third kind of research report commonly encountered is the paper prepared for presentation at a meeting of a scholarly group. An important feature of the annual meetings of the American Psychological Association, the American Educational Research Association, the Society for Research in Child Development, and other similar organizations is the presentation of research papers. Members are regularly solicited to present their current research activities at these meetings for two reasons. First, because of the length of time it takes journals to review material for publication and prepare issues, these presentations bring to public notice current research efforts a year or two before they will appear in print. Second, the meetings bring together people who have similar research interests, and thus a forum for discussion of current research efforts is provided. The papers given at such presentations are very similar in format to articles prepared for publication. However, due to time limitations, they are usually more condensed.

All three kinds of reports are prepared with similar sections and writing style. The format and writing style are determined largely by the makeup of the audience. That is, if a paper is prepared for psychologists, the format and writing style of the American Psychological Association will be used.* In addition, technical words used by psychologists would be common in the report. However, if the same paper were prepared for teachers, a style and vocabulary more familiar to educators would be used.†

Regardless of style, length, and audience, research reports all have the common format described here. Specific audiences, of course, require minor alterations in format. For this reason, a student preparing to write a master's thesis or doctoral dissertation must ascertain the specific requirements of his or her university before beginning. Similarly, before starting to write a paper for publication or for presentation at a learned society, a researcher should obtain instructions for format and style from the journal or organization.

---

* *Publication manual of the American Psychological Association* (3rd ed.) (1983). Washington, D.C.: APA.
†For example, *A manual of style* (13th ed.) (1982). University of Chicago Press.

Sections, Divisions, or Chapters

Figure 12-3 shows the typical organization of research reports. Notice that all three types of reports have a title page, introduction, methods, results, discussion and conclusions, and references. Longer reports typically contain acknowledgments, a table of contents, lists of tables and figures, and appendices as well.

Longer reports, such as dissertations and theses, are usually divided into chapters; in shorter reports, the divisions are indicated by headings and subheadings. Papers presented at meetings may be organized and written according to the format in Figure 12-3, but the divisions will typically not be indicated in the paper because they are not easy to follow in a paper that is presented orally.

Title, Introduction, and Method

The title, introduction, and method sections of the detailed research report are very similar to those of the proposal. In fact, if the proposal was done well, the title, introduction, and method sections with minor changes should serve as the first two divisions of the detailed research report (see Figures 12-1 and 12-2). There are only two differences between the introduction and method sections of the proposal and the same sections of the research report. The first

FIGURE 12-3
Contents of components of the three kinds of research reports, where X means "included," B means "brief," D means "detailed," and O means "occasionally included."

	Detailed report	Journal article	Presented paper
Title page	X	X	X
Acknowledgments	X		
Table of contents	X		
List of tables	X		
List of figures	X		
Abstract	X	X	X
Introduction section	XD	XB	XB
Background of problem	X	XB	XB
Statement of problem	X	XO	XO
Review of research	XD	XB	XB
Theoretical or conceptual formulation	XD	XB	XB
Specific hypotheses or research expectations	X	XO	XO
Definition of terms	X	XO	XO
Importance of study	XD	XB	XB
Method	XD	XB	XB
Subjects	XD	XB	XB
Materials	XD	XB	XB
Procedures	XD	XB	XB
Results	XD	XB	XB
Discussion and conclusion	XD	XB	XB
Summary	X	XO	XO
References	X	X	X
Appendices	XO		

difference concerns tense. The proposal discusses what *will be* done. All the procedures are described in the future tense. By the time the research report is written, the research has been completed and hypotheses *were* tested, data *were* collected and analyzed, and so on. So the first task in adapting a proposal introduction and method sections involves changing from future to past tense. Updating the review of the literature may also be necessary if the proposal was completed some time before the data were collected.

The second adaptation lies in the method section. That is, a number of things are deliberately not discussed or else left vague in a proposal because the researcher may not know them. For example, the exact size of the sample, the exact number of female and male subjects, or the average mental age of the subjects might not be known until after the subjects who participated in the study are selected. In addition, the researcher will not have anticipated certain chance events which occurred during data collection that should be included in the final report. For example, the researcher might have proposed to use a videocassette as a training device. But because the cassette arrived from the distributor in damaged condition, he used a videocassette of a similar film that was made available to him. In short, the method section of the research report should reflect what has been done, not necessarily what was proposed, but the study should still be as close as possible to what was proposed.

Results

The results section of a research report tells what happened in the study. Usually, the results of each hypothesis tested are listed in the order that the hypotheses were stated in an earlier section. The results section contains a narrative description of the data collected and statistical analyses. It includes tables and figures depicting scores, statistical tests, and graphs that simplify the description of the results.

The results section contains no interpretation of the findings. Information is presented simply and objectively. Since the study has already been completed, the writing is in the past tense. Furthermore, the third person is usually used because it is associated with objectivity in writing. Consider the following sentence from a results section:

The hypothesis test provides us with the comforting knowledge that group 1 performs better than group 2.

The sentence would have been better stated as:

Group 1 performed significantly better than group 2.

This illustration emphasizes that the writing style for results sections should be dispassionate and objective. Some people complain that the writing style in scientific reports is dull. The purpose of scientific writing is to inform rather than entertain, although good writing is never a crime. Sentences should be in proper grammatical form, and the material should be presented in a clear and objective manner.

Discussion and Conclusion

The section in which the results are discussed and conclusions stated is where researchers place interpretations, generalizations, and inferences regarding their hypotheses and the underlying theory. However, the researcher must be careful not to generalize beyond the data obtained in the study. Earlier, we looked at the notion of causality and questioned whether anything really ever causes anything else. In addition, we discussed the inappropriateness of causal interpretations of correlation coefficients. For these reasons, researchers who try to attribute causes may often be going beyond what is contained in their data.

The discussion and conclusion section is the proper place to relate the findings to previous research. Recommendations for future research are also appropriate here. It is not unusual to indicate the limitations and weaknesses in the study and to speculate about how the findings might have been different with different procedures and conditions.

Summaries and Abstracts

Figure 12-3 indicates that detailed research reports typically have both a summary and an abstract, although published reports and presented papers may not. The summary and the abstract are similar. Both are written to provide a synopsis of the study. The summary is typically included at the end of the report to emphasize or highlight important aspects of the study. Summaries may be as long as 10 or 12 typewritten pages. Usually they are shorter, but there is no established or preferred length. Abstracts, on the other hand, are usually between 100 and 200 words. They include a brief sentence or two describing each of the following: (1) the hypotheses or variables studied, (2) the subjects, (3) the methods and procedures, (4) the results, and (5) conclusions. Abstracts usually precede articles in research journals. They are also found in many research indexes, such as *Psychological Abstracts* and *Mental Retardation Abstracts*. They are designed to inform an interested reader of the substance of the study with a minimum investment of time.

Reference Citations

References cited in the text are listed at the end of the research report. There are several different formats for reference lists, just as there are different ways to reference works in the text of an article. For example, using the format suggested by the American Psychological Association, a sentence in the review of the literature section might be as follows:

An alternative explanation has been suggested in which previous training predominates (Smith & Brown, 1983).

According to the *Manual of Style* of the University of Chicago Press, the entry would be

An alternative explanation has been suggested in which previous training predominates (Smith and Brown, 1983).

The reference list at the end of the report would also be slightly different using these two styles. For APA, the correct listing would be

Smith, A., & Brown, W. C. (1983). Learning motor skills and job performance among telephone workers. *Journal of Applied Psychomotor Education, 142,* 121–123.

The University of Chicago Press style presents the same information slightly differently:

Smith, Arnold, and Brown, William C. ''Learning Motor Skills and Job Performance among Telephone Workers.'' *Journal of Applied Psychomotor Education* (1983), 142, 121–23.

There are many other styles as well. The one used should be consistent throughout the paper and appropriate to the circumstances in which the report is being written. In choosing a style for a research paper, one should consider the target audience. For example, if the report is being written for presentation to the educational psychology department, the most appropriate format would be that in the American Psychological Association's *Publication Manual*. However, if the paper is being prepared for a journal in sociology, the requirements of the American Sociological Association should be addressed. Most publication outlets—journal, monograph, and book publishers—furnish their authors with guidelines for the preparation of manuscripts. In addition, graduate programs generally provide students with instructions for preparing their thesis and dissertation manuscripts.

Appendices

Appendices, rarely seen in journal articles or papers, are common in detailed reports of research. Authors often find it convenient to place in appendices at the end of the report copies of their testing instruments, special instructions to subjects, or other information too lengthy to include in the text but necessary to someone who might want to replicate the study.

EVALUATION OF RESEARCH REPORTS

Both researchers and users or consumers of research must be able to evaluate written reports of research. Researchers must determine which studies are significant for their own work. Furthermore, researchers should be able to recognize good research in order to form the best possible basis for decision making. There are two fundamental aspects to the evaluation of research articles. First, and most important, is the research itself; that is, the formation of the hypotheses, methodology, results, and conclusions. This was covered extensively in Chapter 11. The second important area is the format, adequacy, and clarity of the writing of the report. Figure 12-4 contains a checklist of points to consider in the evaluation of a research report. For description of the items on the checklist, refer to the earlier sections of this chapter and the section on evaluation of research in Chapter 11.

The research report should be written so that there are no questions about what was done, what happened, or how it happened. There should be enough information presented so that the study can be replicated by someone who reads it. Also, the report should be appropriate for the intended audience. The author should not assume that those who read the report are as familiar with the topic as he or she is. Technical jargon should be avoided. Professional words and language should be defined when their use will be familiar only to those expert in the field.

SUMMARY

Research activities begin with an idea and end with a research report that should lead to new ideas and more research. From the idea stage, the proposal is developed. It begins with an introduction that describes the problem, gives background, contains a review of relevant research, and states the research hypotheses. In addition, terms are defined and implications of the proposed study included. The second section of the proposal contains the method, procedures, and materials that will be used to test the research hypotheses. The subject population is identified and data-analysis procedures described. Logistical considerations, such as funding, obtaining of special apparatus, and any unusual needs, are also discussed in the method section of the proposal.

After the data are collected and analyzed, a research report is prepared. Reports may be highly detailed, such as dissertations, or they may be more condensed, such as research reports published in professional journals or presented at meetings of learned societies. The format of the research report is fairly standard, regardless of length, and is outlined in Figure 12-3. The introduction and method sections of the proposal may be readily adapted to the report. The report should be written clearly and objectively and in a format appropriate for the intended audience. Specific guidelines may be obtained from professional organizations, journal editors, book publishers, a graduate school or department, and other sources.

Researchers and practicing professionals should be able to evaluate written research reports in their fields. Research reports should be considered in terms of the quality of the research first and only second in terms of the quality of the reporting and writing. The report should be complete enough so that the study

Section of Report	Adequate	Marginal	Inadequate or not included
Title 1. Appropriateness of words 2. Clarity 3. Focuses on topic			
Abstract			
Introduction 1. Purpose of research 2. Problem 3. Background and/or theoretical basis 4. Review of the literature 5. Hypotheses or research expectations 6. Definitions of terms			
Method 1. Subjects 2. Materials and apparatus 3. Procedures for data collection			
Results 1. Organization 2. Data analysis procedures 3. Objectivity 4. Use of charts, tables, graphs			
Discussion and Conclusions 1. Within framework of study 2. Appropriate to data 3. Conclusions appropriate to hypotheses tested 4. Recommendation for further research 5. Realistic assessment of limitations 6. Appropriateness of recommendations regarding practical implications 7. Appropriate cautions made in inferences and interpretations			
Summary (when included) 1. Clear and concise 2. Describes essential elements of study 3. Includes findings			
References 1. All references cited in the text are included in reference list 2. Reference list includes only references cited in text 3. Essential references to support problem and hypothesis 4. Format of references is appropriate and provides essential information			
Overall 1. Adequate information 2. Clarity and objectivity of the writing 3. Article appropriate for the intended audience			

FIGURE 12-4
A checklist for evaluation of research reports.

can be replicated by other researchers, using the same materials, methods, and procedures.

PROBLEMS FOR THOUGHT AND DISCUSSION

1 For each of the following titles of research projects:
   a Identify the probable dependent and independent variables.
   b Discuss the nature of the relationship implicit in the title (e.g., directional, nondirectional, correlational).
   c Identify the population of interest.

   Attitudes toward Education and IQ Test Score in Elementary School Children
   Effects of Word Length and Parts of Speech on Children's Comprehension
   Employment Aspirations and Personal Interests: A Study of War Veterans

2 Shorten each of the following titles to increase their clarity and effectiveness:
   a The Effects of Two Stages of Interpersonal Interaction on the Behavior of Male High School Graduates, Female High School Graduates, Male College Students, and Female College Students in Two Communities in the South
   b A Study of the Experimental Effects of Familiarity with Argument Content versus Nonfamiliarity with Argument Content upon Deductive Reasoning among Criminal Offenders Who Have Been Convicted of Violent Crimes, Theft, Crimes of Passion, and Fraud

3 Select a research study reported in a journal, and develop a proposal to do that research. Everything that is needed to write a proposal should be available in the article.

4 Develop a brief proposal for your own research, using the outlines in Figures 12-1 and 12-2 and the guidelines for writing proposals contained in this chapter.

5 Determine the adequacy of the following titles of research reports. When there are problems, redo the titles in more acceptable form.
   a The Adequacy of Each of Four Approaches to the Teaching of Mathematics in Grades One, Two, Three, Four, and Five by Teachers from Two Different Racial Groups According to Differences in Student Reading Level
   b Race, Personality, and Learning: A Research Investigation
   c Learning Style, Personal Values, and Personal Needs in 8-Year-Old Boys

6 Obtain two abstracts of research that precede articles in journals or appear in *Psychological Abstracts*. Determine whether each abstract contains information about (1) the variables or hypotheses, (2) the subjects, (3) the methods used, (4) the results, and (5) the conclusions.

7 Select a published research report from a professional journal. On the basis of what is contained in the report, can the conditions of the study be replicated by someone who wishes to do so? Does the researcher report enough information about how to test the hypotheses?

8 Go back to the discussion of the scientific method in Chapter 2. Is there an apparent relationship between the steps of the scientific method and the organization of a research report? Consider each section of the research report and its purpose in your answer.

9 Select a research article reported in a professional publication. Evaluate it, using the checklist in Figure 12-4. Would you have done anything differently if you were the author of the article? Would you have written the report differently?

10 Obtain copies of two or three different manuals for writing research reports. What are the major differences among them? What are the major similarities?

REFERENCES

Alessi, S. M., & Trollip, S. R. (1985). *Computer-based instruction.* Englewood Cliffs, NJ: Prentice-Hall.

Bower, G. H., & Hilgard, E. R. (1981). *Theories of learning* (5th ed.). Englewood Cliffs, NJ: Prentice-Hall.

Bramble, W. J., & Mason, E. J. (1985). *Computers in the schools.* New York: McGraw-Hill.

Weisel, E. (1973). *The oath.* New York: Random House.

SUPPLEMENTARY READINGS

Gibaldi, J., & Achtert, W. S. (1984). *MLA handbook for writers of research papers* (2nd ed.). New York: Modern Language Association.

Locke, L. F., & Spirduso, W. W. (1976). *Proposals that work: A guideline for planning research.* New York: Teachers College.

A manual of style (1982). The University of Chicago Press.

Publication manual of the American Psychological Association (3rd ed.) (1983). Washington: American Psychological Association.

Strunk, W., & White, E. B. (1979). *The elements of style* (3rd ed.). New York: Macmillan.

Turabian, K. L. (1973). *A manual for writers of term papers, theses, and dissertations* (4th ed.). The University of Chicago Press.

13

EVALUATION

Evaluation holds a special position in the spectrum of educational and behavioral science research activities because of the diversity of methods, approaches, purposes, and perspectives evaluation can assume. Evaluation is growing and changing so rapidly, a complete discussion of its methods and techniques would be impossible in a single chapter. Because evaluators routinely use many of the available techniques of the social sciences and education, evaluation appears very much like other research activities (e.g., research designed to support the development of theory). However, the basis for doing an evaluation, the perspectives taken, and concern for communicating about the evaluation to a designated constituency render the field of evaluation different from other kinds of systematic inquiry. In this chapter, we will consider definitions of *evaluation,* several evaluation approaches, and ways to determine the adequacy of an evaluation.

WHAT IS EVALUATION?

Evaluation has been defined a number of ways. However, the basic definition that we used in Chapter 2 may serve as a starting point: *Evaluation* is the process of determining the adequacy of a product, objective, process, procedure, program, approach, function, or functionary. One problem with this definition is that it sounds as if the ultimate purpose of evaluation is to hold people accountable. This is not the case. The purpose of evaluation is educative. It is to obtain information about whatever is being evaluated. It is true that if the information gathered during an evaluation reveals that a program is not meeting its objectives, certain personnel might be held responsible, but accountability is a management, not an evaluation, responsibility.

Nevo (1983) suggested that "any entity" (p. 124) can be the object of evaluation. He further identified four purposes of educational evaluation: formative, summative, sociopolitical, and administrative. The formative purpose of evaluation is to provide information for improvement of a program, project, or other "entity." The summative purpose is to help management make decisions regarding selection and accountability. The sociopolitical purposes of evaluation might include developing information for the purpose of supporting a political view with respect to a program, project, or other concern. Finally, the administrative functions of evaluation have to do with the exercise of authority and responsibility, such as occurs when a school administrator institutes a staff-evaluation procedure.

Worthen and Sanders (1987) distinguish evaluation from research. Their definition of *evaluation* is simple but encompassing: "Evaluation is the determination of a thing's value" (p. 22). They define *research* as "the activity aimed at obtaining generalizable knowledge by testing claims about relationships among variables, or describing generalizable phenomena" (p. 23). These definitions are useful for understanding the similarities and differences between evaluation and research. Both involve *systematic inquiry;* that is, good careful scholarship in investigating questions and seeking information. However, research seeks to develop information that can be generalized to a broader population (that can be placed in a knowledge structure such as a theory or model) and is useful simply for the reason that it is knowledge. Evaluation has a more limited target group, those participating in or otherwise having an interest in a particular entity. The information generated by evaluation is intended to apply only to that entity. Thus generalizations in evaluation tend to be more restricted in purpose and in practice.

Evaluators disagree on the purposes and methods of evaluation. Some argue that the designers and producers of a product or program should state their goals explicitly. Then the evaluator judges the worth of their products by determining the degree to which the products actually meet the goals. Others argue that information relative to attainment of the goals stated by the developers and producers of products and programs needs to be supplemented by judgments about the value of the stated objectives (e.g., through comparing these objectives with needs of the ultimate users of the products). Controversy over the narrowness of the definition of *evaluation* we have given may arise because most modern evaluators visualize the role of the evaluator as encompassing more than determining the worth of things. They see evaluators as having other important roles, such as determining needs, assisting during the development of educational materials by pilot-testing them, and providing data that suggest improvements. The position we are taking in this book is that the definition of *evaluation* we have given above is a good one, particularly in that it stresses the central purpose of evaluation. However, we note that in doing an adequate job of evaluation, the evaluator often serves in a number of other roles and furnishes other kinds of information.

Before proceeding to some of the approaches to evaluation, we will briefly identify certain key concepts in evaluation: its constituency, goals and objectives, and needs assessment. These concepts are basic to understanding evaluation.

Who Is the Constituency for Evaluation?

Five groups of people affected by evaluation have been identified by Worthen and Sanders (1987). The first is the *sponsor,* which authorizes the evaluation and provides the funds for it. A sponsor might be a large government funding agency, such as the National Institute for Child Health and Development, or the department of education of a state. The second group with which evaluation is concerned is, collectively, the *client.* The client requests the evaluation. Typically, the client is the agency responsible for operating the project or program. The sponsor and the client are occasionally the same. For example, when a state health department initiates, funds, and administers a community health education program, it is both sponsor and client. *Participants* constitute the third group in evaluation. The participants are the people with whom the evaluator works during the course of an evaluation. Some groups of participants include representatives of the sponsor or client groups. A participant group might also include staff or those whom the program or project seeks to serve (e.g., family members, students, etc.). *Stake holders* are those who have the most interest in the evaluation results. They might include clients or sponsors who have an interest in the continuation of the program or teachers, students, parents, or others who stand to benefit from improved or continued services. Sometimes the major stake holders are not directly involved in the program. For example, consider a project in which children who are experiencing difficulty in arithmetic are removed from their regular classes and given individually tailored instruction in small groups for 30 minutes a day. Although the children receiving the special instruction are clearly stake holders, so are the other children in the class, who are able to cover more arithmetic in class during their absence and thus gain more during a semester when the teacher does not have to gauge presentation by the slower students. The fifth group is the *audience* for the evaluation. Again, this includes some of the people in the other four groups, but it might also include a wider audience, such as people who might want to emulate the program in other settings or who are involved in similar programs already and feel their operations or services could benefit from the findings of an evaluation of another program.

Clearly, there is much overlap in the five constituent groups. However, it is useful to think of the different needs of the five groups from the perspective of the evaluator. This points to another difference between evaluation and many other forms of scholarly research. The evaluator is asked to provide information in forms that will be useful to specific constituent groups. A researcher involved in theory-oriented studies does not generally have to couch findings in forms that will be useful for any constituent purposes.

Goals and Objectives

Goals express general purposes. They are statements that provide clarity of intention. Goals may be established for individuals, programs, organizations, projects, schools, or other groups, tasks, or categories. For example, a goal might be for a tourist to learn to speak Spanish before going on a trip to Mexico or for a university to build a clinical child-services center. Notice that the goals in our examples lack specificity. We do not specify how *much* Spanish the tourist is to learn within a certain time frame or the size, capacity, or opening date of the child-services unit. This sort of specificity is done with objectives.

Objectives state exactly what will be accomplished and by whom. Thus objectives have more specificity and precision than do goals. For example, an objective of the tourist who wants to learn to speak in Spanish might be to "learn, in one week, to recognize, pronounce, and know the meaning of 200 Spanish words and phrases." Objectives are more important than goals in evaluations because of their specificity and clarity. However, in some instances, goals may also be useful. For example, when a project is in its early planning stages, goals may help guide thinking as objectives are developed.

Needs Assessment

A *needs assessment* is a systematic study of what is needed to attain the identified goals and objectives. One common approach to needs assessment is to systematically analyze what already exists regarding the objectives and to compare that with what should exist to attain them. The discrepancy between what should exist and what exists is the result of a needs assessment. This discrepancy forms the basis for planning the project or program. Needs assessment can be considered part of the evaluation process, although it is sometimes confused with evaluation itself (Auvenshine & Mason, 1982).

In the following sections, we will consider several approaches to evaluation. These approaches should be considered philosophical perspectives as well as systematic methodologies. Evaluators tend to tailor their studies to the needs at hand, rarely relying on a single approach or type of information.

THE TYLER-BLOOM APPROACH

The evaluation model proposed by Tyler (1942, 1969) and elaborated on by Bloom (Bloom, Hastings, & Madaus, 1971) initially followed rather closely the definition of *evaluation* presented above but has developed to the point where it would now require a broader definition. At the center of the approach is the notion that a developer of curricula, products, or materials has a set of broad goals for the creation. As Tyler (1969) pointed out, sources of educational goals or objectives include studies of the learners themselves, studies of contemporary life outside the school, suggestions from specialists in a field of knowledge, the philosophical position of the person stating the goals (as well as of other persons interested in education), and the psychology of learning. These educational goals can serve as general criteria for judging the worth of an educational product, but only in an indirect way. Since these goals typically involve general actions for instructors (e.g., "Teach the students multiplication") or vague outcomes for the students (e.g., "Students will understand euclidean geometry"), performance of these objectives is not easily measured. Because adequate measures of performance may not be available, judgments about the worth of the products are difficult at best.

The proposed solution to this problem is to transform general goal statements into *behavioral objectives*. For example, the goal statement

to teach the students multiplication

may be transformed to a series of behavioral objectives, such as:

The student can recall products from the multiplication table through the 10s.

The student can solve multiplication problems involving one-, two-, and three-digit numbers.

Given behavioral objectives such as these, it is possible to construct test items or other devices which indicate mastery or nonmastery of the behavioral objectives by a student. Thus, to measure performance on the first behavioral objective, the evaluator uses items such as

What is 5 times 2?
What is 6 times 8?

To measure performance on the second behavioral objective, the evaluator constructs items such as

$$427 \qquad 632 \qquad 43$$
$$\times\,32 \qquad \times\,929 \qquad \times\,6$$

Notice that it is essential to phrase statements of behavioral objectives in terms of some specific thing the student can do after being exposed to the curriculum, program, product, materials, etc., in order for the performance on the objective to be measurable. Behavioral objectives are not things for the teacher to do (e.g., show the students how to multiply three-digit numbers). Behavioral objectives cannot be stated as vague internalized abilities students theoretically possess, such as "understand the multiplication of numbers," because these phenomena are not easily measured.

The Taxonomies of Educational Objectives

The taxonomies of educational objectives developed by Bloom and others represent an attempt to provide a scheme for classifying behavioral objectives in the field of education. The scheme is in some ways similar to the classification of life forms in biology. Taxonomies were developed for behavioral objectives in three domains: cognitive, affective, and psychomotor. The most commonly used taxonomies are presented in the *Taxonomy of Educational Objectives: The Classification of Educational Goals. Handbook 1. Cognitive Domain* (Bloom, 1956), and *Handbook 2. Affective Domain* (Krathwohl, Bloom, & Masia, 1964). The classifications of objectives in these taxonomies can be used with behavioral objectives from any content area.

Taxonomy of Cognitive Objectives The taxonomy for the cognitive domain includes objectives having to do with thinking, knowing, and problem solving. Objectives in the cognitive domain are classified from simple to complex. The categories of objectives are hierarchical in nature. Each category is assumed to involve behavior that is more complex and abstract than the previous category and is, in turn, broken down into subcategories that are again ordered by complexity. A listing of the major and minor categories of the taxonomy of objectives in the cognitive domain follows (Bloom et al., 1956, pp. 201–207).

1.00 Knowledge
  Remembering specific pieces of information is emphasized.
 1.10 Knowledge of Specifics
 1.11 Knowledge of Terminology
 1.12 Knowledge of Specific Facts
 1.20 Knowledge of Ways and Means of Dealing with Specifics
 1.21 Knowledge of Conventions
 1.22 Knowledge of Trends and Sequences
 1.23 Knowledge of Classifications and Categories
 1.24 Knowledge of Criteria
 1.25 Knowledge of Methodology
 1.30 Knowledge of the Universals and Abstractions in a Field
 1.31 Knowledge of Principles and Generalizations
 1.32 Knowledge of Theories and Structures
 2.00 Comprehension
  The ability to use the information that is known, but not relating it to other knowledge or material in order to understand its full implications, is emphasized here. This might be called a very low level of understanding.
 2.10 Translation
 2.20 Interpretation
 2.30 Extrapolation
 3.00 Application

The use of abstractions such as general methods, ideas, rules, principles, or theories in actual specific situations

4.00 Analysis

Material is broken down into its various parts, and the relationships or hierarchy among the parts is made clear. This should facilitate communication of the organization and effects of ideas.

4.10 Analysis of Elements
4.20 Analysis of Relations
4.30 Analysis of Organizational Principles
5.00 Synthesis

Parts are put together to form a meaningful whole in a way that is not evident when the parts are considered separately.

5.10 Production of a Unique Communication
5.20 Production of a Plan or Proposed Set of Operations
5.30 Derivation of a Set of Abstract Relations
6.00 Evaluation

Judgments regarding how well materials and methods serve purposes as established by comparison with standard criteria

6.10 Judgments in Terms of Internal Evidence
6.20 Judgments in Terms of External Criteria

Taxonomy of Affective Objectives　The hierarchical principles organizing the affective taxonomy of educational objectives (Krathwohl et al., 1964) were more difficult to determine than were the cognitive taxonomy. In the affective domain, objectives deal with attitudes, values, interests, and appreciation. The taxonomy is restricted to positive or desirable outcomes of the educational process and does not include deviant or maladaptive behaviors. Objectives in the affective domain are arranged from receiving (attending) at the lowest level to characterization by a value or value concept at the highest level, as follows (pp. 176–185):

1.0 Receiving (Attending)

Awareness of, or sensitivity to, stimuli or characteristics of the environment and willingness to attend them

1.1 Awareness
1.2 Willingness to Receive
1.3 Controlled or Selected Attention

2.0 Responding

Contains an element of motivation so that the learner responds by attending more actively. This is the beginning of interest.

2.1 Acquiescence in Responding
2.2 Willingness to Respond
2.3 Satisfaction in Response

3.0 Valuing

A sense of worth or value is attached to an object, idea, phenomenon, or behavior as a function of the person's own internalized experiences and assessments and society's values.

3.1 Acceptance of a Value

3.2 Preference for a Value

3.3 Commitment

4.0 Organization

Values are organized or structured so that they can be called upon as appropriate in different situations.

4.1 Conceptualization of a Value

4.2 Organization of a Value System

5.0 Characterization by a Value or Value Complex

A consistent and dependable value structure which characterizes an individual and aids in developing a philosophy of life

5.1 Generalized Set

5.2 Characterization

Using the Taxonomies of Educational Objectives

The taxonomies are useful to the evaluator of programs and products in a number of ways. First, the taxonomies focus on behavior. Thus the emphasis in these taxonomies is in the proper place for evaluation purposes. Precise statements of behavioral objectives provide the basis for measuring and judging the worth of phenomena.

The taxonomies of educational objectives encourage consideration of a wider array of objectives than might otherwise be considered. Those using the taxonomy are more likely to include more complex objectives (e.g., application of principles) than to overemphasize the recall of factual material. At the same time, the affective consequences can be systematically brought into the process of evaluation. The importance of affective concerns such as student interest can hardly be overemphasized. In using the affective taxonomy, one is encouraged to consider the entire range of affect from awareness through characterization by a value complex. The outcomes of this process of specification of behavioral objectives are (1) more precise descriptions of objectives and (2) precise definitions of what is supposed to occur so that performance on these objectives can be measured.

Construction of Evaluation Instruments

The taxonomies of educational objectives are useful in another way. In stating objectives, a content-by-objectives grid may be constructed. An example of such a grid is presented in Figure 13-1 for the individualized junior high school course in general science mentioned earlier. Only four content areas (the universe and solar system, atomic theory, electricity and magnetism, and weather and erosion) are included in the chart, although additional content areas would obviously be included in the course. The six categories of the taxonomy make up the rows of this chart, though only a portion of them might be used in many courses. Each of the cells of this content-by-objectives grid becomes a specific

	Content			
Objectives of Instructions	Area I The universe and solar system	Area II Atomic theory	Area III Electricity and magnetism	Area IV etc. Weather and erosion
I. Knowledge				
Specifics				
Ways and means of dealing with specifics				
Universals and abstractions				
II. Comprehension				
Translation				
Interpretation				
Extrapolation				
III. Application				
IV. Analysis				
Elements				
Relations				
Principles				
V. Synthesis				
Unique communication				
Plan or set of operations				
Derivation of abstract relations				
VI. Evaluation				
Internal evidence				
External criteria				

FIGURE 13-1
Content-by-objectives grid.

area in which behavioral objectives can be stated. The degree of importance for objectives in the cells of the grid is determined by those designing the program. The cell at the intersection of knowledge of specifics and the universe and solar system might contain the following behavioral objective:

The student can recall the names of the nine planets in our solar system.

At the intersection of comprehension (interpretation) and atomic theory, the following objective might be found:

The student can state the atomic number of an element when given the number of protons and neutrons in the nucleus.

In the cell at the intersection of application and electricity and magnetism, the following behavioral objective might be found:

The student can construct a simple electrical circuit.

These objectives, in the way they are stated, are useful to the evaluator because they suggest how they might be measured.

In selecting an evaluation instrument for the measurement of performance, the content-by-objectives grid allows for the comparison of an available test with the behavioral objectives that have been stated for the course. If a suitable instrument is not found, one may be developed from the behavioral objectives included in the grid. With the Tyler-Bloom evaluation approach, any and all methods of measuring performance on the objectives can be considered. Most often, achievement tests are of the paper-and-pencil type (e.g., matching, multiple choice, completion, essay). Items are included in the test based on a sampling scheme that allows for representation of the cells in the grid proportionate to the emphasis placed on them. (Chapter 9 includes a more thorough description of various types of tests and the construction of items.)

Once an adequate test has been constructed, it is pilot-tested on a sample of subjects, and the items are refined and modified accordingly (see Chapter 9 for a brief description of item-analysis procedures). The revised and refined test can then be used for the evaluation of the program. A total score for the test, as well as part scores in content areas and specific items, can be obtained. These scores are then analyzed to determine strengths and weaknesses for particular educational objectives or content areas. Weak spots in the program can thus be identified and strengthened.

In the evaluation of an individualized junior high school science program, the evaluator would work closely with the course developers to obtain statements of the objectives and content to be covered. A final version of the objectives-by-content grid would emerge that contains only those objectives deemed appropriate for the course, including the full list of content areas. Behavioral objectives would be carefully stated and items developed to measure their attainment. These items would collectively constitute an achievement test for the course. Alternatively, several achievement tests could be designed that correspond to the major portions of the course. The course would be tried out, using a portion of the students in the school district. At the appropriate time, the course could be evaluated by administering the achievement test or tests. From the scores on the tests, the overall success or failure of the course could be determined and students' grades could be assigned as well. The average test score for the students and average scores for each objective or content area can also be determined. Responses to individual items allow for the pinpointing of particular weaknesses in the program.

FORMATIVE AND SUMMATIVE EVALUATION

A distinction between two types of evaluation, formative and summative, was proposed by Scriven (1967). Scriven distinguished between the goals and the roles of evaluation. He pointed out that at the methodological level, the purpose of evaluation is to judge the worth of a process or product. Thus, in terms of the stated goals, questions such as "How well does this curriculum perform?" "What merits or drawbacks does this program have?" or "Is the use of this product worth what it is costing?" may be asked. However, the roles of evaluation may be broader. One role has to do with the process of program development. In this regard, evaluation may seek answers to specific questions about a program as it is being developed. For example, some questions raised in this context might be "Is the curriculum too difficult for the students?" and "Does it take too long to make a particular point?" If meaningful feedback can be provided during the development of a curriculum or product, revisions can be made in the material prior to its completion. This is the formative role of evaluation, and so it is called *formative evaluation*. A second role for evaluation is to provide decision makers with information about whether to use the final form of the product or program. This is more closely related to what we considered in the discussion of the Tyler-Bloom model and is known as *summative evaluation*.

Formative evaluation, which Scriven used in connection with curriculum improvements, is regarded by Bloom, Hastings, and Madaus (1971) as applicable also to improving the processes of curriculum development, teaching, and student learning. To do a successful job of formative evaluation, the evaluator must (1) develop the most useful evidence, (2) report the evidence well, and (3) be objective.

Bloom et al. contrast formative evaluation with what they call *diagnostic* and *summative evaluation*. Diagnostic evaluation, when performed prior to instruction, has as its primary function the placement of students at the proper starting point within a particular instructional program. It may suggest that a student should proceed to more advanced work, or it may suggest remedial work. Diagnostic evaluation is sometimes performed during a course of instruction as well, in order to determine the reasons for repeated deficiencies in a student's learning that have not responded to remedial instruction. Summative evaluation, on the other hand, as in Scriven's description, occurs after all or much of the course has been given. In a summative evaluation, a judgment is made about the student, teacher, and/or program regarding effectiveness.

A single program evaluation may well involve all three types. Diagnostic evaluation, when applied to a program or course of study, would be used for initial student placement and the identification of individual problems. Formative evaluation would occur during the course to allow for the improvement of the course itself, the teaching of the course, or the performance of students taking the course. Summative evaluation would occur at the end or after the completion of the major portions of the program to allow for judgments about the effectiveness of the program, instructional methods, and student performance.

To convey a better idea of the Bloom, Hastings, and Madaus concepts of formative evaluation, we now return to the individualized science course. These authors view formative evaluation within a particular instructional model. They assume that most of the students, those of average or high science aptitude, are capable of learning the material with proper instructional programming; and, of course, those students with below-average or poor science aptitude will experience more difficulty. If all students received an equal amount of instruction, the resulting achievement-test scores should be distributed over a wide range. The majority of students would score close to some middle point, with a few students scoring very well or very poorly. However, if students can be provided with appropriate methods and enough time for learning in areas they find difficult, it is hypothesized that they will (except in a small minority of the cases) achieve mastery of the material. This is a simplified description of the mastery learning model described by Bloom (1968).

Formative as well as diagnostic evaluation holds a very important place within the mastery learning model. Diagnostic tests are given at the beginning of the science course to determine whether students have the requisite skills for the course and to determine their starting point. During the course, diagnostic examinations are also used to identify specific learning difficulties. In implementing the formative evaluation, the science course is broken down into a number of logical units. For each unit of the course, a content-by-behavior grid similar to that shown in Figure 13-1 is constructed. Specification of the elements within the grid reflects the instructional emphases of the unit. Items are constructed to measure the behavioral objectives in the same way they were constructed for the achievement test described earlier. These items are put together to form unit examinations, or *formative examinations*.

The formative examinations are administered after the completion of each instructional unit. When mastery is indicated by the test score, the student progresses to the next instructional unit. When mastery is not indicated, prescriptions for additional study are determined from the particular items missed. After some further instruction in the problem areas, the student again takes the formative examination (or, more likely, a parallel or similar form of it), and the process is repeated until mastery of that unit is achieved. Upon passing the formative examinations over a block of units, the student is able to take the summative examination for that block and, ultimately, for the entire science course. Results on the formative examinations can be used to determine modifications that may be needed in the program.

The mastery learning approach to instruction has become more and more popular since it was proposed in the late 1960s (Guskey, 1985). Applications of formative evaluation to many instructional areas are included in Bloom, Hastings, and Madaus (1971). Although we have emphasized applications dealing with school curriculum, the formative, summative, and diagnostic approaches to evaluation can be applied to a variety of programs and projects.

STUFFLEBEAM'S MODEL: CIPP

The model proposed by Stufflebeam (1970) in the Phi Delta Kappa National Study Committee on Evaluation report entitled *Educational Evaluation and Decision Making* and Stufflebeam et al. (1971) does not discount many of the activities involved in the Tyler-Bloom approach or the formative and summative evaluation ideas described in the preceding section. Rather, the model is more comprehensive and includes, as well, activities that might not be considered *evaluation* in the strict sense of the term. According to Stufflebeam, the evaluator performs an active role in furnishing information to the decision makers responsible for educational program or product development. Stufflebeam's definition of *evaluation* includes but goes beyond our original notion of evaluation as judging the worth of a product. To Stufflebeam, educational evaluation is "the process of delineating, obtaining, and providing useful information for judging decision alternatives" (Stufflebeam et al., p. 40).

The Stufflebeam model, conceptualized as an aid to decision making, is the ongoing cyclical process depicted in Figure 13-2. In the upper diagram, the cyclical process of decision making, leading to program activities that are evaluated and that allow additional decisions, etc., is depicted. The lower diagram depicts the activities carried out by the evaluator, including delineating, obtaining, and providing information. The delineation and provision of information are activities which require close collaboration with the decision maker. The obtaining of information is a technical activity largely executed by the evaluator. The size of the task of providing information is closely related to the decision making required.

The types of educational decisions with which the evaluator is concerned

FIGURE 13-2
The relationship of evaluation to decision making. (From Stufflebeam, Foley, D. L., Gephart, W. L., Guba, E. J., Hammond, R. L., Merriman, H. O., & Provus, M. M. (1971). *Educational evaluation and decision making.* Itasca, IL: F. E. Peacock, p. 216. Reproduced by permission of Phi Delta Kappa, Inc.)

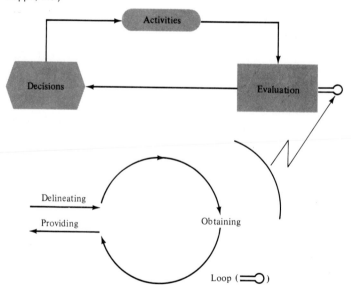

are depicted in Table 13-1. For each type of decision, a corresponding type of evaluation is listed. It is because of these four types of evaluation (context, input, process, and product) that the Stufflebeam model is referred to as the CIPP model. Here, context and input evaluation reflect the intentions of the program, whereas process and product evaluation reflect the actual program accomplishments. Furthermore, the input and process evaluations concern the means to reach project goals, and the context and product evaluations involve the goals (or ends) themselves.

Context Evaluation

Context evaluation concerns the environment of the program being evaluated. In a context evaluation, the existing and desired conditions of the program setting are studied. Unmet needs and problems that prevent needs from being met are identified. This information contributes to decisions regarding what must be done in the program. Therefore, the context evaluation will take place before the project is defined and will contribute to the decisions regarding the formulation of the project.

Input Evaluation

Input evaluation is instituted once the project objectives have been identified. Its purpose is to obtain information about how to utilize available resources to achieve the stated objectives. Thus capabilities are studied. Possible strategies for achieving the objectives are identified, and procedures for implementing the strategies are prepared. On the basis of information provided by the input evaluation, the method of attaining the objectives is determined.

Process Evaluation

Process evaluation provides information to persons who are responsible for operation of the project. It provides a basis for correcting procedural difficul-

TABLE 13-1
TYPES OF DECISIONS AND CORRESPONDING TYPES OF
EVALUATION

Decisions	Evaluation
Planning decisions to determine objectives	Context
Structuring decisions to design procedures	Input
Implementing decisions to foster operational utilization, improvement, and control of the products	Process
Recycling decisions to respond to accomplishments and progress	Product

ties, keeps the administrators informed about progress, and provides a continuous record of the project.

Product Evaluation

Product evaluation is performed during and at the end of a project cycle. In product evaluation, the degree to which the project attained the objectives established for it is studied. Thus the attainments of the project are compared to predetermined standards in order to make decisions regarding the total program. For example, on the basis of product evaluation, a school administrator may decide to scrap an innovative program that was being tried in one school or to expand the program to several schools.

Design and Application of the CIPP Model

The structure of an evaluation design for any of the four types of evaluation consists of six major parts. These are (1) focusing the evaluation, (2) collecting the information, (3) organizing the information, (4) analyzing the information, (5) reporting the information, and (6) administering the evaluation. To illustrate the use of the CIPP evaluation model, consider again the evaluation of a junior high science course. The evaluator would work closely with the developers of the science course and aid them in making planning, recycling, structuring, and implementing decisions. The decision makers might be faced with some of the questions that follow:

Planning decision	What science skills do the students in the district typically bring with them into the science course?
Structuring decision	What is the best approach to familiarizing the students with the computerized portions of individualized instruction?
Implementing decision	Are the particular instructional sequences employed in the computerized versions of various course units effective?
Recycling decision	Are the instructional objectives met for the various portions of the course?

According to Stufflebeam's six steps, the focus of the evaluation must be determined; the information collected, organized, analyzed, and reported; and the evaluation administered.

As an example, consider the evaluator providing information on the first question listed above concerning the skills that students in the district typically bring with them into a science course. The focus of the information is to allow the course developers to identify the starting points for each instructional unit. The evaluator determines that a standardized achievement test in the science area is adequate for the purpose. A random sample of 100 students in the school district is selected and the test administered to this sample by classroom teachers. The tests are sent back to the central office and average scores tabulated in a number of subareas of science achievement. A report summarizing these average scores is prepared and given to the course developers.

USING COMPARATIVE STUDIES

In the experimental and quasi-experimental designs discussed in Chapter 4, effects of treatments were determined by comparing observations obtained under one set of conditions to observations made under other conditions. Therefore, this type of study is called *comparative*. Evaluations that use the comparative approach are usually quasi-experimental because of the lack of opportunity for random assignment to treatments and the unavailability of control groups (Rossi & Freeman, 1985). Quasi-experimentation has evolved considerably in terms of how it is applied in evaluation. For example, there is a growing realization of the importance of human judgment in interpreting evaluation data, the need for multiple perspectives, the significance of means and processes as well as outcomes, and the importance of the underlying social science and behavioral theory of a program or project (Bickman, 1987; Trochim, 1986).

Some Problems with Comparative Studies

Comparative studies have much to recommend them in selecting among alternative forms of instruction. However, there are problems in conducting such studies and interpreting the results. Several difficulties with the use of comparative studies are illustrated through the example of the study of modern versus traditional mathematics instruction.

The first problem is largely a measurement problem. Consider three possible measuring instruments for measuring mathematics achievement, the dependent variable in the study. Test A has items dealing with the conceptual understanding of mathematical principles, test B is composed largely of computational items in which quick and accurate elementary mathematical computations are emphasized, and test C is a standardized mathematics achievement test regularly administered in the school where the study is being conducted. The average scores for the two instructional groups on these measures are given in Table 13-2. If the study is run using test A, which emphasizes an understanding of principles, we expect the students instructed under the modern mathematics approach to do better than the students instructed by the traditional method. However, if we measure performance on test B, which emphasizes computational skills, we expect the traditional mathematics group to perform better. Thus the choice of measures influences the results of our study. The problem can be even more severe when one of the available standardized tests is used. The outcome when such a test is used is indicated by the two question marks in Table 13-2. The relative performances of the two groups varies here with the choice of standardized tests. Tests that emphasize

TABLE 13-2
EXPECTED MATHEMATICS ACHIEVEMENT SCORES ON
THREE TESTS

	Group	
Test	**Modern math**	**Traditional math**
Principles	Higher	Lower
Computation	Lower	Higher
Standardized	?	?

computation favor the traditional mathematics group, and tests that emphasize conceptual understanding of principles favor the modern mathematics group. Standardized tests that include a mixture of theoretical and computational items or items of an entirely different nature, such as problems requiring application of trigonometric principles, may give mixed results.

In comparative studies, the selection of the measure of performance is one determinant of the outcome of the study. Thus the evaluator needs to understand what is measured by the test chosen for the study. In selecting the appropriate test an evaluator has at least two alternatives. The first is to use a test that has separate measures of a number of aspects of achievement (e.g., scales that measure each of several levels of objectives from the taxonomies of objectives) and to compare the average performance of the groups on each of these variables (see Chapter 7 for a brief introduction to procedures for doing this). Using this approach, differences (e.g., the modern mathematics group performs better on the test of principles, but the traditional mathematics group performs better on the computation test) can be identified. The alternative is to decide in advance which particular objectives should be met by the program based on either stated overall program objectives or what the evaluator or others feel the objectives should be. Thus, in the example of mathematics instruction, the school personnel responsible for the study might decide that understanding mathematics is not nearly as important as the ability to balance one's checkbook and might opt for a test emphasizing computational skills. Obviously, a careful determination of the *appropriate* measure of performance is difficult in many situations.

A second problem with the comparison approach to evaluation arises because of the need for careful definition of the instructional methods to be used for each group. Narrowly defined treatments present a problem in comparative studies. Often, the instructor is encouraged to improvise solutions for problems that arise using alternate materials, etc., which thus changes the nature of the treatment. On the other hand, if the instructor stays within the boundaries of a narrowly defined instructional situation, the resulting artificiality may seriously limit the quality of the results.

A third problem with this approach arises in assigning students to the treatment groups. The ideal situation from a research-design point of view would be one in which the evaluator can draw a random sample from a well-defined population of students, form treatment groups through random assignment, and randomly assign treatments to groups. In practice, the evaluator may study only the students in a single school or school district (perhaps a single classroom). Thus the population that can be studied is often very restricted. To further complicate matters, students are grouped by classrooms, and classrooms are grouped into schools. The evaluator cannot often change these groupings to suit a study. This makes dealing with intact groups of students necessary, and the initial equivalence of treatment groups is therefore open to question. In a small study, where only a few classrooms are assigned to each treatment, the generalization of results to additional classrooms is questionable. If a large number of classrooms is used, the evaluator can consider the classroom as the experimental unit and randomly assign classrooms to treatments. The statistical procedures for handling a problem of this type are somewhat advanced for the present text, however (see Hays, 1981; Reichardt & Gollob, 1986).

Before we leave this discussion of problems with comparison-group evaluations, it should be stressed that other methods suffer from these same problems and that well-designed comparison-group methods may be more powerful and less subject to these problems than other methods. Furthermore, there is an additional problem area in most evaluation which we will mention here. Evaluation studies are usually performed with specified groups under conditions that may very well be unique. Therefore, results of such studies cannot necessarily be generalized to other settings and groups.

Some Advantages of Comparative Studies

Now that we have discussed some of the problems with the comparison-group approach to evaluation, let us look at some advantages of the approach. First, if the study is designed well, there is a gain in experimental precision and, hence, internal validity. Second, there is the increased opportunity for educational decision makers to make rational choices regarding educational programs and products when information from comparative studies can be coupled with cost data. Third, in many, if not most, evaluation studies there is at least an implied comparison group. This is important because of the need to have some standard against which to judge performance. Even though an achievement test has been constructed to measure performance of behavioral objectives, responses to items on the test do not reveal achievement in the absolute sense. The evaluator must rely on experience—his or her own or that of others—to determine the level of response that represents mastery of an objective. In forming judgments about the level that constitutes mastery, the evaluator refers to a hypothetical group of students. In this sense, there is an implied comparison group added to the single-group evaluation design. From a strict experimental-design point of view, we would say that the control group should be a formal part of the experiment. However, most evaluators would not argue for conjuring up alternative treatment groups to allow for comparison methods if the information needed for evaluation can be obtained using a single-group procedure.

Let us turn to an example of an individualized science course. The main question to be answered by a comparative study might be whether the new individualized science course, with its slightly higher cost per student, should be used in the school district. In order to obtain information to facilitate making a decision, students are to be assigned to two groups: the science course as it has been taught and the science course with the new individualized approach. Since classrooms of students are to remain intact during the study, the classroom is considered the experimental unit (the smallest unit to which the treatments can be applied). Random assignment of students to classrooms is desirable but, for various reasons, impractical. Thus four science classrooms are chosen from each of a number of randomly selected schools in the district. At each school, two classes are randomly assigned to each type of course. All this random assignment seems complicated, but it is necessary to allow for the theoretical equating of groups through randomization. Appropriate measures of success are chosen as dependent variables. Perhaps scores are computed for several levels of objectives from the cognitive taxonomy. Measures of affective objectives are also included. Then, using rather sophisticated statistical procedures, the performances of students in the two courses can be compared using these several outcome measures. When combined with cost information, the results of these comparisons may allow administrators and teachers to make a rational decision regarding the full-scale implementation of the course.

QUALITATIVE APPROACHES TO EVALUATION

Qualitative approaches to evaluation include a broad range of methods designed to uncover important aspects of a program that are not easily quantifiable. Distinguishing between quality and quantity will help clarify how the two approaches contribute differently to an evaluation. *Quality* refers to the character, nature, and meaning of something; *quantity* addresses only the amount of something. Consider the evaluation of a training session. One could report attendance figures and the pre- and posttest scores of the participants and call it an evaluation of sorts. On the other hand, one could add considerably to the evaluation if the interest level and enthusiasm of the participants could be established. For example, photographs were used with other kinds of information (e.g., interviews and observations recorded in notes) by Covert and Stahlman (1984) to evaluate a professional conference. This approach permitted the evaluators to capture much of the flavor of the conference in their report. Issues like low attendance at sessions on the last day, fatigue in meetings held later in the day, and the enthusiasm with which opportunities were taken for informal get-togethers at meals and in the hotel lobby could be documented with photographs and vignettes and integrated with more traditional data (e.g., participants' ratings of satisfaction with the sessions) to enable the evaluators to provide a much more complete picture of the conference.

Much of the methodology of qualitative evaluation comes from ethnology and anthropology (Britan, 1981; Van Maanen, Dabbs, & Faulkner, 1982). These approaches emphasize the social and environmental contexts of an evaluation. Methods used in such approaches might include participant observation; content analysis of materials and other documents related to the program; in-depth interviews; and systematic study of the historical, economic, cultural, and other antecedents to the program. An illustration of such an evaluation was provided by Britan in regard to a project designed by a professional group to stimulate law-related educational programs in elementary schools. A traditional evaluation determined that most of what had been planned was being done. However, a qualitative evaluation determined that quality was lacking in the program and that the vagueness of the goals and of the leadership led to different objectives for involvement in the program at different locations. Because of a lack of central focus, it was impossible to determine whether the initiatives taken by the participants were due to the program or to other influences. A completely quantitative orientation would not have been as effective in revealing these shortcomings. Qualitative analysis is considered a powerful tool of the evaluator.

JUDGING THE ADEQUACY OF AN EVALUATION

It might appear from the past discussion that part of the judgment of how useful an evaluation is depends upon the method of evaluation employed. However, it cannot be said that one method is better than another without knowing the context. Moreover, because of the context of an evaluation and the questions being asked, an evaluator may alter one of the well-known methods to suit the needs of a situation. For that reason, we cannot rely upon the conceptual model of the evaluation to ensure its adequacy.

Several authors have presented criteria for judging the adequacy of evaluation studies (see, for example, Gephart, Ingle, and Remstad, 1967; Scriven, 1974). *Meta-evaluation* is the term used for the evaluation of an evaluation. A generally accepted set of standards is required to evaluate evaluations. Perhaps the most comprehensive standards for determining the quality of an evaluation were developed by a joint committee composed of representatives from a dozen professional organizations in the fields of psychology, curriculum development, teaching, and related areas.* The committee proposed 30 stan-

---

* The committee was composed of representatives from the American Association of School Administrators, American Educational Research Association, American Federation of Teachers, American Personnel and Guidance Association, American Psychological Association, Association for Supervision and Curriculum Development, Council for American Private Education, Education Commission of the States, National Association of Elementary School Principals, National Council on Measurement in Education, National Education Association, and National School Boards Association.

dards in the areas of utility, feasibility, propriety, and accuracy (Joint Committee on Standards for Educational Evaluation, 1981). These standards are summarized below.

A Utility

The utility standards deal with the degree to which the evaluation provides useful information to those for whom it was prepared.

1 *Audience Identification.* The audience for whom the evaluation is intended should be explicitly identified.

2 *Evaluator Credibility.* Evaluation should be conducted by persons who are competent and trustworthy.

3 *Information Scope and Selection.* The information selected and collected should be capable of answering the questions adequately in terms of the needs and perspectives of the intended audience.

4 *Valuational Interpretation.* The values, perspectives, procedures, and rationales for interpreting data should be clear so that the bases for making judgments are known.

5 *Report Clarity.* The report should be written so that the intended audience can understand it.

6 *Report Dissemination.* Dissemination of the report should be made to all persons who have a right or a need to know the results of the evaluation.

7 *Report Timeliness.* Reports should be made in a timely manner.

8 *Evaluation Impact.* The plan and implementation of the evaluation should permit and encourage the audience to take action as a result of it.

B Feasibility

Standards in the feasibility group deal with prudent and effective use of resources and appropriateness within the context in which the evaluation is done.

9 *Practical Procedures.* Procedures should be practical so that disruption to participants is minimal.

10 *Political Viability.* The evaluation plan should anticipate the various crosscurrents from opinion and interest groups within the context of the entity being evaluated, and the evaluation should be conducted so as to minimize the effects of these influences on the outcome.

11 *Cost-effectiveness.* Costs of the evaluation should be justified by the information it produces.

C Propriety

The standards under propriety have to do with the protection of the welfare, privacy, and rights of the persons involved in the evaluation and the ethical and legal concerns common in all settings involving human subjects (see Chapter 11).

12 *Formal Obligation.* All parties should agree in writing to what is being done, when, how, and by whom.

13 *Conflicts of interest.* Potential conflicts of interest should be recognized and dealt with openly and honestly.

14 *Full and Frank Disclosure*. Evaluation reports should be honest and open in the portrayal of the evaluation and its findings.

15 *Public's Right to Know*. All information that can ethically and legally be made available to the public should be.

16 *Rights of Human Subjects*. The rights and welfare of human subjects should be protected.

17 *Human Interactions*. Persons involved in the evaluation should be treated with respect and dignity.

18 *Balanced Reporting*. The evaluation should be balanced in its recognition of both strengths and weaknesses.

19 *Fiscal Responsibility*. Expenditures and budget for the evaluation should be prudent and handled ethically and in accordance with accepted accounting procedures.

D Accuracy

The evaluation should produce accurate and dependable information that reflects the true value and merit of the entity being evaluated.

20 *Object Information*. The program, project, or other entity being evaluated should be viewed in sufficient detail to permit clear identification and description.

21 *Context Analysis*. The environment and context of the evaluation should be described in sufficient detail to enable identification of contextual influences affecting the evaluation and the entity being evaluated.

22 *Described Purposes and Procedures*. Evaluation purposes and procedures should be recorded and described.

23 *Defensible Information Sources*. The origins of the information obtained in the evaluation should be described in sufficient detail so that the adequacy of the information can be assessed.

24 *Valid Measurement*. Measurement instruments should be valid for the purposes and contexts in which they are used.

25 *Reliable Measurement*. Measurement instruments should be valid for the purposes and contexts in which they are used.

26 *Systematic Data Control*. Care should be taken in collecting, processing, and reporting data so as to minimize the possibility of error.

27 *Analysis of Quantitative Information*. Quantitative data analyses should be proper, thorough, and systematic so as to provide clear and defendable interpretations.

28 *Analysis of Qualitative Information*. The analysis of qualitative information should be so proper, thorough, and systematic as to provide clear and defensible interpretations.

29 *Justified Conclusions*. Conclusions should be justified by the data and the analyses.

30 *Objective Reporting*. Procedures should be included in the evaluation to insure that the final report does not reflect the biases of any of the participants or any special-interest or pressure groups.

OTHER ISSUES IN EVALUATION

Although there are many other important issues in evaluation, the following deserve some special attention in this chapter.

Comparison of Goals and Needs

In our discussion of evaluation, we recognized the importance of obtaining clear, precise statements of goals in solving the problem of determining what to measure in a meaningful evaluation. However, in considering the process of stating goals, we paid scant attention to identifying them. Determination of the worth of the goals stated for a project is an evaluation activity of considerable importance. A program or product may well meet the goals stated for it and yet be worthless. For example, consider the folly of instituting an expensive accelerated reading course in an inner-city school where 80 percent of the students read substantially below grade level. Clearly, the need of the school is in the area of remedial reading, and yet the solution provided is for advanced readers. An important part of evaluation is thus a consideration of the congruence between the *needs* of the target group and the *goals* of the program or product.

Internal versus External Evaluation

The issue of the degree of congruence between needs of the group and the goals of the program or product leads us to another consideration. Should the evaluation of an educational program or product be done by an internal or external individual or team? The internal evaluator, as part of the staff, is familiar with the developmental efforts, is in a position to conduct meaningful formative evaluation and aid in decision making. This type of evaluator is familiar with the program or product to the extent that he or she may do a better job of designing measurement instruments, drawing an appropriate sample, etc. However, the internal evaluator may be unable to separate him or herself from the production effort and may, perhaps unconsciously, have an emotional investment in the project goals and products that detracts from his or her objectivity.

The outside evaluator, on the other hand, is not part of the program staff and therefore is not as familiar with the program or product and the developmental process. Also, he or she has little opportunity to do formative evaluation or help in everyday decision making. But the outside evaluator is often in a better position to be objective about the adequacy of the program or product goals, since he or she is not necessarily personally committed to them. Thus he or she can approach the situation slightly differently, realizing that the project staff will have stated goals and that the internal evaluation, if there is one, will be concerned with the degree to which those goals are met. Though concerned with this issue, the outside evaluator focuses on the broader question of the congruence of goals and needs. To do this, he or she may conduct thorough and comprehensive studies of needs and judge the goals and outcomes against the needs which are identified.

Should an internal or external evaluation be conducted? For a developmental project of any substantial scale, both types probably should be conducted so that the strengths of both approaches may be utilized.

Cost-Benefit Analysis

The worth of programs or products in terms of the costs and benefits is seldom, if ever, adequately assessed in educational evaluations. Instruction in the intricacies of cost studies or cost-benefit analysis is not included in the training of most educational researchers and evaluators. The nearest approximations to cost studies are strict dollar calculations relative to production cost for educational program and product development. Benefits are determined merely by the average number of items correct on an achievement test or the increase in the average number of items correct under a new program as compared to an old one. Neither the determination of costs or benefits under these schemes is adequate for educational decision making. On the cost side, things such as capital (e.g., equipment) costs (including the interest which would accrue on money not put into capital expenditures), opportunity costs (costs associated with eliminating alternative opportunities by spending money for the product development), and so forth need to be considered. Benefits, such as affective consequences, side effects (which are properly classified as costs when negative), societal consequences, and so forth need to be considered.

One of the major obstacles to benefit-cost evaluation is the problem of assigning value to measures and observations relevant to an evaluation study (Thompson, 1980; Thompson, Rothrock, Strain, & Palmer, 1981). For example, how does one attach monetary value to a high school student's change of attitude towards smoking? First, there is the problem of establishing the meaning of a change in attitude. The calibration of that change into monetary units is the second difficulty. Cost-effectiveness, another approach, does not require reducing everything to a common monetary value (Rossi & Freeman, 1985). In this approach, the effectiveness of programs with similar goals and objectives can be determined by comparing costs.

The importance of costs in any program cannot be overstated. Without the necessary funds, the best-designed projects will not be done. In an era of limited funding for educational and social programs, costs become an important item of study. Cost-effectiveness and benefit-cost analysis procedures for evaluation have developed considerably in recent years. It is probably safe to assume that this field will continue to develop as an important aspect of evaluation studies.

Politics of Evaluation

Political concerns are an integral element of every evaluation and can originate from a variety of levels and sources. Consider the example of a project to evaluate three alcoholic-treatment programs with the aim of selecting one to be funded by the state agency for human resources. The program with the best record in treating chronic alcoholism will get a lucrative contract to provide services for an established number of referrals from the state agency. The state agency will pay all counseling fees for the cases they refer. There is naturally an element of competition among the programs participating in the evaluation. All three programs provide counseling services to alcoholics, but program F specializes in treating family units, program H works primarily with individuals, and program A emphasizes the treatment of adolescent alcohol abusers. Obviously, each of the programs has an interest in determining the criteria of the evaluation (F would like family services emphasized, A would like the evaluation to focus on services for adolescent clients, etc.). Add to this pressure on the evaluator the pressure from several state legislators, each interested in seeing a contract funded by the state go to the program located in his or her district. At the same time, politics among the workers within each program to gain influence and compete for resources contributes to the political crosscurrents with which the evaluator must be prepared to deal.

Evaluators generally expect to have to deal with legitimate political interests as part of the overall setting of an evaluation. Of greater concern are political efforts to influence the evaluation unethically. For example, the director of a project might intimate to the evaluator that awarding the project's evaluation contract for the following year might be dependent on a favorable report for the present year. Another example would be the client who tells the evaluator at the start what the results will be at the end or who changes the data and interpretations after the final report is submitted. Brickell (1978) makes a number of practical suggestions for dealing with political influences in evaluation settings.

Evaluations done in the public-policy area often face the problem of divergent goals. On the one hand, the evaluator tries to formulate an evaluation that will be used by the audience to affect policy. The audience, in this case, might be legislators on the state or federal levels. On the other hand, legislators are generally trying to represent points of view that they believe are consistent with the wishes and common good of the majority of their constituents. In other words, politicians may genuinely want the best information from an evaluation, but the best information is useless to them if it does not support their unique needs and point of view. Chelmski (1987) takes the position that in order to do evaluation in this kind of environment, an evaluator must be able to translate legislative needs and political imperatives into evaluation questions and procedures and then translate the findings back into policy and political terms so that the results are useful.

Evaluators who choose to ignore the realities of the political context are going to find it difficult to produce useful evaluations. Their reports and recommendations will not be valued by their audiences. This is because the results are not provided in ways and forms that can be used within the political context in which the audience must work. One of the most important skills an evaluator can develop is that of structuring an evaluation to make it useful within the political context without compromising the integrity of the design or the findings.

Dissemination of Evaluation Results

The main point to be made about dissemination is that the evaluator's job has only begun with the production of a final report written in technical language and placed on a shelf to gather dust. The evaluator should, unless legally or ethically constrained for some reason, consider the various audiences for which the information may be useful and prepare materials accordingly. For each of these audiences, the results should be presented in a readable, understandable, and accessible form. For one audience, this may mean presenting the results at professional meetings, publishing them in scholarly journals, or entering comprehensive reports in the ERIC system. For other audiences, the dissemination of results may include giving formal presentations to school boards, informal presentations at PTA meetings, and so forth. The important point here is that relevant and accurate information should be made available to persons who need it, and providing this information is often the responsibility of the evaluator.

SUMMARY

It may seem as if evaluation is one of the great frontiers in education and the behavioral sciences, and it probably is. The field is expanding rapidly. The decade between 1975 and 1985 saw much growth in evaluation, including the establishment of a professional association (the American Evaluation Association), the development of standards for evaluation by the Joint Committee on Standards for Educational Evaluation (1981; Rossi, 1982), an emerging philosophy of evaluation (House, 1983), and numerous new methodologies and approaches (e.g., data envelopment analysis, program theory, adversary evaluation, etc.).

An evaluator has to be prepared to use theoretical foundations from such diverse fields as social change, economics, psychology, systems theory, political science, management, statistics, anthropology, sociology, and education, sometimes in a single evaluation. This is because evaluation must be tailored to the questions and needs of the setting. As evaluation becomes more sophisticated, so do the problems it addresses. Evaluation is emerging as a major area of expenditure in the policy-related and applied research of government, education, and human services agencies (Rossi & Freeman, 1985). *Evaluation* was initially defined as "judging the worth of an educational process or product." However, as we discussed several alternative evaluation models, a broader definition was required, particularly when we considered alternative roles of evaluation.

The Tyler-Bloom evaluation model was considered first. It involved the careful determination of content and objectives for a curriculum and the precise statement of behavioral objectives. Instruments were designed to measure performance in terms of these behavioral objectives, and the worth of the program could be determined from the responses on such devices. The cognitive and affective taxonomies of educational objectives were considered as valuable guides in choosing and stating objectives. Next, Scriven's distinction between formative and summative evaluation was discussed. *Formative evaluation* is the use of systematic evaluation in program construction, teaching, and learning in order to improve these processes. Summative evaluation occurs after the use of much or all of an educational process or product in order to make a judgment about its worth. The notions of formative and summative evaluation as they apply to the mastery learning model were discussed.

Stufflebeam's CIPP evaluation model was also presented. In this model, the role of the evaluator is that of an aid to decision makers. Four basic types of evaluation are conducted: context, input, process, and product (whence the acronym CIPP). Context evaluation provides information for planning decisions, input evaluation provides information for structuring decisions, process evaluation provides information for implementing decisions, and product evaluation provides information for recycling decisions. The structure for any of these four types of CIPP evaluation consists of the following parts: focusing the evaluation, collection of information, organization of information, analysis of information, reporting of information, and administration of the evaluation.

The use of comparative studies in evaluation was considered. The difficulty in determining the relevant measure of the dependent variable was discussed, as well as the tendency of this selection to influence the results of the comparative study. The problems of defining the treatments and problems associated with the nature of student grouping into classroom, school, and district were considered. The conclusion was reached that for some purposes (e.g., where choosing among alternatives is required), comparative studies are useful. However, the artificial creation of alternative groups for comparison studies in cases where single-group evaluation studies can serve the purpose was deemed unnecessary. In addition, qualitative approaches to evaluation, such as ethnographic studies, content analyses, and other approaches that emphasize the qualitative rather than the quantitative aspects of a program were discussed. Thirty standards for educational evaluations developed by the Joint Committee on Standards for Educational Evaluation were presented. These standards fall into the categories of utility, feasibility, propriety, and accuracy. Other topics covered were comparisons of needs and goals, internal versus external evaluation, cost-benefit analysis, the politics of evaluation, and the dissemination of evaluation results.

In some respects, a high-quality evaluation study may be more difficult to do than a good theory-oriented or basic research study. This is true for a number of reasons. First, most evaluation studies are done in a field where the researcher has little control over many of the environmental conditions. Second, there is usually political or environmental pressure for a particular result. Third, good evaluation requires that a variety of methods and perspectives be used. Often, this kind of effort has not been properly anticipated in the program budget. Further, this kind of multiplicity of views and techniques often stretches the research training and capabilities of the person designated as evaluator. As our understanding of evaluation grows, the importance of training evaluators in a variety of methods will become clearer.

PROBLEMS FOR THOUGHT AND DISCUSSION

1 Write behavioral objectives for each of the following programs, and tell how attainment of the objective can be assessed.
a A basic high school algebra program
b Self-assertiveness training offered by a psychology clinic
c Vocational rehabilitation training provided to parolees from a state penal institution.
2 A private philanthrophic organization wants to fund a music education program for preschool children who are being raised in orphanages or foster homes.
a Discuss the evaluation of such a program, using the Bloom approach and formative and summative evaluation.
b Consider the evaluation of the program using the CIPP model.
c Would the Bloom approach provide information that the CIPP model would not? Explain your answer.
d What kinds of information would be more likely to be provided by a CIPP approach than by Bloom's approach? Explain your answer.
3 An evaluator is asked to assess the effectiveness of a program designed to alleviate the adjustment problems of convicted felons who return to society after completing their time in prison. The program provides for vocational training, counseling for emotional problems, help in locating a place to live, and also a social center in the community for rehabilitated former convicts.
a Develop an evaluation of the program, using an experimental design.
b Discuss appropriate criterion measures.
c Discuss how the evaluation might be strengthened by addition of a qualitative aspect to the evaluation.
4 You are asked to design an evaluation of the teacher education program at your college. What would be the advantages and disadvantages of choosing each of the following evaluation approaches?
a Cost-benefit
b Comparative groups
c Formative-summative
d Qualitative

REFERENCES

Auvenshine, C. D., & Mason, E. J. (1982). Needs assessment in planning rehabilitation services. *Journal of Rehabilitation Administration, 6,* 56–62.

Bickman, L. (1987). The unctions of program theory. In Bickman, L. (Ed.), *Using program theory in evaluation.* San Francisco: Jossey-Bass.

Bloom, B. S. (Ed.) (1956). *Taxonomy of educational objectives. Handbook I: Cognitive domain.* New York: McKay.

Bloom, B. S. (1968). Learning for mastery. *Evaluation Comment, 1* (2), 1–12.

Bloom, B. S., Hastings, J. T., & Madaus, G. F. (1971). *Handbook on formative and summative evaluation of student learning.* New York: McGraw-Hill.

Brickell, H. M. (1978). The influence of external political factors on the role and methodology of evaluation. In Cook, T. D., Del Rosario, M. L., Hennigan, K. M., Mark, M. M., & Trochim, W. M. K., (Eds.), *Evaluation studies review annual* (vol. 3). Beverly Hills, CA: Sage.

Britan, G. M. (1981). Contextual evaluation: An ethnographic approach to program assessment. In Conner, R. F. (Ed.), *Methodological advances in evaluation research.* Beverly Hills, CA: Sage.

Chelmski, E. (1987). The politics of program evaluation. In Cordray, D. S., Bloom, H. S., & Light, R. (Eds.), *Evaluation practice in review.* San Francisco: Jossey-Bass.

Covert, R. W., & Stahlman, J. I. (1984). *Evaluation '83. Reinventing the wheel: An evaluation of an evaluation conference.* Unpublished manuscript. Charlottesville: University of Virginia Evaluation Research Center, School of Education.

Gephart, W. J., Ingle, R. B., & Remstad, R. C. (1967). A framework for evaluating comparative studies. In Cody, H. (Ed.), *Conference on research in music education.* U.S. Office of Education Cooperative Research Report no. 6-1388.

Guskey, T. (1985). *Implementing mastery learning.* Belmont, CA: Wadsworth.

Hays, W. L. (1981). *Statistics* (3rd ed.). New York: Holt.

House, E. R. (1983). *Philosophy of evaluation.* San Francisco: Jossey-Bass.

Joint Committee on Standards for Educational Evaluation (1981). *Standards for the evaluation of programs, projects, and materials.* New York: McGraw-Hill.

Krathwohl, D. R., Bloom, B. S., & Masia, B. B. (1964). *Taxonomy of educational objectives. Handbook II: Affective domain.* New York: McKay.

Levin, H. (1987). Cost-benefit and cost-effectiveness analyses. In Cordray, D. S., Bloom, H. S., and Light, R. J. (Eds.), *Evaluation practice in review.* San Francisco: Jossey-Bass.

Nevo, D. (1983). The conceptualization of educational evaluation: An analytic review of the literature. *Review of Educational Research, 53,* 117–128.

Reichardt, C. S., & Gollob, H. F. (1986). In Trochim, W. M. K. (Ed.), *Advances in quasi-experimental design and analysis.* San Francisco: Jossey-Bass.

Rossi, P. H. (Ed.), (1982). *Standards for evaluation practice.* San Francisco: Jossey-Bass.

Rossi, P. H., & Freeman, H. E. (1985). *Evaluation: A systematic approach.* Beverly Hills, CA: Sage.

Scriven, M. (1967). The methodology of evaluation. In Stake, R. E. (Ed.), *Curriculum evaluation.* American Educational Research Association Monograph 1. Chicago: Rand McNally.

Scriven, M. (1974). Standards for the evaluation of educational programs and products. In Borich, G. D. (Ed.), *Evaluating educational programs and products.* Englewood Cliffs, NJ: Educational Technology Publications.

Stufflebeam, D. L. (June 24, 1970). *An introduction to the PDK book—Educational evaluation and decision making.* Address delivered at the eleventh annual PDK Symposium on Educational Research. Columbus: Ohio State University.

Stufflebeam, D. L., Foley, W. J., Gephart, W. J., Guba, E. G., Hammond, R. L., Merriman, H. O., & Provus, M. M. (1971). *Educational evaluation and decision-making in education.* Itasca, IL: Peacock.

Thompson, M. S. (1980). *Benefit-cost analysis for program evaluation.* Beverly Hills, CA: Sage.

Thompson, M. S., Rothrock, J. K., Strain, R., & Palmer, R. H. (1981). Cost analysis for program evaluation. In Conner, R. F. (Ed.), *Methodological advances in evaluation research*. Beverly Hills, CA: Sage.

Trochim, W. M. K. (1986). Editor's notes. In Trochim, W. M. K. (Ed.), *Advances in quasi-experimental design and analysis*. San Francisco: Jossey-Bass.

Tyler, R. W. (1942). General statement on evaluation. *Journal of Education Research*, *35*, 492–501

Tyler, R. W. (1969). *Basic principles of curriculum and instruction*. Chicago: University of Chicago Press.

Van Maanen, J., Dabbs, J. M., & Faulkner, R. R. (Eds.) (1982). *Varieties of qualitative research*. Beverly Hills, CA: Sage.

Worthen, B. R., & Sanders, J. R. (1987). *Educational evaluation: Alternative approaches and practical guidelines*. New York: Longmans.

SUPPLEMENTARY READINGS

Arnstein, J., II. (1975). The outcome. *Phi Delta Kappan, 57*, 188–190.

Borich, G. D. (Ed.) (1974). *Evaluating educational programs and products*. Englewood Cliffs, NJ: Educational Technology.

Cronbach, L. J. (1982). *Designing evaluations of educational and social programs*. San Francisco: Jossey-Bass.

Kaufman, R., & Thomas, S. (1980). *Evaluation without fear*. New York: New Viewpoints.

Palumbo, D. (Ed.) (1987). *The politics of program evaluation*. Beverly Hills, CA: Sage.

Provus, M. (1971). *Discrepancy evaluation*. Berkeley, CA: McCutchan.

Wergin, J. F. (1976). The evaluation of organizational policy making: A political model. *Review of Educational Research, 46*, 75–115.

Wolf, R. (1975). Trial by jury: A new evaluation method. *Phi Delta Kappan, 57*, 185–187.

CHAPTER 14

SOME PERSPECTIVES ON RESEARCH AND REALITY

Up to this point, we have discussed research in education and the behavioral sciences extensively. However, we have not yet considered the place of research within the larger world of reality. Over the years, researchers have come to believe that the social context of research is probably as important as anything else in determining what will be investigated, using which methods, and by whom.

In this chapter, we will consider the environmental context of research in education and the behavioral sciences. We will look at the role of relevance in research, governmental influences, and the scope of activities which fall under the term "research." We shall also speculate on the future of research.

RELEVANCE

Research that is relevant has immediate utility, practicality, and relationship to the real, everyday problems of society. Many nonresearchers think good research is relevant to the issues and problems facing modern society. On the other hand, scientists sometimes feel that research design and procedures suffer when an attempt at relevance is made. They contrast "laboratory" research, in which the variables are highly controlled and contrived, to "field" research, in which variables are studied as they exist and the researcher exercises little or no control over them. With the decrease in control, the results become more difficult to interpret. This can be illustrated using two hypothetical examples of research to improve preschool children's verbal ability. The first, a laboratory study, utilizes a social learning paradigm (see Bandura,

1986, for an explanation of social learning) that hypothesizes that children who observe highly verbal peers will become more verbal. Preschool children are randomly assigned to see a film showing highly verbal children playing together with blocks or to see a film showing children playing with blocks who do not speak to one another. The two groups are then compared, using a specially prepared test of verbal ability. The second is a field study in which it is hypothesized that preschool children who are placed in a class with highly verbal preschool children will become more verbal themselves. Children are randomly assigned to a class of verbal children or a less verbal class, and the two groups of children are compared on the test of verbal ability.

The same problem is investigated in the two studies. However, as the researcher moves from the laboratory to the classroom, a considerable amount of control is sacrificed. In the laboratory study, the researcher did not have to be concerned with things such as social cliques among the children who were serving as models, the role of the teacher in the classroom, and the kinds of structure provided for group activities. Any of these variables, as well as several others, could influence the results of the field study and, consequently, must be considered when interpreting the results. Yet it is precisely these intruding influences that make the field study more relevant.

Uri Bronfenbrenner, the well-known social psychologist, addressed the problem of relevance of research (Bronfenbrenner, 1976) and suggested, as a solution, what he called the *ecological perspective*. This perspective requires observations of more than mere behavior in research investigations. The influences present in the environment must be considered simultaneously with the observations that are made. Moreover, when an experiment is replicated in a new setting, any differences recorded should be viewed in the context of the difference between the settings.

Bronfenbrenner's ecological model should not be mistaken for field research. Nor was Bronfenbrenner rejecting controlled laboratory experimentation in pursuit of knowledge about human development and behavior. Rather, he was concerned with the traditional similarity of these two approaches in that behavior is observed and reported with minimal consideration of the contexts in which it occurred. Bronfenbrenner's admonition to consider research data in ecological perspective is something that should be given careful consideration by the research community. Evaluation seems more comfortable considering contexts rather than other forms of inquiry in the behavioral sciences and education at the present time (Worthen & Sanders, 1987).

THE EXPECTATIONS OF SOCIETY

In the United States, nearly everyone has had experience with the educational system and may consequently feel that he or she is an expert on education. This attitude has affected educational research because people expect that educational research will produce findings that are immediately understandable by the general public and are applicable to everyday problems. What is not generally understood is the complexity of behavioral science phenomena, particularly as they apply in education. Thus on the one hand, there is a public that sees deficiencies in areas such as reading and mathematics and wants research to find ways of alleviating these problems. On the other hand, the same public does not understand the complexities of the problems and sometimes demands solutions prematurely. This situation is not peculiar to education and the behavioral sciences. Medicine, engineering, and the physical sciences are all victims of this need to have social problems solved immediately.

In an environment where the public wants answers now, the politics of research are played. Politicians usually try to represent their constituencies so that they can remain in favor the next time the electors go to the polls. Thus politicians tend to favor support for research designed to produce short-term benefits or to tackle current issues of concern. They tend not to favor research that will take years and perhaps produce long-term benefits which will not be appreciated fully for generations. One of the more blatant examples of political power attempting to influence research was the "Golden Fleece" of Senator Proxmire (Van den Berghe, 1979). To further complicate the issue of support for research, international contexts and pressures, personal greed, national priorities, and other influences all have their effect. Arthur E. Wise (1976) described the politics which affected the formation and early years of operation of the now defunct National Institute of Education (NIE). This agency was originally chartered to support development of systematic, generalizable knowledge in education. In his article, Wise quoted from a letter written by Daniel Patrick Moynihan to the *Wall Street Journal* which pretty well described the situation we are discussing here. Moynihan wrote of his testimony before Congress, "One Congressman, very junior, had asserted something to the effect that my people need answers now! I had answered, in effect, that they weren't going to get them because nobody had them" (p. 63). The successor to NIE, the Office of Educational Research and Improvement, has been no less subject to political influence and public impatience (Finn, 1988; Shavelson & Berliner, 1988; Bennett, 1987).

Support for research in this country tends to follow fads that arise from social and economic pressure rather than from theoretical or conceptual scientific breakthroughs. Further, the influence of popular opinion and the general public upon research funding through representative government is great. All this is raised to support the argument presented by Start (1975) and others (e.g., Krathwohl, 1974) that researchers must become more sophisticated about the world in which they live. They must better understand the social context in which educational and behavioral science research is conducted. Furthermore, they must recognize the daily stresses that result in problems crying out for immediate attention. For example, no moratorium on crime occurs while behavioral researchers put together a theory of penal practice, and children continue not to learn to read and write while educational researchers work out a solution to these problems. Thus, after facing its problems all day long, society is in more of a mood to support the frantic search for solutions than to wait patiently for good theory to be developed. The point here is not that applied research is better or worse than theoretical research; rather, that one kind of research is being emphasized at the expense of another. That both have a place should be better recognized.

The experimental psychologist William Bevan (1976) suggested that behavioral scientists and scientists in general have an obligation to understand society at the same time that society must come to a better understanding of science. Bevan placed some of the responsibility for upgrading society's understanding of science on the educational establishment. At the same time, he suggested that behavioral scientists develop greater appreciation of the applied needs of society. Bevan's admonitions have even broader implications with the increasing role of technology and scientific innovation affecting all aspects of modern life (Naisbett, 1982).

THE SCOPE OF THE RESEARCH ENTERPRISE

The scope of the research effort in behavioral and social areas is vast. Research in education alone spans the fields of anthropology, psychology, sociology, management sciences, medicine, nutrition, economics, neuropsychology, psychopharmocology, and other disciplines. Traxler (1954), reviewing educational research at the midpoint of the twentieth century, identified three fields of research which were being emphasized at that time. They were (1) the humanities, including the social foundations of education; (2) organization, administration, and legal aspects; and (3) human learning and development. Traxler felt that the third area was receiving the greatest amount of attention at midcentury.

Since midcentury, very few changes have taken place in terms of the major areas of research in education. However, the conduct of research investigations, the sophistication of the methods, and the kinds of questions that are investigated have changed somewhat. In the past two or three decades, researchers have become more sophisticated about the logic and quantitative methods of research. More recently, qualitative methods are being incorporated with increasing frequency. Moreover, the number of settings in which the scientific research approach is applied have multiplied. Research methods are currently brought to bear upon practical and applied questions to a far greater extent than was previously the case. Furthermore, the multidisciplinary approach to the solution of research problems has become more dominant over the years. This has resulted in less isolation among the sciences and more cooperation among disciplines to develop solutions to problems. Nevertheless, even greater interdisciplinary cooperation seems desirable for increased understanding of phenomena in the behavioral sciences and education.

Trends in Research

Early research in education largely emphasized the philosophical approach. Edward L. Thorndike's work represented an early attempt at empiricism in educational and psychological research (e.g., Thorndike, 1917). In their book titled *The Psychology of Reading,* Gibson and Levin (1975) refer to the period from 1920 to 1960 as a time of "curriculum research," which produced no knowledge that could be usefully applied to the understanding of reading. During this period, researchers were scurrying about comparing the results of one method of teaching reading with another, caring little about the more important questions of what reading is or how it is learned. What Gibson and Levin described in the field of reading was happening in other educational and behavioral research fields as well.

In addition to the "curriculum research" character of the activities of the 1920s to the 1960s, researchers were relatively naive about quantitative methods and research design. For example, as late as the 1960s, it was reported that less than half the doctoral programs in education in 76 institutions in the United States that were sampled offered a course in experimental design (Krathwohl, 1965).

Until 1956, educational research was virtually unfunded by the federal government. In 1956, the U.S. Office of Education funded the Cooperative Research Program at a level of $1 million. The program had been expanded to $11.5 million by 1964 (Tyler, 1965). The amount available for educational research was further increased in 1965 with the funding of the Elementary and Secondary Education Act of 1965, which, among other things, provided funds for research in education. The increase in funding produced a serious personnel shortage of educational researchers, which had an effect on the graduate training programs. With a ready market for graduates, colleges and universities were inclined to improve their programs in research, statistics, measurement, and evaluation.

During this period of increased activity in the training of researchers, government funding agencies were moving towards an emphasis upon program-oriented research and curriculum development (Stanley, 1967). Also during this period, the number of agencies active in educational and behavioral science research increased drastically. In addition to the United States Department of Education, the National Science Foundation (NSF) began to become interested in curriculum innovation in science and mathematics, and the National Institute of Mental Health (NIMH) funded a variety of behavioral science research programs and provided money for training students. Other governmental agencies are also heavily committed to supporting research and program development in education and the behavioral sciences. For example, the Office of Child Development (OCD), National Institutes of Health (NIH), Bureau of Indian Affairs (BIA), and Bureau of Prisons (BP) all provide for research on educational and behavioral problems. The National Institute of Education (NIE), which we mentioned earlier, established in 1972 specifically to support research in education has been replaced by the Office of Education Research Innovation (OERI). Thus funding for research in these areas since 1956 had increased geometrically to the point where the current annual total budget for educational and behavioral science and related research in the United States reaches into the billions of dollars.

Research and Development

It has been suggested that the increased money for educational research came at a time when the field was not ready for it. The money fostered an attitude that any recognized problems could be solved (Howe, 1976). This attitude is nowhere more evident than in the research and development (R&D) movement.

During the 1960s, USOE provided funding for research and development centers that were charged with focusing on a problem area once it had been identified. There have been varying numbers of R&D centers in operation over the years, depending upon the funding situation. For example, the Learning Research and Development Center (LRDC) was established at the University of Pittsburgh to study methods of developing educational innovations. The center located at the University of Wisconsin was dedicated to development of methods that would enhance cognitive learning in educational settings. The center at the University of Texas focused on teacher education. Other centers have emphasized administration, social psychological aspects of education, career education, vocational education, and educational policy making, among other areas.

In addition to R&D centers, Regional Educational Laboratories (REL) were developed to focus on regional problems relating to education. Over the years, funding for the regional laboratories has been reduced, and, consequently, the scope and focus of problems considered by the RELs changed somewhat over their first decade of existence. At one time, there were as many as 20 regional laboratories, but this number has since been reduced considerably.

The R&D movement represented an important development for educational and behavioral science researchers. That is, a middle position was established between theory-oriented research activities and the application of research findings to practical problems in education (Travers, 1983). Snelbecker (1974) suggested the importance of an intermediate position which he called "psycho-educational design" to bridge the gap between theory-oriented psychological research and the more applied problems of the classroom. The R&D centers and regional laboratories emphasized the use of basic knowledge and theory to design and test educational materials, procedures, and methods.

SPECULATIONS FOR THE FUTURE

Speculation about the future of educational and behavioral science research must take into account the fact that these fields, as they are presently constituted, will probably change considerably as a result of advances in knowledge and theory. It has been suggested, for example, that there really is no field of educational research (Cronbach and Suppes, 1969; Howe, 1976). Rather, there is basic research in the disciplines of psychology, sociology, anthropology, and biology that contributes to the solution of problems in education. Further, the development of theories applicable in education must emanate from the other disciplines. Educational research, on the other hand, may become a highly specialized decision-oriented field. It is also possible that the decision-oriented, fact-oriented research of the past may have been useful in the short term but will not provide long-term understanding of the questions facing educators regarding the teaching and learning processes. The development of long-term solutions requires theory-oriented research. The dynamic growth of interest in policy studies and evaluation in education seems to support this position.

Multidisciplinary Cooperation

Research in the behavioral sciences and education is becoming increasingly multidisciplinary. As the different sciences become aware of the complexity of the variables that they investigate, they seek the expertise of other disciplines. Years ago, Tyler (1965) noted an increase in multidisciplinary research in education. This idea has been reinforced more recently by Howe (1976). Furthermore, Bronfenbrenner's (1976) notion of ecological validity, in which the environmental setting and external influences on a research investigation are considered in the interpretation of the findings, is supportive of the multidisciplinary point of view. That is, to thoroughly understand the environment in which a research investigation occurs, the skills of several disciplines may be required.

Along with multidisciplinary cooperation, behavioral research appears to be turning less rigidly empirical. To use the concepts of Royce (1974), which were discussed in Chapter 1, educational researchers, psychologists, and others who do research in behavioral phenomena will probably come to accept the notion that there may be types of knowledge which are metaphorical or rational as well as empirical. Thus educators, who to date have had problems in defining empirically such variables as achievement and learning style, will begin to find additional perspectives, including qualitative ones, to help them investigate these complex issues.

Research and Change

Educational and behavioral science researchers will probably experience continued difficulty in getting their findings recognized and accepted in the future (Eisner, 1984, Baker, 1984). This is because these findings concern values, habits, and customs. Society does not change its ways immediately when an important finding is reported in the professional literature. People, agencies, institutions, and organizations become set in their ways and, consequently, have a strong tendency to resist change that is not superficial. The natural, physical, medical, and biological sciences do not seem to experience this problem to the same degree. For example, if a new theory of instruction were developed that would revolutionize education, require teachers and administrators to be retrained and school buildings to be rebuilt, and the evidence provided in support of the theory was so substantial that little argument could be made against it, there would still be traditional schools for some time. In a way, this is not a bad characteristic for it protects society from change that seems attractive but would be harmful in the long run.

Computers and Research

Probably one of the most important advances for researchers investigating behavioral science and educational problems has been the computer. High-speed digital computers have been and will continue to be used to process large amounts of data rapidly. Computers have facilitated the formulation and utilization of data banks for research. Also, computers have enabled sophisticated statistical processing of data to take place. In addition, computers have been used for simulation studies; control of experimental situations, including presentation of stimuli and recording of responses; analysis of complex behavior, such as voice, brain wave, and eye movements; and storage of data. Further, more complex and precise measurement of multiple variables can be simultaneously achieved with computer technology. These functions were discussed more completely in Chapter 10. It is safe to assume that the utilization of computers in research will continue to expand in the future to an even greater extent.

Cross-Cultural Perspective

With an increased awareness of the effects of environment on research, there will probably be an increase in research in different cultures and settings. The rationale for this movement will be that findings replicated in different settings will be more dependable than findings demonstrated in only one environmental setting. The International Project on the Evaluation of Educational Achievement, in which characteristics and school achievement of random samples of students from several countries are studied, represents an effort towards this kind of research. Recently, the importance of cross-cultural perspectives in research has received emphasis from organizations with a multicultural or cross-cultural perspective, such as UNESCO, the East-West Center, and the International Association of Cross-Cultural Psychology. International competition and the global nature of world markets have made international and multicultural perspectives in education more important. As this trend continues, more research will be needed in this area. In addition, the cultural complexity of a pluralistic society increases the need for multilingual and multicultural understanding and thus adds more impetus to research in education and culture.

Measurement Methods

The techniques of measurement used in the behavioral sciences and education have not changed radically in the past half century. However, recent innovations in criterion-referenced assessment using behavioral objectives, the concept of mastery, and some novel methods of scaling and calibrating of tests have been suggested that may lead to significant changes in how measuring is done in the behavioral sciences and education. Computerized testing is being combined with advances in scaling techniques (e.g., latent traits, discussed in Chapter 8) to produce innovative possibilities for measurement and testing, such as adaptive testing, performance assessment with realistic simulations (e.g., pilot training with a simulator), and unobtrusive curriculum embedded assessment. As researchers become familiar with these techniques, more sophisticated studies of learning and knowledge acquisition will become possible.

Research in the area of validity has lagged considerably. This is largely due to the relationship between what is known about a construct and the way it is measured. This, the major problem in behavioral and educational assessment, will therefore not be solved until more is known about the constructs considered in these areas. Perhaps Bereiter (1965) was alluding to this when he said that improvement in educational research must wait until the educational field itself improves. Paradoxically, this knowledge may be difficult to come by with the inadequate measuring instruments and techniques currently available, although it is expected that noteworthy advances in the measurement field will have a powerful effect upon research of the future.

CONCLUSION

We have toured educational and behavioral science research intensively in the chapters of this text. We hope that you see the field as dynamic, expanding, interesting, and diverse in scope, method, and purpose. Moreover, we hope that you appreciate better its importance. In view of what mankind has been able to learn about the world through investigation of the natural, physical, and biological sciences, the only way to describe current understanding of human behavior, learning, and instruction is to say that it is at the genesis stage. As society becomes more complex, understanding society and its people becomes increasingly important.

We have tried to present more than merely the methods of research. The quality of knowledge produced by different kinds of research strategies and techniques has been emphasized as well. The reader is encouraged to continue to recognize these qualitative aspects of knowledge as he or she continues to develop professionally. The reader is also cautioned to be wary of simple or obvious solutions. If there is anything that should be obvious from past behavioral science and educational research, it is the need for a healthy respect for the complexity of human behavior and the elusiveness of fact.

SUMMARY

Research exists in a social context larger than the laboratory. It is impelled or frustrated by the needs and pressures of society. Although field studies may seem to make research more relevant, complex natural settings also make results more difficult to interpret. However, the expectations of society for research to provide answers to questions tends to make field research more attractive than theory-oriented research.

National funding for research is highly political and sensitive to pressures in society. To protect their interests, educational and behavioral science researchers must be sensitive to the needs and pressures within society. Furthermore, they should take responsibility for educating the public about what they do and the importance of it.

Research in education and the behavioral sciences is a vast enterprise, involving billions of dollars annually. This support for research has come about only in the past few decades. A large part of this support is for research and development. For example, R&D laboratories and centers were established around the country to work on applied problems in education by the U.S. Office of Education.

In the future, behavioral science and educational researchers will probably address themselves more directly to policy issues and the complex environmental influences in which research findings occur. Research will probably be increasingly qualitative and multidisciplinary and will involve computers and other technological advances. Furthermore, measurement of the variables studied will improve with knowledge about those variables. Finally, an increasingly cross-cultural perspective will be evident in future research.

REFERENCES

Baker, E. L. (1984). Can educational research inform educational practice? Yes! *Phi Delta Kappan, 65,* 453–455.

Bandura, A. (1986). *Social foundations of thought and action.* Englewood Cliffs, NJ: Prentice-Hall.

Bennett, W. J. (March 18, 1987). The nation's report card. Statement by U.S. Secretary of Education, Horace Mann Learning Center. U.S. Dept. of Education.

Bereiter, C. (1965). Issues and dilemmas in developing training programs for educational researchers. In Guba, E., and Elam, S. (Eds.), *The training and nature of educational researchers.* Bloomington, IN.: Phi Delta Kappa.

Bevan, W. (1976). The sound of the wind that's blowing. *American Psychologist, 31,* 481–491.

Bronfenbrenner, U. (April 1976). *The ecology of education.* Paper presented at the annual meeting of the American Educational Research Association. San Francisco.

Cronbach, L. J., & Suppes, P. (1969). *Research for tomorrow's schools.* New York: Macmillan.

Eisner, E. W. (1984). Can educational research inform educational practice? *Phi Delta Kappan, 65,* 447–452.

Finn, C. E. (1988). What ails educational research. *Educational Researcher, 17* (1) 5–8.

Gibson, E. J., & Levin, H. (1975). *The psychology of reading*. Cambridge, MA: M.I.T.

Howe, H. (1976). Education research—The promise and the problem. *Educational Researcher, 5*(6), 2–7.

Krathwohl, D. R. (1965). Current formal patterns of educating empirically oriented researchers and methodologists. In Guba, E., and Elam, S. (Eds.), *The training and nature of educational researchers*. Bloomington, IN: Phi Delta Kappa.

Krathwohl, D. R. (1974). An analysis of the perceived ineffectiveness of educational research and some recommendations. *Educational Psychologist, 11*, 73–86.

Naisbett, J. (1982). *Megatrends: Ten new directions transforming our lives*. New York: Warner.

Shavelson, R. J., & Berliner, D. C. (1988). Erosion of the education research infrastructure: A reply to Finn. *Educational Researcher, 17* (1), 9–12.

Snelbecker, E. G. (1974). *Learning theory, instructional theory, and psychoeducational design*. New York: University Press of America.

Stanley, J. C. (1967). On improving certain aspects of educational experimentation. In Stanley, J. C. (Ed.), *Improving experimental design and statistical analysis*. Chicago: Rand McNally.

Start, K. B. (1975). Reality for the researcher. *American Educational Research Journal, 12*, 323–336.

Thorndike, E. L. (1917). Reading as reasoning: A study of mistakes in paragraph reading. *Journal of Educational Psychology, 8*, 323–332.

Travers, R. M. W. (1983). *How research has changed American schools: A history from 1840 to the present*. Kalamazoo, MI: Mythos Press.

Traxler, A. E. (1954). Some comments on educational research at midcentury. *Journal of Educational Research, 47*, 359–366.

Tyler, R. W. (1965). The field of educational research. In Guba, E., and Elam, S. (Eds.), *The training and nature of educational researchers*. Bloomington, IN: Phi Delta Kappa.

Van den Berghe, P. (1979). Tarts, seagulls, and Senator Proxmire: The politics of obscurantism. *Academe, 66*, 424–426. (There are two sides. See also Senator Proxmire's reply on pages 426–428 of the same issue of *Academe*.)

Wise, A. E. (1976). The taming of the National Institute of Education: A personal view. *Educational Researcher, 58*, 62–65.

Worthen, B. R., & Sanders, J. R. (1987). *Educational evaluation: Alternative approaches and practical guidelines*. New York: Longmans.

SUPPLEMENTARY READINGS

Gage, N. L. (1981). *Hard gains in the soft sciences: The case of pedagogy*. Bloomington, IN: Phi Delta Kappa.

Jacob, E. (1987). Qualitative research traditions: A review. *Review of Educational Research, 57*, 1–50.

Jensen, A. E. (1984). Political ideologies and educational research. *Phi Delta Kappan, 65*, 460–462.

McCall, R. B. (1988). Science and the press: Like oil and water. *American Psychologist, 43*, 87–94.

Park, R. L. (1986). The muzzling of American science. *Academe, 72* (5), 19–23.

Tobias, S. (1985). New directions for educational psychologists. *Educational Psychologist, 20*, 96–101.

What works: Research about teaching and learning (1986). U. S. Department of Education.

GLOSSARY OF TERMS

action research investigation designed to facilitate change in real settings.

algorithm system of steps to follow in solving a mathematical problem.

alternative hypothesis the possibility or possibilities not suggested in the null hypothesis; often postulates differences among population groups.

analysis of variance a statistical technique for testing null hypotheses based on partitioning variance into systematic and error components.

ANOVA analysis of variance.

applied research investigations that search for solutions to practical problems.

a priori probability the theoretical probability that an event will occur. It is equal to the number of times the event occurs in a set of possible outcomes divided by the total number of outcomes in the set.

basic research research oriented towards development of theory.

case study investigates the condition or status of a person or group and is designed to increase understanding as it exists in real-life settings.

central limit theorem a mathematical theorem which states that in a population of mean μ and variance σ^2, as sample size increases, the distribution of sample means over repeated samples of size n approaches a normal distribution, with mean μ and variance σ^2/n.

central tendency statistic a single value, such as the mean, median, or mode, which represents the "typical" score in a set of scores.

cluster sampling selection of clusters of elements to study from a population of clusters.

compiler a computer program that translates symbols from a user-oriented computer language to machine language for processing by a computer.

computer an electronic machine that can perform simple operations extremely rapidly and accurately.

computer program a set of instructions to a computer.

concurrent validity the degree to which test performance can reflect a criterion that exists presently.

construct a concept devised to facilitate scientific research and explanation.

construct validity the extent to which a test measures a construct.

content validity the ability of a test or measure to reflect or represent a universe of content.

control group subjects in a research study that do not receive the experimental treatment whose performance or traits are compared to subjects who do receive the treatment.

correlation index that summarizes relationships between variables.

correlational research investigation of relationships among variables.

criterion-related validity predictive or concurrent validity.

cross-sectional research different age or developmental groups studied at the same time to investigate trends.

debugging finding the errors in a computer program and correcting them.

deduction reasoning from the general to the particular.

dependent variables variables upon which the measurements of effects are made in a research study.

descriptive research describes existing or past situations or phenomena.

descriptive statistics statistics used to summarize data.

effect difference between group mean and grand mean in analysis of variance (see also: interaction effect).

empirical probability probability of an event determined on the basis of the number of times the event has been observed divided by the total number of outcomes observed.

error score the component of an observed score due to random fluctuation.

evaluation process of obtaining information for use in judging the adequacy or effectiveness of an individual, event, product, objective, or program.

experimental group group that receives the treatment in an experiment.

experimental research studies in which the researcher has control over treatment conditions and extraneous influences.

ex post facto research investigation using data that have been collected in the past or investigation of past events.

external validity the degree to which the results of research may be generalized to a wider group than the sample studied.

factor classification variable or independent variable in analysis of variance; underlying variable identified in factor analysis.

factor analysis statistical procedure for identifying variables that have common aspects or that overlap.

factor loadings correlations of variables with factors in a factor analysis.

formative evaluation evaluation of a product or program while it is being developed to optimize the quality of the final product or program.

historical research collection and interpretation of data from the past.

hypothesis a tentative declarative statement about the relationship between two or more variables.

independent variables variables manipulated by the researcher or hypothesized to contribute to observed effects.

induction reasoning from the specific to the general.

inferential statistics statistics used to characterize populations with estimates based on sample data.

interaction effect analysis-of-variance effect due to influences of two or more factors in combination.

internal validity the degree to which an experimental or treatment combination rather than uncontrolled influences is responsible for observed treatment effects.

interval scales measurement scales having the properties of nominal and ordinal scales, and additionally the intervals between consecutive points on the scale are equally spaced.

intervening variables variables that contaminate or obscure the effects in an experiment.

latent trait scaling method of scaling a test based on underlying trait identified through statistical analysis.

law a statement about a relationship between two or more variables that has an extremely high probability of confirmation by observation and that is not contrary to known facts.

longitudinal research studying trends in the same group over a period of time.

main effects analysis-of-variance effects due to a single factor.

mastery level of achievement based on attainment of objectives.

mean the arithmetic average of a list of scores.

measurement assigning numbers to objects or events according to rules.

median the point on a scale above and below which are 50 percent of the scores in a list.

meta-analysis study of effect size across several studies.

meta-evaluation evaluation of an evaluation.

mode most frequently occurring score in a list.

model a representation of abstract ideas in real terms.

nominal scale measurement scale in which numbers are used as names of categories.

null hypothesis the proposition of no differences or no relationships in a population.

objective tests tests that can be scored relatively free of scorer bias and interpretation.

observed score the score obtained on a test.

ordinal scale measurement scale that indicates relative amount or rank-order of a trait or characteristic.

parameter characteristic of population.

phenomenon fact or event which can be observed.

policy study research to support policy planning or decision making.

predictive validity the degree to which performance on a test can predict a criterion in the future.

preexperimental designs research designs that use only one group or two predetermined groups for comparisons.

problem a research question about conditions or relationships among or between variables.

projective tests tests that contain unstructured stimuli which are used to elicit responses reflecting an individual's inner feelings, beliefs, values, and personality.

quasi-experimental design research plan that has some but not all the validity features of an experimental design.

random sample a sample in which each member of a population has an equal probability of being chosen for inclusion.

ratio scale has all the properties of an interval scale and a true zero point.

regression procedure for predicting or estimating values of a dependent variable from one or more independent variables.

reliability the consistency or dependability of a test.

research search for answers to questions.

sampling drawing a sample from a population.

sampling distribution distribution of estimates of a parameter computed from samples of a certain size.

science systematic development and organization of a body of knowledge.

scientific method a procedure often followed in systematic research which is based on making observations in response to questions.

standard deviation a statistic for the summarization of the dispersion in a list of interval scores.

standard error of measurement standard deviation of the error component of observed scores.

standard error of the mean standard deviation of a sampling distribution of means.

standardized tests tests that have clear, concise instructions for administration and scoring and have standard materials and procedures.

standard scores scores expressed in terms of standard deviations from the mean.

statistic an estimate of a parameter value.

statistical significance a term applied to results not likely to occur by chance if the null hypothesis is true.

stratified random sample a sampling procedure in which members of the sample are chosen randomly from strata or groups that comprise the population.

summative evaluation research designed to provide information about the usefulness or worth of a completed project or product.

theory a set of formulations designed to explain and predict facts and events that can be observed.

trait an enduring characteristic of an individual to respond in a particular way.

true score the portion of an observed score not due to random error.

Type I error decision to reject a null hypothesis when it is true.

Type II error decision not to reject a null hypothesis when the alternative is true.

validity the degree to which a test measures what it is supposed to measure; the degree to which the results of an experiment are attributable to the treatments.

variables characteristics of persons, objects, groups, events, etc., which can be assigned qualitative or quantitative values.

STATISTICAL TABLES

Table B.1 / One-, two-, and three-digit random numbers.

1	6	4	3	1	1	3	4	9	0
1	7	7	0	1	7	5	3	7	7
1	1	5	6	4	8	5	6	1	3
2	6	4	7	5	5	9	7	3	4
1	8	2	4	3	5	9	9	8	8
4	5	7	4	1	8	9	9	3	7
1	2	8	8	2	3	8	8	9	2
0	1	7	3	4	2	5	5	1	6
0	5	5	1	4	9	9	8	6	5
2	7	9	8	1	9	8	4	3	1
1	7	1	7	6	5	8	0	4	5
1	7	2	5	7	7	4	6	3	7
6	0	9	9	8	3	2	0	0	1
7	8	6	9	5	8	4	5	9	6
3	1	1	9	0	5	9	2	8	8
6	5	3	9	9	8	7	4	5	3
5	8	7	9	7	3	4	9	2	4
0	1	1	7	8	8	4	1	0	4
0	7	8	5	6	9	1	1	2	3
8	0	7	7	3	4	8	2	0	4

Table B.1 / One-, two-, and three-digit random numbers (continued)

0	6	4	0	5	4	2	6	2	3
4	2	6	9	2	1	5	3	0	7
8	5	5	5	7	2	8	7	2	6
8	7	4	3	3	0	5	7	7	1
2	0	5	5	2	7	1	3	3	8
7	4	9	8	2	0	9	2	7	9
3	7	2	0	8	7	6	7	4	9
2	0	8	3	0	3	6	2	7	8
7	2	0	7	4	4	5	9	7	2
7	9	1	7	0	0	5	9	9	2
2	2	3	2	8	2	7	5	8	6
1	0	3	7	4	0	4	8	9	7
3	3	6	8	6	8	5	2	5	5
7	6	2	6	2	3	3	7	9	6
2	0	8	0	9	9	5	0	7	6
2	9	4	6	8	3	9	5	0	2
5	2	4	4	4	0	7	7	7	5
6	4	7	5	1	5	1	4	2	7
4	4	1	5	3	0	8	4	6	4
5	8	3	2	1	8	0	0	2	9
8	3	7	8	4	1	7	5	7	7
6	9	8	4	0	9	4	7	9	7
3	1	5	4	1	2	6	4	9	8
4	0	8	8	9	2	7	5	4	7
8	5	3	6	9	5	9	6	0	4
1	4	2	2	7	9	0	5	2	4
0	2	3	6	4	6	2	4	6	2
1	1	1	6	5	9	2	5	6	9
7	4	9	0	6	9	6	5	9	5
8	2	2	5	0	3	1	2	2	1
3	65	50	88	21	69	14	26	39	21
34	60	36	6	38	21	17	43	90	46
72	74	69	45	40	2	73	21	91	84
24	9	87	17	89	20	84	33	27	90
90	81	97	93	75	99	50	8	45	85
26	7	6	3	50	13	39	49	26	94
43	9	25	80	20	82	82	19	45	97
22	87	49	46	72	75	35	69	34	38
43	36	69	56	47	10	76	43	3	50
58	29	69	21	32	85	35	38	9	58

Table B.1 / One-, two-, and three-digit random numbers (continued)

93	57	80	99	69	88	72	60	44	39
39	30	60	71	47	86	28	67	52	74
91	58	35	35	60	21	16	62	9	97
99	80	67	65	34	51	40	66	83	8
68	56	85	74	65	18	91	32	19	77
20	16	7	58	82	46	84	0	67	89
5	88	76	77	11	10	86	7	24	39
44	80	89	41	21	46	54	41	43	30
17	85	53	52	26	85	48	85	40	26
1	91	13	40	71	89	99	35	51	84
95	39	49	34	91	93	33	26	54	13
45	90	89	22	21	36	67	57	45	4
10	89	91	23	5	82	99	3	86	6
57	18	42	35	43	64	89	1	10	99
49	10	29	3	9	44	43	81	78	37
83	93	95	4	68	85	54	76	77	26
51	71	5	91	25	14	34	22	61	24
61	81	70	9	38	21	12	47	72	3
2	50	80	32	98	91	67	77	81	2
60	67	42	14	46	59	89	42	41	84
81	61	37	95	13	46	68	32	42	22
32	92	79	81	47	49	1	40	49	50
58	98	36	22	60	77	89	52	12	3
63	59	3	7	37	19	29	53	32	62
51	76	92	38	78	14	69	45	83	47
43	19	19	64	32	17	49	90	7	18
90	32	88	38	92	70	66	30	88	86
57	17	51	48	60	69	58	71	68	51
28	10	18	41	30	78	52	54	11	28
53	5	43	15	36	45	83	89	53	3
68	69	68	96	28	24	30	33	34	40
76	26	39	20	81	84	34	47	69	47
46	27	22	50	31	86	34	83	6	24
87	31	73	18	52	57	93	79	8	18
8	37	39	57	32	67	50	21	96	89
57	44	79	73	22	80	62	13	99	67
74	25	18	28	40	81	23	91	33	5
24	53	98	8	37	62	77	24	4	24
76	86	27	92	61	40	52	24	20	92
43	41	73	76	29	83	16	26	88	39

Table B.1 / One-, two-, and three-digit random numbers (continued)

109	616	461	397	145	179	332	485	916	0
192	775	791	45	126	750	591	331	736	722
167	100	592	698	453	891	551	625	170	327
276	627	434	782	578	591	988	766	391	460
149	858	271	412	389	526	970	971	818	821
410	501	717	429	129	842	924	924	384	778
119	282	863	862	274	311	810	805	942	281
25	187	723	313	480	286	541	515	195	680
74	576	573	113	411	918	951	843	687	551
213	775	926	860	147	933	842	418	364	182
130	709	160	701	628	544	810	76	476	508
138	745	233	550	757	711	415	618	395	780
660	90	955	986	889	366	200	25	79	112
713	831	629	970	518	300	464	584	922	645
338	177	176	939	99	504	985	279	816	863
603	582	396	906	933	819	727	416	598	373
578	894	787	981	715	376	496	985	244	464
40	126	157	731	832	882	432	167	83	427
33	702	859	560	647	905	127	129	296	381
834	81	739	779	395	493	870	273	29	443
7	668	482	37	528	421	258	689	239	322
490	254	646	979	255	178	536	332	59	761
880	512	538	534	781	271	892	786	206	667
864	781	407	398	387	25	523	731	700	148
260	72	599	575	288	708	108	305	342	888
788	406	933	865	246	24	943	251	750	992
382	784	204	20	879	768	683	758	418	957
200	47	821	328	55	388	608	292	760	814
759	224	88	786	423	416	501	927	791	270
750	916	138	768	39	1	533	930	908	287
293	235	305	276	884	281	775	555	887	663
172	86	399	725	442	59	415	879	920	757
391	398	642	861	697	820	518	280	533	577
792	610	265	636	203	393	367	767	920	647
233	81	808	66	942	974	542	82	723	685
271	992	460	673	817	304	940	588	49	286
523	222	482	442	423	53	764	788	789	550
698	400	754	596	187	580	123	430	292	727
479	405	186	595	311	5	860	486	646	411
591	826	326	206	181	803	50	44	246	918

Table B.1 / One-, two-, and three-digit random numbers (continued)

811	398	707	805	431	130	780	582	734	766
603	948	817	457	7	901	441	780	930	783
312	100	536	494	161	232	622	436	975	804
443	71	859	850	905	279	764	597	478	776
850	524	323	650	978	582	981	654	91	412
114	498	208	250	715	976	10	552	242	488
33	273	342	652	491	617	228	420	631	221
172	148	176	656	504	914	279	555	603	928
729	434	975	69	606	931	617	546	938	582
827	269	263	508	98	360	190	274	201	132

percentage of the curve to the left.

Table B.2 / Cumulative normal distribution. *

z	X	Area	z	X	Area
−3.25	$\mu - 3.25\sigma$	.0006	−1.00	$\mu - 1.00\sigma$	.1587
−3.20	$\mu - 3.20\sigma$	.0007	− .95	$\mu - .95\sigma$	.1711
−3.15	$\mu - 3.15\sigma$	.0008	− .90	$\mu - .90\sigma$	.1841
−3.10	$\mu - 3.10\sigma$	.0010	− .85	$\mu - .85\sigma$	.1977
−3.05	$\mu - 3.05\sigma$	.0011	− .80	$\mu - .80\sigma$	.2119
−3.00	$\mu - 3.00\sigma$	.0013	− .75	$\mu - .75\sigma$	.2266
−2.95	$\mu - 2.95\sigma$	.0016	− .70	$\mu - .70\sigma$	.2420
−2.90	$\mu - 2.90\sigma$	.0019	− .65	$\mu - .65\sigma$	.2578
−2.85	$\mu - 2.85\sigma$	.0022	− .60	$\mu - .60\sigma$	.2743
−2.80	$\mu - 2.80\sigma$	.0026	− .55	$\mu - .55\sigma$	.2912
−2.75	$\mu - 2.75\sigma$	.0030	− .50	$\mu - .50\sigma$	.3085
−2.70	$\mu - 2.70\sigma$	.0035	− .45	$\mu - .45\sigma$	.3264
−2.65	$\mu - 2.65\sigma$	.0040	− .40	$\mu - .40\sigma$	.3446
−2.60	$\mu - 2.60\sigma$	.0047	− .35	$\mu - .35\sigma$	.3632
−2.55	$\mu - 2.55\sigma$	.0054	− .30	$\mu - .30\sigma$	.3821
−2.50	$\mu - 2.50\sigma$	.0062	− .25	$\mu - .25\sigma$	.4013
−2.45	$\mu - 2.45\sigma$	.0071	− .20	$\mu - .20\sigma$	.4207
−2.40	$\mu - 2.40\sigma$	.0082	− .15	$\mu - .15\sigma$	.4404
−2.35	$\mu - 2.35\sigma$	.0094	− .10	$\mu - .10\sigma$	.4602
−2.30	$\mu - 2.30\sigma$	.0107	− .05	$\mu - .05\sigma$	.4801
−2.25	$\mu - 2.25\sigma$	.0122			
−2.20	$\mu - 2.20\sigma$	.0139			
−2.15	$\mu - 2.15\sigma$	.0158	.00	μ	.5000
−2.10	$\mu - 2.10\sigma$	.0179			
−2.05	$\mu - 2.05\sigma$	.0202			
−2.00	$\mu - 2.00\sigma$	.0228	.05	$\mu + .05\sigma$	.5199
−1.95	$\mu - 1.95\sigma$	.0256	.10	$\mu + .10\sigma$	.5398
−1.90	$\mu - 1.90\sigma$	.0287	.15	$\mu + .15\sigma$	.5596
−1.85	$\mu - 1.85\sigma$	.0322	.20	$\mu + .20\sigma$	.5793
−1.80	$\mu - 1.80\sigma$	.0359	.25	$\mu + .25\sigma$	.5987
−1.75	$\mu - 1.75\sigma$	.0401	.30	$\mu + .30\sigma$	.6179
−1.70	$\mu - 1.70\sigma$	.0446	.35	$\mu + .35\sigma$	.6368
−1.65	$\mu - 1.65\sigma$	.0495	.40	$\mu + .40\sigma$	.6554
−1.60	$\mu - 1.60\sigma$	.0548	.45	$\mu + .45\sigma$	.6736
−1.55	$\mu - 1.55\sigma$	.0606	.50	$\mu + .50\sigma$	.6915
−1.50	$\mu - 1.50\sigma$	.0668	.55	$\mu + .55\sigma$	.7088
−1.45	$\mu - 1.45\sigma$	.0735	.60	$\mu + .60\sigma$	.7257
−1.40	$\mu - 1.40\sigma$	.0808	.65	$\mu + .65\sigma$	.7422
−1.35	$\mu - 1.35\sigma$	.0885	.70	$\mu + .70\sigma$	.7580
−1.30	$\mu - 1.30\sigma$	.0968	.75	$\mu + .75\sigma$	.7734
−1.25	$\mu - 1.25\sigma$	.1056	.80	$\mu + .80\sigma$	.7881
−1.20	$\mu - 1.20\sigma$	.1151	.85	$\mu + .85\sigma$	.8023
−1.15	$\mu - 1.15\sigma$	.1251	.90	$\mu + .90\sigma$	.8159
−1.10	$\mu - 1.10\sigma$	.1357	.95	$\mu + .95\sigma$	.8289
−1.05	$\mu - 1.05\sigma$	.1469	1.00	$\mu + 1.00\sigma$	.8413

* From Dixon, W. J., and Massey, F. J., *Introduction to Statistical Analysis* (3rd Ed.). New York: McGraw-Hill, 1969.

Table B.2 / Cumulative normal distribution (continued)

z	X	Area	z	X	Area
1.05	$\mu + 1.05\sigma$	.8531	−4.265	$\mu - 4.265\sigma$	.00001
1.10	$\mu + 1.10\sigma$	.8643	−3.719	$\mu - 3.719\sigma$	.0001
1.15	$\mu + 1.15\sigma$	.8749	−3.090	$\mu - 3.090\sigma$	.001
1.20	$\mu + 1.20\sigma$	.8849	−2.576	$\mu - 2.576\sigma$	.005
1.25	$\mu + 1.25\sigma$	.8944	−2.326	$\mu - 2.326\sigma$	.01
1.30	$\mu + 1.30\sigma$	.9032	−2.054	$\mu - 2.054\sigma$	.02
1.35	$\mu + 1.35\sigma$	.9115	−1.960	$\mu - 1.960\sigma$	.025
1.40	$\mu + 1.40\sigma$	.9192	−1.881	$\mu - 1.881\sigma$	.03
1.45	$\mu + 1.45\sigma$	.9265	−1.751	$\mu - 1.751\sigma$	.04
1.50	$\mu + 1.50\sigma$	.9332	−1.645	$\mu - 1.645\sigma$	.05
1.55	$\mu + 1.55\sigma$	.9394	−1.555	$\mu - 1.555\sigma$	.06
1.60	$\mu + 1.60\sigma$	.9452	−1.476	$\mu - 1.476\sigma$	.07
1.65	$\mu + 1.65\sigma$	.9505	−1.405	$\mu - 1.405\sigma$	.08
1.70	$\mu + 1.70\sigma$	.9554	−1.341	$\mu - 1.341\sigma$	.09
1.75	$\mu + 1.75\sigma$	.9599	−1.282	$\mu - 1.282\sigma$	.10
1.80	$\mu + 1.80\sigma$	.9641	−1.036	$\mu - 1.036\sigma$	.15
1.85	$\mu + 1.85\sigma$	.9678	−.842	$\mu - .812\sigma$	.20
1.90	$\mu + 1.90\sigma$	.9713	−.674	$\mu - .674\sigma$	.25
1.95	$\mu + 1.95\sigma$	.9744	−.524	$\mu - .524\sigma$	.30
2.00	$\mu + 2.00\sigma$	.9772	−.385	$\mu - .385\sigma$	.35
2.05	$\mu + 2.05\sigma$	.9798	−.253	$\mu - .253\sigma$	.40
2.10	$\mu + 2.10\sigma$	.9821	−.126	$\mu - .126\sigma$	.45
2.15	$\mu + 2.15\sigma$	.9842	0	μ	.50
2.20	$\mu + 2.20\sigma$	.9861	.126	$\mu + .126\sigma$	.55
2.25	$\mu + 2.25\sigma$	.9878	.253	$\mu + .253\sigma$	.60
2.30	$\mu + 2.30\sigma$	.9893	.385	$\mu + .385\sigma$	.65
2.35	$\mu + 2.35\sigma$	.9906	.524	$\mu + .524\sigma$	.70
2.40	$\mu + 2.40\sigma$	.9918	.674	$\mu + .674\sigma$	.75
2.45	$\mu + 2.45\sigma$	.9929	.842	$\mu + .842\sigma$	.80
2.50	$\mu + 2.50\sigma$	.9938	1.036	$\mu + 1.036\sigma$	.85
2.55	$\mu + 2.55\sigma$	.9946	1.282	$\mu + 1.282\sigma$	.90
2.60	$\mu + 2.60\sigma$	.9953	1.341	$\mu + 1.341\sigma$	.91
2.65	$\mu + 2.65\sigma$	.9960	1.405	$\mu + 1.405\sigma$	.92
2.70	$\mu + 2.70\sigma$	.9965	1.476	$\mu + 1.476\sigma$	.93
2.75	$\mu + 2.75\sigma$	.9970	1.555	$\mu + 1.555\sigma$	.94
2.80	$\mu + 2.80\sigma$	.9974	1.645	$\mu + 1.645\sigma$	.95
2.85	$\mu + 2.85\sigma$	.9978	1.751	$\mu + 1.751\sigma$	.96
2.90	$\mu + 2.90\sigma$	.9981	1.881	$\mu + 1.881\sigma$	.97
2.95	$\mu + 2.95\sigma$	.9984	1.960	$\mu + 1.960\sigma$	.975
3.00	$\mu + 3.00\sigma$	.9987	2.054	$\mu + 2.054\sigma$	.98
3.05	$\mu + 3.05\sigma$	.9989	2.326	$\mu + 2.326\sigma$	.99
3.10	$\mu + 3.10\sigma$	.9990	2.576	$\mu + 2.576\sigma$	.995
3.15	$\mu + 3.15\sigma$	.9992	3.090	$\mu + 3.090\sigma$	.999
3.20	$\mu + 3.20\sigma$	.9993	3.719	$\mu + 3.719\sigma$	.9999
3.25	$\mu + 3.25\sigma$	.9994	4.265	$\mu + 4.265\sigma$	.99999

Table B.3 / Table of *t* for two-tailed test*

df	P = .9	.8	.7	.6	.5	.4	.3	.2	.1	.05	.02	.01
1	.158	.325	.510	.727	1.000	1.376	1.963	3.078	6.314	12.706	31.821	63.657
2	.142	.289	.445	.617	.816	1.061	1.386	1.886	2.920	4.303	6.965	9.925
3	.137	.277	.424	.584	.765	.978	1.250	1.638	2.353	3.182	4.541	5.841
4	.134	.271	.414	.569	.741	.941	1.190	1.533	2.132	2.776	3.747	4.604
5	.132	.267	.408	.559	.727	.920	1.156	1.476	2.015	2.571	3.365	4.032
6	.131	.265	.404	.553	.718	.906	1.134	1.440	1.943	2.447	3.143	3.707
7	.130	.263	.402	.549	.711	.896	1.119	1.415	1.895	2.365	2.998	3.499
8	.130	.262	.399	.546	.706	.889	1.108	1.397	1.860	2.306	2.896	3.355
9	.129	.261	.398	.543	.703	.883	1.100	1.383	1.833	2.262	2.821	3.250
10	.129	.260	.397	.542	.700	.879	1.093	1.372	1.812	2.228	2.764	3.169
11	.129	.260	.396	.540	.697	.876	1.088	1.363	1.796	2.201	2.718	3.106
12	.128	.259	.395	.539	.695	.873	1.083	1.356	1.782	2.179	2.681	3.055
13	.128	.259	.394	.538	.694	.870	1.079	1.350	1.771	2.160	2.650	3.012
14	.128	.258	.393	.537	.692	.868	1.076	1.345	1.761	2.145	2.624	2.977
15	.128	.258	.393	.536	.691	.866	1.074	1.341	1.753	2.131	2.602	2.947
16	.128	.258	.392	.535	.690	.865	1.071	1.337	1.746	2.120	2.583	2.921
17	.128	.257	.392	.534	.689	.863	1.069	1.333	1.740	2.110	2.567	2.898
18	.127	.257	.392	.534	.688	.862	1.067	1.330	1.734	2.101	2.552	2.878
19	.127	.257	.391	.533	.688	.861	1.066	1.328	1.729	2.093	2.539	2.861
20	.127	.257	.391	.533	.687	.860	1.064	1.325	1.725	2.086	2.528	2.845
21	.127	.257	.391	.532	.686	.859	1.063	1.323	1.721	2.080	2.518	2.831
22	.127	.256	.390	.532	.686	.858	1.061	1.321	1.717	2.074	2.508	2.819
23	.127	.256	.390	.532	.685	.858	1.060	1.319	1.714	2.069	2.500	2.807
24	.127	.256	.390	.531	.685	.857	1.059	1.318	1.711	2.064	2.492	2.797
25	.127	.256	.390	.531	.684	.856	1.058	1.316	1.708	2.060	2.485	2.787
26	.127	.256	.390	.531	.684	.856	1.058	1.315	1.706	2.056	2.479	2.779
27	.127	.256	.389	.531	.684	.855	1.057	1.314	1.703	2.052	2.473	2.771
28	.127	.256	.389	.530	.683	.855	1.056	1.313	1.701	2.048	2.467	2.763
29	.127	.256	.389	.530	.683	.854	1.055	1.311	1.699	2.045	2.462	2.756
30	.127	.256	.389	.530	.683	.854	1.055	1.310	1.697	2.042	2.457	2.750
∞	.12566	.25335	.38532	.52440	.67449	.84162	1.03643	1.28155	1.64485	1.95996	2.32634	2.57582

* From Fisher, R. A. *Statistical Methods for Research Workers* (13th Ed.). London: Oliver and Boyd, 1958. Reproduced by permission of the Publisher.

Table B.4 / A Table of chi-square*

df	$\alpha = .99$	.98	.95	.90	.80	.70
1	.000157	.000628	.00393	.0158	.0642	.148
2	.0201	.0404	.103	.211	.446	.713
3	.115	.185	.352	.584	1.005	1.424
4	.297	.429	.711	1.064	1.649	2.195
5	.554	.752	1.145	1.610	2.343	3.000
6	.872	1.134	1.635	2.204	3.070	3.828
7	1.239	1.564	2.167	2.833	3.822	4.671
8	1.646	2.032	2.733	3.490	4.594	5.527
9	2.088	2.532	3.325	4.168	5.380	6.393
10	2.558	3.059	3.940	4.865	6.179	7.267
11	3.053	3.609	4.575	5.578	6.989	8.148
12	3.571	4.178	5.226	6.304	7.807	9.034
13	4.107	4.765	5.892	7.042	8.634	9.926
14	4.660	5.368	6.571	7.790	9.467	10.821
15	5.229	5.985	7.261	8.547	10.307	11.721
16	5.812	6.614	7.962	9.312	11.152	12.624
17	6.408	7.255	8.672	10.085	12.002	13.531
18	7.015	7.906	9.390	10.865	12.857	14.440
19	7.633	8.567	10.117	11.651	13.716	15.352
20	8.260	9.237	10.851	12.443	14.578	16.266
21	8.897	9.915	11.591	13.240	15.445	17.182
22	9.542	10.600	12.338	14.041	16.314	18.101
23	10.196	11.293	13.091	14.848	17.187	19.021
24	10.856	11.992	13.848	15.659	18.062	19.943
25	11.524	12.697	14.611	16.473	18.940	20.867
26	12.198	13.409	15.379	17.292	19.820	21.792
27	12.879	14.125	16.151	18.114	20.703	22.719
28	13.565	14.847	16.928	18.939	21.588	23.647
29	14.256	15.574	17.708	19.768	22.475	24.577
30	14.953	16.306	18.493	20.599	23.364	25.508

For larger values of n, the expression $\sqrt{2\chi^2} - \sqrt{2n-1}$ may be used as a normal deviate with unit variance.

* From Fisher, R. A. *Statistical Methods for Research Workers* (13th Ed.). London: Oliver and Boyd, 1958. Reproduced by permission of the Publisher.

.50	.30	.20	.10	.05	.02	.01
.455	1.074	1.642	2.706	3.841	5.412	6.635
1.386	2.408	3.219	4.605	5.991	7.824	9.210
2.366	3.665	4.642	6.251	7.815	9.837	11.345
3.357	4.878	5.989	7.779	9.488	11.668	13.277
4.351	6.064	7.289	9.236	11.070	13.388	15.086
5.348	7.231	8.558	10.645	12.592	15.033	16.812
6.346	8.383	9.803	12.017	14.067	16.622	18.475
7.344	9.524	11.030	13.362	15.507	18.168	20.090
8.343	10.656	12.242	14.684	16.919	19.679	21.666
9.342	11.781	13.442	15.987	18.307	21.161	23.209
10.341	12.899	14.631	17.275	19.675	22.618	24.725
11.340	14.011	15.812	18.549	21.026	24.054	26.217
12.340	15.119	16.985	19.812	22.362	25.472	27.688
13.339	16.222	18.151	21.064	23.685	26.873	29.141
14.339	17.322	19.311	22.307	24.996	28.259	30.578
15.338	18.418	20.465	23.542	26.296	29.633	32.000
16.338	19.511	21.615	24.769	27.587	30.995	33.409
17.338	20.601	22.760	25.989	28.869	32.346	34.805
18.338	21.689	23.900	27.204	30.144	33.687	36.191
19.337	22.775	25.038	28.412	31.410	35.020	37.566
20.337	23.858	26.171	29.615	32.671	36.343	38.932
21.337	24.939	27.301	30.813	33.924	37.659	40.289
22.337	26.018	28.429	32.007	35.172	38.968	41.638
23.337	27.096	29.553	33.196	36.415	40.270	42.980
24.337	28.172	30.675	34.382	37.652	41.566	44.314
25.336	29.246	31.795	35.563	38.885	42.856	45.642
26.336	30.319	32.912	36.741	40.113	44.140	46.963
27.336	31.391	34.027	37.916	41.337	45.419	48.278
28.336	32.461	35.139	39.087	42.557	46.693	49.588
29.336	33.530	36.250	40.256	43.773	47.962	50.892

Table B.5 / .05 (lightface type) and .01 (boldface type) points for the distribution of F *

Between

df_1 degrees of freedom (for the numerator)

degrees of freedom (Within)

df_2†

	1	2	3	4	5	6	7	8	9	10	11	12
1	161	200	216	225	230	234	237	239	241	242	243	244
	4,052	**4,999**	**5,403**	**5,625**	**5,764**	**5,859**	**5,928**	**5,981**	**6,022**	**6,056**	**6,082**	**6,106**
2	18.51	19.00	19.16	19.25	19.30	19.33	19.36	19.37	19.38	19.39	19.40	19.41
	98.49	**99.00**	**99.17**	**99.25**	**99.30**	**99.33**	**99.34**	**99.36**	**99.38**	**99.40**	**99.41**	**99.42**
3	10.13	9.55	9.28	9.12	9.01	8.94	8.88	8.84	8.81	8.78	8.76	8.74
	34.12	**30.82**	**29.46**	**28.71**	**28.24**	**27.91**	**27.67**	**27.49**	**27.34**	**27.23**	**27.13**	**27.05**
4	7.71	6.94	6.59	6.39	6.26	6.16	6.09	6.04	6.00	5.96	5.93	5.91
	21.20	**18.00**	**16.69**	**15.98**	**15.52**	**15.21**	**14.98**	**14.80**	**14.66**	**14.54**	**14.45**	**14.37**
5	6.61	5.79	5.41	5.19	5.05	4.95	4.88	4.82	4.78	4.74	4.70	4.68
	16.26	**13.27**	**12.06**	**11.39**	**10.97**	**10.67**	**10.45**	**10.27**	**10.15**	**10.05**	**9.96**	**9.89**
6	5.99	5.14	4.76	4.53	4.39	4.28	4.21	4.15	4.10	4.06	4.03	4.00
	13.74	**10.92**	**9.78**	**9.15**	**8.75**	**8.47**	**8.26**	**8.10**	**7.98**	**7.87**	**7.79**	**7.72**
7	5.59	4.74	4.35	4.12	3.97	3.87	3.79	3.73	3.68	3.63	3.60	3.57
	12.25	**9.55**	**8.45**	**7.85**	**7.46**	**7.19**	**7.00**	**6.84**	**6.71**	**6.62**	**6.54**	**6.47**
8	5.32	4.46	4.07	3.84	3.69	3.58	3.50	3.44	3.39	3.34	3.31	3.28
	11.26	**8.65**	**7.59**	**7.01**	**6.63**	**6.37**	**6.19**	**6.03**	**5.91**	**5.82**	**5.74**	**5.67**
9	5.12	4.26	3.86	3.63	3.48	3.37	3.29	3.23	3.18	3.13	3.10	3.07
	10.56	**8.02**	**6.99**	**6.42**	**6.06**	**5.80**	**5.62**	**5.47**	**5.35**	**5.26**	**5.18**	**5.11**
10	4.96	4.10	3.71	3.48	3.33	3.22	3.14	3.07	3.02	2.97	2.94	2.91
	10.04	**7.56**	**6.55**	**5.99**	**5.64**	**5.39**	**5.21**	**5.06**	**4.95**	**4.85**	**4.78**	**4.71**
11	4.84	3.98	2.59	3.36	3.20	3.09	3.01	2.95	2.90	2.86	2.82	2.79
	9.65	**7.20**	**6.22**	**5.67**	**5.32**	**5.07**	**4.88**	**4.74**	**4.63**	**4.54**	**4.46**	**4.40**
12	4.75	3.88	3.49	3.26	3.11	3.00	2.92	2.85	2.80	2.76	2.72	2.69
	9.33	**6.93**	**5.95**	**5.41**	**5.06**	**4.82**	**4.65**	**4.50**	**4.39**	**4.30**	**4.22**	**4.16**
13	4.67	3.80	3.41	3.18	3.02	2.92	2.84	2.77	2.72	2.67	2.63	2.60
	9.07	**6.70**	**5.74**	**5.20**	**4.86**	**4.62**	**4.44**	**4.30**	**4.19**	**4.10**	**4.02**	**3.96**

* Reprinted by permission from *Statistical Methods*, sixth edition, 1967, by George W. Snedecor and William G. Cochran. Copyright © 1967 by Iowa State University Press, Ames.

† Degrees of freedom for the denominator.

											df_2
14	16	20	24	30	40	50	75	100	200	500	∞
245	246	248	249	250	251	252	253	253	254	254	254	
6,142	6,169	6,208	6,234	6,258	6,286	6,302	6,323	6,334	6,352	6,361	6,366	
19.42	19.43	19.44	19.45	19.46	19.47	19.47	19.48	19.49	19.49	19.50	19.50	
99.43	99.44	99.45	99.46	99.47	99.48	99.48	99.49	99.49	99.49	99.50	99.50	
8.71	8.69	8.66	8.64	8.62	8.60	8.58	8.57	8.56	8.54	8.54	8.53	3
26.92	26.83	26.69	26.60	26.50	26.41	26.35	26.27	26.23	26.18	26.14	26.12	
5.87	5.84	5.80	5.77	5.74	5.71	5.70	5.68	5.66	5.65	5.64	5.63	4
14.24	14.15	14.02	13.93	13.83	13.74	13.69	13.61	13.57	13.52	13.48	13.46	
4.64	4.60	4.56	4.53	4.50	4.46	4.44	4.42	4.40	4.38	4.37	4.36	5
9.77	9.68	9.55	9.47	9.38	9.29	9.24	9.17	9.13	9.07	9.04	9.02	
3.96	3.92	3.87	3.84	3.81	3.77	3.75	3.72	3.71	3.69	3.68	3.67	6
7.60	7.52	7.39	7.31	7.23	7.14	7.09	7.02	6.99	6.94	6.90	6.88	
3.52	3.49	3.44	3.41	3.38	3.34	3.32	3.29	3.28	3.25	3.24	3.23	7
6.35	6.27	6.15	6.07	5.98	5.90	5.85	5.78	5.75	5.70	5.67	5.65	
3.23	3.20	3.15	3.12	3.08	3.05	3.03	3.00	2.98	2.96	2.94	2.93	8
5.56	5.48	5.36	5.28	5.20	5.11	5.06	5.00	4.96	4.91	4.88	4.86	
3.02	2.98	2.93	2.90	2.86	2.82	2.80	2.77	2.76	2.73	2.72	2.71	9
5.00	4.92	4.80	4.73	4.64	4.56	4.51	4.45	4.41	4.36	4.33	4.31	
2.86	2.82	2.77	2.74	2.70	2.67	2.64	2.61	2.59	2.56	2.55	2.54	10
4.60	4.52	4.41	4.33	4.25	4.17	4.12	4.05	4.01	3.96	3.93	3.91	
2.74	2.70	2.65	2.61	2.57	2.53	2.50	2.47	2.45	2.42	2.41	2.40	11
4.29	4.21	4.10	4.02	3.94	3.86	3.80	3.74	3.70	3.66	3.62	3.60	
2.64	2.60	2.54	2.50	2.46	2.42	2.40	2.36	2.35	2.32	2.31	2.30	12
4.05	3.98	3.86	3.78	3.70	3.61	3.56	3.49	3.46	3.41	3.38	3.36	
2.55	2.51	2.46	2.42	2.38	2.34	2.32	2.28	2.26	2.24	2.22	2.21	13
3.85	3.78	3.67	3.59	3.51	3.42	3.37	3.30	3.27	3.21	3.18	3.16	

Table B.5 / .05 (lightface type) and .01 (boldface type) points for the distribution of F (continued)

df₁ degrees of freedom (for the numerator)

df_2	1	2	3	4	5	6	7	8	9	10	11	12
14	4.60	3.74	3.34	3.11	2.96	2.85	2.77	2.70	2.65	2.60	2.56	2.53
	8.86	**6.51**	**5.56**	**5.03**	**4.69**	**4.46**	**4.28**	**4.14**	**4.03**	**3.94**	**3.86**	**3.80**
15	4.54	3.68	3.29	3.06	2.90	2.79	2.70	2.64	2.59	2.55	2.51	2.48
	8.68	**6.36**	**5.42**	**4.89**	**4.56**	**4.32**	**4.14**	**4.00**	**3.89**	**3.80**	**3.73**	**3.67**
16	4.49	3.63	3.24	3.01	2.85	2.74	2.66	2.59	2.54	2.49	2.45	2.42
	8.53	**6.23**	**5.29**	**4.77**	**4.44**	**4.20**	**4.03**	**3.89**	**3.78**	**3.69**	**3.61**	**3.55**
17	4.45	3.59	3.20	2.96	2.81	2.70	2.62	2.55	2.50	2.45	2.41	2.38
	8.40	**6.11**	**5.18**	**4.67**	**4.34**	**4.10**	**3.93**	**3.79**	**3.68**	**3.59**	**3.52**	**3.45**
18	4.41	3.55	3.16	2.93	2.77	2.66	2.58	2.51	2.46	2.41	2.37	2.34
	8.28	**6.01**	**5.09**	**4.58**	**4.25**	**4.01**	**3.85**	**3.71**	**3.60**	**3.51**	**3.44**	**3.37**
19	4.38	3.52	3.13	2.90	2.74	2.63	2.55	2.48	2.43	2.38	2.34	2.31
	8.18	**5.93**	**5.01**	**4.50**	**4.17**	**3.94**	**3.77**	**3.63**	**3.52**	**3.43**	**3.36**	**3.30**
20	4.35	3.49	3.10	2.87	2.71	2.60	2.52	2.45	2.40	2.35	2.31	2.28
	8.10	**5.85**	**4.94**	**4.43**	**4.10**	**3.87**	**3.71**	**3.56**	**3.45**	**3.37**	**3.30**	**3.23**
21	4.32	3.47	3.07	2.84	2.68	2.57	2.49	2.42	2.37	2.32	2.28	2.25
	8.02	**5.78**	**4.87**	**4.37**	**4.04**	**3.81**	**3.65**	**3.51**	**3.40**	**3.31**	**3.24**	**3.17**
22	4.30	3.44	3.05	2.82	2.66	2.55	2.47	2.40	2.35	2.30	2.26	2.23
	7.94	**5.72**	**4.82**	**4.31**	**3.99**	**3.76**	**3.59**	**3.45**	**3.35**	**3.26**	**3.18**	**3.12**
23	4.28	3.42	3.03	2.80	2.64	2.53	2.45	2.38	2.32	2.28	2.24	2.20
	7.88	**5.66**	**4.76**	**4.26**	**3.94**	**3.71**	**3.54**	**3.41**	**3.30**	**3.21**	**3.14**	**3.07**
24	4.26	3.40	3.01	2.78	2.62	2.51	2.43	2.36	2.30	2.26	2.22	2.18
	7.82	**5.61**	**4.72**	**4.22**	**3.90**	**3.67**	**3.50**	**3.36**	**3.25**	**3.17**	**3.09**	**3.03**
25	4.24	3.38	2.99	2.76	2.60	2.49	2.41	2.34	2.28	2.24	2.20	2.16
	7.77	**5.57**	**4.63**	**4.13**	**3.86**	**3.63**	**3.46**	**3.32**	**3.21**	**3.13**	**3.05**	**2.99**
26	4.22	3.37	2.98	2.74	2.59	2.47	2.39	2.32	2.27	2.22	2.18	2.15
	7.72	**5.53**	**4.64**	**4.14**	**3.82**	**3.59**	**3.42**	**3.29**	**3.17**	**3.09**	**3.02**	**2.96**

												df_2
14	16	20	24	30	40	50	75	100	200	500	∞	
2.48	2.44	2.39	2.35	2.31	2.27	2.24	2.21	2.19	2.16	2.14	2.13	14
3.70	3.62	3.51	3.43	3.34	3.26	3.21	2.14	3.11	3.06	3.02	3.00	
2.43	2.39	2.33	2.29	2.25	2.21	2.18	2.15	2.12	2.10	2.08	2.07	15
3.56	3.48	3.36	3.29	3.20	3.12	3.07	3.00	2.97	2.92	2.89	2.87	
2.37	2.33	2.28	2.24	2.20	2.16	2.13	2.09	2.07	2.04	2.02	2.01	16
3.45	3.37	3.25	3.18	3.10	3.01	2.96	2.89	2.86	2.80	2.77	2.75	
2.33	2.29	2.23	2.19	2.15	2.11	2.08	2.04	2.02	1.99	1.97	1.96	17
3.35	3.27	3.16	3.08	3.00	2.92	2.86	2.79	2.76	2.70	2.67	2.65	
2.29	2.25	2.19	2.15	2.11	2.07	2.04	2.00	1.98	1.95	1.93	1.92	18
3.27	3.19	3.07	3.00	2.91	2.83	2.78	2.71	2.68	2.62	2.59	2.57	
2.26	2.21	2.15	2.11	2.07	2.02	2.00	1.96	1.94	1.91	1.90	1.88	19
3.19	3.12	3.00	2.92	2.84	2.76	2.70	2.63	2.60	2.54	2.51	2.49	
2.23	2.18	2.12	2.08	2.04	1.99	1.96	1.92	1.90	1.87	1.85	1.84	20
3.13	3.05	2.94	2.86	2.77	2.69	2.63	2.56	2.53	2.47	2.44	2.42	
2.20	2.15	2.09	2.05	2.00	1.96	1.93	1.89	1.87	1.84	1.82	1.81	21
3.07	2.99	2.88	2.80	2.72	2.63	2.58	2.51	2.47	2.42	2.38	2.36	
2.18	2.13	2.07	2.03	1.98	1.93	1.91	1.87	1.84	1.81	1.80	1.78	22
3.02	2.94	2.83	2.75	2.67	2.58	2.53	2.46	2.42	2.37	2.33	2.31	
2.14	2.10	2.04	2.00	1.96	1.91	1.88	1.84	1.82	1.79	1.77	1.76	23
2.97	2.89	2.78	2.70	2.62	2.53	2.48	2.41	2.37	2.32	2.28	2.26	
2.13	2.09	2.02	1.98	1.94	1.89	1.86	1.82	1.80	1.76	1.74	1.73	24
2.93	2.85	2.74	2.66	2.58	2.49	2.44	2.36	2.33	2.27	2.23	2.21	
2.11	2.06	2.00	1.96	1.92	1.87	1.84	1.80	1.77	1.74	1.72	1.71	25
2.89	2.81	2.70	2.62	2.54	2.45	2.40	2.32	2.29	2.23	2.19	2.17	
2.10	2.05	1.99	1.95	1.90	1.85	1.82	1.78	1.76	1.72	1.70	1.69	26
2.86	2.77	2.66	2.58	2.50	2.50	2.36	2.28	2.25	2.19	2.15	2.13	

Table B.5 / .05 (lightface type) and .01 (boldface type) points for the distribution of F (continued)

df_1 degrees of freedom (for the numerator)

df_2	1	2	3	4	5	6	7	8	9	10	11	12
27	4.21	3.35	2.96	2.73	2.57	2.46	2.37	2.30	2.25	2.20	2.16	2.13
	7.68	**5.49**	**4.60**	**4.11**	**3.79**	**3.56**	**3.39**	**3.26**	**3.14**	**3.06**	**2.98**	**2.93**
28	4.20	3.34	2.95	2.71	2.56	2.44	2.36	2.29	2.24	2.19	2.15	2.12
	7.64	**5.45**	**4.57**	**4.07**	**3.76**	**3.53**	**3.36**	**3.23**	**3.11**	**3.03**	**2.95**	**2.90**
29	4.18	3.33	2.93	2.70	2.54	2.43	2.35	2.28	2.22	2.18	2.14	2.10
	7.60	**5.42**	**4.54**	**4.04**	**3.73**	**3.50**	**3.33**	**3.20**	**3.08**	**3.00**	**2.92**	**2.87**
30	4.17	3.32	2.92	2.69	2.53	2.42	2.34	2.27	2.21	2.16	2.12	2.09
	7.56	**5.39**	**4.51**	**4.02**	**3.70**	**3.47**	**3.30**	**3.17**	**3.06**	**2.98**	**2.90**	**2.84**
32	4.15	3.30	2.90	2.67	2.51	2.40	2.32	2.25	2.19	2.14	2.10	2.07
	7.50	**5.34**	**4.46**	**3.97**	**3.66**	**3.42**	**3.25**	**3.12**	**3.01**	**2.94**	**2.86**	**2.80**
34	4.13	3.28	2.88	2.65	2.49	2.38	2.30	2.23	2.17	2.12	2.08	2.05
	7.44	**5.29**	**4.42**	**3.93**	**3.61**	**3.38**	**3.21**	**3.08**	**2.97**	**2.89**	**2.82**	**2.76**
36	4.11	3.26	2.86	2.63	2.48	2.36	2.28	2.21	2.15	2.10	2.06	2.03
	7.39	**5.25**	**4.38**	**3.89**	**3.58**	**3.35**	**3.18**	**3.04**	**2.94**	**2.86**	**2.78**	**2.72**
38	4.10	3.25	2.85	2.62	2.46	2.35	2.26	2.19	2.14	2.09	2.05	2.02
	7.35	**5.21**	**4.34**	**3.86**	**3.54**	**3.32**	**3.15**	**3.02**	**2.91**	**2.82**	**2.75**	**2.69**
40	4.08	3.23	2.84	2.61	2.45	2.34	2.25	2.18	2.12	2.07	2.04	2.00
	7.31	**5.18**	**4.31**	**3.83**	**3.51**	**3.29**	**3.12**	**2.99**	**2.88**	**2.80**	**2.73**	**2.66**
42	4.07	3.22	2.83	2.59	2.44	2.32	2.24	2.17	2.11	2.06	2.02	1.99
	7.27	**5.15**	**4.29**	**3.80**	**3.49**	**3.26**	**3.10**	**2.96**	**2.86**	**2.77**	**2.70**	**2.64**
44	4.06	3.21	2.82	2.58	2.43	2.31	2.23	2.16	2.10	2.05	2.01	1.98
	7.24	**5.12**	**4.26**	**3.78**	**3.46**	**3.24**	**3.07**	**2.94**	**2.84**	**2.75**	**2.68**	**2.62**
46	4.05	3.20	2.81	2.57	2.42	2.30	2.22	2.14	2.09	2.04	2.00	1.97
	7.21	**5.10**	**4.24**	**3.76**	**3.44**	**3.22**	**3.05**	**2.92**	**2.82**	**2.73**	**2.66**	**2.60**
48	4.04	3.19	2.80	2.56	2.41	2.30	2.21	2.14	2.08	2.03	1.99	1.96
	7.19	**5.08**	**4.22**	**3.74**	**3.42**	**3.20**	**3.04**	**2.90**	**2.80**	**2.71**	**2.64**	**2.58**

												df_2
14	16	20	24	30	40	50	75	100	200	500	∞	
2.08	2.03	1.97	1.93	1.88	1.84	1.80	1.76	1.74	1.71	1.68	1.67	27
2.83	**2.74**	**2.63**	**2.55**	**2.47**	**2.38**	**2.33**	**2.25**	**2.21**	**2.16**	**2.12**	**2.10**	
2.06	2.02	1.96	1.91	1.87	1.81	1.78	1.75	1.72	1.69	1.67	1.65	28
2.80	**2.71**	**2.60**	**2.52**	**2.44**	**2.35**	**2.30**	**2.22**	**2.18**	**2.13**	**2.09**	**2.06**	
2.05	2.00	1.94	1.90	1.85	1.80	1.77	1.73	1.71	1.68	1.65	1.64	29
2.77	**2.68**	**2.57**	**2.49**	**2.41**	**2.32**	**2.27**	**2.19**	**2.15**	**2.10**	**2.06**	**2.03**	
2.04	1.99	1.93	1.89	1.84	1.79	1.76	1.72	1.69	1.66	1.64	1.62	30
2.74	**2.66**	**2.55**	**2.47**	**2.38**	**2.29**	**2.24**	**2.16**	**2.13**	**2.07**	**2.03**	**2.01**	
2.02	1.97	1.91	1.86	1.82	1.76	1.74	1.69	1.67	1.64	1.61	1.59	32
2.70	**2.62**	**2.51**	**2.42**	**2.34**	**2.25**	**2.20**	**2.12**	**2.08**	**2.02**	**1.98**	**1.96**	
2.00	1.95	1.89	1.84	1.80	1.74	1.71	1.67	1.64	1.61	1.59	1.57	34
2.66	**2.58**	**2.47**	**2.38**	**2.30**	**2.21**	**2.15**	**2.08**	**2.04**	**1.98**	**1.94**	**1.91**	
1.98	1.93	1.87	1.82	1.78	1.72	1.69	1.65	1.62	1.59	1.56	1.55	36
2.62	**2.54**	**2.43**	**2.35**	**2.26**	**2.17**	**2.12**	**2.04**	**2.00**	**1.94**	**1.90**	**1.87**	
1.96	1.92	1.85	1.80	1.76	1.71	1.67	1.63	1.60	1.57	1.54	1.53	38
2.59	**2.51**	**2.40**	**2.32**	**2.22**	**2.14**	**2.08**	**2.00**	**1.97**	**1.90**	**1.86**	**1.84**	
1.95	1.90	1.84	1.79	1.74	1.69	1.66	1.61	1.59	1.55	1.53	1.51	40
2.56	**2.49**	**2.37**	**2.29**	**2.20**	**2.11**	**2.05**	**1.97**	**1.94**	**1.88**	**1.84**	**1.81**	
1.94	1.89	1.82	1.78	1.73	1.68	1.64	1.60	1.57	1.54	1.51	1.49	42
2.54	**2.46**	**2.35**	**2.26**	**2.17**	**2.08**	**2.02**	**1.94**	**1.91**	**1.85**	**1.80**	**1.78**	
1.92	1.88	1.81	1.76	1.72	1.66	1.63	1.58	1.56	1.52	1.50	1.48	44
2.52	**2.44**	**2.32**	**2.24**	**2.15**	**2.06**	**2.00**	**1.92**	**1.88**	**1.82**	**1.78**	**1.75**	
1.91	1.87	1.80	1.75	1.71	1.65	1.62	1.57	1.54	1.51	1.48	1.46	46
2.50	**2.42**	**2.30**	**2.22**	**2.13**	**2.04**	**1.98**	**1.90**	**1.86**	**1.80**	**1.76**	**1.72**	
1.90	1.86	1.79	1.74	1.70	1.64	1.61	1.56	1.53	1.50	1.47	1.45	48
2.48	**2.40**	**2.28**	**2.20**	**2.11**	**2.02**	**1.96**	**1.88**	**1.84**	**1.78**	**1.73**	**1.70**	

Table B.5 / .05 (lightface type) and .01 (boldface type) points for the distribution of F (continued)

df_1 degrees of freedom (for the numerator)

df_2	1	2	3	4	5	6	7	8	9	10	11	12
50	4.03	3.18	2.79	2.56	2.40	2.29	2.20	2.13	2.07	2.02	1.98	1.95
	7.17	**5.06**	**4.20**	**3.72**	**3.41**	**3.18**	**3.02**	**2.88**	**2.78**	**2.70**	**2.62**	**2.56**
55	4.02	3.17	2.78	2.54	2.38	2.27	2.18	2.11	2.05	2.00	1.97	1.93
	7.12	**5.01**	**4.16**	**3.68**	**3.37**	**3.15**	**2.98**	**2.85**	**2.75**	**2.66**	**2.59**	**2.53**
60	4.00	3.15	2.76	2.52	2.37	2.25	2.17	2.10	2.04	1.99	1.95	1.92
	7.08	**4.98**	**4.13**	**3.65**	**3.34**	**3.12**	**2.95**	**2.82**	**2.72**	**2.63**	**2.56**	**2.50**
65	3.99	3.14	2.75	2.51	2.36	2.24	2.15	2.08	2.02	1.98	1.94	1.90
	7.04	**4.95**	**4.10**	**3.62**	**3.31**	**3.09**	**2.93**	**2.79**	**2.70**	**2.61**	**2.54**	**2.47**
70	3.98	3.13	2.74	2.50	2.35	2.23	2.14	2.07	2.01	1.97	1.93	1.89
	7.01	**4.92**	**4.08**	**3.60**	**3.29**	**3.07**	**2.91**	**2.77**	**2.67**	**2.59**	**2.51**	**2.45**
80	3.96	3.11	2.72	2.48	2.33	2.21	2.12	2.05	1.99	1.95	1.91	1.88
	6.96	**4.88**	**4.04**	**3.56**	**3.25**	**3.04**	**2.87**	**2.74**	**2.64**	**2.55**	**2.48**	**2.41**
100	3.94	3.09	2.70	2.46	2.30	2.19	2.10	2.03	1.97	1.92	1.88	1.85
	6.90	**4.82**	**3.98**	**3.51**	**3.20**	**2.99**	**2.82**	**2.69**	**2.59**	**2.51**	**2.43**	**2.36**
125	3.92	3.07	2.68	2.44	2.29	2.17	2.08	2.01	1.95	1.90	1.86	1.83
	6.84	**4.78**	**3.94**	**3.47**	**3.17**	**2.95**	**2.79**	**2.65**	**2.56**	**2.47**	**2.40**	**2.33**
150	3.91	3.06	2.67	2.43	2.27	2.16	2.07	2.00	1.94	1.89	1.85	1.82
	6.81	**4.75**	**3.91**	**3.44**	**3.14**	**2.92**	**2.76**	**2.62**	**2.53**	**2.44**	**2.37**	**2.30**
200	3.89	3.04	2.65	2.41	2.26	2.14	2.05	1.98	1.92	1.87	1.83	1.80
	6.76	**4.71**	**3.88**	**3.41**	**3.11**	**2.90**	**2.73**	**2.60**	**2.50**	**2.41**	**2.34**	**2.28**
400	3.86	3.02	2.62	2.39	2.23	2.12	2.03	1.96	1.90	1.85	1.81	1.78
	6.70	**4.66**	**3.83**	**3.36**	**3.06**	**2.85**	**2.69**	**2.55**	**2.46**	**2.37**	**2.29**	**2.23**
1,000	3.85	3.00	2.61	2.38	2.22	2.10	2.02	1.95	1.89	1.84	1.80	1.76
	6.66	**4.62**	**3.80**	**3.34**	**3.04**	**2.82**	**2.66**	**2.53**	**2.43**	**2.34**	**2.26**	**2.20**
∞	3.84	2.99	2.60	2.37	2.21	2.09	2.01	1.94	1.88	1.83	1.79	1.75
	6.64	**4.60**	**3.78**	**3.32**	**3.02**	**2.80**	**2.64**	**2.51**	**2.41**	**2.32**	**2.24**	**2.18**

												df_2
14	16	20	24	30	40	50	75	100	200	500	∞	
1.90	1.85	1.78	1.74	1.69	1.63	1.60	1.55	1.52	1.48	1.46	1.44	50
2.46	**2.39**	**2.26**	**2.18**	**2.10**	**2.00**	**1.94**	**1.86**	**1.82**	**1.76**	**1.71**	**1.68**	
1.88	1.83	1.76	1.72	1.67	1.61	1.58	1.52	1.50	1.46	1.43	1.41	55
2.43	**2.35**	**2.23**	**2.15**	**2.06**	**1.96**	**1.90**	**1.82**	**1.78**	**1.71**	**1.66**	**1.64**	
1.86	1.81	1.75	1.70	1.65	1.59	1.56	1.50	1.48	1.44	1.41	1.39	60
2.40	**2.32**	**2.20**	**2.12**	**2.03**	**1.93**	**1.87**	**1.79**	**1.74**	**1.68**	**1.63**	**1.60**	
1.85	1.80	1.73	1.68	1.63	1.57	1.54	1.49	1.46	1.42	1.39	1.37	65
2.37	**2.30**	**2.18**	**2.09**	**2.00**	**1.90**	**1.84**	**1.76**	**1.71**	**1.64**	**1.60**	**1.56**	
1.84	1.79	1.72	1.67	1.62	1.56	1.53	1.47	1.45	1.40	1.37	1.35	70
2.35	**2.28**	**2.15**	**2.07**	**1.98**	**1.88**	**1.82**	**1.74**	**1.69**	**1.62**	**1.56**	**1.53**	
1.82	1.77	1.70	1.65	1.60	1.54	1.51	1.45	1.42	1.38	1.35	1.32	80
2.32	**2.24**	**2.11**	**2.03**	**1.94**	**1.84**	**1.78**	**1.70**	**1.65**	**1.57**	**1.52**	**1.49**	
1.79	1.75	1.68	1.63	1.57	1.51	1.48	1.42	1.39	1.34	1.30	1.28	100
2.26	**2.19**	**2.06**	**1.98**	**1.89**	**1.79**	**1.73**	**1.64**	**1.59**	**1.51**	**1.46**	**1.43**	
1.77	1.72	1.65	1.60	1.55	1.49	1.45	1.39	1.36	1.31	1.27	1.25	125
2.23	**2.15**	**2.03**	**1.94**	**1.85**	**1.75**	**1.68**	**1.59**	**1.54**	**1.46**	**1.40**	**1.37**	
1.76	1.71	1.64	1.59	1.54	1.47	1.44	1.37	1.34	1.29	1.25	1.22	150
2.20	**2.12**	**2.00**	**1.91**	**1.83**	**1.72**	**1.66**	**1.56**	**1.51**	**1.43**	**1.37**	**1.33**	
1.74	1.69	1.62	1.57	1.52	1.45	1.42	1.35	1.32	1.26	1.22	1.19	200
2.17	**2.09**	**1.97**	**1.88**	**1.79**	**1.69**	**1.62**	**1.53**	**1.48**	**1.39**	**1.33**	**1.28**	
1.72	1.67	1.60	1.54	1.49	1.42	1.38	1.32	1.28	1.22	1.16	1.13	400
2.12	**2.04**	**1.92**	**1.84**	**1.74**	**1.64**	**1.57**	**1.47**	**1.42**	**1.32**	**1.24**	**1.19**	
1.70	1.65	1.58	1.53	1.47	1.41	1.36	1.30	1.26	1.19	1.13	1.08	1,000
2.09	**2.01**	**1.89**	**1.81**	**1.71**	**1.61**	**1.54**	**1.44**	**1.38**	**1.28**	**1.19**	**1.11**	
1.69	1.64	1.57	1.52	1.46	1.40	1.35	1.28	1.24	1.17	1.11	1.00	∞
2.07	**1.99**	**1.87**	**1.79**	**1.69**	**1.59**	**1.52**	**1.41**	**1.36**	**1.25**	**1.15**	**1.00**	

ANSWERS TO SELECTED PROBLEMS

CHAPTER 1

Pages 25 to 27

1 **a** Yes
  b Yes
  c No
2 **a** Yes
  b No
  c Yes
3 The testing of hypotheses for theory development in the natural and physical sciences involves induction. Organization, description, and prediction more often involve deduction. The one that is more powerful is the one that is used appropriately in a given situation.
4 Deductive, inductive, inductive, deductive
5 **a** basic—used for theory development
  b applied—practical rather than theoretical
  c applied—practical use for testing professionals
6 Some bias factors include the following:
  a *topic selection*—formulation of the problem, selection of facets of the problem for study
  b *sample or subjects*—selection of certain groups or individuals, ignoring other groups or individuals
  c *observation, measurement procedures*—selection of biased measures, determining what does and doesn't get measured
  d *design procedures*—selection of a design that will or will not likely allow for the detection of certain effects or interactions, putting the experimental group at a subtle disadvantage
  e *data collection*—biased observers, biased instrumentation, differential care in obtaining complete data from comparison groups

  f data analysis—focusing on positive results and ignoring others, biased scoring procedures

  g *interpretation of results*—adjusting probability levels to show significant results, identification of trends in the absence of statistical significance, choosing scales on graphs that magnify differences

CHAPTER 2

Pages 60 to 61

5 a Survey research. No.

  b No. The type of research was inappropriate to address the problem.

  c Through historical research

  d The study measured opinions about the significance of the items in forming state laws on public education.

6 a evaluation

  b the effectiveness of the materials in terms of student learning outcomes

  d The research is applied. The intent is not the development of general theories about curriculum or learning.

CHAPTER 3

Pages 91 to 92

1 a No, but it is intended to be a law.

  b It is more properly a theory.

  c More specific operational definitions of "work" and "time available for completion" are needed in order to test the hypothesis.

5 It should raise a question about a relationship between variables, be stated clearly and concisely, and suggest a method of researching the question.

9 Library research is needed to determine whether comparative information is available. The difficulty is that the research calls for an experimental study and yet the comparison group is no longer available.

11 Valid tests of hypotheses depend upon the stating of the hypothesis prior to data collection. That is not to say that researchers should ignore serendipitous findings, as these findings may point the way for further research.

12 Some problems are:

  a lack of precise definition of "brighter"

  b the independent variable (one year of graduate school) lacks precision and should not be in question form

  c definitions of "better" and "mathematics students" are imprecise

  d "impulsive," "reflective," and "read" all need more precise definition

CHAPTER 4

Pages 123 to 124

1 Research example A

  a R X O

    R   O

b The design is strong in internal validity.

c External validity may be a problem since the entire group of subjects for the study is not a random sample from a larger population.

Research Example B

a R   O   X   O
  R   O   O

b While there is random assignment to experimental groups, it is at the class section level. There are only two sections per group, and this may influence the results if the sections differ.

c Pretesting may be a problem with the design since the pretest may interact with the treatment.

2 a The study is a static-group comparison and suffers from the threats to validity of that type of research, particularly regression.

b The performance of extreme groups tends to regress towards the mean upon subsequent measurement. This may produce the smaller gains in mathematics achievement in the high ability group.

CHAPTER 5

Pages 144 to 145

1 A counterbalanced design might be used, and the corresponding threats to internal and external validity will be present, depending on the situation.

CHAPTER 6

Pages 158 to 160

1 a Ordinal
  b Nominal
  c Nominal
  d Interval or ratio
  e Interval or ratio
  f Interval
  g Interval
  h Ratio
  i Ratio
  j Ordinal

2 Mode if he wishes to show high productivity, with no measure of dispersion for the mode.

3 Median with such a skewed distribution

4 a Mean, median, mode, range, variance
  b Median, mode, range
  c Mode, frequency distribution
  d Median, range

5 a Mode = 5.0, median = 5.0, $\bar{X} = 5.0$
  b Inclusive range = 7
    Exclusive range = 6
  c $S_x = 1.65$

Pages 182 to 186

1 Mode = 30
 Median = 27.5
 $\overline{X}$ = 24.33
 All indicate a "typical" score for the distribution. The mean is more affected by the extremely low scores than the mode or median.

2 **a** Mode is white (category 1)
 b The median level of skill is 17
 c The mean is 10.44

3 **a** $z = -.50$
 b .3085, .6915
 c $z = 1.50$
 d .9332
 e .6247

4 $r_{xy} = -.65$

5 **a** $r_{xy} = .25$
 b Relationship somewhat curvilinear, reduces r_{xy}

6 $\overline{X} = 128.98$, Sx = 12.94

 10   0 4
 11   1 2 2 3 4 8 9 9
 12   1 1 1 2 3 3 4 5 6 6 7 8 8 8 8 9 9 9 9 9
 13   0   0 2 2 3 4 4 5 5 5 6 8
 14   0 3 7 8 8
 15   9
 19   4

 From the analysis it appears that the distribution is positively skewed.

7 Not exactly. For many kinds of scores the distribution will be approximately normal.

8 **a** Normal
 b Nonnormal
 c Nonnormal
 d Normal
 e Nonnormal

9 $\overline{X} = 6.125$, $S_x = 1.25$

X	z	T
8	1.50	65
4	− 1.70	33
7	.70	57
6	− .10	49
6	− .10	49
5	− .90	41
6	− .10	49
7	.70	57

10 $z = 1.00$ in math; $z = -.50$ in history.

11 93.3 percent below 650; 99.4 percent score below 750.

12 $S_{xy} = (-27.11)$ There is a negative linear relationship between map reading and maze tracing.

$r_{xy} = -.90$ There is a high negative linear relationship between map reading and maze tracing.

13

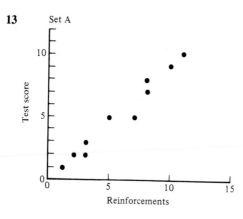

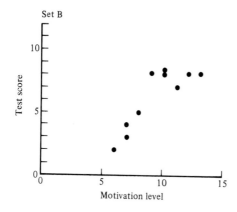

The relationship depicted in set A is linear.
That depicted in set B is curvilinear.

The relationship depicted in Set A is linear. That depicted in Set B is curvilinear.

CHAPTER 7

Pages 197 to 198

2 a Subset
b Empty set

c Subset
d Universal set
e Universal set for that college subset for all students
f Subset

3a

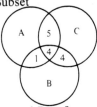

b A and B = 5
  A and C = 9
  B and C = 8
c union of A and B = 33
  union of A and C = 28
  union of B and C = 33
  union of A, B, and C = 40
d union of the intersections of A and C with B and C minus the intersection of A, B, and C $\cdot$ = 13
e $P = \frac{13}{40} = .325$

4 While a formal test goes beyond the information provided in this chapter, the probability of a randomly sampled voter casting a vote for candidate A is .54 as opposed to .42 for candidate B. Hence, we may infer that candidate A won the election.

5 a Biased
  b Biased
  c Unbiased
  d Biased

Pages 220 to 224

2 Increase sample size and $\sigma_{\bar{x}}$ becomes smaller
3 a 1.00
  b 16.35, 17.65
  c 15.35, 18.65
4 a $\mu_M > \mu_W$
  b $p_{bs} > p_{bf}$
  c $\sigma_u^2 = \sigma_r^2$
6 a $H_0 : \mu_M = \mu_F$
  $H_1 : \mu_M \neq \mu_F$
  b t for independent samples (the sample size is really too small for this test in actual practice).
  c $t = .175$, 8 df, do not reject H_0
8 Replication addresses the issue of the validity and generalizability of statistical findings.
9 a $H_0 : \mu_H = \mu_L$
  $H_1 : \mu_H \neq \mu_L$
  b t for correlated samples, $\alpha = .05$
  c reject H_0 if $t > 2.262$ or $t < -2.262$

$t = -3.48$, reject H_0

10 a $\chi^2 = 4.267$, critical value for $\chi^2 (\alpha = .05)$ with 2 df is 5.991; therefore hypothesis of independence is not rejected.

11 a They would not be expected to be exactly the same.
  b No.
  c No, verbal presentation was not studied.
  d Generalization is a problem because the students are not a random sample from a larger population.

Page 251

5 Factor analytic research is more like descriptive research.

CHAPTER 8

Pages 274 to 275

2 a Construct, criterion
  b Construct
  c Construct
  d Construct, content
  e Construct, criterion
  f Construct, criterion
  g Construct, content
  h Construct, predictive

5 $r_{xx} = .89$ using Spearman-Brown formula
  SEM = 4.17

6 a content
  b The test should match the curriculum. The difficulty and emphasis may be affected by expected student performance and the purposes of the research.

7 When $r_{xx} = 1.0$, the SEM = 0. When $r_{xx} = 0$, the SEM = S_O. Thus the maximum value for SEM is S_O, the standard deviation of the observed scores, and the minimum value is 0.

Page 282

3 A criterion referenced test would allow the principal to better determine the nature of precisely what has been learned under the two approaches.

CHAPTER 9

Pages 313

2 Intelligence was not a target variable of the project and should not have been so important in the evaluation. The program should have been evaluated more in terms of the children's mental and physical health.

CHAPTER 12

Page 384

1 a *independent*   *dependent*
    (1) attitude   IQ
    (2) word length/
        parts of speech   comprehension
    (3) personal interests   employment aspirations
  b (1) directional
    (2) nondirectional
    (3) correlational
  c (1) elementary school children
    (2) children
    (3) war veterans

2 a The Effects of Interpersonal Interaction on the Behavior of High School Graduates and College Students
  b The Effect of Familiarity of Argument Content upon Deductive Reasoning among Criminal Offenders

CHAPTER 13

Page 413

4 Advantages
  a Provides information about costs and benefits of the program and its components.
  b Can provide valid information about the effectiveness of competing strategies that can be used in the program.
  c Allows for improvements to be made as the program undergoes evaluation, as well as providing an overall analysis of its effectiveness.
  d Provides information about aspects of the program which may not be easily quantifiable.

Disadvantages
  a Narrow focus.
  b May be difficult and expensive and be of narrow focus.
  c Formative evaluation leads to changes in the program and affects summative evaluation. May ignore costs/benefits analysis and qualitative factors.
  d Often lacks scientific rigor and fails to provide "hard evidence" regarding costs and program effectiveness.

NAME INDEX

Abel, E. R., 26
Achenbach, T. M., 46, 61
Achtert, W. S., 385
Adair, J. G., 366
Alessi, S. M., 372, 385
Alexander, K. L., 77, 92
Allen, M. J., 271–272, 281–282
American Psychological Association, 355, 365, 368, 377, 380, 381, 385
Anastasi, A., 69, 92, 268, 282, 291, 313
Anastasio, E. J., 241, 251
Anbar, A., 41, 43, 61
Anderson, R. C., 27
Anderson, R. E., 182, 186
Andrade, E. N., 4
Argulewicz, E. N., 26, 27
Arnstein, J., II, 415
Auvenshire, C. D., 389

Backman, M. E., 38–39, 42–43, 50, 61, 413
Baker, E. L., 422, 425
Baker, F. B., 283
Baker, R. L., 62
Bandura, A., 73–76, 88, 92, 425
Barclay, James R., 17, 27, 306, 313–314
Barlow, D. H., 137, 145

Beck, S. J., 309, 314
Bennett, W. J., 418, 425
Benwar, C. A., 113, 124
Bereiter, C., 424–425
Berenson, M. L., 186
Bergan, J. R., 92, 224, 251
Berk, R. A., 277–278, 282
Berliner, D. C., 418, 426
Bevan, W., 418, 425
Bickman, L., 401, 413
Bloom, B. S., 277, 283, 389, 391, 395–397, 413–414
Bloom, H. S., 414
Bloom, L. J., 111, 114, 124
Borg, W., 105, 124
Borich, G. D., 414–415
Bornstein, P. H., 136, 145
Bower, G. H., 20, 27, 373, 385
Boyce, W. T., 125
Bramble, W. J., 26–27, 332, 334, 372, 385
Brandwein, A. C., 141, 145
Bray, J. S., 252
Brickell, H. M., 410, 414
Britan, G. M., 405, 414
Bronfenbrenner, U., 417, 422, 425
Broudy, H. S., 27, 37, 61
Brown, J. O., 291, 314

459

SUBJECT INDEX

11. Page 213. Formula for t should be:

$$t = \frac{\bar{X}_1 - \bar{X}_2}{\sqrt{\dfrac{(n_1 - 1)S_1^2 + (n_2 - 1)S_2^2}{n_1 + n_2 - 2}\left(\dfrac{1}{n_1} + \dfrac{1}{n_2}\right)}}$$

12. Page 214. Formula for t should be shown as follows (with equal sign after whole equation):

$$t = \frac{21.5 - 17.8}{\sqrt{\dfrac{9(7.167) + 9(10.844)}{10 + 10 - 2}\left(\dfrac{1}{10} + \dfrac{1}{10}\right)}} = 2.76$$

13. Page 243. All of the \ marks in Table 7-12 should be the symbol $<$ (less than) (e.g., for Task (A) under last column (Cohesiveness), first entry should be < 1).

14. Page 269 and 270. Lower parentheses in equation as follows:

$$r_{xx} = \frac{1}{k - 1}\left(1 - \frac{\Sigma pq}{S_o^2}\right)$$

Also lower parentheses for equation at bottom of page 270 for the equation for α:

$$\alpha = \left(\frac{k}{k - 1}\right)\left(\frac{S_o^2 - S_i^2}{S_o^2}\right)$$

15. Page 362. In checklist, under **Validity of research design**: should read:

"(Review Figure 5.5)"

Errata Sheet

for

Mason and Bramble

Understanding and Conducting Research:
Applications in Education and the Behavioral Sciences (2nd ed.)
(ISBN: 0-07-040703-7)

1. **Page 175.** Third equation should be: $Y_i = 5 + .5X_i$

2. **Page 176.** Second equation should be $\hat{Y} = -6.0 + .32X$

3. **Page 178.** The two equations for estimating beta should be shown as:

$$\hat{\beta}_1 = .82 \frac{(4.05)}{(10.37)} = .32$$

$$\hat{\beta}_0 = 10 - .32(50) = -6.0$$

4. **Page 180.** After the word **where** at the middle of page, the beta should be shown as: β_0

5. **Page 184.** The equation shown in item 4 should be:

$$r_{xy} = \frac{\Sigma XY - (\Sigma X)(\Sigma Y)/n}{\sqrt{\left(\Sigma X^2 - \frac{(\Sigma X)^2}{n}\right)\left(\Sigma Y^2 - \frac{(\Sigma Y)^2}{n}\right)}}$$

6. **Page 197.** Near the bottom of the page, the number **2** should be a **5**.

7. **Page 198.** The number **3** near the top of the page should be a **6**.

8. **Page 203.** H_0 and H_1 in the middle of page should be:

$$H_0: \mu_s \leq 500$$

$$H_0: \mu_s > 500$$

9. **Page 209.** H_0 should be: $H_0: \mu_s = 500$

10. **Page 209.** Should show square root sign in the denominator:

$$\sigma_{\bar{x}} = \frac{100}{\sqrt{100}} = 10$$